# THE CAITHNESS BOOK

# The Caithness Book

EDITOR

DONALD OMAND

*Printed and published by*

HIGHLAND PRINTERS LTD
DIRIEBUGHT ROAD
INVERNESS
SCOTLAND

*First Edition 1972*

# Contents

FOREWORD                                     *Neil M. Gunn*

INTRODUCTION TO THE COUNTY                   *D. Omand*

## PART I — NATURAL ENVIRONMENT

## PART II — HISTORICAL

## PART III — GENERAL

# List of Plates

# List of Figures

# Acknowledgments

I wish to thank the following people for supplying material and/or giving advice on chapter content:

JOHN SINCLAIR, Lord Lieutenant of Caithness.

MR D. YOUNG (Fochabers).

DR F. ROBERTSON, MR D. FRASER AND MR D. MILLER (Wick).

MR W. G. MOWAT (Lybster).

MR J. ROSIE (Lybster).

MR R. GUNN AND MR D. SINCLAIR (Halkirk).

MR A. GUNN AND MR D. STARK (Castletown).

MR J. GUNN (Reay).

MR L. J. MYATT (Thurso).

Gamekeepers: MESSRS J. BAIKIE, J. CAMERON, J. MACKAY, T. MACKAY AND J. MILLER.

MR A. ALLATHAN AND MR P. ALLEN of the North of Scotland College of Agriculture (Thurso).

DR W. F. H. NICOLAISEN, formerly of the School of Scottish Studies, University of Edinburgh.

DR ISOBEL HENDERSON, National Library of Scotland, Edinburgh.

MESSRS R. B. K. STEVENSON AND A. FENTON, National Museum of Antiquities, (Edinburgh).

LORD THURSO (Thurso).

DEPARTMENT OF THE ENVIRONMENT, Edinburgh.

MR E. W. MACKIE, Hunterian Museum, University of Glasgow.

STAFF OF THE RED DEER COMMISSION, Inverness.

Material for the chapter 'SOME CAITHNESS PLACE NAMES' was supplied by MR D. GRANT AND MISS H. MUNRO (Thurso).

MR W. FITZPATRICK AND MISS A. GUNN (Thurso) provided valuable secretarial assistance.

Acknowledgment is made to the FORESTRY COMMISSION for use of their material for the "Woodland" chapter.

I am grateful to AEROFILMS LIMITED for permission to reproduce an aerial view of Stroma.

The Table showing the products obtainable from peat (CHAPTER 8) came from a paper by W. A. P. BLACK given at a symposium on the Natural Resources of Scotland in Edinburgh in 1960.

I wish to thank the MACAULAY INSTITUTE for Soil Research, Aberdeen, for use of their material for the "Soils" chapter.

I owe particular gratitude to MR D. GRANT, (Thurso,) for so willingly making available his extensive knowledge of the County — a knowledge which has contributed to many of the chapters in this book.

All maps were drawn by MR J. I. BRAMMAN, the diagrams by MR J. SAXON.

MRS BARBARA MYATT (Thurso) designed and painted the dust jacket.

Finally, I wish to thank CAITHNESS EDUCATION COMMITTEE for their interest in this work and for their financing of the many initial costs incurred.

D.O.

# Foreword

NEIL M. GUNN

A glance over the table of contents will indicate the wide-ranging nature of this authoritative book on Caithness, all the way from its Geology and Early Inhabitants to its Fishing Industry and Agriculture, from its ruined brochs to its shining nuclear buildings. And this may arouse the interesting reflection that just as Caithness would appear to have been the head once upon a time of what may be called the broch culture, distinguished by its circular towers, so in our age it took the lead in a new departure in nuclear physics distinguished architecturally by a great silver sphere cupped in Dounreay. There may even be those who might add that it was not just chance that created it the physical or geographical head of an island of some historic renown. Certainly astonishing things can happen within its borders. A friend tells me that while travelling south in a first-class railway carriage the other day he conversed with a lady who confessed that the social life in atomic Thurso was so hectic she was going home to London for a rest.

So solemn an experience stirred my imagination, and I thought that just as the Caithness Book gives all the basic facts, human and physical, searchingly displayed and commented upon, how interesting it would be if a complementary book could be composed dealing with the infinitely varied aspects of human life, past and present, experienced at first hand, and got together from its distinctive districts. If this may seem an extravagant notion, are there not schools in Caithness where senior pupils do in fact write essays on the history and affairs of their local districts? By contact with old folk and other sources of research a given area could not only be documented in the customary factual way but heightened in interest by being brought alive.

Whereupon I began to think of my own Dunbeath district with its strath beyond compare. (A remark which I first made in youthful innocence to an equally youthful, red-haired, vivid cousin who lived in Latheronwheel. "What!" she replied, "Dunbeath strath the most beautiful? Nonsense! As everyone knows Latheronwheel strath is the most beautiful strath in the whole of Caithness"). However, let me stick to Dunbeath and its river which rises near mountains and winds through miles of moorlands; a real Highland river with its salmon and spawning beds, on the way to that spot marked on the map as Picts' Houses. Many a night have I camped amid their ruins and had long thoughts about my ancestors as they came up from the river, moved around the ancient foundations and passed on to the endless moor. To listen to the near silence and then to the silence beyond the distant cry of a curlew . . . to far standing stones or stones in a sun circle. Then in the morning light back to the river, the Falls Pool, the endless variety of pools, with their known spots where the salmon lie, down to the Tulach, the green eminence on which the ancient broch stands. The guard chamber in the wall; which, as a boy, I never failed to scan carefully before entering the courtyard and crossing over to the low small entrance in the high wall and coming erect again in the inside chamber, shaped like a slightly crushed beeskep, with a high corbelled roof that made us wonder what "kept up" the stones, for the chamber in my boyhood was as perfect as when it had first been built. Outside again; and, beyond the burn below, rose the copious rolling ruins of religious settlements going back possibly to the first Christian missionaries . . . to St Columba in Inverness . . . to Europe. And at school we had to swot up stuff like the Wars of the Roses and who was John of Gaunt (a name I have never forgotten so possibly I was once "kept in" for utterly failing to remember him or his dates). For of course Dunbeath and its strath had no history, nothing to learn, much less write home about, or (may the dry Caithness humour keep its savour) tell the world.

So let us get back again to the refreshing waters of our Highland river and on to where they met the sea in the harbour. The sea, the winter fishing boats, the "small lines" each with its 600 baited hooks, shot in the dark, and then the return to the harbour on the morning tide.

Summer, and the launching of the big boats for the herring fishing, the gutting crews of cheerful quick-witted women, the excitement of this whole gamble of the sea, with the occasional big catch and the silver herring coming tripping in over the gunnel and into the hold. I can still see one elderly face, beneficent, suntanned and sweating, calling them his silver darlings.

All very parochial no doubt, certainly far away from school books and learning, but alive with life. Times change, but each change has its own life. Standing still, listening in that corbelled chamber in the broch wall, we sometimes even imagined we could hear history. Even historical times and places can intermix on a normal occasion in a fascinating fashion. Some two or three years ago I was fishing for salmon at the head of the Thurso river and at lunch time, standing outside the bothy, my attention was caught by a gentleman wearing a fore-and-aft cap whose earflaps and strings had come somewhat adrift, a thick muffler knotted under his left ear, loose-fitting Harris tweeds, fishing boots whose high tops had tumbled down to his ankles, and holding in his right hand with careful negligence a half-empty bottle of whisky, from which he was generously helping his angling companions. He seemed so like a figure out of an older age that I quietly asked my friend if he knew who he was, and even more quietly my Caithness friend replied, "He's high up in the Atomics."

I'm afraid I did not intend to write like this in a sober foreword, and can but plead that these chapter headings in the Caithness Book stirred some ancient memories and got the better of me. May they get the better of a few more, and especially of the imaginative young, alive in their own day and age.

# Introduction to the County

The County of Caithness, population 28,000, whose 10 parishes (see fig. 1) cover 177,414 hectares (685 square miles), has been described as the 'Lowlands beyond the Highlands.' This is an apt description of the northern triangle of the County, a low-lying windswept and almost treeless landscape carved from fossiliferous sediments laid down millions of years ago in a huge fresh-water basin. The fertile soil of this gently-undulating lowland contrasts markedly with the bleak interior moorland which is bordered to the south and west by a much more highland landscape culminating in the eroded hulk of Morven.

Undoubtedly the most dramatic land forms in Caithness are found along the sculptured coastline of 'geos', arches, stacks, and skerries which offer some of the finest rock scenery in Britain. On the massive cliffs are high densities of breeding sea birds.

Travelling by rail the visitor can hardly be impressed as he traverses mile after monotonous mile of desolate moor from the Sutherland boundary to near Scotscalder. Scenically, the better approach, is by the east coast road on which the traveller would twist and turn his way past noble hills, across wooded glens, incised valleys, picturesque hamlets and view some of the widest panoramas in the north of Scotland.

Yet, the County's wide expense of moorland is not without interest. Apart from its great reserve of peat it has many flourishing colonies of moorland plants. Because of its northern latitude Caithness has many alpine plants growing at low altitudes.

The oldest known written reference to Caithness appears to have been by the geographer Siculus, who lived at the time of Julius Caesar. Siculus refers to 'Cape Orcas', which has been interpreted as Dunnet Head, the northernmost promontory in Caithness. Yet, people were living in Caithness long before Caesar's invasion of Britain. Excavations at Keiss over a century ago revealed the oldest middle stone age site then known in Scotland. At a much later date the incoming 'Megalithic' people left behind their burial cairns, standing stones, stone rows and stone circles. But the most typical of all ancient monuments is the broch, of which Caithness has more than any other county in Scotland.

Evidence of the Norse invasion from across the 'Pictland' or Pentland Firth is strongly reflected in the place names of the fertile lowlands, which the Viking farmers developed into the granary of the North.

Thurso, a town before the Vikings came, now houses many of the people who work at the nearby Atomic Energy Establishment at Dounreay, where the world's first Fast Breeder Nuclear Reactor was established.

Wick, the County town, has evolved from combining the very old settlement of that name with the planned burgh of Pulteneytown on the south side of the river. At the height of the fishing industry in Caithness, Wick was the herring metropolis of the world.

Caithness, on land, had considerable isolation until the development of communications during the 19th century. Visitors today are still astonished to find on arriving at Inverness that Wick is 258 rail km (161 miles) farther north!

With recent and projected developments in the Moray Firth area, promised factories for Caithness and proposed schemes to span the Beauly, Cromarty and Dornoch Firths, an economic revolution of the 'Land of the Catti' may be just around the corner.

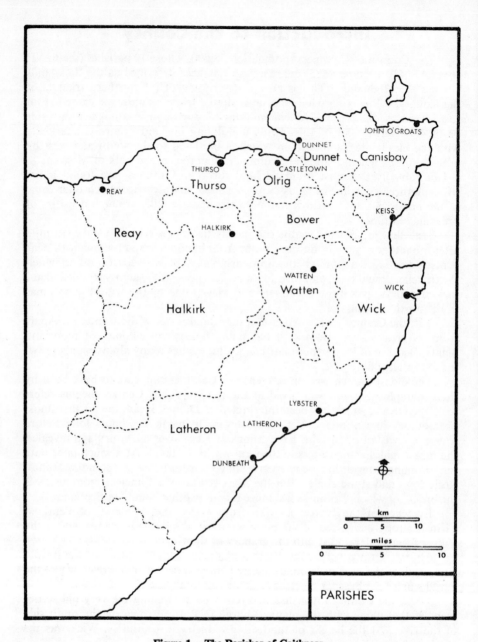

**Figure 1. The Parishes of Caithness**

# PART I

# *Natural Environment*

# CHAPTER 1

# GEOLOGY

## Introduction

In Caithness and the adjoining north-east corner of the Scottish mainland there occur on the surface examples of the three main rock types — igneous, sedimentary and metamorphic.

Some of these rocks were formed at widely separated times, and the great differences in properties and characteristics between some of them give rise to changes in the landscape and vegetation.

For those who are not well briefed in geology, there are appendices in which two of the basic concepts of geology are described — the classification of rocks into their three main types and the geological time scale.

## Historical Geology

The study of when and how all the rocks in a given region were formed, and the way in which they all fit together and combine to form the overall rock structure of the region, is called historical geology, or stratigraphy.

The geologist often likens the overall structure of many regions to that of a block of flats. As he stands on the surface, he imagines himself standing on top of the block of flats. The earth's crust beneath him is made up of different layers or 'storeys', with the very oldest one at the bottom, and a succession of younger ones with finally the youngest one at the top forming the surface.

This is broadly the position over much of Caithness, where there are three distinct horizons of very different rocks, each of greatly differing age and nature. We shall now look systematically at all the rocks in this region, starting with the basement (the most ancient) rocks of the area.

The Lewisian Gneiss which outcrops on the surface in north-west Scotland and the Hebrides is probably the oldest rock in Britain; indeed, it is among the oldest rocks in the world, being identified with the ancient rocks of the Scandinavian and Canadian Shield areas.

Gneiss is a metamorphic rock, which is to say that it was formed by the complete alteration of the original rock under conditions of extreme heat and pressure. It is made up mainly of the minerals quartz, felspar and mica. Frequently, these constituents tend to separate out, giving layers enriched in particular minerals; such a layered rock is said to be 'foliated'. This gives the gneiss a roughly and broadly banded or striped appearance.

The first still detectable metamorphic alteration of these rocks has been placed, using radiometric dating techniques, at about 2,600 million years ago, and since this time, these rocks have undergone several periods of metamorphism.

The Lewisian Gneiss is immensely thick, and has no discernible base. Along the eastern boundary of its exposure, it is overlain by a relatively thin covering of younger Cambro-Ordovician sedimentary rocks, and slightly farther east

3

again, along a line which geologists call the Moine Thrust Line (see figures 2-3), these rocks, dipping towards the east, become covered by a different type of rock. Once 'underground', the thin layer of Cambro-Ordovician rocks tapers out after some distance, but the Lewisian Gneiss is not discontinous and under-lies all the rocks found in northern Scotland. And so it is probably safe to say that the basement rock in Caithness, lying thousands of metres under the more recent rocks and never itself outcropping on the surface, is the Lewisian Gneiss.

The next group of rocks which go to make up the geology of Caithness are the Moine series schists and granulites. These, too, are metamorphic rocks, although they are much younger than the Lewisian Gneiss and have probably only been metamorphosed once.

Originally, the Moine rocks were a sedimentary series, being laid down some 800 to 1,000 million years ago in a quiet, shallow water sea or lake, upon a floor of Lewisian Gneiss. When these soft sediments were compacted into rocks, they gave a series of impure sandstones and shales, with occasional thin bands of low grade impure limestone. The total thickness of these sedimentary rocks was probably at least 6,000 metres (20,000 ft.).

Then, about 480-400 million years ago, in a period of intense and massive geological activity, these sedimentary rocks, together with their base of Lewisian Gneiss, were severely folded, buckled, and sucked down into the earth's crust, where they were affected by severe heat and pressure. In time, through uplift and erosion of the rocks on top, the resulting metamorphic rocks found their way to the surface again; these are the rocks which now form the Moine series.

The metamorphic rocks resulting from the original Moine sedimentary series are many and varied. The impure sandstones have become psammites. The commonest variety is a quartz — felspar-granulite — which is usually a massive, granular, light-coloured, vaguely banded rock. The shales have given rise to a group of metamorphic rocks collectively called pelites. The pure shales have become flaky, shiny mica or garnet schists, or sometimes, when more intensely metamorphosed, massive, crystalline, regularly banded felspathic schists, while the lime-rich shales have been changed into either flaky, friable, black hornblende schist, or else amphibolite, a black rock consisting mainly of hornblendic minerals with some felspar.

All these metamorphic rocks can be found on the surface in the extreme western and southern parts of Caithness, or in adjacent Sutherland.

The Caithness mountain of Scaraben (ND 066268) and its neighbours Creag Scalabsdale (ND 970240), Cnoc an Eirannaich (ND 957277) and Cnoc Coire na Fearna (ND 935298) on the Caithness-Sutherland border, are all composed of quartzite, a pure white variety of psammite resulting from the metamor-phosis of pure sandstones.

In the Moine series of metamorphic rocks a general trend can be discerned over the whole area of their outcrop — the metamorphic grade gradually increases moving across them from south-west to north-east. The mineral make-up of the igneous rock granite is, roughly speaking, about 60% felspar, 30% quartz, and 10% micaceous minerals. In the region just to the east of Strath Halladale, in the far north-east corner of the Moine Series outcrop, the condi-tions imposed during the alteration of the original rocks were so drastic that these minerals have been produced in roughly the same proportions as they occur in granite. Thus, from a mineralogical point of view, these rocks are

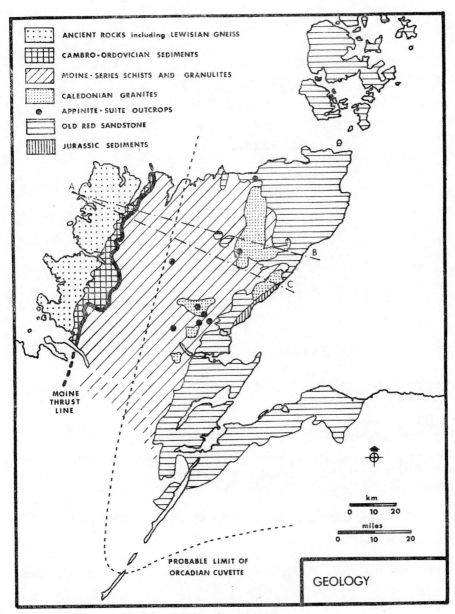

Figure 2.  Geology

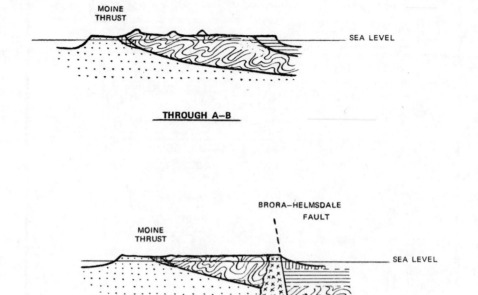

**THROUGH A-B**

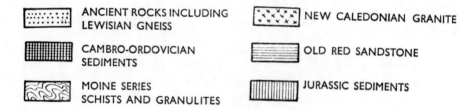

:::::::: ANCIENT ROCKS INCLUDING
LEWISIAN GNEISS

CAMBRO-ORDOVICIAN
SEDIMENTS

MOINE SERIES
SCHISTS AND GRANULITES

NEW CALEDONIAN GRANITE

OLD RED SANDSTONE

JURASSIC SEDIMENTS

Figure 3.   Schematic sections through **AB and AC** (see Figure 2.)

granites. However, like most metamorphic rocks, they have a banded appearance, these bands sometimes having been folded later. This banding is due to the frequent tendency of the minerals to segregate out into more concentrated layers, whereas in a 'true' granite, of purely igneous origin, the constituent minerals are much more evenly dispersed, to give a uniform looking rock. These Strath Halladale rocks are variously referred to as 'The Old Caledonian Granites' or 'the foliated granites'. Being, as they are, the product of the extreme metamorphosis of the original Moine sedimentary series, they share the same metamorphic age of about 450-410 million years as the rest of the surrounding Moine series, into which they sometimes shade without any sharp boundaries.

Other granite, as well as the Old Caledonian Granite, was formed in the Caledonian mountain building period.

Late in this period of very active geological mountain building, a whole family of granites, which has members all over Scotland, was formed. The members of this series are known as the New Caledonian Granites. These granites unlike the Old Caledonian Granite, are 'true' granites in as much as they are solely of igneous origin, i.e. they were formed when molten material from very deep down in the earth's crust was forced upwards, pushing aside the rocks above (an intrusion). The molten material solidified before it reached the surface, which it did only after prolonged erosion and removal of the rocks above. Many of these intrusions have clear, sharp, steep boundaries with the surrounding rocks. It is the northern-most member of this group, the Helmsdale granite, which outcrops partly in Caithness.

As all granites do, the Helmsdale granite consists mainly of the minerals felspar, quartz and mica. A notable feature of the Helmsdale granite is the very deep pink colour of its orthoclase felspar, which gives the whole intrusion its characteristic red colour. The date of the Helmsdale Granite intrusion is about 400 million years ago.

Throughout the Highlands there runs a series of small neutral, basic and ultra-basic igneous intrusions which are found in close association with the Caledonian Granites, particularly the New Caledonian Granites. This group of rocks is known as the Appinite Suite and is generally believed to be a by-product of the formation of the much larger granitic intrusions.

The main member of this group to outcrop in Caithness is the Reay diorite, which extends for 1.6 km. (1 mile) or so east, west and south of the village of Reay. This intrusion, larger than many in the suite, is of generally neutral igneous composition, comprising mainly the minerals hornblende, biotite, felspar and quartz. These give the rock a generally black and white speckled appearance, but like many members of the suite, the whole intrusion is not of a completely uniform composition. A notable feature of this intrusion is that it is cut by many veins of a pinkish igneous rock known as pegmatite, which is composed of the minerals felspar and quartz. All these features can be clearly seen in the old quarry (ND 936646) on the northern side of the A836, just west of Sandside, where the diorite was once worked for road metal.

Two other members of the Appinite Suite occur in the north-east mainland. Both of these are relatively small intrusions, and are of ultra-basic nature, consisting almost entirely of dark ferro-magnesian minerals.

The first of these is the classical site for a type of coarse-grained unfoliated ultra-basic igneous rock called scyelite, which derives its name from Loch Scye, about 1.6 km (1 mile) south of the intrusion (ND 010567). The outcrop, some

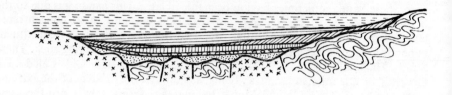

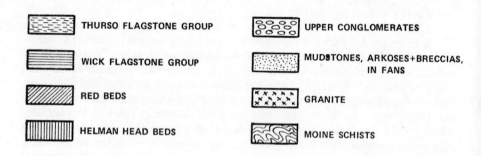

**Figure 4.** Schematic horizontal section through the rocks of Lake Orcadie.

30 m. (90 ft.) in diameter, appears as a green grassy hummock.

The second intrusion occurs about 1.6 km. (1 mile) east of Auchentoul Lodge on the A897 (ND 876359). This is a larger intrusion than the one at Loch Scye, but for much of its area the outcrop is covered by thick layers of peat, and it can only be seen in burn cuttings. The rock is a scyelite type, but in general it is less weathered and altered than the Loch Scye outcrop.

## THE OLD RED SANDSTONE

**General**

A glance at the geological map of Caithness will show that most of the rocks cropping out at the surface belong to the Middle Old Red Sandstone. The name "Devonian" was coined in 1839 to describe the rocks laid down between the Silurian and the Carboniferous. Being readily translated into other languages it passed quickly into international use, whilst the older name, the Old Red Sandstone, being longer and more awkward to translate, fell generally into disuse. However, in 1855, the name "Old Red Sandstone" was revived and used to describe those Devonian rocks in Britain which were laid down on the ancient continent and which contained no marine fossils. The Old Red Sandstone, then, represents sediments laid down in the mountains, valleys, lakes and other fresh water regions of the Devonian continent. The Old Red Sandstone, like the Devonian system itself, can be divided into three distinct units: the Lower, Middle, and Upper Old Red Sandstone. In the geographical region stretching from the Moray Firth to Shetland it can be shown that this consists almost entirely of the middle division of the Old Red Sandstone.

Elsewhere in Britain the middle division is completely absent. The common development is to find the lower division overlaid unconformably by the Upper division, i.e. the Middle division is missing. This curious fact is difficult to explain unless we assume that, during Lower Old Red Sandstone times, the northern part of the continent was being elevated, possibly by the Caledonian mountain-building epoch, while the other parts formed basins of deposition. During Middle Old Red Sandstone times it can be assumed that the situation was reversed and that the northern province of the ancient continent was steadily depressed to form a basin of deposition while the other areas were possibly raised and slowly eroded until any Middle Old Red sediments which may have accumulated were removed. The process may then have been again reversed after Upper Old Red Sandstone times as the northern province has only isolated remnants of a supposed Upper Old Red Sandstone cover laid down unconformably on Middle Old Red strata.

**Lake Orcadie**

Geikie in 1878 coined words for these various basins of deposition in Britain. They were Lake Orcadie to the north of the Grampians, Lake Caledonia occupying the central valley of Scotland, Lake Cheviot in south-east Scotland and northern England, the Welsh Lake near the borders of Wales and the Bristol Channel, and the lake of Lorne in the north of Argyllshire. We shall be concerned only with "Lake Orcadie".

To give these areas the name "lake" is rather too sweeping a generalisation. They are more properly basins of deposition or *Cuvettes* (the French word which is internationally used to describe them). They probably consisted of very variable bodies of water, sometimes of the proportion of inland seas, but sometimes during drought, reduced to strings of lakes, pools and puddles separated by dismal mud flats, baking and cracking under the hot sun. The mountains which bordered the cuvette consisted of the crystalline schists and granites mentioned earlier in this chapter and they would have formed an exceedingly rough and rugged landscape. Steep ridges and peaks must have risen out of the very floor of the cuvette to dominate the shallow waters and flats and would have contributed their marginal conglomerates and breccias. Vast quantities of sediments were swept into the cuvette so that, sometimes, they actually broke the surface of the water to form mud-banks. At other times the lake basin would suddenly subside and the silting up would begin again. Thus, for immense periods of time, subsidence and sedimentation kept pace with each other until thousands of metres of sediment had been deposited. The nature of this phenonemon gave rise to more or less regular cycles of sedimentation or *cyclothems* as they are called.

Sometimes they repeat themselves regularly according to the pattern:

4. Mudstones with desiccation cracks.
3. Sandstones, often current-bedded and sometimes containing a "slump" horizon at the top.
2. Dark fissile flags.
1. Dark fissile limestone.

These cyclothems are often 6m to 15m (20ft to 50ft) in thickness and the fossil fishes are usually restricted to the lower elements. The mineral dolomite is usually the cementing medium for the limestone and flagstone and is not of immediate organic origin. The dolomitic limestones which crop out on a line from Durness to the Isle of Skye may have formed part of the watershed of the river system which fed the Orcadian cuvette and the mineral may have been derived from these deposits. The presence of considerable outliers of probable Old Red Sandstone at Tongue and other places may be an indication that the Orcadian lake extended westwards at one time over much of the adjacent county of Sutherland.

The uppermost divisions of the Middle Old Red Sandstone are better developed in Orkney than in Caithness and there they seem to indicate a change in sedimentary pattern consisting of the dying out of flagstones and the development of sandstones. This suggests an uplift of some area of erosion in the watershed of the Orcadian cuvette, heralding the sandstone facies of the Upper Old Red Sandstone as developed at Dunnet Head and on the island of Hoy.

### The Barren Sediments

In Caithness there are vast quantities and great thicknesses of barren sediments, long thought to form a more or less continuous basement to the fossiliferous lacustrine sediments of the Orcadian cuvette and to be of possible Lower Old Red Sandstone age. The lowest of the conglomerates recognised, however, consists of the Helmsdale granite, one of the forceful newer Caledonian granites. No radiometric datings are available for this granite but datings for three of the other granites formed during the same epoch indicate an age which is not far removed from that of the Middle Old Red Sandstone itself. As we must allow sufficient time for the overlying rocks to be weathered away it is probable that these barren sediments are no earlier than the Middle Old Red Sandstone itself and probably continued to develop throughout the period of the Middle and possibly into that of the Upper Old Red Sandstone. The absence of fossils from these beds precludes an actual correlation and we must await for a new method before the problem can be completely solved.

These so-called barren basement sediments are not seen in Orkney, the lowest conglomerates known being probably well within the flagstone series equivalent to the lowest fossiliferous horizons of Caithness. Basement conglomerates are, however, developed at widely different geographical locations in the Orcadian cuvette.

It can easily be seen that many of the conglomerates are very angular and have formed as screes by sub-aerial weathering of nearby rocks, against which they lie. Others again show the effects of rolling and are probably river and lake-margin shingle banks.

There are also great thicknesses of barren chocolate-brown sandstones with banks of arkose. Some of these can be seen to occupy troughs in the uneven floor of the cuvette and may represent the muds deposited in the valleys which were the channels of the original drainage system.

Finally, there is an upper and very coarse conglomerate which probably marks a period of uplift in the Caledonian mountain-building epoch. It is interesting to speculate whether this is the movement which gave rise to the late sandstones in Orkney and Dunnet Head.

The order in which the beds of Caithness were laid down has been the subject of a great deal of research work because nowhere do we see a complete succession, the beds being folded and faulted. We therefore correlate the beds using the rock types (lithology), their order seen in unfaulted sections, and by the fossils they contain. Thus we can draw up a table of the following sort:

**Table 1. Rock Sequence in Caithness**

| | | |
|---|---|---|
| UPPER OLD RED SANDSTONE | Dunnet Head Sandstone | No known fossils |
| | | ? *unconformity* |
| MIDDLE OLD RED SANDSTONE | John O'Groats Sandstone Mey Beds Spittal Beds Wick Beds Local Basement | |

GRANITE-SCHIST COMPLEX

The names given to the different beds are those where the rock type was first recognised.

We will now examine some of the areas where various rock types occur.

**Barren Group**

It is difficult to be certain of this group of rocks. In some places the flagstones lie directly on the granite-schist complex but at others there is a local basement of conglomerate derived directly from the underlying rock. We are on safer ground with the clearly marginal deposits. A conglomerate is developed in the Ousdale burn which consists of, and lies on, the Helmsdale granite. It is often impossible to say where the granite leaves off and the conglomerate starts. This is a breccia formed by the mechanical weathering of the granite itself.

In the new road cutting on the south side of Ousdale we again see the Helmsdale granite but here there is no junction seen between the jointed granite and the overlying rocks. A little farther up the road cutting we see purplish and chocolate-brown mudstones and thin bands of arkose. The coarsest arkose is developed in the disused quarry on the left hand side of the road travelling northward. Here one should note that the arkoses consist of angular crystals of orthoclase felspar which indicates that the weathering mechanism was mechanical and that, although there are current-bedded structures in the arkoses, the crystals can not have rolled far or their corners would have been knocked off.

For a really coarse conglomerate it is necessary to climb to the top of Morven where angular blocks of the crystalline schists and granites can be seen, embedded in a matrix of arkose.

### Wick Beds

The best examples of the Wick Beds are probably to be found at the North Head and South Head, Wick, where dark flagstones are well developed. At Helman Head one can see a cyclothem of the type described earlier.

### Spittal Beds

These can be seen between Broad Haven and Noss Head, including the rocks below the twin castles of Sinclair and Girnigoe. They can, of course, also be seen at Spittal quarry. One will note that the rocks in these beds weather pale grey, blue, green, and ochre and are not dark like the Wick Beds.

### Mey Beds

The shore section from Mey to Castletown consists largely of the Mey Beds. They weather rather like the Spittal Beds but have a curious "nodule" horizon in the cylothems.

Ackergill Shore to Freswick Bay is also a Mey Beds locality.

### John O'Groats Sandstones

The John O'Groats Sandstones are quite distinctive, being often brick-red in colour and generally coarser than the beds below them. Flagstones are poorly developed. The classical localities are from just west of John O'Groats to Sannick Bay, from St John's Head to Canisbay, and on the north side of Freswick Bay.

### Upper Old Red Sandstone

Dunnet Head is the classical locality for this deposit. These sandstones closely resemble those of the John O'Groats Sandstones.

### Volcanic Rocks

There are two volcanic necks in Caithness, one cutting the Upper Old Red Sandstone at Brough on Dunnet Head and one cutting the John O'Groats Sandstones at the Ness of Duncansby. Their ages are not known. There are also a number of volcanic dykes. The most notable are the monchiquite dykes at Dunnet Head.

### Fault Systems

The major fault systems of Caithness are not well known. One line of faulting follows the course: Lower Forss Water–Loch Calder–middle reaches of

Thurso River–Little River–Loch Rangag–Latheron. Another important fault is one which is seen on the shore at Lybster. A reversed fault passing through Brough throws down the Upper Old Red Sandstone against the Mey Beds at Dunnet Head. A further fault at St John's Head throws down the John O'Groats Sandstones against the Mey Beds. The north side of Freswick Bay marks a line of faulting which throws down the John O'Groats Sandstones against the Mey Beds.

A fault at Broad Haven, just north of Wick, throws down the Spittal Beds against the Wick Beds. The escarpment to the south-east of Holborn Head, which overlooks Scrabster, marks the line of a fault, the rocks of Thurso Bay being thrown down. A further fault, marked by the end of the line of cliffs just west of the beach at Thurso, throws down the rocks to the west against those of the Kirk Ebb, and Thurso East shore on the east bank of the Thurso River.

The major fault system which produces the magnificent sea cliffs on the south-east coast of the County is not seen in Caithness. This is the Brora-Helmsdale fault which is probably part of the Great Glen Fault system. Smaller faults and joints run parallel to it and can be seen at Latheron, Forss Shore and other places.

### Joints

Joints generally occur as a result of stress relaxation after movement has taken place along a fault. Many shore sections reveal a net-work of joints roughly at right angles to each other. The joints and, to a lesser extent, the faults, govern the weathering of the cliffs to produce the characteristic rectangular geos, sea-caves and gloups (blow-holes) which make up the magnificent coast-line of Caithness.

### APPENDIX 1
### CLASSIFICATION OF ROCKS

Rocks can be formed in one of three ways and depending upon the mode of origin may be classified as igneous, sedimentary or metamorphic.

IGNEOUS ROCKS are formed when molten material, usually originating from deep in the earth's crust, solidifies. Igneous rocks are sometimes called **primary rocks,** because in the beginning, when the crust of the earth was just solidifying, they must have been the first of the rock types to be formed.

The physical make up or **texture** of an igneous rock is that of interlocking mineral crystals or grains — rather in the fashion of a 3-dimensional jigsaw puzzle, with the usually irregularly shaped mineral grains each locking into all their neighbours.

Igneous rocks are classified in two ways:
(i) on their grain size.
(ii) on their mineral composition; in particular, on the amount of silica (quartz, $SiO_2$) which they contain.

The **grain size classification** is simple; there are three subdivisions:
(i) Coarse-grained, with mineral grains on average over about 1 mm (0.04 in) in size.
(ii) Medium-grained with mineral grains able to be distinguished with the naked eye, and up to about 1 mm (0.04 in) size.
(iii) Fine-grained, whose mineral grains cannot be distinguished with the naked eye.

The grain size that a given igneous rock has depends upon the rate at which it solidified and cooled. If it was allowed to cool slowly, then it will have large crystal grains, but if it was chilled rapidly, then it will have very fine grains.

An **igneous rock** is said to be **acid** if its overall silica content is over 65%. With such a silica content there is usually a fair amount of free quartz in the rock.

A **neutral igneous rock** has an overall silica content of between 55% and 65%; such rocks contain little or no free quartz.

A **basic igneous rock** has an overall silica content of less than 55%, and contains no free quartz.

It is important to note that as the silica content changes, the nature of the mainly silicate minerals of the rock also changes. This change in the chemical and physical nature of the constituent minerals in the rock is the basis for a useful 'rule of thumb' for the classification of igneous rocks — namely that the lighter-coloured the igneous rock, the greater the acidity. Using this rule, we can quickly classify the white and pink igneous rocks as acid, the black and white speckled ones as neutral, and the dark green black ones as basic.

A **SEDIMENTARY ROCK** is made up of layers, or strata, of material.

This material can either be the debris of pre-existing rocks, deposited in **beds** by the action of wind or water, to give **clastic** sedimentary rocks, such as sandstone or shale; or it can be a compound, deposited by chemical or biological action to give a **non-clastic** sedimentary rock such as oolitic limestone or dolomite.

**Clastic sedimentary rocks** consist of pieces or grains of rock debris, and are sub-divided according to the size of these grains.

Rudaceous rocks — contain debris greater than 2 mm (0.08 in) in diameter, e.g. conglomerates, breccia.

Arenaceous rocks — are formed by particles between 0.1 mm (0.004 in) and 2 mm (0.08 in) in diameter e.g. sandstone.

Argillaceous rocks — are formed of particles less than 0.1 mm (0.004 in) in diameter, e.g. shales, mudstones.

Often, one of the factors helping to hold the grains of clastic rock together, is a mineral glue or **cement.** This can form when the naturally occurring ground water, which sometimes circulates through the rocks, contains a mineral dissolved or suspended in it. This it can deposit at the points of contact of the sedimentary grains, so that when the ground water disappears and the rocks dry out again this deposited mineral also dries out and acts as a cement between the mineral grains.

The chemical composition of this mineral cement affects the nature of the clastic rock. For example, calcite cemented rocks are creamy coloured, while iron hydroxide cemented rocks are very reddish. Rocks containing mica cement are easily split down the planes rich in mica.

**Non clastic sedimentary rocks** are named according to their chemical composition. Calcium carbonate deposits are limestones, sodium chloride deposits are rock salt, etc.

A **METAMORPHIC ROCK** is one which has been altered from its original state.

Both igneous and sedimentary rocks can be metamorphosed, and the conditions which can cause a metamorphic change, include an increased temperature, or an increased downward load, or a sideways crushing pressure, or any combination of these factors. Each of these factors produces its own type of metamorphism, with its own characteristic change in the rock.

When a rock undergoes metamorphosis, the amount of change in it is called its **metamorphic grade.** Three grades are generally referred to — low, medium and high. These represent, respectively, minor, considerable and extensive changes in the original rock.

The metamorphosis which affected the rocks in northern Scotland was due to both an increased temperature and an increased load. This is known as **regional metamorphism,** and it is usually of a medium or high grade.

Sedimentary rocks which have suffered regional metamorphism show several characteristic changes. Their texture becomes one of interlocking mineral grains, similar to that of an igneous rock; new, often high density, minerals form, and frequently some of these new minerals align themselves into definite bands, or **foliations.** If these foliations are very close together, then the rock will often flake or split easily along them. Such a rock is called a **schist.**

## APPENDIX 2
### GEOLOGICAL TIME SCALE

Ever since man first studied the different layers of rock and rock structures he has repeatedly asked the question "How old are they?"

The very early geologists were able to derive some basic techniques for the relative dating of different rocks on a small local scale. If for example a cliff face were made up of layers of sedimentary rocks then the uppermost strata were nearly always the youngest, each succeeding layer of sedimentary rocks being younger than the one immediately beneath it. Further, if there were a band of igneous rock reaching up through the cliff face, cutting all the strata of sedimentary rock, then this igneous rock must have been emplaced after the formation of the sedimentary series, and was thus younger than it. This type of guide is still used today to tell the relative ages of different rocks on a local basis.

During the first part of the 19th century, two scientific advances allowed great progress to be made in the relative dating of sedimentary rocks. First, the exact nature of fossils was realised. Then, the theory was accepted that life had evolved slowly and steadily from very primitive forms in ancient times to the sophisticated forms of today. Using these two concepts in conjuction, deductions could be made which allowed the interdating of sedimentary rocks over huge regions of the earth's surface.

First, it was realised that at any particular time in the geological past, any given form of life had probably evolved to much the same degree over a very wide area. Thus, when the fossils found in the rocks of one region closely resembled those from the rocks of another region, then the ages of the two fossil-bearing strata were able to be approximately equated. An extension of this practice was the detailing of the fossil populations in certain well-studied classical localities. Then, as new areas were explored, any rocks which contained the same fossil population as one of the classical localities were said to be of the age of this classical area. So, when some of the sedimentary rocks in north-west Scotland were discovered to contain the same fossil population as a well-studied type-site in Wales, these Scottish rocks were said to be of Cambrian age (from Cambria, in Mid Wales).

Secondly, came the idea that the relative ages of sedimentary rocks could be roughly estimated from the sophistication of the fossil life which occurred in them. Using this notion the present geological time scale was built up. This was done by placing in order all the classical type-sites, so that the succession of their fossil life showed a complete biological evolution from the most simple forms in the most ancient rocks to the most advanced in the youngest ones.

By the end of last century, the geological time scale as we know it today (page 16) was complete; the recorded fossil life from each succeeding geological period and system formed an unbroken chain of biological evolution. All fossil-containing rocks could now be placed somewhere in the geological succession and thus the relative age of the rocks could be estimated.

It was not until the last decade or so that a technique known as radiometric dating was evolved. Using this sensitive and complex method, the age of an igneous or metamorphic rock could be estimated in terms of millions of years by finding out how long ago the mineral crystals in it had been formed.

Now, many of the major geological events of the earth's past can be dated to an accuracy of $\sim$ 15 million years. By using this technique a 'guestimate' of 4,500 million years has been made for the age of the earth.

## GEOLOGICAL COLUMN

| Era | System | Approx. Age (millions of years) | Events in Northern Scotland (millions of years) | Approx. First occurrence of some Living Species |
|---|---|---|---|---|
| | Holocene (recent) | | | |
| | Pleistocene (glacial) | | | |
| | | 1 | | |
| | Pliocene | | | |
| Cainozoic (recent life) | | 11 | | |
| | Miocene | | | |
| | | 25 | | |
| | Oligocene | | | |
| | | 40 | | |
| | Eocene | | | |
| | | 60 | | |
| | Palaeocene | | | |
| | | 70 | | |
| | Cretaceous | | represented in parts in Golspie-Ord Point section | |
| Mesozoic (mediaeval life) | | 135 | | |
| | Jurassic | | | |
| | | 180 | | |
| | Triassic | | | |
| | | 225 | | |
| | Permian | | | |
| | | 270 | | |
| | Carboniferous | | | |
| | | 355 | | |
| | Devonian (Old Red Sandstone) | | Lake Orcadie 380-360 | |
| Palaeozoic (ancient life) | | 400 | | |
| | Silurian | | Metamorphosis of Moines and associated events 480-400 | |
| | | 440 | | |
| | Ordovician | | | |
| | | 500 | | |
| | Cambrian | | Cambro-Ordovician sedimentary series of North-West Highlands c. 600-490 | |
| | | 600 | | |
| | | | Moines and Torridonian laid down as sediments 1,000-800 | |
| | | | Events in metamorphic make-up of Lewisian Gneiss 2,600-1,600 | |
| | Oldest known minerals | 3,000 | | |
| | Estimated origin of earth | 4,500 | | |

First occurrence of some Living Species (listed along vertical lines, from left to right): modern man (homo sapiens) — ape man (hominid) — grass and flowering plants — Birds — mammals — reptiles — amphibians — land plants — fishes — simple sponges and seaweeds

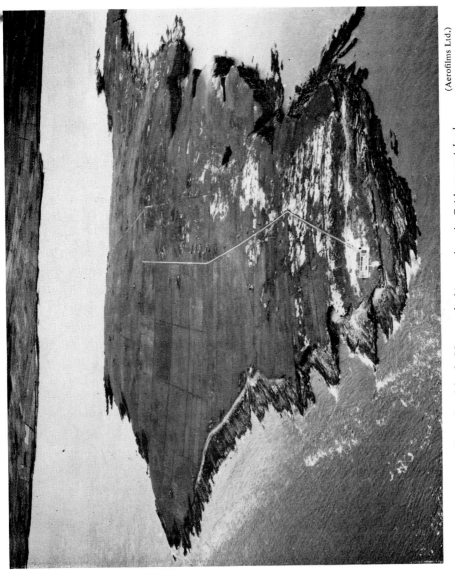

(Aerofilms Ltd.)

PLATE 1.   *Island of Stroma, looking south to the Caithness mainland.*

(A. Luciani)

PLATE 2.   *Frost-shattered rock on Scaraben.*

PLATE 3.   *The stacks of Duncansby.*

(A. Luciani)

# CHAPTER 2

# MINERALS

### Mineralisation in Caithness

The minerals in Caithness have been formed by two main methods. One of each of these predominates in the two main rock formations in the County, the resulting mineralisation in each area, therefore, having a different character.

### The igneous/metamorphic complex

In the igneous/metamorphic complex to the south-west of the County, there are many small veins and lodes, some of them containing unusual minerals. Most of these minerals undoubtedly originated from the mass of igneous material which is now the Helmsdale granite. Some of them travelled out from this once very hot body to where they are now found in the surrounding Moine metamorphic rocks. Common among this type of mineral are veins of pure white milky quartz; some of those which cut across the Moine schists of the Helmsdale valleys are up to 30 cm (12 in.) thick—just south of the A897 bridge over the Kildonan burn (ND 911213), for example.

Other minerals, some of which almost certainly originated in the same intrusive igneous body, now fill cracks in the parent granite. An example of this type of mineralisation occurs at Ousdale (ND 067204) where the north end of the A9 road cutting bares an outer edge of the Helmsdale granite. Here, small cracks in the granite—possibly contraction cracks formed as the igneous rock cooled—are filled with Blue John. Blue John is a relatively unusual blue variety of the otherwise common colourless mineral Fluorspar ($CaF_2$), and owes its colour to a trace impurity of the element manganese.

A famous example of mineralisation caused by the Helmsdale granite, and the only one to be of any economic importance, is the 'Kildonan gold' of the Helmsdale valley, just within the Sutherland boundary. This mineral, like the quartz veins previously mentioned, also migrated from the igneous body into the surrounding metamorphic rocks.

The presence of gold in any quantity was confirmed early in 1869 by R. N. Gilchrist of Helmsdale. This prospector, with much experience gained in the Australian gold fields, suspected, sought for and found gold in his own native valley. His systematic search revealed gold in worthwhile quantities in the Kildonan, Suisgill, Kinbrace and Torrish burns. A gold rush quickly followed, and by the end of that year, what was then estimated to be £10,000 worth of gold had been panned. However, the 500 or so prospectors caused considerable damage and upheaval in the valleys, and when, the following year, the landowners refused them permission to extend the field of their original diggings, the rush was over.

The gold is in the form of small flakes and nodules. It probably occurs within, or is closely associated with, the numerous quartzic and pegmatitic veins

17

which cut across the Moine schists and quartzites of Cnoc na Eirannaich and Cnoc Coire na Fearna region. The total amount of gold in the rocks of the region is probably quite small; the reason that so much of it was panned from the burns lies in the 'concentrating' action which the burns have. This action is due to the density of gold, which is at least five or six times that of most other rocks and minerals. The weathering action of the wind, rain and frost breaks up the rocks of the hillsides, which are then washed into the burns and rivers. In time of spate, the larger rocks are broken up and tumbled and swept downstream together with the smaller debris. The gold flakes in all this debris, being relatively heavy and presenting such a small area to be swept by the current, tend to fall to the stream bed, collect there, and thus are not moved very far. The few kilograms of gold which were panned from the stream beds were therefore the remnants of the vast quantities of material which had been weathered from the hillside since the height of the Ice Age, all the rest of the material having been washed down the river.

In fact, the Helmsdale 'gold' is not pure gold. It is the commonest of the gold minerals, an alloy of gold and mainly silver, known as electrum. A recently found and analysed sample gave approximately 80% gold, most of the rest being silver.

It seems quite possible that there is still sufficient gold left in the area to be commercially worthwhile. Prospecting has never been allowed in two of the Caithness streams, the Berriedale and the Langwell, which rise very close to the Kildonan and Suisgill burns and whose head-waters flow over the same rock system. Further, in 1964 the Institute of Geological Sciences re-surveyed the Kildonan region of the Helmsdale valley, and suggested that a modern open-cast excavation technique might produce sufficient gold to be commercially viable. However, as was the case 100 years ago, the landowners would probably refuse permission to dig on the grounds of the considerable disturbance that this mining technique would certainly cause in the stream valleys.

### The Old Red Sandstone

Apart from the igneous/metamorphic complex, the rest of the surface of Caithness is made up from the deposits of the Orcadian basin. Above a discontinuous basement of arid semi-desert deposits, lie the Caithness flagstones series, which represent the existence in the basin of a near permanent lake. The rocks of this flagstone series now form the major part of the land surface of Caithness, and it is the mineralisation in this rock series which gives Caithness most of its minerals.

The smaller mineral occurrences in the flagstones series are due entirely to ground water deposition, while the larger ones are probably of a complex origin.

The rocks of the Caithness flagstone series contain many natural joints, fractures and faults. In any region, such features frequently contain small amounts of various minerals, all deposited from the ground water. This occurs when the water in the rocks below the water table has had minerals dissolved or in suspension in it. While it is circulating and percolating through the rocks, the water retains the minerals, but on reaching a cavity, fissure, or a different rock, the water stagnates and the minerals deposit out. Such minerals as calcite ($CaCO_3$), fluorspar ($CaF_2$), barytes ($BaSO_4$), hematite ($Fe_2O_3$), iron pyrites ($Fe_2S$), and copper pyrites ($FeCuS$) are common in fissures in the Caithness flagstones, and can be seen in joints in many cliff and quarry faces.

The mineralisation of the flagstone in the area just south of Wick contains a very high proportion of pyrites, including copper pyrites. It has a bright, shiny, gold or brass colour, and occurs as either discrete little crystals, often set in quartz or calcite, or else as nodules. Although amounts of copper in the region were never substantial, it is recorded that one of the richer veins of copper pyrites was once mined, probably about 1760. No certain trace of these old workings near the Castle of "Auld" Wick now remains.

Another ground-water induced mineralised vein occurs just east of Achvarasdal, Reay (ND 986647). This is a larger mineralised vein; it is some 450 m (500 yards) long, and runs in a N.N.E. direction across the burn valley just to the east of Achvarasdal.

Here, along a line of buckling and breaking of the country rocks known as a crush fault, oxides of iron, principally hematite, have collected and been deposited. Besides strongly staining and colouring the broken lumps of smashed native flagstone which fill the crush fault, some iron oxide is also present in the form of large pure nodules. It was these lumps, very rich in iron, which led to the exploitation of the vein between 1870 and 1873. During this period, the iron ores were quarried by means of three shallow pits sunk into the vein. However, it seems that the vein was not as rich as had been hoped, as only one boat load of 150,000kg (150 tons) of selected ore was ever taken from Sandside harbour—which had been specially built to ship the ore from the quarries.

In the Caithness Old Red Sandstone, there is one other line of mineralisation. This is a very much larger and more complex zone than any of the others so far discussed, and the details of its origin are not yet known with certainty. However, in recent times an estimate of its position and a picture of its general nature have been built up from reports and pieces of information collected over many years.

The first recorded report of a section of this line dates from 1804, and refers to the Hill of Sour, Skinnet, north of Halkirk. Then, Sir John Sinclair was advertising the mining rights of a recently discovered mineralised vein in the hill; the vein was reported to contain about 30cm (12 in) of galena ($PbS$), together with some iron pyrites and barytes. Within the past few years, a second mineral vein has been discovered on the Hill of Sour. This is on North Calder Farm, on the western slope of the hill, and it contains about 30cm (12 in) of pyrites.

In 1914, C. B. Crampton recorded two other mineral occurrences which had been discovered. The larger of these had at this date, apparently been known for many years. It was of a good vein of barytes at Roy Geo on Clyth Shore, with a second exposure slightly inland at Warehouse. The exposure at Roy Geo (ND 270352), is in the notch of the geo, and is about 1.2m (4 ft) wide in the cliff face, with a north-west trend and a dip of between 75° and 80° to the north-east. Later, during the First World War, this vein was worked for its barytes by means of three shafts driven into it, one at beach level, one at 15m (50 ft) and one at 23m (75 ft). The lengths of these shafts varied from 60m to 120m (200 ft to 400 ft). Inside the mine, the vein increased in width to a maximum of 2.7m (9 ft) and over the four-year period 1915-1918, some 2.5 million kg (2,450 tons) of barytes were won. However, it was thought that the actual vein of barytes was nearly worked out. Traces of the workings can still be seen. The second discovery which Crampton recorded dated from 1912, when smallish veins of galena with barytes were reported from the Spittal area.

Then, later in 1914, Captain W. Murray Treipland reported the discovery of a large mineralised vein on Achanarras Hill. The vein, which was about 2m (6 ft) wide at the surface, was found to run about 45° to 50° north-west, with a dip of between 70° and 85° to the north-east. It contained, along with broken lumps of country rock, good amounts of galena and barytes, together with some calcite, pyrites and zinc blende (ZnS). This vein also was exploited during the First World War. Early trial pits proved the length of the mineralised vein to be at least 550m (600 yards). A shaft sunk for 36m (120 ft.) did not reach the bottom of the vein, whose average width over this distance was about 1½m (5 ft.). Galleries were led off this shaft at 12m (40 ft) and 24m (80 ft) in order to work the lead. It was reckoned at the time that had the proper plant been available, 100,000 kg (100 tons) of payable ore could have been mined per day. Unfortunately, the mining equipment available was minimal, and the working was frequently interrupted by flooding. Later trials proved the mineralised zone to extend for 3.2 km (two miles) to the south-east of Achanarras Hill, and several smaller "off-shoots" of the main vein were also discovered. The mine was closed in 1919, when the capital required to buy the plant needed for proper commercial operation could not be raised. A report made on the area during the Second World War suggested that the vein could be exploited with profit by one or two small workings, but no action was ever taken. The remains of the old workings (ND 152544) are still visible on Achanarras Hill.

It will be seen that these mineral occurrences — from Occumster and Warehouse through Spittal and Achanarras to Skinnet—all lie very nearly on a single straight line, running approximately north-west. Also, the two major mineral veins, at Occumster and Achanarras, both dip about 70° to 80° to the northeast. This has given rise to the idea that all these occurrences belong to a single mineralised zone.

CHAPTER 3

# FOSSILS

### Fossils and Evolution

The earliest known fossils appear in the Pre-Cambrian period; these are often vague and problematic remains of soft-bodied organisms. Life probably began, a long time before the advent of these fossil remains, as the result of complex chemical and physical processes.

In the Cambrian period, however, we find the first recognisable life-forms. There were crustacea of many sorts with well-developed organs, gastropods, molluscs, corals, sponges and a host of other animals whose hard parts were particularly well-developed and therefore left fine fossil remains. The Ordovician period saw further development and the Silurian which followed shows the beginnings of the vertebrate fauna. The Devonian epoch marked the great evolutionary period of the fishes and probably saw the first colonisation by the vertebrates of the dry land. The Carboniferous was the era of the great forests and of the amphibia, while the Permian and Triassic gave us advanced reptiles. The Jurrassic and Cretaceous saw the reptiles evolve to colonise not only the land but also the air and the oceans. It also saw their almost complete extinction. Primitive birds, mammals and flowering plants came into being during this epoch but their greatest evolution came in the Tertiary period. The Quaternary, however, saw the mammals rapidly on the decline and today the number of genera and species is still falling, many having become extinct in historical times, and many others are in imminent danger of extinction. The exceptions are man and his domestic animals, the latter being submitted to a form of artificial evolution by selective breeding to provide special animals for various purposes. The others on the increase are those which live unwelcomed of man's efforts, such as rats and mice.

The fossil record shows the gradual progress of evolution through the ages but at no place is the record complete. It is rather like an old story where there are many copies of the book in existence, none of these complete, and all of different editions. We have to painstakingly complete the story from many sources.

In Caithness we have a whole chapter on the Middle Devonian, a paragraph on the Upper Devonian, a few sentences on the Upper Jurassic, a few words on the lower Cretaceous, a footnote on the Pliocene and several passages on the Quaternary.

### The Fossils of the Middle Old Red Sandstone

A glance at the geological map on page 5 will show that the Devonian system in Caithness is represented by the Middle Old Red Sandstone and one solitary relic of supposed Upper Old Red Sandstone. A vast thickness of sediment accumulated in the basin known as the Orcadian Cuvette, the method of sedimentation being by repeated silting up and subsidence so that the two roughly kept pace. This gave us the system known as a cyclothem (cf. page 10). The fossil fishes are always found in the lower part of the cyclothem, many cyclothems being superimposed one on another. The ideas of a catastrophic destruction must therefore be largely discounted as we would require a considerable number of catastrophies to account for the fossil record. What was their environment? The lack of evaporites suggests a large body of shallow water which was fed and drained by a substantial river system. Some people think that the fishes inhabited the rivers and perished in the more brackish waters of the lake after being swept there by floods. Others again think they were lake dwellers. The truth probably lies between both theories. Some fishes may have kept always to the lake whereas others may have migrated upstream just as lake trout "run" the rivers to spawn.

In many cases the fishes are intact. This is a puzzle, in a way. When a modern fish dies its abdominal cavity fills with gas as the animal decomposes under the action of bacteria. The belly swells, the fish floats, belly up, and drifts. The distended belly eventually bursts and the fish then can sink to the bottom. Alternatively, it could strand itself on a sandbank. Neither of these things appears to have happened. The fish are frequently whole or almost whole and there are no 'sole marks' in the rocks to indicate stranding. The fact that the fish are whole suggests that there were no scavengers, which is also a puzzle.

There are two mechanisms suggested, the first being that the lake became periodically poisonous which killed the fish and the bacteria of decomposition; it also kept away the scavengers. This suggests a long period when the lake water must have been poisonous. The second theory is that the shallow lake froze solid in winter leaving a few deeps where some fish could survive. Hard freezing for short spells would leave no evidence behind. The theory that the fish were left stranded in shrinking pools does not seem feasible on the grounds that the lower part of the cyclothem suggests the **deepest water conditions.** In addition one would also expect sole marks in the mud to indicate that the fishes had moved about in the shallow water before dying. The problem of their environment and cause of death must remain an enigma.

### The Fossil Fishes

The fossil fishes can be divided and sub-divided into classes (classification) but it would be a mistake to think that we could be as certain with fossil forms as with living ones that our classification was really correct. Three classes are represented in Caithness: the Agnatha, the Placodermi and the Osteichthyes.

### Agnatha

Some zoologists do not regard the Agnatha as fishes at all. They have no jaws, no body skeleton, a notochord in place of a spinal column and they lack the two pairs of fins which fishes normally have. They were much commoner in the Lower Devonian and the Silurian than in the Middle Devonian. Only one genus is known from the Middle Old Red Sandstone of Caithness—*Cephalaspis*. There are recent reports of *anaspids* being found, but the genus has not yet been determined. Modern jawless fishes include the Hagfish and Lampreys.

### Placodermi

The Placodermi, are for the most part, heavily armoured, and seem to hold an intermediate place between the Agnatha and the Osteichthyes. They appear to be ancestral to the sharks with which they have a great deal in common: a visceral skeleton which did not normally ossify, a primitive gill structure lacking an operculum, and, in some genera, clear evidence of a copulating habit as distinct from the spawning habit of the Osteichthyes.

## Osteichthyes

These are the bony, as distinct from the cartilaginous, fishes and are ancestral to most modern fishes and probably the land vertebrates only.

### The Classified List

In the classified list, A. S. Romer's model in "Vertebrate Palaeontology," (Chicago) has been followed but R. S. Miles has been used in placing the subclass Acanthodii and the Order Acanthodiformes in the Class Osteichthyes though they appear to hold a position midway between the Placodermi and the Osteichthyes.

The problematical fish *Palaeospondylus* cannot easily be placed in the classified list.

The names in brackets are either synonyms or names which have been superceded.

In the following list *Asterolepis* has been included. So far it has not been recorded from Caithness but, by anology with Orkney, it ought to occur (and probably does) in the Mey Beds.

### Classified List of Caithness Fossil Fishes

CLASS AGNATHA
  ORDER OSTEOSTRACHI
  Cephalaspidae
  *Cephalaspis*

CLASS PLACODERMI
  ORDER ARTHRODIRA
  SUB ORDER BRACHYTHORACI
  Coccosteidae
  *Coccosteus, Dickosteus, Watsonosteus, Millerosteus.* (Formerly all these genera were referred to as *Coccosteus*).

  Homosteidae
  *Homosteus* (*Homostius*). (Early writers confused this fish with *Asterolepis*).

  ORDER PTYCTODONTIDA
  Ptyctodontidae
  *Rhamphodopsis*

  ORDER ANTIARCHI
  Asterolepidae
  *Asterolepis* (*Homosteus* was mistaken for this fish by early writers)
  *Pterichthyodes* (*Pterichthys*), *Microbrachius*

SYSTEMATIC POSITION UNCERTAIN
  *Palaeospondylus*


CLASS OSTEICHTHYES
  SUB CLASS ACANTHODII
    ORDER CLIMATIIFORMES
      SUB ORDER DIPLACANTHOIDEI
        Diplacanthidae
          *Diplacanthus, Rhadinacanthus*

    ORDER ACANTHODIFORMES
      Mesacanthidae
        *Mesacanthus* (Mistakenly called *Acanthodes* by some early writers)
      Cheiracanthidae
        *Cheiracanthus*

  SUB CLASS ACTINOPTERYGII
    INFRA CLASS CHONDROSTEI
      ORDER PALAEONISCIFORMES
        SUB ORDER PALAEONISCOIDEI
          Cheirolepidae
            *Cheirolepis*

  SUB CLASS CHOANICHTHYES (OR SARCOPTERYGII)
    ORDER CROSSOPTERYGII
      SUB ORDER RHIPIDISTIA
        SUPER FAMILY OSTEOLEPIDOIDEA
          Osteolepidae
            *Gyroptychius* (*Diplopterus, Diplopterax* in some texts)
            *Osteolepis, Thursius*

          Rhizodontidae
            *Tristichopterus*

        SUPER FAMILY HOLOPTYCHOIDEA
          Holoptychidae
            *Glyptolepis* (*Holoptychius* in some early papers)

  ORDER DIPNOI
    Dipteridae
      *Dipterus, Pentlandia* (*Dipterus*)

### The Invertebrates

The invertebrate fauna of the Middle Old Red Sandstone is fairly poor. There are trace fossils which may be worm tracks. These occur right through the entire fossil record. There are giant eurypterids which are found from fairly low horizons to fairly high ones. These lobster or scorpion-like creatures may have reached well over a metre (3 ft) in length and are characteristic of the Lower Devonian and Silurian rather than of the Middle Old Red Sandstone. One of these has been described and placed in the genus *Pterygotus*, its specific name being *dicki*. A further giant eurypterid found recently at John O'Groats has so far not been described but it is of another genus. There is also a single record of a limuloid, a creature which resembles a trilobite. The Branchiopod *Asmussia murchisoniana* is locally abundant in the Mey Beds.

### The Plants
Little is known of the fossil flora of the Middle Old Red Sandstone. Well-preserved plants from the Chert beds at Rhynie in Aberdeenshire show us what kinds of plants grew here.

We know that they were land plants because they have a vascular structure which is not present in primitive water plants such as algae. The normal type of plant was one with a creeping stem habit which threw up woody shoots and rudimentary hair fibres from time to time. The terminals of the shoots bore sporangia and further propagation by wind-blown spores was likely. Some had scaly leaves clinging close to the stem like the lepidodendrons of the Carboniferous. Others had radiating leaves located at nodes on the stem like the calamites of the Carboniferous. They were mainly bog-type plants which exceptionally grew to the size of small trees. It is probable that there was a seasonal growth and decay.

Algae were also present but they were small in size and have left few remains.

This rather monotonous vegetation cover was probably restricted to the damp margins of lakes and rivers and to very shallow water, although it could, by its very nature, probably survive a certain amount of drought.

### Upper Old Red Sandstone
The Upper Old Red Sandstone is confined to the faulted block of Dunnet Head. No fossils are known from these rocks.

### Jurassic and Cretaceous
The Brora-Helmsdale Fault, which is never far out to sea off the south-east coast of Caithness, faults down the Kimmeridgian and Lower Cretaceous. Blocks of fossiliferous rock or isolated fossils of this period are not uncommon on the shores of Caithness and are found as derived fossils in the glacial till. These fossils consist of fragments of land plants and shallow water marine organisms, probably from a lagoon-type environment. There are gastropods, lamellibranchs, brachiopods, echinoderms, hexacorals and other organisms typical of the Kimmeridgian and Lower Cretaceous horizons in England. There are also fragments of coniferous vegetation and occasional fern fronds.

### Pliocene
The Pliocene period was one of erosion and no Pliocene fossils are known.

### Pleistocene
The glacial till of the Pleistocene contains marine shells north-east of a line from about Berriedale to Reay where it is referred to as the "shelly boulder clay." Most of the shells are fragmented but occasionally whole shells, usually very friable, can be found. The commonest appear to be *Turritella* and *Cyprina islandica*, both of which are common in British waters today.

# CHAPTER 4

# THE ICE AGE

**General**

Evidence of former glaciations on a widespread scale throughout the world is overwhelmingly conclusive. At the present time over one-tenth of the earth's surface is covered with ice, but during the most recent Ice Age this proportion rose to nearly one-third.

There are clear indications of at least three Ice Ages recurring every 250-300 million years. During glacial times the world's average temperature may have dropped to 6°C (42°F); in between, it may have averaged 22° C (72°F). We are now living in a relatively warm interglacial period, with average world temperatures of some 15°C (58°F).

Apart from these major fluctuations of temperature, smaller but very significant variations have occurred within the past thousand years. For example, North Atlantic climate appears to have been warmer when the Vikings were making their colonising voyages. In the early 12th century contemporary accounts mention the vineyards of southern England—and those of Caithness! But by the the 1420s, the climate had become so cold that the Swedish army was able to march over the frozen Baltic and Henry VIII, in 1537, rode a carriage down the frozen Thames. From the mid 16th to the mid 19th century conditions were cold enough for this period to be dubbed the 'Mini Ice Age.' For the ensuing century a much milder climate was enjoyed—this was shown by the dramatic shrinkage of the European glaciers. Since 1950, however, there have been signs of a colder climatic trend.

The cause of these milder fluctuations in climate are unknown. But what initiated the Ice Ages? Some of the suggested explanations are:

1. Land uplift leading to a lowering of temperature.
2. Variations in the sun's output of radiation.
3. Changes in the radiation received by the earth owing to some interfering medium.
4. 'Wandering' of the Poles.
5. 'Drifting' of the continents.
6. Changes in oceanic circulation.

Yet, what sparked off Ice Ages still remains a subject of controversy. There is no general agreement on the cause(s)—probably a combination of factors is involved.

It was not until 1840, through the work of the famous geologist Louis Agassiz, that it was appreciated that Britain had been overwhelmed by ice. Agassiz correctly identified the superficial deposits (drift) associated with ice and ice/water deposition. He assigned these to the most recent of the Ice Ages, called the Pleistocene.

26

During the multiple glaciations of the Pleistocene, great drift sheets were spread over the lowland areas of Britain, with the exception of the southern extremities of the country which remained unglaciated.

Most of the evidence pointing to glaciation in Scotland dates from 25,000 to 10,000 years ago (Sissons). Earlier deposits were eroded or buried, so that it is often difficult to establish what happened in previous ice movements. Scotland south of the Highlands was totally submerged by ice. In the Highlands it was certainly well over 915 m (3,000 ft) thick and the assumption has been made that all this area was overwhelmed by ice.

The general movement of ice out from the Highlands of Scotland showed a simple radial pattern to the west. To the east this pattern was broken by the presence of Scandinavian ice close to and sometimes encroaching on the coast.

**Caithness**

The pre-glacial landscape of Caithness (see Chapter 5) consisted of a number of planed surfaces which were probably uplifted fairly rapidly not long before the beginning of the Ice Age. Into these surfaces the rivers cut incised V-shaped valleys. Evidence of a warmer climate at this time is shown by areas where rock is deeply chemically weathered—e.g. Dunnet Head and Berriedale. Therefore, masses of loosely-consolidated, weathered material would have been available for the ice to scour away. The onset, too, of a cold climate preceding the ice advance would, by a freeze-thaw effect, have shattered the bedrock.

The glacial phenomena of Caithness have for a long time attracted the attention of geologists. As yet, the sequence and ages of ice movements in Caithness have not been satisfactorily determined so the following is an account of our state of knowledge at the present time.

Perhaps the most interesting of the County's Ice Age deposits is the shelly till (a mixture of clay, stones, etc.) deposited at the base of the ice. The earliest comprehensive account of this till was given by Jameson over a century ago. He described it as being of a "deep leaden grey or slate colour", and as a "coarse, gritty mud." The fine, dark-coloured materials of this till are probably due in the main to pulverised flagstone but may in part be the result of fine materials dredged by the ice from the bed of the North Sea. However, the colour of this tenacious, compact deposit depends (to a considerable extent) on the colour of the bedrock. For instance, in the area of the John O'Groats sandstone, the overlying till may assume the reddish hue of the underlying rock. Many sections of the till are rich in shell fragments and occasionally whole shells may be uncovered, e.g. turritella. The earliest accounts of these shells were given by Hugh Miller, who obtained most of his specimens from Robert Dick of Thurso. Dick, in the 1840s, had already come to the conclusion that the deposit was of glacial origin and not marine, as had been believed. Although the stones in this shelly till consist mainly of fragments of Caithness flag, many rock types, much younger in age than those outcropping in Caithness, have also been found. Common among these transported erratics are: gneiss, granite, mica-schist, quartzite, Jurassic sandstone, chalk and chalk-flint—particularly abundant in North Stroma. Some of these rock types border the east coast of Sutherland and Ross-shire and extend under the North Sea. Erratics of the peculiar, angular conglomerate found in place in the Sarclet area can be traced in a north-north-westerly direction leading from the outcrop.

Undoubtedly the most remarkable of these ice-transported masses is the

Cretaceous sandstone erratic found at Leavad, 6.4 km (4 miles) south of Spittal. In the summer of 1910 ten bores were made in and around the area of the deposit, which had been used as a sand pit. These bores showed that the erratic was 220 m (720 ft) long, 137 m (450 ft) wide and nearly 8 m (26 ft) thick. This mass must have been carried inland from the sea over cliffs and hills exceeding 150 m (500 ft) in height, to arrive in its present location some 90 m (300 ft) above sea level.

The predominant movement of the ice sheet which deposited the shelly till was from south to north, the ice coming in from the North Sea, which was probably dry land at that time. It is worthy of note that this ice movement was in conformity with the strike of the rocks and many lines of crush. As well as the evidence of shell-bearing till and erratics, the many ice scratches (striations) on the rocks testify to this northerly movement. Such striated surfaces are not well preserved if the rock has long been exposed to weathering. Good examples may be seen where superficial deposits have recently been removed; e.g. Dunnet Head and Borrowston Quarry 2.5 km (1½ miles) south of Thrumster. Crossed striations are particularly well displayed on the shores of Achkinloch.

In northern Caithness the trend of the striations assumes a more pronounced south-east-to-north-west alignment, until, on Dunnet Head, the orientation is almost east-west. The cause of this increasingly westward trend has been ascribed to the presence off-shore of the Scandinavian ice sheet which had pushed across the North Sea. This Scandinavian sheet may even have intruded on to the Caithness landscape but no evidence of such a happening has yet been found.

The depth of the ice sheet over Caithness at this time is unknown. Ice was certainly thick enough to overrun Ben-a-Chielt 287 m (942 ft) but there is no evidence that Morven was submerged—although it must be admitted that evidence of glaciation could by now have been obliterated by weathering.

In its passage from the North Sea on to the Caithness land, the ice met considerable obstacles in the steep landward approach from sea, the high cliffs and the scarp faces along the east coast—particularly in the area between Occumster and Ulbster. It is mainly to the north of the latter area that the striations trend so markedly towards the north-west. In this eastern area of the County (Occumster-Ulbster), glacial action has been predominantly erosive and the mantle of glacial deposits (drift) is very thin. The ice has etched out the softer bands of bedrock leaving an ice-moulded ridge and furrow effect in the landscape. On the South Head, Wick, a collection of local boulders called the 'Grey Bools' was probably snapped off by the ice from the seaward-dipping sedimentary rocks and deposited in situ.

To the west, north and south of the eastern area of erosion the drift is still thin, commonly just over 1 m (3 ft) thick, except in the valleys and some bays where it has accumulated to great depths—e.g. the valleys of Dunbeath, Langwell, Berriedale and the bays of Scrabster, Gills and Dunbeath.

Many of our biggest lochs, e.g. Watten and Calder, lie in depressions aligned to the movement of ice across the Caithness lowland. It seems likely that these lochs and others within the shelly till area are all rock basin ones.

Of particular interest is the fact that one of the bores at Leavad passed through a deposit of brown till containing no shells. Opposite Langwell House a section shows a bank of dark till sandwiched between two deposits of reddish-brown till. Similar juxtapositions of the tills have been observed at Harpsdale, as well as in the valleys of the Berriedale, Dunbeath and Latheronwheel valleys. Investigation of these sites may indicate a local ice movement which pre-dates the arrival of the shelly till from the North Sea. Striations, trending generally in a north-easterly direction may be associated with this movement.

In the area to the west of the shelly till deposit (see figure 5) there is a complete divergence in the trend of ice markings. Here there is evidence of ice moving from the higher ground to the lowlands and the coast. Near Berriedale the striations trend south-east, at Loch More towards the east, and in the Sandside Burn to the north. It has been suggested that this radial movement, which deposited a reddish coloured till, was of later date than the shelly till. However, it is possible that the two tills are of similar age, the pressure of ice sweeping in from the North Sea forcing the local ice to change direction.

This deposit of reddish-brown till produced by local ice may be seen in a splendid section at the mouth of the Sandside Burn, where it is overlain by a dune of blown sand. The rocks contained in the till are found in situ in the vicinity—e.g. pink granite, quartzite, red mudstones, breccia, diorite and mica-schist. No evidence of shells has been found in this deposit. On the south slopes of Ben Ratha, 242 m (795 ft)— some two miles south-west of Reay—are beauti-fully polished rock surfaces, testifying to the erosive power of this ice movement. Erratics on Creag Leathan 128 m (418 ft) show this hill was submerged by ice. However, ice moulded features, such as occur in the area of shelly till deposition, are not found. The many lochs within the area of this deposit are generally dammed by drift or peat, unlike those occurring within the shelly till deposit.

That a subsequent local glaciation occurred following the events already des-cribed is clearly indicated. Many moraines (ice-deposited mounds consisting of sand, clay and boulders) and sand/gravel deposits resting on the tills, indicate its distribution. Charlesworth, who mapped the distribution and limits of this later movement stated that, 'Caithness had a Caithness Glacier which expanded to the E. and N. and a Knockfin Snowfield to the S. which fed the Glutt glacier on the N.E. and the Three South Caithness Glaciers, viz. those of Dunbeath, Berriedale and Langwell'.

The ice surface is believed not to have exceeded 460 m (1,500 ft), so many hills would have stood above the ice as nunataks (ice free peaks). Such nunataks must have been subjected to intense frost shattering.

The major lobes of the Caithness Glacier pushed out towards Reay, Forss, Calder, Thurso, Castletown and Wick. Moraines formed at this time are well-pronounced in the Dunn-Bilbster area. In the lower parts of the valleys fed by the Knockfin Snowfield moraines are well developed. The limit of the Langwell Valley glacier is clearly seen at a point some 5 km (3 miles) from the mouth of the river. The glacier in the Berriedale valley reached An Dun. The lobe of ice which pushed down the valley of the Wick River barely reached the coast, while the glacier in the Thurso valley seems to have reached the sea.

In general, the effects of the passage of ice have been to smooth the pre-existing landscape, which does not seem to have suffered severe erosion during the various ice movements. Although the covering of drift is extensive, it is thick only in the deeply slotted valleys which were partially filled to depths exceeding 30 m (100 ft). Lesser valleys were competely obliterated by glacial debris. Exhumation of these valleys by the existing rivers is far from complete. In fact, some have failed to regain their old courses (see Chapter 5). A similar situation occurs on the coast, where the sea has failed to

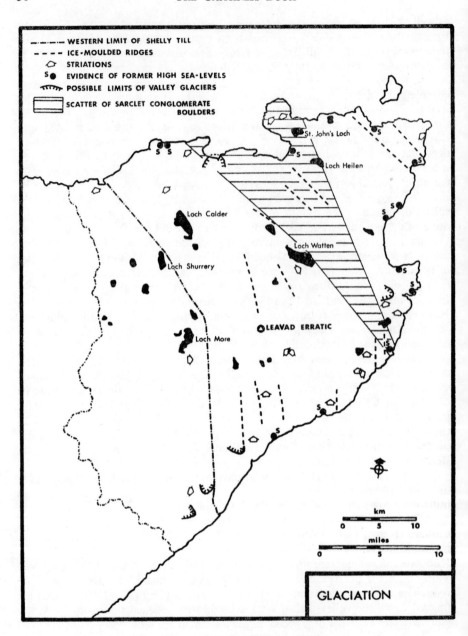

Figure 5. Features of the glaciation of Caithness

remove all the drift in the geos which were formed before ice traversed the land.

With warming of the climate, vast volumes of water must have poured on, in and under the ice, eventually making their mark on the underlying landscape. The sand/gravel ridge at Dalemore and like deposits (eskers) in the Acharole Burn are remnants of such former water courses. Well-marked features remain where glacial meltwater formerly flowed. Such channels may be seen in the lower portion of the Acharole Burn, upstream from the bridge at Watten. In the Dirlot area dry valleys mark former meltwater courses and similar cuts may be seen at Camster Lodge, Stirkoke Mill and between the lochs of Watenan and Yarrows.

Some dry ravines occur deeply cut into the landscape: the most impressive are those at Scrabster and Carsgoe, near Halkirk. Their formation may be attributed to glacial meltwater or to stream excavation when a much wetter climate prevailed some 5-7,000 years ago, long after the ice had disappeared.

With the abstraction of sea water piled up on the land as ice, sea level obviously falls. Conversely, sea level rises again when the ice melts. During the maximum accumulation of ice, sea level fell over 90 m (300 ft). Surprisingly, however, each time the ice sheets melted away, the rising sea failed to regain its original level. Land, once released of its ice load, recovers from its depression by springing back, leaving remnants of old shorelines at high altitudes. Such old shorelines of late-glacial age stand far above the high water mark. Definite evidence of late-glacial beaches has not been found in Caithness, although small sections of beach-like material, at altitudes exceeding 25 m (80 ft), occur at Dunbeath, Latheronwheel and Achastle.

There are deposits of post-glacial raised beach pebbles mainly less than 4.5 m (15 ft) above O.D. at Berriedale, Dunbeath, Latheronwheel, Achastle, Ceann Hilligoe, Sarclet, Ackergill, Keiss, Dunnet, Gills Bay and to the east of Brims Castle.

On the other hand a number of boreholes suggest evidence of a much *lower* sea level at one time around the Caithness shores. At Lybster harbour a bore passed through 6 m (20 ft) of till without touching rock; near the new bridge at Latheronwheel 27 m (90 ft) of till was bored before rock was met; at Wick harbour a 21 m (70 ft) bore failed to reach rock. These depths of till choking former valleys might imply that at one time the rivers had to cut down to meet a sea level much lower than the present one. Moreover, many caves which are water-filled at L.W.M. appear to have been formed during a period of lower sea level.

Rafts of peat occur below H.W.M. under the sand at Dunnet Bay and Sinclair's Bay. The former is occasionally still visible. Submarine peats have also been reported from the Bays of Wick, Lybster and Thurso. The peat deposits, if in place, must have accumulated during a phase of lower sea level.

### Cold Climate Evidence

Fringing the ice would have been a zone of sparse vegetation and Arctic-like climate. In such an environment is formed a suite of characteristic landforms. Examples of these in Caithness are listed below.

1. The aforementioned climatic conditions facilitate the downhill movement of materials. Many of the smooth, concave slopes in the County may be attributed to such down-slope flow.

2. Sections of till and moraine show severe disturbance and frost-shattering

of the contained stones, the fissile flagstones being particularly susceptible.

3. Sometimes, about 1 m (3 ft) from the surface a compacted layer occurs; above it is the fossil 'freeze-thaw' layer where stones are often vertically orientated.
4. Angular deposits of frost-shattered material (head) are not uncommon and may be seen on the western slopes of Ben-a-Chielt, at Sarclet Haven, Ousdale and to the south of Loch Yarrows.
5. Evidence of severe frost action is indicated by angular blocks littering the slopes beneath the escarpments at Dunnet Head, Badbea, the pebble-strewn summit of Morven (the pebbles being obtained from the conglomerate) and the quartzite blocks on Scaraben.
6. Also on Scaraben are found lobes and step-like terraces running parallel to the contours.
7. In the Leavad erratic dyke-like masses of till were found piercing the sandstone. A photograph taken in 1908 shows these to be fossil frost wedges.

So, in the recent past and during a short space of geological time this dramatic climatic change was inaugurated. With some 10% of the earth's surface still under ice, we have no reason to assume that the climatic conditions which led to repeated glaciations have disappeared.

The following is a list of readily accessible locations where some of the features mentioned in this chapter may be seen.

| Feature | Location | Map Reference |
|---|---|---|
| Shelly Till Sections | Latheronwheel | ND 192323 |
| | Scrabster | ND 098702 |
| Red Till (no shells) | Sandside | ND 961653 |
| Moraines | Watten | ND 2056 |
| Esker | Dalemore | ND 1349 |
| Striations | Borrowston Quarry | ND 326433 |
| Crossed Striations | Achkinloch | ND 187422 |
| | (Loch Stemster on 1″ Map) | |
| Erratic | Leavad | ND 173460 |
| Meltwater Cut | Stirkoke | ND 3249 |
| Dry Ravines | Scrabster | ND 098698 |
| | Carsgoe | ND 139632 |
| Rock Notch | Latheronwheel | ND 191320 |
| Raised Platforms | Sarclet | ND 353434 |
| | Ellen's Goe | ND 328403 |
| Raised Beach Pebbles | Sarclet | ND 353434 |
| | Keiss | ND 355614 |
| Ice Choked Valley | Occumster | ND 264354 |
| Head | Sarclet | ND 353434 |

PLATE 5.  *The Meadow Well, Thurso.*

(R Stewart)

PLATE 4.  *Ellen's Geo, Ulbster.*

(E. J. Fulton)

PLATE 6. *Fossil fish, Thursius pholidotus. The head is poorly preserved but the squamation and fins can be clearly seen. Mey Beds.* (J. Selby)

# CHAPTER 5

# RELIEF AND DRAINAGE

Adjectives such as featureless, flat and monotonous have been used to describe the Caithness landscape. Its monotony is debatable, its flatness non-existent and it is far from featureless!

### Erosion Surfaces

In the northern, central and eastern parts of the County—in the area approximating to where the sandstone/flagstone sediments have been laid—is a gently undulating surface which has been planed by the agencies of erosion. This planed surface, varying in height between 90 m (300 ft) and 180 m (600 ft), slopes to the north and north-east. Godard believed this surface was eroded in late Tertiary times and called it the "Pliocene level." Below the 50 foot contour, the extensive area of lowland bordering Sinclair's Bay may be part of another surface. To the south-west of Halkirk the junction of sedimentary/metamorphic rocks is not reflected in the landscape, as the "Pliocene level" cuts right across it leaving no surface evidence of the transition from one rock type to the other. Above the erosion surface stand a number of bold residual reliefs, the most pronounced of which are the Dorrery Hills. A series of steep scarp faces occurs on Dunnet Head and on the east coast between Clyth and Ulbster. The former is the outer edge of a basin-like structure (syncline) and the latter, part of an upfold (anticline).

Godard describes two other erosion surfaces in Caithness, both older and much less extensive than the "Pliocene level," but still carved out in Tertiary times. The younger of these two levels, which occurs between 260 m (850 ft) and 280 m (920 ft), he terms the "Scottish Surface". This clearly marked level cuts across a variety of rock types: mica-schist, gneiss and granite, and makes pronounced nicks in the quartzite of the Scarabens. Moreover, it leaves isolated a number of buttes which are reminiscent of landforms carved out in a more humid and warmer environment.

The oldest erosion surface, termed by Godard the "Intermediary" is found between 350 m (1150 ft) and 400 m (1300 ft) and is conserved within the "Scottish surface" model. It, too, truncates a variety of rock types but is mainly developed on the granitic area known as the Knockfin Heights and forms one of the most extensive erosion surfaces at this altitude in the British Isles.

Old elements of the landscape have been exhumed from beneath younger sediments. The most prominent of these is the long quartzite spine of the Scarabens trending for 2.5 km (4 miles) in a west-south-west to east-south-east direction and perched boldly above the "Intermediate" Surface. It is possible that the chiselling out of the conical-shaped hills, e.g. Morven, at 705 m (2313 ft) the highest summit in the County, occurred when Scaraben was exhumed.

33

In the rest of the County the very regular surface developed on the Old Granites may pre-date the formation of Lake Orcadie.

Since the deposition of the Lake Orcadie sediments, considerable movements of the crust have taken place (see Chapter 1). The major dislocations and lines of crush trend in a north-south direction. Their influences in the relief are not all that dramatic except along the cliff-line where they have exerted a powerful influence on coastal sculpture.

### Rock Type and Landscapes

Except along joint planes and lines of fracture the rocks occurring in Caithness are commonly impermeable.

The correlations between rock type and landscape may be summarised as follows:

Granites and associated types decay deeply, yielding smooth flowing outlines, e.g. along the western County boundary.

The diorite of Reay forms a basin of erosion, the residual hills giving an irregular knob-like landscape.

Mica-schists are characterised by a subdued relief, part of which forms the "Pliocene level."

Quartzite is slow to decay and forms upstanding masses, viz. the Scarabens. This rock type is particularly susceptible to frost action, disintegrating to an angular debris which buries the hill tops and clothes the slopes in screes.

Conglomerates form the only prominent hills apart from quartzites. These outliers of the Middle Old Red Sandstone series are typically cone-shaped and butte-like in character, e.g. Maiden Pap and Morven.

A subdued and gently-undulating relief characterises the flagstones and sandstones which form the underlying geology of lowland Caithness.

The Upper Old Red Sandstone of Dunnet Head, the most northerly promontory on the British mainland, gives rise to a bold scarp and dip landscape.

"Tors" are upstanding masses of rounded, dissected joint blocks of rock outcrop. They probably underwent a two-stage process in formation: extensive sub-surface rotting, followed by later exhumation with subsequent removal of rock decay products. Tors have been formed on the conglomerate summits of Morven, Smean and Maiden Pap.

### Rivers

The major watershed of the County runs through Ben Alisky, the hills of Caplaich, Stemster, Spittal and Olrig, through Duncansby Head and possibly at one time it passed through Stroma into South Ronaldsay (see figure 7).

Two river systems have developed on either side of the watershed. The northerly-flowing streams have progressed at the expense of those flowing into the Moray Firth, by capturing their headwaters.

The main rivers show strong discordance with structure; particularly good examples are the Berriedale and Langwell Waters, the courses of which are in the main transverse to the underlying structure probably indicating their superimposition from some ancient surface.

Between Watten and Wick the zig-zag course of the Wick River may be attributed to glacial influences, the tributaries of Haster and Winless following an ice-cut groove.

The course of the County's longest river, the Thurso 53 km (33 miles), is

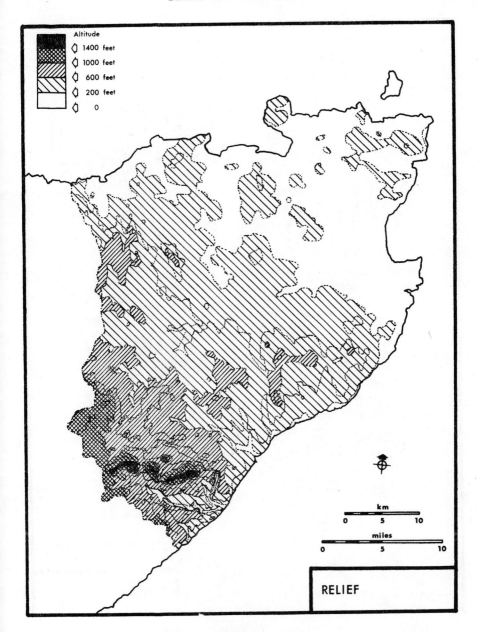

Figure 6. Relief of Caithness

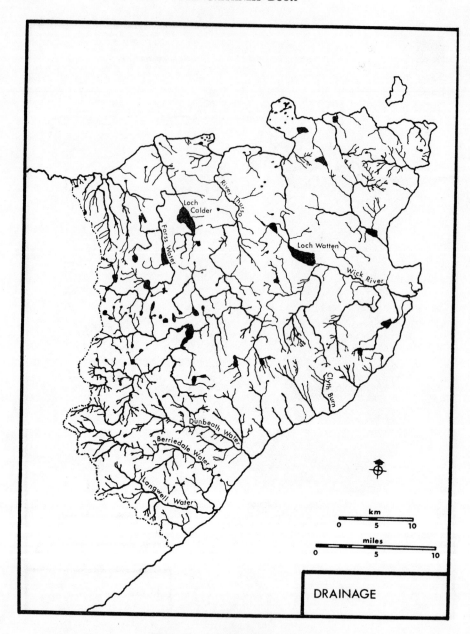

**Figure 7. Drainage of Caithness**

characterised by a series of rectangular bends. Above Dalemore is the long north-east stretch of Strathmore water. Between Dalmore and Olgrinmore it probably follows a north-west to south-east crush line which faults the eastern shore of Loch Calder and follows the lower course of the Forss Water. From Olgrinmore to Halkirk the series of right-angled bends may be attributed to the regional slope of the ground and ice moulding of the landscape. Below Halkirk the river opens out in a wide alluvial flat and cuts a gorge in the moraine some 4 km (2½ miles) from Thurso.

Forss Water has a similar configuration to Thurso River, with north-south and east-west segments. The former are in conformity with the strike of the rocks and a crush zone, the latter with the regional slope.

The short, sub-parallel, easterly-flowing streams have much steeper gradients and straighter courses than the rivers.

Well-developed terraces have been cut along the major water courses and occur at considerable heights in the Dunbeath, Langwell and Berriedale valleys. These terraces are sometimes capped by water-laid boulders and coarse gravelly materials which are in marked contrast to the fine-grained alluvial plains of the lower courses of the Wick and Thurso Rivers, where extensive flooding can occur.

It would seem that parts of certain water courses failed to find their old channels following choking by glacial debris. In the Achorn Burn a fine chasm headed by a waterfall is attributed to a change of course, as also is the gorge on the Dunbeath River 0.5 km (⅓ mile) above Ballantrath. The Reisgill Burn is believed to have excavated a 30 m (100 ft) rock channel between the A9 road and the sea, having departed from its old channel immediately to the north.

At Occumster the old choked channel of the Clyth Burn can be clearly seen from the sea and 0.8 km (½ mile) north the re-routed stream plunges into the sea over a 25 m (80 ft) waterfall.

## Lochs

In the following brief account of Caithness Lochs, maximum depths sounded, before damming, are indicated.

The shallow flat-bottomed Lochs of Scarmclate, 1.5 m (5 ft), Watten, 3.7 m (12 ft), and Hempriggs, 2.4 m (8 ft), drain into the large Wick River basin. Loch Watten, over 5 km (3 miles) long and 376 hectares (930 acres) in area, is the biggest water body in the County.

Of the many small lochs feeding into the Thurso Basin only Loch More, 2.1 m (7 ft), was sounded.

Calder, 26 m (85 ft), and Shurrery 2.1 m (7 ft), are the main lochs of the Forss Basin. The former, having been dammed to provide the County's principal reservoir, now has a maximum depth of 37 m (120 ft). Loch Calder is exceptional in depth and rather peculiar in configuration, being very deep only near its faulted eastern shore.

The shallow lochs of Wester, 1 m (3 ft), Heilen, 1.5 m (5 ft), and St John's 2.1 m (7 ft), drain by separate streams to the sea.

At several localities deposits of marl have been uncovered from under the overlying peat, implying that small lochs have been infilled and buried by the extensive peat growth. Water courses traversing the flagstone outcrops dissolve lime from the parent rock, subsequently depositing it in the lochs to form marl. The shallow and warmer water of the loch is unable to dissolve as much lime as the colder stream (lime dissolves more easily in cold water) and so a deposit of marl is built up.

The evidence of pre-existing lochs is still marked by a number of prominent flats, e.g. the flat at Lochend area, 2.5 km (1½ miles) to the east of Loch Heilen. Other good examples occur at Achvarasdal, near Reay and at Occumster, near Lybster.

Such water bodies were drained to obtain marl and/or to increase agricultural land. Some lochs, e.g. Achkinloch, had their levels lowered so that marl could be obtained.

### The Coast

The explosive force generated by storm waves crashing against the coast is enormous. Stones have broken the windows of Dunnet Head Lighthouse, which is 90 m (300 ft) above the level of the sea. Local fishermen will readily endorse this comment regarding the Pentland Firth* " . . . when a swell is opposed to the tidal stream, a sea is raised which can scarcely be imagined by those who have never experienced it." During the great storm of 1862 the sea swept over the north end of Stroma up cliffs over 60 m (200 ft) high and rushed in torrents across the island.

Undoubtedly the most spectacular scenery in Caithness is to be found along its 167 km (105 miles) of fretted coast. Great variety occurs in the sedimentary rocks, those of the Old Red Sandstone series giving rise to characteristic coastal forms. Only in a number of open shallow bays where sand has accumulated is the magnificent cliff line broken.

The initial stage in the production of a cliff is the formation of numerous headlands and bays. The cliff form progresses and is maintained by the undermining of the seaward edge of the land. Jointing, faulting, dip-strike relationships, exposure to marine erosion and the direction of greatest fetch (which in Caithness is from the north-east) account for the variety in coastal scenery.

The most striking evidence of undercutting is provided by caves which are excavated along belts of weakness. Well jointed rocks are particularly susceptible to cave formation.

The roof of a cave may eventually communicate with the surface by means of a vertical chimney, forming a blow-hole or "gloup," such as at Holborn Head. Subsequent collapse of the cave roof may form the best-known feature of the Caithness landscape—the "geo" or "goe"—a long, narrow, steep-sided inlet. Geos occur in sandstone and flagstone rocks but are better developed in the latter. The simplest form of geo follows a narrow fissure; wider, sub-parallel geos are excavated between two fractures. Composite geos are formed where any zone of complicated faulting and fissuring occurs, e.g. Wife Geo. Where controlled by joints geos trend perpendicular to the strike of the rocks; where fault controlled they follow the line of weakness irrespective of direction.

Glacial debris still lies in the backwalls of some geos and it is clear that the sea is still in process of re-excavating a fossil coast-line. Marine erosion since the Ice Age would seem to be of only limited extent.

When two caves on opposite sides of a headland unite, the result is a natural arch, e.g. Brig o' Trams to the south of Wick. Later, the roof of the arch fails and an isolated stack results. The pyramidal sandstone giants known as the Stacks of Duncansby are among the most impressive in the British Isles. Flat-topped stacks, usually called "cletts," are formed where the bedding is nearly horizontal, e.g. The Clett at Holborn Head.

*North Sea Pilot, Volume 2, (1959)

It seems likely that most of the east coast of Caithness is influenced by north-ward extensions of the Brora-Helmsdale fault. From Berriedale Ness southward to the County boundary the ancient continental slope of the Ord granite forms the highest cliffs, towering to 120 m (400 ft). Near Berriedale, cliffs cut in sandstone rise to 90 m (300 ft) while the highest flagstone cliffs, which exceed 60 m (200 ft), occur immediately to the west of Thurso and between Wick and Thrumster. Submarine contours come closest to the land where the top of the cliff is a promontory whose altitude declines inland, viz. at the headlands of Holborn, Dunnet and Duncansby.

Beach materials are often derived from glacial deposits, but local boulders may accumulate at the cliff foot, e.g. at the Ord and Dunnet Head. In areas where beach materials cannot accumulate, a combination of atmospheric weathering of joints and marine erosion will produce an abrasion platform such as may be seen during low water in Thurso Bay. The outer margin of such a platform may indicate the former position of the cliff front.

A variety of coast profiles occur:

1. A cliff may be surmounted by a steep rocky slope, e.g. from the Ord to Ous-dale, at Knockinnon and at Bruan.
2. The cliff top recedes in a series of scarps and drift-covered ledges, e.g. at Sarclet and Clyth.
3. A nearly horizontal cliff top may have little or no drift but frequently has a covering of peat, e.g. between Skirza Head and Duncansby Head.
4. The cliff top may be flat or gently sloping seawards, with a thick layer of drift overlying the rock, e.g. westwards from Reay, at Wick, Sarclet, Achastle, Latheron and Latheronwheel.
5. Steep terracetted cliffs of till scarred by gullies occur at Dunbeath, Thurso Bay and Gills Bay. The grass in many of these formerly stable gullies has ruptured and at Scrabster this has led to rapid retreat of the cliff face.

The coastal sand dunes and links may be grouped into three categories:

1. At Keiss and Dunnet a long dune range parallel to the coast is backed by a sandy machair-type flat containing a number of subsidiary dunes. "Blow outs" in the dunes quickly cause erosion and permit the landward movement of sand.
2. At Freswick and Reay the dunes are more irregularly distributed. Here, flat stretches of sand are absent.
3. The links of John O'Groats consist of low, fixed dunes of shell sand. Similar accumulations are found at the Bay of Sannick. In both localities the deposit may consolidate into a coarse, compact material called calcrete.

Blown sand, derived from glacial deposits, has accumulated round the shores of a number of lochs in the interior of the County—particularly at Lochs More and Shurrery.

The most abundant and widespread recent deposit is peat, which still covers some two-thirds of Caithness and was formerly much more extensive. In peat areas farthest removed from streams are found the 'dubh lochans' (water-filled hollows in the peat). They are particularly common in Killimster Moss and the Knockfin Heights. Over most of the central part of Caithness peat forms a continuous cover, masking the underlying landscape and attaining thickness of over 6 m (20 ft). It imparts a wildness to the interior of the County and may have prompted a 19th century author to write " . . . the appearance of Caithness is frightful!"

## CHAPTER 6

# CLIMATE AND WEATHER

## Introduction

This chapter contains a brief and, in places, rather subjective account of the type of weather to be expected in Caithness and of how this compares with other parts of the country. The local weather has a bigger impact on the lives and consciousness of people here than would be true of more sheltered environments for two reasons. Firstly, there is a large section of outdoor workers whose lives are especially vulnerable to the vagaries of the rapidly changing weather, and secondly, the particular nature of the local terrain itself makes for awareness of the weather. The landscape is open, with few trees, buildings or mountains, and this allows an uninterrupted view of the movement of the daily pageant of weather sequences across an enormous expanse of visible sky. One characteristic feature of the Caithness climate is the clearness of the air. This is because the air, which usually originates from high latitudes of the North Atlantic, is clear and cold. Because the bottom layers of this air have been warmed by a long passage over the relatively warm waters of the Atlantic, it has been rendered unstable and the result in Caithness is days of fresh winds, crystal clear air and blue sky filled with towering cumulus clouds. The horizon, whether of sea or of distant hill, has a characteristically sharp edge on such days, and this may be temporarily blurred from time to time by curtains of rain or hail falling from rapidly moving showers.

Although enjoying the benefits of clean maritime air, the Caithness climate is by no means a wet one and the County is favoured in this respect by its position, since rainfall in the Highlands tends to decrease to the north and east. Much of the water has already been removed from the maritime air reaching Caithness by the mountains of the western sea-board of Scotland which experiences, in consequence, one of the wettest climates in Europe. The climate of Caithness, then, is essentially a maritime one, with cool summers and mild winters but less rain than might be expected.

## Temperature

Let us now look in more detail at the main individual weather features which make up our climate, starting with temperature. The variation of mean daily and monthly temperatures at Wick over the year is shown in Table 2. These figures are typical of the populated north-east corner of the County and describe a fairly mild, equable climate with a small range of annual temperature variations.

Thus, Wick in January (mean temperature 3.4 °C, 38.1 °F) is very similar to London (Kew mean temperature 4.3 °C, 39.7 °F), but in July (mean 12.9 °C, 55.2 °C), Wick is very much cooler than Kew (mean 17.6 °C, 63.7 °F). The coolness of the summer months in the north of Scotland is quite remarkable and it

40

Table 2

**Temperatures at Wick**

| Month | Mean Daily Maximum | | Mean Daily Minimum | | Monthly Mean (1930-1960) | |
|---|---|---|---|---|---|---|
| | °C | °F | °C | °F | °C | °F |
| January | 5.5 | 42 | 1.5 | 35 | 3.4 | 38.1 |
| February | 6 | 43 | 1.5 | 35 | 3.5 | 38.3 |
| March | 7 | 45 | 2 | 36 | 4.8 | 40.6 |
| April | 8.5 | 48 | 3 | 38 | 6.4 | 43.5 |
| May | 10.5 | 51 | 5.5 | 42 | 8.4 | 47.1 |
| June | 13.5 | 56 | 7.5 | 46 | 10.8 | 51.4 |
| July | 15 | 59 | 10 | 50 | 12.9 | 55.2 |
| August | 15 | 59 | 10 | 50 | 12.7 | 54.9 |
| September | 14 | 57 | 8 | 47 | 11.5 | 52.7 |
| October | 11 | 52 | 6 | 43 | 9.0 | 48.2 |
| November | 8 | 47 | 3.5 | 39 | 6.4 | 43.5 |
| December | 6.5 | 44 | 2.5 | 37 | 4.7 | 40.5 |
| YEAR | 10 | 50 | 5.5 | 42 | 7.9 | 46.2 |

is necessary to go to within the Arctic Circle to find similar summer temperatures on the Continent.

The largest influence on temperatures in Caithness over the year is the presence of the surrounding ocean, the temperature of which changes only slightly over the year (between 6°C and 12°C, 44°F and 54°F) and prevents great extremes of summer heat or winter cold. It also means that the temperature in spring is slow to warm and in the autumn slow to cool and this is reflected in the growing season (defined as the part of the year with mean temperature above 5.5°C, 42°F), which extends from early April to mid November in an average year, according to the figures in Table 2.

As we leave the coast and proceed inland the sea exerts a decreasing influence upon the climate: the winters become colder and the summers a little warmer. In winter and early spring the factor which has the greater effect upon temperatures is height above sea level, rather than distance from the sea. Thus the main road south from Wick frequently experiences severe winter weather and snow drifts at the Ord of Caithness where, although only a mile from the sea, the land rises to 230 m (750 ft) above sea level. The reason for this effect of altitude is the rapid decrease in temperature with height, of unstable maritime air. The effect is most noticeable when sea level temperatures are just a little above freezing point and on such days there can be a marked deterioration in road conditions between, say, Thurso and the top of Scrabster Hill, which is a rise of little more than 75 m (250 ft).

### Precipitation

Caithness has a low rainfall, with annual total increasing westwards across the County from 76 cm (30 in) per year near the east coast to 100 cm (40 in) or more in the west and south-west. This is a low total for Scotland and the only drier parts are the extreme east coast and inner Moray Firth. The climate gives the impression of being wetter than these figures indicate, probably because measureable rain falls often—about 250 days per year. However, rates of evaporation can be high on windy days and the total rainfall is not excessive—at least for agricultural purposes. Very heavy rain was experienced over North Scotland during 16th and 17th December, 1966 and caused serious flooding in the Conon valley and surrounding area. Much of this rain was orographic in character and occurred with south-westerly winds. It showed the shielding effect which

### Table 3

### Average Annual Sunshine and Rainfall Totals at Wick (1916—1950)

| MONTH | Monthly Rain | | Daily Rain | | Monthly Sun | Daily Sun |
|---|---|---|---|---|---|---|
| | mm | inches | mm | inches | hours | hours |
| January | 74.3 | 2.92 | 2.40 | .094 | 44 | 1.43 |
| February | 50.9 | 2.00 | 1.82 | .071 | 70 | 2.51 |
| March | 46.1 | 1.82 | 1.49 | .058 | 106 | 3.41 |
| April | 51.8 | 2.04 | 1.73 | .068 | 152 | 5.08 |
| May | 45.9 | 1.81 | 1.48 | .058 | 176 | 5.69 |
| June | 52.4 | 2.06 | 1.75 | .069 | 164 | 5.48 |
| July | 65.4 | 2.57 | 2.11 | .083 | 139 | 4.48 |
| August | 67.3 | 2.65 | 2.17 | .085 | 144 | 4.66 |
| September | 74.0 | 2.91 | 2.47 | .097 | 100.5 | 3.35 |
| October | 79.1 | 3.11 | 2.55 | .100 | 73 | 2.35 |
| November | 80.2 | 3.16 | 2.67 | .105 | 52 | 1.74 |
| December | 75.2 | 2.96 | 2.43 | .095 | 22 | .72 |
| YEAR | 76.3 | 30.0 | 2.07 | .082 | 1242 | 3.41 |

the mountains give to Caithness at such times, because although parts of Ross-shire had 25 cm (10 in) of rain during this 48 hour period, Caithness received less than 2.5 cm (1 in).

Snow is a regular feature of the Caithness climate and falls fairly frequently; the long-term average for the number of days on which snow was observed to fall at Wick is 35 days per year but this seems to have increased in recent years to nearer 50. The snow seldom lies for any length of time on the coast, although inland it falls more frequently and lies longer. Heavy falls of snow are quite rare and the fall on most of the 50 days will consist only of brief showers of snow or mixed snow and hail. Nevertheless, the effect of even light falls is accentuated by the wind, which quickly forms snow drifts. Most snow falls from an unstable northerly airstream blowing down from the Arctic between a high pressure area to the west, extending south from Greenland, and a low to the East and over Scandinavia. Heavy falls are always possible in this situation when disturbances (Polar depressions) form to the north and move south towards Scotland. Some of the heaviest and most protracted falls of recent years occurred in this way during January 1955. Often the onset of the icy north winds is very sudden, and in fierce outbreaks of Arctic air the wind may be of gale force and arrive at the north coast of Scotland with a temperature well below freezing point, even after traversing several hundreds of miles of open sea which separates Caithness from the pack ice to the north. Snow in these conditions is so powdery and the drifting so severe that visibility is reduced to near zero. It is dangerous to venture far on foot and road transport is halted until the weather improves. A severe, although brief, storm of this type arrived on 7th February 1969 and a surprisingly late blizzard, equally severe, occurred on 1st April 1968.

### Sunshine and Wind

The sunshine distribution over the country tends to be the inverse of the rainfall distribution and this is true on a small scale in Caithness, where the eastern side is the sunnier with half an hour sunshine per day more than the west. Most of the year's quota of sunshine occurs during the early summer (see Table 3), and May and June are the sunniest months with about $5\frac{1}{2}$ hours sunshine per day. These sunshine figures show how predominantly cloudy the climate is, since the total for the year at Wick is about 29% of the maximum possible sunshine, and even in the sunniest months clouds cover the sun for more than two thirds of the day. Thus the sun is always welcome and never shines too long or too strongly at this latitude. The sunshine figures, however, leave out of account the quality of the sunlight, which tends to be high locally because of the absence of dust and smoke in the air which remove the shorter wavelengths.

Apart from the clarity of the air, wind is one of the most memorable and obstrusive features of the Caithness climate. Average wind speeds increase northwards and westwards in Britain, and Caithness has one of the most windy climates of all the mainland counties, probably exceeded in storminess only by the islands to the north and west. The most windy part of the County is the exposed north coast, where Dounreay has a mean wind speed over the year of about 30 km/h (19 mile/h), while the corresponding figure for Wick is about 22 km/h (14 mile/h), and for Kew 14 km/h (9 mile/h). In exposed areas the wind can cause considerable erosion and the continual damage to vegetation provides a constant handicap to any trees and shrubs which are not given some form of shelter. Vegetation near the coast has the additional hazard of being burned by salt spray at each onshore gale. In a normal year there are about 30 gales, in which the mean hourly wind speed exceeds 33 knots (61 km/h or 38 mile/h), and most of these occur between October and March. Sometimes, in winter, long spells of stormy weather occur and the effect of these on the wind-battered population is to induce a longing for respite and a period of calm. March 1967, for instance, was such a month, with heavy rain and westerly gales. Gales were recorded at Dounreay on 28 out of 31 days of the month and the mean wind speed for the month was 43 km/h (27 mile/h), which means that an equivalent of 3200 km (20,000 miles) of air had passed over the County—almost equal to once round the earth! Westerly gales are most frequent, but south-easterly gales can be equally trying. This was seen during the week of continuous and very cold easterly gales, in March, 1969, which coated windows in the County with salt. Although the present weather may seem stormy enough, there is evidence of a decrease of wind strength over the last 30-40 years and an increase in northerly and south-easterly winds at the expense of the westerly ones. Such a change is most marked in recent years 1968 and 1969.

### Weather Through the Year

Although the year is nominally divided into four seasons, no very clear division is usual in the weather, which can overlap seasonal boundaries very widely. Winter is best defined as the dark season and its short days are likely to be stormy. Mild wet spells alternate with colder periods of frost and snow and the discomfort of the colder weather is to some extent offset by occasional days of rare beauty. These usually occur after a few days of biting winds and snow showers when a ridge of high pressure moves over and the skies clear. Temperatures usually stay well below freezing during such times, with a deep snow cover and clear skies. As the sun sets the colour of the sky shades slowly from pale orange near the departed sun to the deepest blue or black overhead and in the intensifying frost which follows, auroral flares to the north sometimes add to the impression of an Arctic night. Very low temperatures occur on such nights, particularly in the river valleys, but these remain largely unrecorded. The coldest weather comes with northerly winds bringing outbreaks of Arctic air from the far north, but it is unusual for these to last more than a week or two. Cold continental air from the east, coming from a high pressure area over Scandinavia and Russia, may give months of severe winter weather, as in 1963, but the cold is not then likely to be so intense in Caithness as it is in south-east England. Yearly variations in weather are at their greatest in winter and this was shown recently when the exceptionally cold winter of 1963 was followed by the very mild winter of 1964. Thunder is a winter phenomenon here, in contrast to most of Britain, and is most likely to be heard during heavy showers in unstable maritime air. Overnight fog (radiation fog) is almost unknown in winter even when much of England is blanketed for days on end.

The rapidly increasing heat of the sun during March and April—the heating effect of the sun on a horizontal surface varies by a ratio of 30 to 1 between Christmas and June—is not matched by a similar warming of the air. April storms can be as severe as any in winter and even in May a brief covering of snow is not at all unusual. In fact, there is a quite regular expectation of a wintry and unsettled spell during the first fortnight of May, which is known as the May Gobs. The best chance of a spell of settled weather comes between mid May and mid June, and in most years a week or two of fine weather can be expected, during which the sunshine may be unbroken. Then, the colours of the land and sea show incredible intensity and sharpness of contrast. Unfortunately this is not the whole story because these fine early summer spells usually come with winds from an easterly airt and North Sea coasts are then liable to be affected by haar. This is fog or low cloud which usually forms overnight and results from cooling of the lower layers of the air in crossing the North Sea, It often penetrates 32 km or 48 km (20 or 30 miles) inland during the night and is gradually evaporated by the sun again during the morning. The extreme east coast, however, may continue to have dull, misty weather for days on end, while districts farther west enjoy brilliant and unbroken sunshine.

After the drier months February-June are over, the rainfall in most years increases for the rest of the summer and autumn. Very often, the change to more unsettled weather occurs at the end of June—and coincides with the haymaking! This is just an average trend, however, and a few years, e.g. 1955, continue to have good weather right through the summer. In such a variable climate as that of Caithness, no two seasons are ever more than moderately similar and nothing is certain, except that the weather will continue to be conspicuously capricious!

# CHAPTER 7

# THE SOILS

Soils develop as a result of complex physical, chemical and biological processes which take place in the mineral material at the surface of the earth. The interaction of these soil-forming processes differentiates the material into horizons lying roughly parallel to the surface and differing from each other in properties such as colour, texture, structure, consistency, etc. A vertical section through these horizons from the surface down to relatively unaltered parent material, usually at about 1 m (3 ft to 4 ft), is called the soil profile.

## THE SOIL-FORMING FACTORS

The nature and intensity of the soil-forming processes are governed by the physical and chemical properties of the parent material, the past and present factors of climate, relief and vegetation, and the length of time that these processes have been operating. In addition, Man in his use of the land has been responsible for altering some of the natural features of the soil.

### Parent material

The parent material is the raw geological material in which the soil profile develops. It may be glacial drift, such as till, moraine, sand and gravel, or weathered rock. Sometimes a soil profile may have developed in two contrasting materials, such as a sand deposit overlying till. The properties of the parent material which most affect soil formation are texture, i.e. the relative amounts of sand, silt and clay-sized particles present, and mineralogical composition. Coarse-textured parent materials are those which contain a high proportion of sand and very little clay, and they give rise to sandy soils which are readily permeable and free-draining, while parent materials with fine texture, i.e. high clay content, form clayey soils with poor permeability and which consequently are water-retentive. Loamy parent materials (moderately coarse, medium, and moderately fine textures) have intermediate properties. Stoniness is also a property inherited from the parent material.

The nature of the mineral constituents of the parent material affects the degree of acidity of the soil. Siliceous parent materials (such as those derived from granite) quickly produce acid soils whereas parent materials with a high base content (such as those derived from basalt) become leached less rapidly. Leaching is the process by which materials are removed in solution by percolating water.

The soil parent materials in Caithness consist predominantly of the various drift deposits formed during the Pleistocene glaciation. The main deposit is till, of which two principal types occur. The most widespread is the dark grey moderately fine-textured compact till which occurs in the north and east of the County, and is derived mainly from the rocks of the Caithness Flagstone Series

46

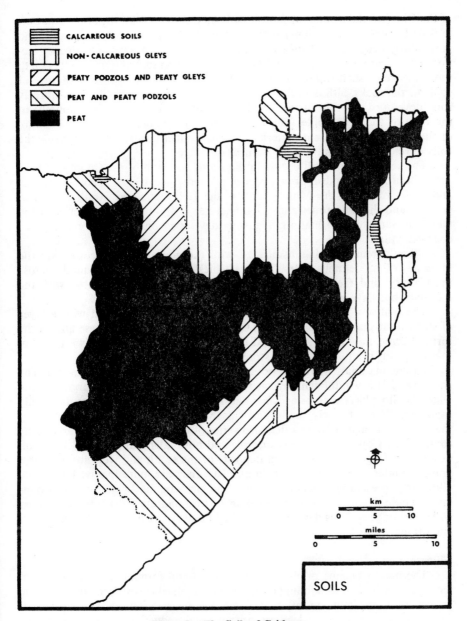

Figure 8. The Soils of Caithness

of the Old Red Sandstone formation. It is of variable thickness, being 1 m (3 ft to 4 ft) in general, but thinner or absent on the higher or steeper ground, and particularly deep where it forms infillings of valleys and bays. The deeper sec- tions are calcareous (i.e. lime rich) below about 1.5 m to 2 m (4 ft to 6 ft) due to the presence of shell fragments as well as to the inherent calcareous nature of some of the rocks, although the upper part is invariably leached. Consequently soils developed on this till are no longer calcareous except occasionally at the base of the soil profile. The moderately fine texture and compact nature of the till make this parent material relatively impermeable and as a result the soils developed on it have poor natural drainage.

The second type of till occurs in the south and west of the County. It con- sists of a brown or reddish-brown deposit of moderately coarse to coarse texture, and is derived from the Moine Schists, the Helmsdale and Strath Halladale granites and the sandstones and conglomerates of the Barren Red Series of the Old Red Sandstone formation. The soils developed on this till are acidic and coarse textured.

Other parent materials associated with the glaciation of the area are the moraines of moderately coarse texture which form a trail of mounds across the County, and the sand and gravel deposits which are associated with the moraines but have a very limited distribution.

The plateaux summits of Scaraben and Morven are covered with a layer of stony frost-shattered debris which extends down the sides of these hills in the form of scree, now mainly stabilized under a vegetation cover. Soils formed on these deposits are thus extremely stony.

Parent materials of recent origin consist of shelly sand and alluvium. The shelly sand is a windblown deposit which is found around the margins of the wider, shallow bays such as at Keiss and Dunnet. Soils developed on the shelly sands are thus extremely sandy and calcareous. River alluvium occurs along the main rivers and streams, often on a series of terrace levels, particularly in the south of the County. Texture is variable and both lateral and vertical variation occurs, but in general the alluvial deposits of the south and west are of coarse gravelly material while in the north and east they are more loamy. Lacustrine alluvium is present in parts of the north and east and marks the sites of former lakes. These deposits tend to be finer in texture and are frequently associated with marl or peat. Soils developed on alluvium are extremely variable in texture and drainage class.

### Climate

The main elements of climate which affect soil formation are rainfall and temperature. Not all rain falling on the soil is involved in soil formation as some is lost in immediate run-off and some by evaporation and transpiration. Decreases in temperature lead to proportional reduction in the amount of water lost by evapo-transpiration and thus soils become wetter as temperatures become lower.

In Britain, annual rainfall exceeds annual evaporation, and the dominant movement of water in the soil is downwards. The natural tendency is, therefore, for the soluble salts to be removed from the surface layers of the soil. Increased rainfall coupled with lower temperatures (conditions which are found in High- land Britain) promotes the accumulation of raw organic matter at the surface, and associated with this is the removal of iron and aluminium compounds from the upper part of the soil profile, a process known as podzolization.

While the climate of Caithness has helped to determine the overall nature of the soils, there is probably insufficient variation within the County to cause local soil differences, except on the summits of the higher hills.

## Relief

Relief affects the soil-water regime. On steep slopes, run-off may be high and consequently a smaller amount of the total rainfall enters the soil to become involved in soil formation, while on gentle slopes and on flatter ground the rate of run-off will be much less; in hollows, there can be no run-off and indeed the site may receive water laterally.

Soils with natural free drainage will thus tend to occur on the more steeply sloping ground, while poorly drained soils occur on the flatter ground.

## Vegetation

The effect of vegetation on soil development is difficult to assess, but the relationship between natural or semi-natural vegetation and major soil group is well marked in the uncultivated soils. This relationship is briefly discussed later in the chapter.

## Time

The time factor relates to the length of time that the soil-forming processes have been operating. One effect of the Pleistocene glaciation was that all pre-existing soils were removed. Consequently. the present soils only date back to the period following the retreat of the ice and the recolonization of the landscape by vegetation. The majority of soils in Caithness are thus about the same age. However, the soils formed on the recent deposits of shelly sand and alluvium are younger and in many cases do not exhibit a well-developed profile, because insufficient time has elapsed for the soil-forming processes to produce well-defined soil horizons.

## Man

Man, in his use of the soil for agriculture and forestry, can change it in a number of ways. The natural vegetation is destroyed and by ploughing, surface horizons become intermixed. The addition of lime and fertilizers combats the natural effect of leaching and thus acidic soils low in plant nutrients are made capable of supporting arable and other crops. Also, by draining and ditching, the soil-water regime is changed.

Cultivated soils in Caithness have probably been reclaimed largely from peaty soils and many, particularly the soils of the crofting regions, still retain their original features, while others have lost these characters due to their long history of cultivation.

## SOIL CLASSIFICATION

Soils are classified into major soil groups and sub-groups according to the nature and arrangement of the horizons which make up the soil profile. For convenience in describing soil profiles, and in making comparison between different profiles, a conventional letter-symbol is allocated to each horizon according to the properties of that horizon, and in such a way that analagous horizons of similar profiles receive the same symbol. Basically, a soil profile

E

consists of an A horizon which is the surface horizon, a B horizon which occurs in the middle of the profile, and the C horizon which is the relatively unaltered parent material. Each horizon may be subdivided further, and other letters added to make the designation more specific.

Examples of horizon nomenclature of two different profiles are given in figure 9.

In Britain, the principal soil groups recognized are: calcareous soils, brown earths, podzols, gleys, and organic soils. Soils of all these groups are present in Caithness, although podzols, gleys and organic soils are most common.

Calcareous soils contain free calcium carbonate throughout the profile. They are developed on calcareous parent materials where little or no leaching has occurred, due either to the very recent age of the material, or to the highly calcareous nature of the parent material. In Caithness the freely drained sub-group of brown calcareous soils is developed on the shelly sand deposits.

Brown earths are leached soils with no free calcium carbonate present in the upper horizons of the profile. The A horizon consists of mixed mineral and organic matter and has a moderately acidic reaction, while the B horizon of the well-drained soil is a uniform shade of brown, reddish brown or yellowish brown. Boundaries between horizons are usually indistinct, one horizon merging with the next. Slight drainage impedance gives rise to the appearance of rusty mottling, and the soils are said to have imperfect drainage. Soils of the sub-group of brown forest soils occur in Caithness but only of minor extent, being restricted to the steeper and lower well-drained slopes around Berriedale.

Podzols are acidic soils, characterized by an H horizon of raw organic matter, underlain by a grey, bleached A2 horizon from which iron and alumminium compounds have been leached, and a brightly-coloured B horizon. They commonly occur on acidic, free-draining, moderately coarse or coarse textured parent materials. Soils of the sub-group of peaty podzols are very characteristic of much of upland Britain, and they occur in Caithness on the coarser-textured drifts of the west and south on moderate to steep slopes under a *Calluna*-dominant vegetation. Important features of the peaty podzol profile (figure 9) are a peaty H horizon, a grey gleyed A2g horizon, and a thin 1.5 mm (1/16 in) iron pan which is generally continuous and impermeable to water and plant roots. Below the iron pan, the B2 horizon is bright-coloured and there is little or no evidence of drainage impedance. Where peaty podzols have been re-claimed for agriculture the H and A horizons become intermixed and modified into a uniform dark brown surface horizon, and profile characteristics may resemble those of brown forest soils, although traces of the former iron pan are frequently present on the upper surface of the B horizon. Such soils occur in Caithness, particularly in the Wick Valley where they are associated with the coarser-textured moundy moraines.

Gleys are soils which have developed under conditions of intermittent (seasonal) or permanent waterlogging and have poor or very poor natural drainage. Horizons are predominantly grey coloured, due to reduction of the iron compounds under anaerobic conditions with ochreous mottling occurring on re-oxidation under intermittent aerobic conditions. Gleys are divided in to surface-water gleys and ground-water gleys. In the group of surface-water gleys, water-logging is greatest in surface horizons due to impermeability caused by fine texture or compaction which prevents water from passing downwards through the soil. Two sub-groups occur in Caithness, developed on the moder-

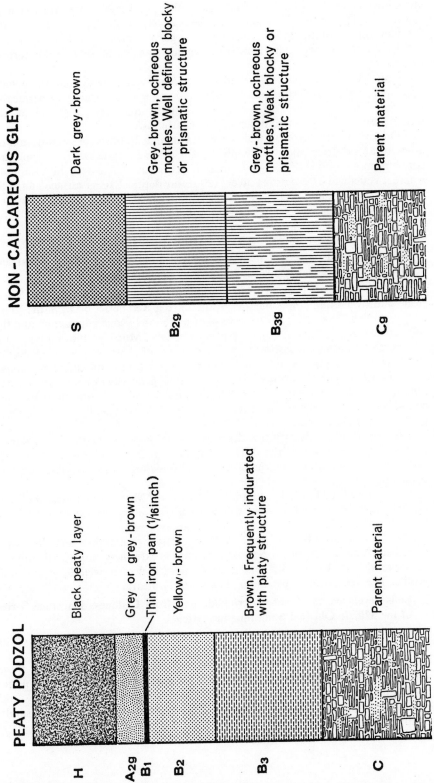

**NON-CALCAREOUS GLEY**

S — Dark grey-brown

B2g — Grey-brown, ochreous mottles. Well defined blocky or prismatic structure

B3g — Grey-brown, ochreous mottles. Weak blocky or prismatic structure

Cg — Parent material

**PEATY PODZOL**

H — Black peaty layer

A2g / B1 — Grey or grey-brown / Thin iron pan (1/16 inch)

B2 — Yellow-brown

B3 — Brown. Frequently indurated with platy structure

C — Parent material

Figure 9. Two soil profiles

ately fine-textured till derived from the Caithness Flags. They are the non-calcareous gleys (figure 9) which occur extensively in lowland Caithness and form an important arable soil, and the peaty gleys, which occur less extensively and have a peaty surface horizon with organic staining present in the horizon below.

The second group of gleys are the ground-water gleys and these have developed under conditions of a high ground-water table, usually in permeable material. The sub-group of calcareous ground-water gleys is found on the wetter parts of the shelly sand deposits in Caithness.

Organic soils are those which contain a high amount of organic matter down to an arbitrary specified depth. Peat is the main type of organic soil and contains more than 60% organic matter, It occurs extensively in Caithness, where it is defined as exceeding 50 cm (20 in) in depth. Excess surface moisture, low temperatures, and acidic conditions, factors which inhibit the decomposition of dead plant remains, are responsible for its formation.

## THE SOILS

### 1. Soils developed on parent materials derived from granite, Moine schist and Middle Old Red Sandstone sandstones and conglomerates.

Parent materials derived from granite, Moine schist, and Old Red Sandstone sandstones and conglomerates of the Barren Red Series occur in the south and west of the County. They are coarse or moderately coarse in texture and the soils developed on them are mainly peaty podzols. Much of the landscape in this part of Caithness consists of gentle slopes with blanket peat, and steeper slopes with peaty podzols developed under a vegetation dominated by *Calluna*. The iron pan, a typical feature of this soil group, is generally present, causing pronounced gleying to occur in the A2g horizon above it. Induration (extreme compaction) in the B horizon is frequently present and usually occurs immediately below the iron pan.

Brown forest soils with free drainage occur on some of the lower slopes around Berriedale, where the drift is derived mainly from Moine schist. The vegetation is usually an acid grassland of *Festuca* and *Agrostis*, with bracken commonly present.

Soils developed on the summit plateaux of Morven and Scaraben are podzols, and are typical of those which occur on the exposed summits of Scottish hills. They are characterized by a coarse-textured, gritty grey A2 horizon, below which occurs a black A/B horizon of humus accumulation, and a browner B horizon. The surface of the Scaraben summit is extremely stony, with angular quartzite debris, but below this there is nevertheless a well-developed soil profile. The vegetation is usually a *Rhacomitrium* heath.

### 2. Soils developed on parent materials derived from Caithness Flagstone Series of the Middle Old Red Sandstone formation.

Soils developed on parent materials derived from Caithness Flags occur over most of the central and eastern parts of the County.

The commonest soils are non-calcareous gleys developed on till and these form the dominant arable soil of the lowland part of Caithness. Grey colours predominate in the sub-surface horizons, associated with coarse ochreous and pale brown mottling, while structure units are typically prisms with grey sandy coatings on the faces.

Peaty gleys, also developed on till, are less common but are widespread—particularly in the crofting region of the north-east where some have been reclaimed for cultivation. A feature of these profiles is the presence of dark brown organic staining at the top of the mineral horizon immediately beneath the peaty surface layer.

Freely drained soils with an indurated B horizon occurring immediately below the plough-layer are developed on moraines of coarser texture than the till, and on steeper slopes where run-off is greater. This indurated horizon is brown in colour, extremely firm, breaking with a sudden fracture, and generally has a marked peaty structure. Traces of an iron pan frequently occur on the upper surface, which indicate that these soils are most probably reclaimed from skinned peat or peaty podzols, although traces of a former peaty layer have usually disappeared during their history of cultivation.

Extremely shallow soils, with bed-rock present at depths of 45 cm (18 in) or less, occur in the relatively drift-free region between Ulbster and Dunbeath, and to a lesser extent in parts of the lowland area. The profile frequently consists simply of a cultivated surface horizon of 20 cm (8 in) overlying rock.

Peaty podzols are mainly associated with rock ridges and steeper slopes in the upland region between Achavanich and Loch of Yarrows. They are developed on thin drift of moderately coarse texture and the profiles are characterized by the presence of a thin A2g horizon, an iron pan, a thin friable B2 horizon, and an indurated B3 horizon, while rock usually occurs at about 60 cm (24 in) below the peaty surface horizon. The vegetation is usually dominated by *Calluna*. Associated with the peaty podzols are very shallow peaty soils in which rock occurs immediately below the A2 horizon.

### 3. Soils developed on Upper Old Red Sandstone sandstone

Sandstones of Upper Old Red Sandstone age occur at Dunnet Head producing a characteristic landscape pattern of steep scarp faces forming long narrow outcrops and gentle slopes and flats which are mainly peat-covered. Peaty podzols occur on the steep slopes and are developed on soft weathered sandstone. A characteristic feature of the profile is the development of a thin black horizon of humus enrichment above the iron pan. *Calluna vulgaris* is the dominant member of the plant community on these soils.

### 4. Soils developed on shelly sand

Calcareous soils are developed on the deposits of shelly sand which occur at Dunnet, Keiss and elsewhere, and consist of brown calcareous soils, calcareous ground-water gleys, and skeletal soils. They are characterized by their extreme sandiness and consistence.

Brown calcareous soils occur in the free draining sites, usually on low stable dunes, and a typical profile consists of a dark brown A horizon of organic matter and sand, a brown B horizon of shelly sand, and a slightly paler-coloured C horizon. Thin dark bands are sometimes present below the A horizon and these represent incipient A horizon development which occurred during short periods of stability in the history of the accumulation of the deposit. The vegetation on these soils is usually pasture containing *Festuca rubra*.

Calcareous ground-water gleys occur in hollows and flatter parts where there is a drainage impedance present due to underlying till or peat. The profile characteristics are a reflection of a fluctuating water table and consist of a dark brown A horizon, a pale brown B horizon with coarse rusty mottling due to seasonal waterlogging, and a grey or dark grey permanently waterlogged C horizon. The vegetation is commonly pasture rich in species.

Skeletal soils supporting marram grass (*Ammophila arenaria*) occur on the recent active dunes that fringe the coastline. Little or no profile development has taken place due to the unstable nature of the deposit.

### 5. Soils developed on Alluvium

Soils developed on alluvium are extremely variable in texture and in drainage class. Texture can vary both laterally and vertically, but in general the soils on the alluvium of the rivers and streams of the south and west of the County have coarse gravelly textures, while the soils on the alluvium of the lowland part of Caithness are usually more loamy. Drainage class is mainly dependent on the depth and seasonal fluctuation of the ground-water table, and alluvial soils vary from those with free drainage to those with very poor drainage.

### Peat

Peat covers approximately two-thirds of the County, and probably was formerly even more extensive, as peat has been removed from some parts to provide fuel and agricultural ground.

The peat occurs in the form of blanket peat, so called because it forms a blanket over the landscape. It is acid in nature, and supports a moorland vegetation of *Calluna*, *Eriophorum* and *Trichophorum*, although flushed sites occur along some of the stream channels giving a vegetation generally dominated by rushes.

Peat is discussed further in Chapter 8.

# CHAPTER 8

# CAITHNESS PEAT

## Introduction

A keen-eyed climber resting half-way up the eastern face of the scree of Morven on an August afternoon might well find his attention diverted to one of a number of scenes by which Scotland might be identified in the eyes of a romantic traveller. A well-pointed stag, knee-deep in heather, proudly astride a not-too-distant knoll to the south, a tweed-coated and hatted angler with rod aquiver against the struggling trout or salmon; a kilted laird recounting his acres with nervous collie twitching at his heels; seine-netters making for their harbours at Helmsdale, Lybster and Wick; and, to the North, the immense central plain of Caithness on which his comment, as he turned once again to struggle upwards, might well be:

"Scots wha hae — nothing but peat,
More peat and still more peat!"

He would be correct in the sense that Caithness contains more peat in a single bog than any other County in Great Britain. Scottish peat has been used in the past for heating Scotland's crofts, making her whisky and smoking her fish, but these uses are rapidly dying out and the deposits of peat continue to grow faster than they are utilised. In their second Report, the Scottish Peat Committee commented:,

"We are impressed by the undoubted potential economic value of the extensive peat resources in Scotland; the problems of exploitation arising not only from inherent characteristics of the material itself but no less from the changing economic environment, difficult as they are, present a challenge to our scientific and technical skills in Scotland".

It was also reported that they "found peat to be a fascinating, absorbing but in some respects a baffling subject" and after having completed their survey some years later they felt they could fully endorse this earlier observation.

This chapter looks at what peat is, or more accurately, at some of the things we know about peat, where and how much of it there is in Caithness and what the prospects are for using it.

## The Origins of Peat

Essentially peat is the result of the continuous accumulation of partly decomposed plant remains whose decay in the usual way has been prevented by excess of moisture or submersion in water at the soil surface. The excess of moisture prevents normal decomposition by excluding atmospheric oxygen and so preventing the bacteria, which need oxygen, from acting on the vegetable matter. In Caithness the low summer temperatures and the generally poor quality of the underlying soil in the bog areas are effective deterrents to the growth of all but the most acid tolerant plants in these uncultivated districts.

Such plants as can survive generally do not decompose rapidly but provide accumulations of organic material at the surface, which, after some 10,000 to 20,000 years, we recognize as peat deposits. In Caithness these deposits spread over the contours of the land and in consequence are known as "Blanket Bogs."

### The Caithness Bogs

There are three large Blanket Bogs in Caithness and these are shown in the map of Figure 8. Their principal characteristics are listed in the table below:

#### Table 4. Caithness Blanket Peat Bogs

|  | Area | | Peat Solids | | Average Depth | |
|  | Hectares | Acres | Million Kilos | Million Tons | Metres | Feet |
|---|---|---|---|---|---|---|
| 1. Altnabreac | 8,537 | 20,996 | 13,440 | 13.2 | 2.1 | 7.2 |
| 2. Achairn Bog | 3,309 | 8,177 | 6,618 | 6.5 | 2.2 | 7.5 |
| 3. Shielton Bog | 1,630 | 4,028 | 3,564 | 3.5 | 2.4 | 8.0 |

These bogs have been extensively surveyed by the Peat Section of the Department of Agriculture and Fisheries for Scotland during the years 1949 and 1961. The survey results have been published in Volume 4 of the Scottish Peat Survey produced by the Department and published by the Stationery Office. The survey report contains data on:

(i) Location of the deposits with special reference to their accessibility and elevation.

(ii) Area, depth, volume of raw peat and tonnage of peat solids present.

(iii) Moisture, ash and fibre contents, bulk density, degree of humification, calorific value, chemical composition and botanical origin of the peat.

(iv) Possible methods of utilisation, with, in special cases, detailed analyses of the economics of alternative schemes.

Most of these terms are self-explanatory and the specialised ones will be defined later in the appropriate section.

The main peat-forming plants in Caithness are species of sphagnum mosses and deer hair-grass (trichophorum caespitosum) intermixed with species of cotton grass particularly eriophorum vaginatum or harestail, cotton grass, and heather (calluna vulgaris). At the bottom of most deposits remains of silver birch, alder, rowan and willow trees can be found — often showing a stump of the original trunk and its larger root members.

### The Nature of Peat

If we look at a bank where peat is being cut, we can recognize the live plants growing on the surface of the deposit and below that a layer of loosely packed vegetable material, usually fairly light in colour. As our eyes travel downwards the layer becomes more compressed, with lessening evidence of the nature of the original vegetation and a darkening in colour, until it becomes nearly black at the bottom of the deposit.

This change in consistency and colour gives a rough indication of what is known as the degree of humification of peat, which normally increases with increasing depth in the deposit. Humification means the process of decay which peat undergoes and is of considerable importance to peat utilisation and value because of its relation to the physical properties (particularly the water-holding capacity) of peat.

Since the botanical origin and the rate of decay and degree of humification of peat deposits can vary very substantially, it will be realised that peat is a generic term covering a wide range of materials whose only common attribute is their vegetable origin, where the rate of accumulation exceeds the rate of decomposition. Peat which has accumulated rapidly remains relatively fresh and lightly humified, while peat which has accumulated only slowly undergoes considerable alteration and exhibits a high degree of humification. Since in the far North the growing season is relatively short and the summer temperatures low, most Caithness peat has accumulated slowly and is, therefore, highly humified. This is a vital factor, full account of which must be made in any proposal for utilising the deposits in the County. Deriving from the degree of humification are some of the basic properties of the typical Caithness material which are tabulated below, as analysed from oven-dried samples.

Table 5.  Some Basic Properties of Caithness Peat

| Bog | Moisture Content % | Volatiles % | Fixed Carbon % | Ash Content % | Calorific Value BTU/lb. |
|---|---|---|---|---|---|
| Altnabreac | 16 | 56 | 26 | 2 | 10,000 |
| Achairn | 6 | 64 | 26 | 4 | 9,900 |
| Shielton | 6 | 63 | 27 | 4 | 9,400 |

As the material has already been extensively dried, the moisture present will represent the water which is retained by the colloidal structure of the material and can only be released together with other chemical volatiles by destructive distillation. Removal of these fluid contents will reduce the material to its fixed carbon and inorganic constituents, and by burning off the carbonaceous material the ultimate inorganic or ash content is determined.

The degree of humification of peat samples is estimated in the field according to the method devised by the Swedish botanist L. von Post. The von Post scale ranges from 1 to 10, the higher the number the higher the degree of humification. The method is entirely subjective as it involves squeezing samples of fresh peat in the hand and noting the amount of free water released; the rate at which the peat can be extruded through the fingers, its consistency and colour. The same person must make all the observations relevant to a particular survey or series of surveys and experience counts for a great deal. The average value of humification of peat in the Caithness Bogs is H7, which represents good fuel peat.

## Utilisation of Peat

Peat can be left where it is and allowed to accumulate, in which case the area remains a virtual desert in that nothing useful can be done with it; using it as a growing medium can be expensive. It can be removed and utilised in a number of different ways, none of which has been demonstrated to be economic, so far as Caithness is concerned.

Peat bogs can be used for agriculture or forestry and the relative merits of doing one or the other are fiercely argued by their respective advocates. The chief argument against intensive afforestation is that it could make eventual working of the bogs difficult, if not impossible. Utilisation for agricultural purposes, which would entail providing an effective draining system, would preserve and probable even enhance the potential value of the bogs, but has the disadvantage of high initial capital outlay. The best solution is probably a judicious use of selected areas of the deposits for forestry so as to provide windbreaks for the areas to be used agriculturally.

In so far as utilisation of the peat itself is concerned the possibilities which have been most extensively explored to date are:

    (i) Its use as a solid fuel for:

        (a) Direct heating in industrial processes or as a domestic fuel. Its use for these purposes would be improved if it were to be accepted as a smokeless fuel.

        (b) As the heating medium for electricity production.

   (ii) Its use in horticulture and agriculture as a soil conditioning agent.

  (iii) Miscellaneous other uses, e.g.

        (a) As a source of chemicals.

        (b) As a source of activated carbon or peat coke.

        (c) As a source of methane gas or other organic by-products as a result of microbiological action of organisms on the peat material.

There are a number of severe handicaps in the way of large scale utilisation of the particular kinds of peat prevalent in Caithness. Some of these are common to peat deposits everywhere, viz:

    (i) The very high water content of the material.

   (ii) The very short, harvesting season of sunny, drying weather which means low utilisation of expensive harvesting plant.

Other more local disadvantages are:

    (i) The general high level of humification of the Caithness deposits which make it less attractive for the horticultural uses that form the principal high volume market in the U.K. today.

   (ii) The high fibre content of the peat.

  (iii) The distance from potential markets which puts a high transport cost penalty on any utilisation scheme involving export of the material.

Generally, high volume production of peat for use as a fuel has to face competition from coal, oil and gas or the electricity produced from these or nuclear power. The possibility of using peat to produce electricity for local use in remote areas of the Scottish Highlands is offset to some extent by the fact that wind-power could be cheaper and equally as reliable.

The prospects for high volume utilisation schemes for the Caithness peat deposit seem, therefore, to be as bleak as the terrain in which they lie. So indeed in the early 1970's they are, but it has to be remembered that they have been accumulating for several thousands of years and while no one has found a profitable use for them yet, things may not always look so bleak.

The vital factor which could bring high volume utilisation schemes nearer the realms of feasibility, is a general increase in the prosperity and standard of living in the U.K. It has been noted in the U.S.A. and other prosperous countries that the use of peat increases as the populace grows richer, because they buy new houses with bigger gardens and need more peat for conditioning the soil. This fact, alone, has accounted for a doubling of peat consumption in the U.S.A. every three years or so, and has led to imports from Germany, Poland and Finland. An increase in general prosperity could also provide more money for much-needed research into the chemical and physical properties of peat, which remain mostly a mystery to us, and for the technological development needed to put this knowledge to work.

Caithness peat is a good fuel because it is rich in chemicals and it is this richness which tends to make it less valuable for horticultural usage. The reason is that during the drying process these chemicals render the peat irreversibly hard and water-repellent and so useless as a soil conditioner. The need for advanced technology lies in solving the question as to what properties peat would have if most of the chemicals were removed from it. A scheme which could be used for this is described on the next page.

Technology would also be needed to devise an economic method of extracting relatively small amounts of these chemicals from the material but modern methods of counter current solvent extraction offer some promise.

In conclusion, then, it is easy to sympathise with the expert's view that "peat is a fascinating — but a baffling subject". It is probably also true to add that only a sizeable economic or technological miracle will succeed in bringing more activity to the Caithness deserts than the scrabbling of rabbits, the hammering of hares, the crunch of deer and the murmuring of heather bees. They are at least unlikely to spoil the potential of the County's most prolific natural resource. It is to be hoped that human beings are no less careful of what one day may prove to be a valuable economic asset.

60

**Table 6**
**AIR-DRY RAW PEAT**

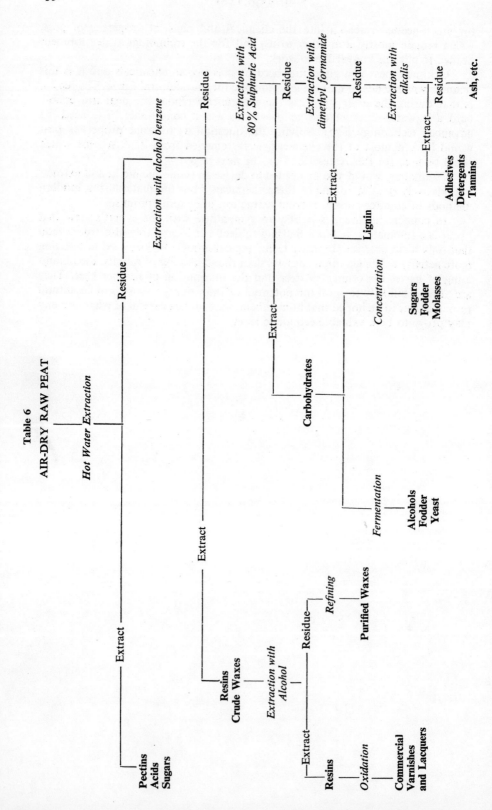

# CHAPTER 9

# THE VEGETATION OF CAITHNESS

The plant population of Caithness is best described according to the nature of the surroundings, or habitat. The study of the relation between a plant and its habitat is called ecology and the principal ecological factors affecting Caithness plants are:

    (i) the nature of the soil, e.g. peat, clay, sand
    (ii) the temperature
    (iii) the wind exposure of the site
    (iv) the water supply
    (v) the supply of mineral salts

The characteristics of the soil are described in detail in Chapter 7. Broadly the major divisions of habitat are stone scree, sand, clay and peat, which each support a different type of plant population.

Temperature is a major factor because it affects survival in different ways. A plant must be able to survive cold winters. Plants which die annually and continue the species only by spreading seed (annuals) generally have no winter problems. Most plants which continue to live for several years (perennials) overwinter as small buds on bulbs, taproots, or rhizomes (underground stems), or as dormant woody structures with small buds. If the dormant plants survive the winter, spring growth begins, for the majority of them when the temperature rises to about 8°C (45°F). In Caithness this temperature is regularly achieved in late April, compared with mid-March in the south of England. The fully developed plants produce flowers and then fruit, Both the rate of plant growth and the ripening of fruit depend on the mean summer temperature as well as on the intensity and frequency of hot spells. The mean summer temperature falls off markedly going north of Inverness, so that in Caithness many temperate-zone plants common in England are unable to produce ripe fruit, or are of stunted growth. Typically, few trees will spread by seed or fruit except hazel, birch, rowan, alder and certain willows. Many others will of course survive if introduced but cannot produce offspring.

Wind exposure is a well-known problem in Caithness. It causes physical damage to tall or slender plants — even bracken is deterred from growing on very exposed sites. The wind also causes excessive evaporation from the leaves of plants resulting in local desiccation or frostbite.

Some leaf structures are more vulnerable than others; for instance gorse and sycamore survive better than oak or beech. Other plants survive well because their growth habit allows some leaves to shelter in the lee of dead wood, so the plant gradually grows away from the wind.

Water and mineral salts are essential to plant growth. In general both are

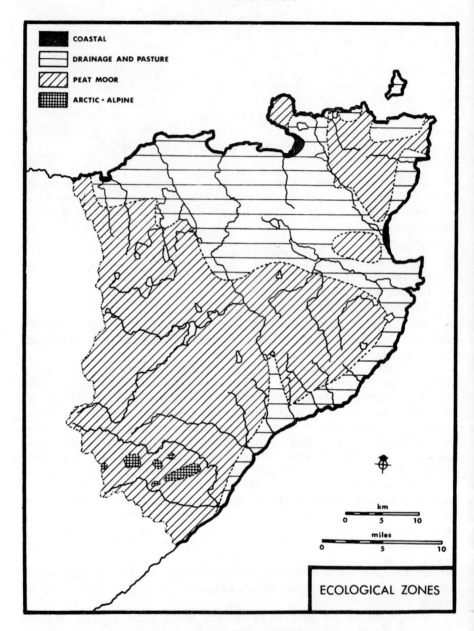

**Figure 10.   Ecological zones of Caithness**

in plentiful supply, but local variations give rise to plants specially adapted to high or low quantities of salts or water.

There are four distinct ecological areas in the County—the Coastal, Moorland, Drainage Zone and Arctic-Alpine habitats. They are quite distinctive in their conditions and in the plant populations growing in them. The distribution of these ecological zones is shown in the map of Figure 10.

Some common plants occur over almost all the ecological zones. They include those many 'weeds' which spread wind-borne seeds. A list of common plants in Caithness, not restricted to specific habitats, is given in Plant List 1. Each plant is named by its common name. It is also named by its internationally known Latin name. The first part of the Latin name is the name of the family group of similar plants. For instance, all buttercups belong to the family *ranunculus*. There are 23 members of the *ranunculus* family known in Britain and each one is called a species. Each species is identified by the second Latin name. Two well-known species are the meadow buttercup, *ranunculus acris* and the lesser celendine, *ranunculus ficaria*. There is sometimes a further division of the species into sub-species (*ssp*) and varieties (*var*). The lesser celendine takes two forms, one reproducing by seed, called *ranunculus ficaria* ssp. *ficaria* and one reproducing from small bulbs on the leaf stems, called *ranunculus ficaria* ssp. *bulbifer*.

All the plants given in List 1 are common plants of the temperate English ecological zone. However, typical southern British zones contain about five times as many species which are equally common, but the rest are unable to survive in Caithness so close to a sub-arctic climate.

## THE COASTAL HABITAT

The coasts are affected by exposure to the unabated blast of sea gales and by the relatively constant sea temperature. Winds carry large quantities of dissolved salts and deposit them on the coasts. The vegetation of the coast, therefore, lives in an exposed, salty, mild-temperature environment. To these features must be added soil type, drainage and rainfall.

The most specialised coastal plants are those which are tolerant of large quantities of common salt and so can live in regions subject to sea-water submersion or to dense sea spray. Such plants are called halophytes — they have a well-developed ability to draw water from strong solutions of salt and often have facilities for preserving or storing water. The leaves and stems are commonly thick and fleshy with a glossy or waxy outer surface. The glossy surface helps to reduce water evaporation from the leaf and the fleshy structure provides water storage in case of drought or excessively high salt concentration.

A second group of specialised coastal plants is called xerophytes. These are tolerant of very dry conditions and so are found growing on loose sand, shingle and on rocky cliff faces, where water rapidly drains away and sunshine and warm winds desiccate the habitat. The two physical attributes which make survival possible are long, strong roots (or rhizome stems) and one or more of the water conserving leaf structures previously described. A typical xerophyte is marram grass (*ammophila arenaria*). It produces a mass of underground stems and fine roots which permeate sand, and are most efficient at extracting water from it. Its leaf is rolled into a hollow cylinder, the outside surface being coated with a glossy waterproof layer to eliminate water evaporation. All leaves have pores (called stomata) which allow controlled 'breathing' and water evaporation. In marram grass they are all situated in grooves on the inside surface of the rolled leaf, so that when the leaf is tightly curled the water loss is quite small and not affected by winds. In rainy weather, however, the leaves will be seen to uncurl and allow rapid loss of water.

The halophytes and xerophytes do not necessarily demand their special conditions. Thrift (*armeria maritima*) — a halophyte, and marram grass, will both grow on ordinary inland soil. However, they are rapidly crowded out by more vigorous plants, which indicates that they survive best on the coast where competition is not so strong.

There is another group of plants, usually called arctic-alpine plants, which demand a high mineral salt concentration, low temperatures and little competition. Such conditions exist in some parts of the north coast of Scotland and this is a specially interesting feature of the coastal vegetation of the area.

### Beaches

The three extensive, sandy beaches in Caithness, at Dunnet, Reay and Keiss, have no sizeable shingle beaches or mud flats. Both are subject to wind and wave action during the frequent northerly gales, making plant survival difficult in shifting sand. The most common plants are the sea rocket (*cakile maritima*), which forms sparse, blue-flowered tangles at the beach drift-line, and the sea sandwort (*honkenya peploides*) forming green mats when the surface of the sand stays stable. In some places, among the sea sandwort, grows the oyster plant (*mertensia maritima*). This plant, which flowers from June to August, used to grow round much of the coast of North Britain but is rapidly declining so that now Caithness, Orkney and Shetland are the only areas where one is sure to find it.

The only other plants which regularly occur on beaches are the sand sedge (*carex arenaria*), the common scurvy-grass (*cochlearia officinalis*) and Babington's Orache (*atriplex glabriuscula*).

### Sand Dunes

At the high water mark on Dunnet beach, especially at the eastern part, are extensive clumps of lyme grass (*elymus arenarius*). It is light green, up to 2 m (6 ft.) high and binds large rafts of sand with its extensive roots. It is tolerant of a dousing in seawater, in contrast to marram grass which is merely tolerant of spray.

Sand dunes are formed by windblown sand piling up on binding grasses — usually marram grass which has a remarkable ability to grow back up to the surface when inundated by sand. Caithness dunes are of small height and not extensive in area, and occur at Dunnet, Reay and Keiss.

Some plants are specially suited to dunes of loose sand. Marram grass dominates, along with sand sedge and sea sandwort. The dark green mouse-eared chickweed (*cerastium atrovirens*) and the mouse-eared hawkweed (*hieracium pilosella*) are common. On the north-west coast the rare 'curved sedge' (*carex maritima*) may be found. This limited variety of plants is a result of the instability of dry sand. Farther inland the loose sand gradually transforms to a fine turf usually called the 'links'. Such areas make good golf courses because drainage is good, the turf fine and the topography interesting. The sward is dominated by three grasses — the red fescue (*festuca rubra*), the sheep's fescue (*festuca ovina*) and the Yorkshire fog (*holcus lanatus*). The flora is rich and varied; one

(E. J. Fulton)

PLATE 7.  *The Scarabens and Morven, viewed from Hillhead, Lybster.*

(A Luciani)

PLATE 8.  *The picturesque waterfall, Forss.*

PLATE 10    Holy Grass (Hierochloe Odorata)

PLATE 9    The Scots Lousewort (Pedicularis Sylvatica)

of the most interesting is Reay Links. It is the home of the eyebright *euphrasia brevipila ssp. reayensis*. It is peculiar among eyebrights in having large floral leaves with white glandular hairs. Reay is the only place in the world where it has been found.

A common pair of late summer link plants are the field gentian (*gentianella campestris*) and the felwort (*gentianella amarella ssp. druceana*). The first of these occurs at Reay in an unusual form previously labelled *gentiana baltica*. The felwort is the northern Scottish sub-species with creamy-white on the inside of the flower.

Dune links is the first habitat to be mentioned which is host to the renowned *primula scotica*. This primrose is found only in Northern Scotland. The leaves which are light green with a mealy grey surface grow in a rosette close to the ground. A single flower stem about 1 cm to 10 cm ($\frac{1}{2}$ in to 4 in) high carries a few small purple primrose flowers. This miniature beauty has become widely known, being taken as the emblem of the National Trust for Scotland and several local organisations. It occurs in considerable quantities along the Caithness coast, as well as in Orkney, Shetland and north-west Sutherland, where it grows in short turf near the sea. Dunnet Links, Keiss Links, Noss Head, Holborn Head, and Sandside Head are all suitable places to find it. The flowering period is from late May to mid-September.

Common dune link plants are given in Plant List 2. In addition many of the plants of List 1 occur.

In moist hollows between the dunes the water supply is more reliable and dead plants form humus in the soil. If these 'dune slacks' are stagnant and badly drained the soil goes sour, giving rise to a vegetation dominated by the spike rush (*eleocharis palustris*), the marsh pennywort (*hydrocotyle vulgaris*) and the water crowfoot (*ranunculus trichophyllus*). If the dune slack is drained the soil is sweet, well aerated and often dressed with fine peat carried by a stream. Such areas carry rich flora giving a brilliant display in July. Plant List 3 gives a typical sample observation from Reay Links.

In certain localities among the dune slacks there occurs the rare Baltic rush (*juncus balticus*) which is distinguished from the common soft rush in that it is shorter and grows in straight lines compared to the clumps of the soft rush.

## Cliffs

Most of the County coastline consists of cliffs of old red sandstone age. They are steep, weathered into horizontal striations, and vertically fissured, providing a good anchorage for rock plants. However, most of the cliffs are subject to violent storms and intense sea spray which reduce the population to a group of hardy well-anchored halophyte-xerophytes. The most common of these is the scurvy-grass which occurs as several species and varieties. Common scurvy grass (*cochlearia officinalis ssp. officinalis*) has large fleshy leaves and produces small, white flowers from May to August. It is closely related to the Alpine scurvy grass (*cochlearia officinalis ssp. alpina*), which has smaller, less fleshy leaves and a different shape of fruit. Both are common in Caithness. Much less common is the Danish scurvy grass (*cochlearia danica*) which has ivy-shaped leaves and flowers from January to April. It is sparsely scattered round the coastline. Even less frequent is the Scottish scurvy grass (*cochlearia scotica*), a plant found only in Northern Scotland, flowering from June to August, and recognised by a small leaf with a squared-off leaf base. It occurs mainly at Sandside and Holborn Heads.

F

The scentless mayweed (*tripleurospermum maritium*), with a large daisy-like flower and much-divided cylindrical leaves, is common along with the thrift or sea pink (*armeria maritima*). Occasionally the only maritime fern, the sea spleen-wort (*asplenium marinum*) occurs, growing in cracks in the cliffs. Two arctic-alpine residents are the rose-root (*sedum rosea*), all round the coast and the *saussuria alpina*, a mountain thistle which was found by Robert Dick, near Thurso, in a rock crevice.

The clifftop is the zone where the coast merges with the adjacent habitat. Here the rigours of the coast are ameliorated by a lesser amount of salt and sometimes more shelter. There is also provision of mature soil or peat from inland. The habitat is often similar to dune links in being a fine turf. In other cases it merges rapidly into acid peat moor.

Where the clifftop is naturally of fine turf it is usually converted into arable land or heavily grazed. It is the most common home of the *primula scotica* which grows alongside the bright blue spring squill (*scilla verna*), the sea pink and the wild thyme (*thymus drucei*). On the east coast there are also large quantities of the Scottish Lovage (*ligusticum scoticum*) growing in mat-grass (*nardus stricta*). The common primrose (*primula vulgaris*) is abundant, and also, rather sur-prisingly, is the cowslip. In England and Wales the cowslip (*primula veris*) is a plant of inland pastures; in Scotland it is not common, being confined to the eastern Border Counties and Perthshire. It then reappears on the north coast, but here it behaves as a strictly coastal plant.

There are several places where the grassy clifftops are well sheltered from the wind. Such havens can develop a rich vegetation based on bushy plants such as the burnet rose (*rosa pimpinellifolia*) and the bush vetch (*vicia sepium*). Among them grow the characteristic plants of the local soil, in luxuriant abundance.

Peat moor clifftops are little different from the rest of the moor. The minia-ture willow (*salix repens*) is rather specialised to this area. The drainage is usually better than on the rest of the moor, so that the coastal strip has generally a 'regressive' nature.

## THE MOORLAND HABITAT

It seems likely that almost all of Caithness was once covered in a layer of peat. The peat was formed in an era of a colder wetter climate than at present. Nowadays the formation of peat has mostly stopped. Figure 10 shows the present peat coverage and those areas, denuded of peat, which have now formed more or less arable soil. The outstanding ecological factor of moorland is the wetness of the top layer of peat. Secondary considerations are available wind shelter and the low summer temperature.

### Progressive Bog

In areas which do not drain there is still a continuing formation of new peat. The ground is waterlogged, excluding free oxygen. As plants die they fall into the wet peat but do not decay. The predominant vegetation is sphagnum moss with cotton sedge. There are more than a dozen species and varieties of spagnum moss occurring in the County. The most common are *sphagnum plumulosum* forming brownish-green hummocks tinged with purple and *sphagnum cus-pidatum*, a long trailing bright green moss which floats in bog pools. The sphag-num mosses all have a spongy structure which helps to maintain the waterlogged nature of the ground, and transports the water uphill to develop hummocks up to 1m (3 ft.) high. Two species of cotton sedge occur, *eriophorum angustifolium*, with a cluster of about four heads on one stem and *eriophorum vaginatum* (the hare's-tail sedge) with a single head.

There are few other plants living in this harsh environment. The sweet gale (*myrica gale*) is a low shrub easily identified by its strong scent, especially when crushed. Three members of the sundew family (*drosera rotundifolia*, *drosera intermedia* and *drosera anglica*) derive the nitrogenous food they require by digesting small insects on their leaves, as does the butterwort (*pinguicula vulgaris*) which traps its prey by rolling up its leaves.

There are numerous local areas of progressive bog, especially on the margins of moorland lochans, but there are no extensive areas remaining in the County.

### Regressive Moorland

The Wick and Thurso rivers have grown to such a size that they now drain away much of the water which once caused peat formation. There are many grades of regressive moor, depending on how dry the moor has become and on the amount of wind shelter available.

Moor which is still wet continues to support the cotton-sedge. It is associated with deer sedge (*trichophorum cespitosum*) which is a light-green thin-stemmed sedge forming dense tufts over large areas of moor. It provides good grazing and gives the moor a light green colour in early summer and a red tinge in the autumn. Other plants in the community are the yellow-flowered bog asphodel (*narthecium ossifragum*), the carnivorous butterwort and the sundews.

Where the moor has been allowed to dry out the dominant plant is heather (*calluna vulgaris*). The form of the plant depends on the amount of shelter available, since its natural luxuriant upward growth is stunted and deflected to the horizontal by strong prevailing wind. Living in association with the heather are, for instance, the ribbed sedge (*carex binervis*), the crowberry (*empetrum nigrum*), the heath bedstraw (*galium saxatile*), the yellow tormentil (*potentilla erecta*) and the blue or pink milkwort in two forms — *polygala vulgaris* with leaves placed alternatively on the stem, and *polygala serpyllifolia* with the leaves in in opposite pairs. Two species of lichen are common on dry peat: *cladonia coccifera* is a horn-shaped structure about 1 cm ($\frac{1}{2}$ in) high with red spore carriers on the rim and *cladonia floerkeana* is similar but not horn-shaped.

In dry, sheltered situations bracken (*pteridium aquilinum*) takes over from heather as the dominant species. Since bracken is susceptible to wind damage and waterlogging there are no extensive bracken-covered areas in Caithness.

Moorland stream banks provide a fruitful habitat. By cutting into peat the stream provides a narrow, wind-sheltered valley. The banks are occasionally flooded with well aerated water, assisting humus formation, so providing a sheltered, moist and fairly sweet-soiled locality. The dominant species are the soft rush (*juncus effusus*), the purple moor grass (*molinia caerulea*), the lady fern (*athyrium filix-femina*) and the whin or gorse (*ulex europaeus*). Other plants of the moorland stream banks are given in Plant List 4. Sometimes a stream cuts a deep, narrow — almost subterranean channel which is cool, dark and moist. This is a good habitat for a most interesting group of plants — the mosses and liverworts which thrive well in the moist shade.

## THE DRAINAGE ZONE AND ARABLE PASTURES

The map of Figure 10 shows that most of the north and east of Caithness is now arable land, owing to the combined efforts of the Thurso and Wick rivers along with the operations of the farmers and crofters. The soil is stiff clay in all parts except the extreme west, easily waterlogged and heavy to cultivate. As a result the poorly drained areas are untilled and used for rough grazing. The dominant flora of this wet, rough pasture is the soft rush (*juncus effusus*) and the compact rush (*juncus conglomeratus var. compactus*) which are almost indistinguishable. There are also mosses and grasses appropriate to the wetness and acidity of the soil. When the soil is very wet and there is some shelter from the wind, the soft rush is displaced by the common sallow (*salix cinerea ssp. atrocinerea*) — a shrub of the willow family standing up to 2 m (6 ft) high. In rough, dry pasture the whin or gorse (*ulex europaeus*) and the creeping thistle (*cirsium arvense*) are common, with the whin sometimes dominant. Such ground is usually heavily grazed so that the only survivors are the meadow grasses, clovers and a few sedges. Where there is no grazing two umbellifers — the cow parsley (*anthriscus sylvestris*) and the hogweed (*heracleum sphondylium*) — predominate, entwined with tufted vetch (*vicia cracca*) and meadow vetchling (*lathyrus pratensis*) and interspersed with tall grasses such as the meadow foxtail (*alopecurus pratensis*) and the cock's-foot grass (*dactylis glomerata*).

Large areas of the County drain to lochs, the characters of which are very variable. The floors may be of sand, gravel, clay, mud or rock. The water may be acid, owing to drainage of peat moor, or more calcinate from either local rock seams or shells in the till. The water may be deep or shallow and the margins of the loch sharp, or boggy and ill-defined.

The underwater flora of the lochs of Caithness has not been properly surveyed and recorded. Lochs in Sutherland commonly have quillwort (*isoestris lacustris*), shore-weed (*littorella lacustris*), water lobelia (*lobelia dortmanna*) and awlwort (*subularia aquatica*). It seems likely that some Caithness lochs have underwater flora similar to those of the Sutherland lochs.

Where a loch margin is sharply defined the wave action deters the growth of a special margin flora except where there is wind shelter, or where the water is shallow. The common margin plants are: flote-grass (*glyceria fluitans*), bog bean (*menyanthes trifoliata*), bulbous rush (*juncus bulbosus*), sharp-flowered rush (*juncus acutiflorus*), spike rush (*eleocharis palustris*) and reed (*phragmites communis*). In such situations are reported two species of the very rare narrow smallreed, (*calamagrostis stricta*) and (*calamagrostis scotica*). The latter was feared to be extinct in Caithness but has been found again in recent years.

The three major rivers are the Wick, Thurso and Berriedale. The Wick river flows through till which is arable land in the upper reaches. The lower reaches have shallow banks dominated by the sharp-flowered rush (*juncus acutiflorus*) and the spike rush (*eleocharis palustris*), with large quantities of the Caithness sedge (*carex recta*) This latter plant is known in only one British locality but does occur in isolated river estuaries in Norway, Sweden, Finland, Iceland and North America. It grows 30 cm to 60 cm (1 ft to 2 ft) high and has thin leaves and dark sedge flowers with the leaves curving over the flowers.

The Thurso River has its origins deep in the peat moors. Its upper reaches are acid and windswept and the banks are dominated by the local moorland flora. As the waters flow into less acid rough pasture the banks become dominated by typical rush brake. In its last 6 km (4 miles) the river flows through a thick deposit of till which has been eroded away to form a steeply banked channel with a flat, flood-plain floor of fine clay loam. The steep clay banks, up to 30 m (100 ft) high give good shelter from the wind. They are lined with dwarf juniper juniper (*juniperus communis ssp. nana*), whin and sallow (*salix cinerea ssp. atrocinerea*). Small colonies of the scarce alpine pyramidal bugle (*ajuga pyramidalis*) occur. On the flood plain there grows a tangle of such common pasture, woodland and fenland flora as are typified by the contents of Plant Lists 1 and 5. The most interesting plant of this locality is the holy grass (*hierochloe odorata*). It is a grass reaching 10 cm to 50 cm (5 in to 20 in) high, and is shown in Plate 28. As it is not easily recognised, it is best sought in the first two weeks of June, when it begins to flower before the other common grasses. When crushed the plant smells strongly of coumarin, the scent of new-mown hay. It is believed to derive its name from a Scandinavian custom of strewing it on church floors to sweeten the air. It was known in south-west Scotland, but was believed to be extinct until discovered in 1834 by the naturalist Robert Dick along the banks of the Thurso river. It is now known in several other localities in Britain, and is common in parts of north Europe, Russia, north Asia and North America.

The Berriedale and Langwell Waters are quite different from the Wick and Thurso Rivers. In their valleys the soil is derived from glacial sand and gravel which is often covered by a thick layer of peat. The rivers begin as streams on the high, sub-alpine moors, and then flow through the moorland valleys. The bottoms of the valleys are filled with a bed of alluvial sand and gravel, often forming a series of terraces. These terraces are dry and porous, bearing fine turf similar to dune links. Sheep's fescue, matgrass (*nardus stricta*) and fiorin grass (*agrostis stolonifera*) predominate, with a sparse sprinkling of other xerophytes. In damp areas the soft rush (*juncus effusus*) and the bulbous rush (*juncus bulbosus*) predominate and in sheltered areas hazel coppices have developed. Near the sea the rivers enter steep-sided, rocky valleys clothed with birch, aspen, rowan, juniper, hazel, birdcherry and willow, with a rich under-growth of wood-land plants such as those of Plant List 6, along with many of the common plants given in Plant List 1. Similar flora also occur in other rocky valleys of the east coast — the Reisgill Burn at Lybster, the Achorn gorge near Dunbeath and the Burn of Latheronwheel.

## THE ARCTIC-ALPINE ENVIRONMENT

The high mountains have a climate dominated by frequent strong winds, low temperatures and high rainfall. The strong winds prevent the survival of trees and all but the strongest and hardiest shrubs. Soil is blasted from the rocks and mats of moss are uprooted. The harsh winter frosts break up the rock to small fragments; the low summer temperatures limit the maturing of fruit and seed, as well as slowing down the conversion of dead plants to humus. The heavy rain dissolves mineral salts out of the rocks and washes away soil and humus. The result is that the high alpine plateaux are rock-strewn deserts. The woolly hair-moss (*rhacomitrium lanuginosum*) grows among the rocks and is the only plant which is reasonably certain to survive. Where this moss is well estab-lished a layer of poor humus forms beneath it. This allows some different plants to grow. Lichens — well adapted to these conditions as they require only clean air and mineral salts — develop among the moss. *Thamnolia vermicularis* and *cladonia subcervicornis* are common alpine lichens. Stunted plants of heather (*calluna vulgaris*) occur, with a range of other plants, according to the nature of the environment. In general, alpine plants need a plentiful supply of mineral salts, and the Caithness hills, being of quartzite or conglomerate, furnish very little. As a result the flora is not rich. It consists of the crowberry (*empetrum nigrum*), the mountain azalea (*loiseleuria procumbens*), the stiff sedge (*carex bigelowii*) and the black bearberry (*arctous alpina*). Small quantities of bilberry (*vaccinium myrtillus*), cowberry (*vaccinium vitis-idaea*) and alpine lady's mantle (*alchemilla alpina*) also occur. In places sheltered from the wind a more luxuriant growth of the same type develops, with a peat base. In some localities it is dominated by bearberry (*arctostaphylos uva-ursi*). Lower down the hill slopes the vegetation merges into high peat moor, still rich in *rhacomitrium* moss down to about 300 m (1000 ft.) above sea level.

Similarly the rocky crags of the hills are also poor in flora, because of the lack of mineral salts. Golden rod (*solidago virgaurea*), alpine lady's mantle, starry saxifrage (*saxifraga stellaris*) and rose root (*sedum rosea*) occur, with the brittle bladder fern (*cystopteris fragilis*), various lichens, liverworts and mosses.

## PLANT LIST 1
### Commonly Occurring Plants

| | |
|---|---|
| Bracken | pteridium aquilinum |
| Meadow buttercup | ranunculus acris |
| Creeping Buttercup | ranunculus repens |
| Lady's smock | cardamine pratensis |
| Common violet | viola riviniana |
| Milkwort | Polygala vulgaris |
| Mouse-eared chickweed | cerastium holosteoides |
| Procumbent pearlwort | sagina procumbens |
| Purging flax | linum catharticum |
| Gorse | ulex europeaus |
| Birdsfoot trefoil | lotus corniculatus |
| Meadow-sweet | filipendula ulmaria |
| Silverweed | potentilla anserina |
| Tormentil | potentilla erecta |
| Rosebay willow herb | chamaenerion angustifolium |
| Cow parsley | anthriscus sylvestris |
| Angelica | angelica sylvestris |
| Hog-weed | heracleum sphondylium |
| Sorrel | rumex acetosa |
| Broad-leaved dock | rumex obtusifolius |
| Stinging nettle | urtica dioica |
| Forget-me-not | myosotis arvensis |
| Germander speedwell | veronica chamaedrys |
| Thyme-leaved speedwell | veronica serpyllifolia |
| Lousewort | pedicularis sylvatica |
| Yellow rattle | rhinanthus minor |
| Self heal | prunella vulgaris |
| Great plantain | plantago major |
| Ribwort plantain | plantago lanceolata |
| Lady's bedstraw | galium verum |
| Goose-grass | galium aparine |
| Scabious | succisa pratensis |
| Ragwort | senecio jacobaea |
| Groundsel | senecio vulgaris |
| Coltsfoot | tussilago farfara |
| Daisy | bellis perennis |
| Spear thistle | cirsium vulgare |
| Marsh thistle | cirsium palustre |
| Knapweed | centaurea nigra |
| Broom | sarothamnus scoparius |
| Cat's ear | hypochoeris radicata |
| Autumnal hawkbit | leontodon autumnalis |
| Mouse-ear hawkweed | hieracium pilosella |
| Dandelion | taraxacum officinale |
| Soft rush | juncus effusus |
| Field woodrush | luzula campestris |
| Dwarf purple orchis | dactylorchis purpurella |
| Common sedge | carex nigra |
| Sheep's fescue | festuca ovina |
| Red fescue | festuca rubra |
| Rye-grass | lolium perenne |
| Annual meadow grass | poa annua |
| Meadow grass | poa pratensis |
| Cock's foot grass | dactylis glomerata |
| Crested dog's-tail grass | cynosorus cristatus |
| Yorkshire fog | holcus lanatus |
| Tufted hair grass | deschampsia cespitosa |
| Bent grass | agrostis tenuis |

| | |
|---|---|
| Sweet vernal grass | anthoxanthum odoratum |
| Mat-grass | nardus stricta |
| Ox-eye daisy | chrysanthemum leucanthemum |
| Primrose | primula vulgaris |

## PLANT LIST 2
### Common Dune Links Plants

| | |
|---|---|
| Sand sedge | carex arenaria |
| Red fescue | festuca rubra |
| Sheeps fescue | festuca ovina |
| Yorkshire fog | holcus lanatus |
| Sea campion | silene maritima |
| Scurvy grass | cochlearia officinalis |
| Thyme | thymus drucei |
| Knapweed | centaurea nigra |
| Lesser burdock | arctium minus ssp. nemorosum |
| Scottish primrose | primula scotica |
| Yellow rattle | rhinanthus minor ssp. monticola |
| Wild pansy | viola tricolor ssp. curtisii |
| Sea plantain | plantago maritima |
| Buck's horn plantain | plantago coronopus |

## PLANT LIST 3
### Dune Link Stream Population

| | |
|---|---|
| Lady's bedstraw | galium verum |
| Birdsfoot trefoil | lotus corniculatus |
| Angelica | angelica sylvestris |
| Ragwort | senecio jacobaea |
| Wild pansy | viola tricolor ssp. curtisii |
| Field woodrush | luzula campestris |
| Marsh horsetail | equisetum palustris |
| Water forget-me-not | myosotis scorpoides |
| Marsh marigold | caltha palustris |
| Silverweed | potentilla anserina |
| Red campion | silene dioica |
| Soft rush | juncus effusus |
| Germander's speedwell | veronica chamaedrys |
| Yellow flag | iris pseudacorus |
| Montbretia | crocosmia x crocosmiflora |
| Monkey flower | mimulus guttatus |
| Dark-hair crowfoot | ranunculus trichophyllus |
| Wall pepper | sedum acre |

## PLANT LIST 4
### Plants of the Moorland Stream Banks

| | |
|---|---|
| Sphagnum moss | sphagnum cuspidatum |
| Juniper moss | polytrichium commune |
| Soft rush | juncus effusus |
| Mat-grass | nardus stricta |
| Wavy-hair-grass | deschampsia flexuosa |

| | |
|---|---|
| Purple moor grass | molinia caerulea |
| Star sedge | carex echinata |
| Common sedge | Carex nigra |
| Fir clubmoss | lycopodium selago |
| Hard fern | blechnum spicant |
| Lady-fern | athyrium filix-femina |
| Male fern | dryopteris filix-mas |
| Common polypody | polypodium vulgare |
| Tormential | potentilla erecta |
| Milkwort | polygala vulgaris |
| Milkwort | polygala serpyllifolia |
| Marsh violet | viola palustris |
| Rowan tree | sorbus aucuparia |
| Lesser spearwort | ranunculus flammula |
| Whin, gorse | ulex europaeus |
| Carnation sedge | carex flacca |
| Butterwort | pinguicula vulgaris |
| Bracken | pteridium aquilinum |
| Moorland spotted orchid | dactylorchis maculata ssp. ericetorum |

## PLANT LIST 5

### Plants of the Lower Thurso River Banks

| | |
|---|---|
| Juniper | juniperus communis ssp. nana |
| Sallow | salix cinerea ssp. atrocinerea |
| Globe flower | trollius europaeus |
| Water horsetail | equisetum fluviatile |
| Lady fern | athyrium filix-femina |
| Marsh marigold | caltha palustris |
| Whin, gorse | ulex europaeus |
| Bulbous buttercup | ranunculus bulbosus |
| Downy pepperwort | lepidium heterophyllum |
| Shepherd's purse | capsella bursa-pastoris |
| Winter cress | barbarea vulgaris |
| Watercress | rorippa nasturtium-aquaticum |
| Creeping yellow cress | rorippa sylvestris |
| Marsh yellow cress | rorippa islandica |
| Violet | viola riviniana |
| Greater stitchwort | stellaria holostea |
| Lesser stitchwort | stellaria graminea |
| Water blinks | montia fontana |
| Hemlock | conium maculatum |
| Comfrey | symphytum officinale |
| Water forget-me-not | myosotis caespitosa |
| Bindweed | calystegia sepium |
| Monkey flower | mimulus guttatus |
| Marsh speedwell | veronica scuttellata |
| Common speedwell | veronica officinalis |
| Buxbaum's speedwell | veronica persica |
| Lousewort | pedicularis sylvatica |
| Water mint | mentha aquatica |
| Pyramidal bugle | ajuga pyramidalis |
| Valerian | valeriana officinalis |
| White butterbur | petasites albus |
| Sneezewort | achillea ptarmica |
| Reddish pondweed | potamogeton alpinus |
| Curled pondweed | potamogeton crispus |

| | |
|---|---|
| Branched bur-reed | sparganium erectum |
| Creeping brown sedge | carex disticha |
| Woodland meadow grass | poa nemoralis |
| Quaking grass | briza media |
| Holy grass | hierochloe odorata |

## PLANT LIST 6
### Plants of the Rocky Valleys of East Caithness

| | |
|---|---|
| Wood sorrel | oxalis acetosella |
| Honeysuckle | lonicera periclymenum |
| Hairy woodrush | luzula pilosa |
| Creeping soft-grass | holcus mollis |
| Beech fern | thelypteris phegopteris |
| Golden saxifrage | chrysosplenium oppositifolium |
| Sweet woodruff | galium odoratum |
| Oak fern | thelypteris dryopteris |
| Slender St John's wort | hypericum pulchrum |
| Wood sage | teucrium scorodonia |
| Pyramidal bugle | ajuga pyramidalis |
| False brome grass | brachypodium sylvaticum |
| Bitter vetch | latharus montanus |
| Wood vetch | vicia sylvatica |
| Eared sallow | salix aurita |
| Carnation sedge | carex flacca |
| Tea-leaved willow | salix phylicifolia |
| Wild hyacinth | endymion non-scriptus |
| Burnet rose | rosa pimpinellifolia |
| Red campion | silene dioica |
| Fragrant orchid | gymnadenia conopsea |
| Golden rod | solidago virgaurea |
| Foxglove | digitalis purpurea |
| Bracken | pteridium aquilinum |
| Bloody cranesbill | geranium sanguineum |
| Wood cranesbill | geranium sylvaticum |
| Herb Robert | geranium robertianum |
| Ramsons garlic | allium ursinum |
| Stone bramble | rubus saxatilis |
| Blackberry | rubus fruticosus |
| Strawberry | fragaria vesca |
| Marsh hawksbeard | crepis paludosa |
| Figwort | scrophularia nodosa |

CHAPTER 10

# THE VERTEBRATE FAUNA OF CAITHNESS

Caithness supports a rich variety of wild life. It has large areas of moorland where wild animals can live a normal existence largely free from man's interference. It has a considerable area of farm land, mostly round the coast and in the valleys of the two rivers, Wick and Thurso, where wild life is sometimes in competition with man. Man is not always sure which animals are his friends and which are his enemies and consequently he sometimes persecutes creatures unnecessarily. In Caithness, however, this persecution has never been so intense or unremitting as to wipe out any well-established species. Caithness has few areas of trees and a consequent lack of some woodland species, though occasionally even species normally associated with woodland, such as the roe deer and red deer have adapted to a treeless environment. Caithness has very few built up areas where wild life has been completely ousted by the density of human population—for in town gardens and homes there are often established complete ecological situations or food chains.

All wild life is interdependent and the natural situation might be summed up in the rhyme:
"Big fleas have little fleas upon their backs to bite  em,
And little fleas have lesser fleas and so ad infinitum."
Into this situation man comes as a disturbing influence. He can upset what is called the balance of nature. To do this is dangerous because no one can foresee the ultimate outcome of such disturbance. For example, man introduced the rabbit to Britain from Europe. Tens of generations of farmers have been regretting this ever since. Direct interference of this sort has not been characteristic of Caithness but today there are those who are worried about the long term effects of the widespread use of chemical pesticides upon creatures we would protect from their influence.

Other factors which will have long term effects on our animal ecology are the increased use of marginal land, the breaking in of moorland pastures, the extension of drainage schemes and afforestation. The range of our fauna then, is not static but is continuously evolving. Let us look at our animals as we find them in 1972.

## DEER

**Red Deer**

To see a herd of Red Deer in the wild is an experience not to be forgotten and we are fortunate that Caithness is one of the few places in Britain where we can do this without difficulty. Anyone who crosses the Ord between dusk and early morning from late autumn to early summer stands a chance of seeing stags and hinds feeding by the roadside. This, the largest British wild animal, is found

75

now mainly in the Scottish Highlands and the Red Deer Commission estimate that there are over 4,000 Red Deer in Caithness. The Red Deer is by origin an animal of open woodland and it is interesting that according to Harvie Brown and Buckley the Red Deer in Caithness rarely leave the deer forest (a wild tract — not necessarily woodland — reserved for deer) for the lower ground. It was thought that the greater part of Caithness was ill-adapted for them. Now Red Deer are found on the moors and hills of the west and south of the County, having adapted completely to living outside woodland. Recently an attempt was made to establish Red Deer in Stroma and a stag and two hinds were imported. The hinds refused to stay and accomplished the incredible feat of swimming across the Pentland Firth and landing in the Gills Bay area.

The life of the Red Deer in Caithness follows an annual cycle in which the stags and hinds have a different pattern. In winter both are found in separate groups on the lower ground where the feeding is better, though the stags come lower down than the hinds.

It takes really severe weather to force the hind to very low ground. Today the deer is going through a difficult time in the south-east of the County where some of their traditional winter feeding grounds have been turned over to afforestation or to the grazing of out-wintered cattle and sheep.

The stags who forage widely may do serious damage to crops such as turnips or cabbage if they raid into cultivated land — a good example of animals in competition with man.

An easterly wind is often the prelude to stag raids for it carries the smell of turnips to the stag who is very fond of 'neeps'. Winter conditions thin out the weaker animals. In their natural wild state few Red Deer survive beyond fifteen years, though hand-fed ones may live for over twenty years. Fewer deer die nowadays from natural causes because considerable numbers are shot either under the auspices of the Red Deer Commission or to satisfy the demands of the venison market that has developed at home and abroad.

Every spring, stags cast their antlers and new ones begin to grow. Each successive pair of antlers will be larger and more branched in a young stag until he reaches full maturity about the age of eight. It was the head of the good stag with a magnificent set of antlers that was so highly prized by the sportsmen of former years. Now, however, many more deer are shot for venison than for their antlers. Thus fewer stags reach full maturity and good heads are rarer.

In summer, while the stag is growing his antlers and gaining condition the hind will rear her single calf, born in June. During its first few days of life the calf lies hidden in the heather until, after ten to fourteen days, it is strong enough to follow its mother. It is during this time that predatory animals, such as the fox, may prey on the young deer.

By autumn the summer feeding will have fattened the stags, hinds and calves and it is now that the famous highland sport of deer stalking is prosecuted. In October the mating or rutting season has arrived. Now the bigger stags round up their harems of hinds and have to exercise eternal vigilance and energy to keep possession of their herds. Other stags are continually trying to woo away the hinds. Big stags present an open challenge and have to be fought while the young stags are an equally exhausting menace, for while they do not fight for possession they are numerous and persistently try to infiltrate among the hinds and have to be chased away. This situation lasts for about three weeks and by the end of it the stags, who have seldom rested or eaten, have lost all their fine condition. They leave the hinds and seek pastures on lower ground to recover.

Winter arrives again and finds the stags in much poorer condition than the hinds. They are less able to withstand a hard winter and have greater need of shelter. Some will be shot on their raiding forays on the farms. The shooting of deer for venison goes on throughout this season and the most highly prized bag will be a "yeld" hind — one that has not had a calf — for she will be much fatter than any of the others. The demand for venison has led some people to think that the farming of deer on hill land might be a practical commercial proposition in Caithness. The estates have always hand-fed some stags kept in parks and have kept some hinds too. This has helped to improve the quality of deer when carried out systematically but the farming of deer has not yet been tried. Afforestation, which at the moment is making life difficult for the deer, might help in the long run by providing winter shelter for the stags.

### Roe Deer

Though the numbers of Roe Deer in the County are small in comparison with those of the Red Deer, this animal is by no means uncommon and all evidence points to an increase in numbers. Roe deer may be found in any part of the County with access to free outrun. Like the Red Deer the Roe is a woodland animal, but it may also be found in very moist areas. Its movements are secretive and in Caithness it has adapted to life in the rushes which provide the cover it requires. It seems to have spread from the Berriedale area since the tree fellings and the great gales of 1951 and 1952.

Though excellent swimmers too the Roe Deer are unlike the larger Red Deer in that they do not form herds but gather in pairs or small family groups. The fawns, usually twins, are born in May having been conceived in July.

### Sika Deer

Some of this Japanese race of deer were taken into the Langwell Estate, it is believed, before the Second World War, and today there are still some to be seen there in the policies. Whilst they have been seen in the Sackville House region and may possibly be in the Bilbster Hill area, no conclusive proof of their establishment in the wild can be obtained. The Sika is somewhat larger than the Roe — 80 cm to 85 cm (32 in to 34 in) at the shoulder as opposed to 65 cm to 75 cm (26 in to 30 in) — and much smaller than the Red, 120 cm to 150 cm (46 in to 58 in). Unlike the other two it has a spotted coat.

## CARNIVORES

### The Fox

Perhaps the most outstanding and natural phenomenon among our wild life in the last 10-15 years is the dramatic increase in the fox population. The farm name Todholes and the Todholes of Dunnet Head testify to the antiquity of the fox in Caithness. ('Tod' is the traditional Scottish word for fox). Formerly, foxes were mainly confined to the higher ground and moors on the west, but in recent years have spread eastwards until they have achieved a fairly uniform coverage of the County. Indeed, there may now be more in the east than in the west. It is a widely held view that the numbers of foxes have increased due to lack of gamekeepers, whose numbers have declined steadily since World War II. In former years these keepers were sufficiently numerous to make effective war on the foxes, whereas now, whilst they still take considerable numbers, large areas are unkeepered and so the foxes multiply. The increasing number of foxes puts a great pressure on their local food supply causing them to forage more widely. This situation has been gravely aggravated by the infection of rabbits by myxomatosis and their consequent gross reduction in numbers. Under normal circumstances the rabbit is the staple diet of the fox and its decimation has meant that the fox has had to look beyond his traditional territory for food.

The spread of the fox has brought him into open conflict with farmers in all parts of the County. He is very fond of poultry and any unsecured henhouse is liable to his depredations. The farmer finds that the main menace of the fox has been to the younger lambs in spring. In the Keiss area tractors have had to be kept running with lights on all night in the sheep folds to keep the fox at bay and even then lambs have been lost. Fox drives have frequently been organised in an attempt to keep down the fox population.

It is a pity that the fox attacks poultry and lambs and the occasional young deer for he is an attractive animal of legendary intelligence. He undoubtedly does much good in his unremitted assault on rabbits, hares, rats, mice and voles which are his natural food. The vixen is a devoted mother, a fact which is often used to tempt her to her own destruction. If a cub is taken from her earth and kept, she will come looking for him and may thus be shot. In winter many foxes range along the shore where they find rich pickings of carrion; many stay near the shore all the year. Others move inland in the spring and summer to breed and it is then that they are most vulnerable to hunters. A vixen gone to earth with her cubs, may be kept there by putting any object she finds unusual at the mouth of the den until the hunter can prepare for their certain extinction.

## The Badger

Badgers exist in two places in Caithness. As far as is known this is the first time that their existence in the County has been recorded in this century. Harvie Brown and Buckley could find no record of the badger in Caithness and Ernest Neal in his recent standard work "The Badger" does not record it as being found in Caithness. To the great satisfaction of all naturalists these interesting animals, little known locally, have taken up residence here.

Whereas the fox is a known rogue, the badger's character is of sterling worth and all the evidence points to his being an animal beneficial to man's interest. He is an omnivorous feeder and so is rarely short of food. His diet comprises wild bulbs, roots and fungi and pests such as rabbits, rats, mice, voles, insects and larvae, slugs and snails. With a range of food like this at his disposal, supplemented by occasional hedgehogs, frogs, worms, grass and berries, it is rare indeed for the badger to be forced by hunger to take any domestic animals. Should he ever take poultry or game birds he will take only one and eat it on the spot.

The badger's sett is a clean and tidy home uncluttered by the nauseous remains of prey found at the fox's den. Badgers have a passion for cleanliness and the female frequently has a spring clean. The Caithness ones have been seen to have their bedding out to air on a fine day. Moreover, they dig special latrines. A large den may sometimes be shared by foxes though each animal will keep to its own area, for the badger could not put up with the fox's habits and if he felt like it would turn the fox out. The sharing of the den, however, has been to the badger's disadvantage for he has often been blamed for the fox's misdemeanours.

## Wild Cat

Recent years have seen no spread of the wild cat which is probably fortunate for other forms of animal life. The wild cat is acknowledged to be the most savage and destructive killer we have. It seems to regard the rest of the world with malice and will kill when it has no hope of eating the victim. The wild cat has always been and still is to be found chiefly in the higher ground to the west and south of the County from Reay, Shurrery, Dalnawillan and Glutt to the Dunbeath and Berriedale Straths. Wild cats have occasionally been found outside this area as far east as Stirkoke in the south and Charleston (ND262717) in the north. Within the last ten years they have become established in the Bower area and two or three have been killed there each year. Domestic cats sometimes go wild in other areas but the true wild cat is a distinct species, larger and heavier, with a striped coat, a thick blunt-ended tail and an untamable nature. The wild cat will kill the domestic cat though the two types have been known to breed together. One female cat in Glutt had kittens though there was no other domestic cat, male or female, within many miles. These kittens proved to be little balls of fire, completely unresponsive to human overtures. Kittens have been taken from a wild cat's den after the mother has been killed but they have never been tamed; often they have refused to eat and have died.

## The Otter

One can think of no other British mammal that has had two naturalists classics written about it. The otter has proved itself worthy of selection by Henry Williamson and Gavin Maxwell to be the subject of their books "Tarka the Otter" and "Ring of Bright Water", two works of superlative quality. Anyone who has read these books will become favourably disposed towards the otter for life and indeed he is generally well regarded in Caithness. The otter is equally at home on land, in fresh water, or in the sea and may be found in any of these habitats. Naturally, he hunts in water, and it is along rivers or by the sea that one is most likely to see him. Though the otter is not scarce in Caithness no animal is more difficult to approach undetected and this, coupled with the fact that it is abroad mostly at night, means that it is not easy to find. His tracks may help his discovery, or the finding of his 'spraint' or droppings which he frequently leaves on a particular spot. The Otter Stone at Loch Scye is so called because generations of otters have used it for their toilet.

It is only on the river that the otter really comes into competition with man. In spring the otter is found in the lower reaches of the river feeding mainly on eels which are then on passage upstream but also taking a number of salmon and trout. People would find this more forgivable if the whole fish were eaten but often only a bite or two from behind the head is taken and the rest of the fish may be left on the riverbank or on a stone. Gamekeepers and River Superintendents agree, however, that provided the number of otters does not rise and force the animals to take more fish, they like having them on the river because of the eels they eat. It is now well established that the otter takes eels in preference to other fish and the eel is the greatest menace to young fish in the river. On the otter's credit side too, he takes old cannibal trout.

As spring lengthens into summer, the otter follows the eels up to the burns

and lochans and when the water is low he may range widely across the countryside or come to the coast. In autumn he feeds again on eels — this time those
migrating downstream to the sea. While on land the otter feeds mainly on rats,
mice, voles, frogs, toads and newts and occasionally on rabbits, earthworms,
slugs and snails. Only if forced by desperate need will it take poultry. Some
otters undoubtedly stay in or near the sea for the greater part of the year where
they live on fish, crabs and mussels. Round the John O' Groats coast at least
three have been found dead in lobster creels in recent years.

	Although those who know the ways of the otter are very tolerant of him,
he has suffered a lot at man's hands either because of ignorance and the thought
that his presence endangers livestock or because of the wish to make a few
shillings out of his pelt. A dead otter is a pathetic sight; the sight of otters playing together or of an otter swimming in a pool is one to stir the blood.

## THE STOAT AND THE WEASEL (Futret)

	These two animals may be confused easily though the weasel is smaller,
does not have a black tip to its tail, and in Caithness does not change colour
to white in winter as does the stoat. As well as being alike physically one might
say that they are alike temperamentally. The stoat displays a ferocity that is
awesome while the weasel displays to an even more concentrated degree the
relentless blood-thirstiness characteristic of this tribe. Despite their savagery
both are worth trying to preserve, within limits, for as tireless hunters they
account for many rabbits, rats, mice and voles. Undoubtedly if they have their
headquarters near a henhouse, they will account for some hens and eggs too
but the balance is in their favour on agricultural land. On game preserves the
picture might be different.

	There is general agreement that though still found, stoats are fewer than
they used to be. Whereas in 1887 Harvie Brown and Buckley say they were
commoner than weasels the reverse is certainly now the case. Some believe there
is a direct correlation between the number of stoats and the number of rabbits,
but others believe that the stoat was on the decline before the decimation of the
rabbits by myxomatosis. Whatever the reason it seems that they are now plentiful only in the Reay area. The corporate courage of a group of stoats is infinite
and should a family be encountered discretion rather than valour should be the
watchword.

	Weasels are much more common than stoats and anyone in the country
or on the road is likely to see one sometime. A family on the move is not an
uncommon sight for the young are often moved if danger threatens. The weasel
has long had a reputation of being able to charm the birds off the trees and we
have one eye-witness account of this behaviour by Alex Gunn of Castletown. He
has seen a weasel tumbling about and contorting its body while a fascinated black-
bird gradually descended a tree until almost within snatching distance of the weasel.
Mr Gunn is sure that had he not interfered the bird would have been taken.

## BATS

### The Pipistrelle or Common Bat

	Bats are not common in Caithness but quite unexpectedly on a calm sum-
mer's night one may be seen twisting and turning in jerky flight, as it hunts for
insects. The disconcerting thing about the bat in Caithness is that one is seen

PLATE 11. *Red Deer at Berriedale.*

(L. Brown)

(J. Selby)

PLATE 12.   *An oyster catcher.*

(J. Selby)

PLATE 13.   *A Ringed plover.*

perhaps on a single evening — then it disappears without a trace. Bats are most often observed in the Dunbeath-Berriedale area but have been seen at Wick, Bilbster, Sackville, Bighouse, Skinnet, Keiss, John O' Groats and Mey. They are known to migrate over very long distances and so they may not breed or hibernate in the County.

## RABBITS AND HARES

### The Rabbit

The inoffensive, cuddly rabbit ranks second only to the rat as the most destructive pest among our native fauna. Little needs to be said about such a familiar creature but mention must be made of the drastic diminution wrought by myxomatosis in their number throughout the County. Only in Stroma did rabbits escape the scourge and there they multiplied prodigiously after the human population left, sufficiently so to make rabbit-hunting safaris to the island occasionally worthwhile. In 1972 however, there is some evidence that myxomatosis may have reached Stroma.

Myxomatosis did not exterminate the rabbits but it made them very scarce for a while. Gradually they have recovered their numbers and some believe that strains of rabbit resistant to the disease may be developing. Others discount this and hold that whenever the density of the rabbit population increases, myxomatosis seems to return. Their numbers at the time of going to press are of controllable proportions but there is no doubt that if they became disease-free they would multiply rapidly causing drastic damage to all growing crops from clover to forest trees. One further point should be made about the rabbit. His disappearance has deprived many predators of their staple diet. This would be good if it meant that these then turned their attention to other pests such as rats, mice, field voles and moles but bad if it forced them to attack lambs and other small livestock. Man used to prey on the rabbit but is now often disinclined to eat them.

### The Brown Hare

In 1961 it was estimated that in Caithness there was an average brown hare population density of 3 to 6 per 405 hectares (1,000 acres) in an area of 24,300 hectares (60,000 acres) of mainly agricultural and marginal land. The brown hare's population was then increasing and indeed in the years that followed the rise in numbers was remarkable corresponding with the shrivelling of the rabbit count. Removal of competition from the rabbit which eats the same food may have been a factor in this increase and the subsequent spread of the fox may account for the fact that in 1970 brown hares are much fewer again except in the Dunbeath area where foxes have not proliferated. Brown hares are still common enough for one to have a chance of viewing the acrobatic antics of the males in spring during the rut; antics which have given rise to the saying "mad as a March hare". The mother or doe will defend her young courageously and one has been seen to "box" a swooping hen harrier and successfully repel all its attacks.

### The Blue Hare

This truly Scottish hare used to be very common on our hills and moors. A smaller species than the brown hare, weighing 2.25 kg to 2.75 kg (5 lb to 6 lb) against 3.5 kg to 4 kg (8 lb to 9 lb), its summer appearance is nevertheless

G

similar. In winter, its coat changes to white and makes it conspicuous on snow-less moorland. Regrettably the blue hare is now very scarce on Caithness up-lands. It is estimated that in some areas there may now be only one twentieth of the blue hare's population of twenty years ago. Hare drives organised in the 1930s might bag 200 to 300 hares on the high moors and in 1947 four guns took 105 blue hares off Strupster in one day. Now in a walk across the same area one would be lucky to see five hares. The fox is again quoted as the villian of the piece and most gamekeepers believe that he has cleared the moors of the blue hare as he has done of the hill-nesting gulls.

Like rabbits, hares often formed part of the Caithness diet especially in those days when the standard of living was not so high. Today, scarity of hares and revulsion at rabbits has meant that neither is eaten often.

## INSECTIVORES

### The Hedgehog

It is a subject of regret that the majority of people are familiar with the hedgehog only as a mangled mass of bloody pulp on the road. Hedgehogs seem to be attracted to the roads in the same way that birds are, in high summer. Possibly they find insects drawn there by the warmth absorbed by the tarmac. On the road their instinctive reaction to danger is of little avail against the crush-ing force of a motor car. Yet it is certain that many could be avoided by drivers with no risk to themselves. Despite the numbers killed on the road and by foxes that can unroll the tight ball and at whose dens the scraped out skins are found, hedgehogs are numerous and have multiplied greatly within the last forty years. With man's assistance they have colonised Stroma. In 1887 (Harvie Brown and Buckley) they were unknown in the wild state. As an insectivore the hedgehog is one of our most beneficial animals eating grubs, slugs, snails and many other pests; in fact his range of food is much wider than this and it may perhaps better be called omnivorous; rats, mice, voles and young rabbits are eaten and the hedgehog is one of the few natural enemies of the adder, which it kills and enjoys. The hedgehog is easily tamed and as a pet, easily fed.

### The Mole

Moles are numerous on all agricultural land where they are most unpopular on account of the earth they throw up covering grazing and leaving the surface uneven. When moleskins were used for clothing in days gone by, mole trappers kept down their numbers but now the market for moleskin is extinct and mole trappers are a vanished race. Moles are still hunted, however, whenever their numbers are such as to interfere with agriculture or gardening. Mole traps are set on their runs, often in those leading to water; or the moles may be poisoned by use of strychnine, a permit for the use of which must be had from the local Board of Agriculture. Foxes and weasels are enemies of the mole, the latter following him along the run to take him. Moles have voracious appetites because of their high metabolic rate and a mole denied food for a few hours will die.

### Shrews (Sheer Mice)

Britain's smallest mammal is the pygmy shrew — body length 43 mm to 64 mm (1.7 in to 2.5 in) and the common shrew is not a great deal larger — body length 58 mm to 87 mm (2.3 in to 3.4 in). Both are present in Caithness and it is likely that most people are familiar with the common shrews, many of which are seen dead in the countryside, having either died a natural death or been taken by cats, which do not eat them probably because of the unpleasant smell given off from their scent glands.

Though different in size both these shrews have similar habits living entirely on insects, worms, woodlice, slugs and snails. Like the moles their appetites are insatiable and they quickly die if deprived of food. Their energetic hunting means they do a tremendous amount of good in the field and garden. Much superstition surrounded them in days of yore and they were believed to poison cattle.

The water shrew is found in Caithness though we are not sure of its range — certainly it exists in the Reay area.

Shrews, and particularly the water shrew, have been associated with a creature that our ancestors in Caithness called the Lavellan. No one seems certain what exactly the Lavellan was but Harvie Brown and Buckley believed it was either the water shrew or the lizard. It would be interesting if anyone could shed more light on the identity of the Lavellan.

## RODENTS

### The Brown Rat (Rottan)

The brown rat (there is no positive evidence of the black rat in Caithness) ranks as public enemy number one among our mammals. Its occurrence is widespread but thankfully its numbers are contained by efficient pest control measures. It is difficult to over-estimate the damage that rats can do not only as rodents but as carriers of human and animal disease. Their fertility is prodigious and one pair can multiply to over 1,000 in one year. In the face of this, attempts at control have to be followed through with perpetual zeal.

### Mice

The mouse is ubiquitous and familiar to all. Control measures effective with rats are also effective with mice. This is fortunate for little in the house is immune from damage during mice infestation.

The field mouse as far as is known does not normally enter houses but is very common out of doors. It is slimmer than the house mouse with larger eyes and ears. It is often called the long-tailed field mouse to distinguish it from the short-tailed field mouse which is not a mouse at all, but the field vole. Field mice, long or short tailed, do considerable damage to gardens and agricultural crops and are not as easily kept down as the house variety. This is one other case where we are dependent upon nature providing a control in the form of predatory animals.

### Voles

The short tailed "field mouse" mentioned above and the "water" rat are neither mouse nor rat but the field vole and the ground vole respectively. The former, as its name implies, is found mostly in the open field where it tunnels just below the ground surface, especially in stubble, in all pastures, and fields. Those seen living in banks or walls are probably bank voles, which have redder coats. These seem to be found at least in the Strathmore area though identification is not positive. The water rat is, it seems, the ground vole and not the water vole. There are apparently two distinct species of similar habits but different range according to Vanden Brink in the 'Field Guide to the Mammals of Europe'. The distinction between the two is controversial but of biological significance and only the ground vole, the smaller of the two, is found along the ditches, burns and rivers of northern Scotland, being well represented in Caithness.

As far as is known this survey covers all the known wild mammals of Caithness in 1972. As agriculture is the subject of a separate chapter domestic animals have not been considered. Other mammals have been known to live ferally in Caithness.

Red squirrels, for example, have lived among the woods at Berriedale and Dunbeath though none has been seen in recent years. Since recorded in 1887 by Harvie Brown and Buckley the polecat has disappeared though evidence of its former existence remains in the name of the Polecat Holes at Duncansby and the Polecat Den at Reay. "To stink like a polecat" was a Caithness simile more common thirty years ago than now, but its use is probably a relic of days when polecats were more familiar. The ferret, the polecat's near relative, is still used by rabbit trappers but though many have escaped, none appear to have bred in the wild. Mink, another near relative of the polecat, have been farmed in Caithness but fortunately none escaped here to become established in the wild as they are believed to have done in Inverness-shire and Ross-shire. Only once has a pine marten been recorded in Caithness and that in the late 1940s when one was shot on Noss Head. It is thought that this one had worked its way northwards and it is believed to have killed hens at Latheronwheel. Guinea pigs and hamsters are common pets in Caithness but though some have undoubtedly escaped, climatic conditions and animal predators have prevented their establishment as wild species.

Worthy of mention as a Caithness mammal now extinct is the semi-wild sheep that used to run on the cliffs and their hinterland at Duncansby Head. These sheep, called "Keerie Sheep" by Harvie Brown and Buckley, belonged to an ancient breed, like those of St Kilda or North Ronaldsay, but larger. The local people called them "Rockies" and the flock was shared among the crofters who would round them up at Shin's Cliff to clip the hairy wool and share out those unmarked. The mutton was good and its availability probably accounts for the old nickname "Mutton Eaters" given to the people of Duncansby. The "Rockies" died out in the first decade of this century.

## REPTILES

**The Adder (Nether)**
The adder is the only Caithness snake but it is very common on all the moors with the exception of Dunnet Head. A poisonous snake, the adder excites alarm where he is seen and humans when they have spotted him rarely let him away with his life. Yet it is the adder's natural inclination to seek cover when disturbed and it bites only if trodden on or interfered with. There have been few cases of human victims of adder bites.

Gamekeepers fear the adder for the sake of their dogs. A gun dog will "point" an adder and is therefore apt to be bitten. If this happens the fang wounds are opened and treated with potassium permanganate which the keeper often carries against such a contingency.

**The Slow Worm**

Slow worms are found in the south-east of the County in Latheron Parish. The slow worm is neither worm nor snake but a legless lizard easily distinguishable from the adder by its uniform greeny bronze colour which contrasts with the mottled back and sides of the adder. Far from slow in its movements the slow worm is quite harmless and indeed makes a good garden pet for it is particularly fond of slugs.

**The Common Lizard**

Lizards in Caithness are found on dry heath or sand dunes throughout the County. They have been seen at Bloody Quoys, Dunn, Reay, Strathmore, Dunbeath and Keiss. Is this the Caithness Lavellan or is the Lavellan a purely mythical creature?

All three reptiles retain their eggs inside the body till the young are fully developed and so the young usually appear to be born rather than hatched.

## AMPHIBIA

**The Common Frog ("Puddag")**

The "Puddag" whose life history is familiar to all youngsters is too well known all over Caithness, including Stroma, to need much mention.

**Common Toad**

Though less well known than the frog and less numerous, the toad is found generally throughout the County. In contrast with the gelatinous mass of the frog's eggs, those of the toad are laid in a string. It spends less time in the water and its skin has a much drier and more warty appearance.

**The Smooth Newt**

This animal is known to be in the Castletown and Keiss areas but is probably found much more generally. Its eggs are laid singly on aquatic plants and after the breeding season it takes to the land.

All amphibia go through the tadpole stage but the tail of the newt is retained on the adult. All must spend some time out of water as well as in it — a fact not always known to those who try to keep them in tanks. If this facility is not afforded to tadpoles reaching maturity, they die.

## CAITHNESS FRESH WATER VERTEBRATE FAUNA

Water not being man's natural environment, he is normally less familiar with the creatures found therein than he is with those on land. Though the burns, rivers and lochs teem with heterogeneous forms of life we can only note those most likely to be seen. The mammals and amphibians have been mentioned in the previous section.

**Salmon**

Caithness offers some of the best accessible salmon fishing in the British Isles, (see Table 7) as indeed it does sea and brown trout fishing.

Table 7.

Thurso River Salmon Catches 1960-69

|      | Jan | Feb | Mar | Apr | May | June | July | Aug | Sept | Oct | Total |
|------|-----|-----|-----|-----|-----|------|------|-----|------|-----|-------|
| 1960 | —   | —   | 60  | 183 | 75  | 50   | 29   | 260 | 306  | 53  | 1,016 |
| 1961 | —   | —   | 59  | 189 | 103 | 43   | 191  | 224 | 107  | 54  | 970   |
| 1962 | 2   | 8   | 48  | 128 | 202 | 143  | 180  | 858 | 360  | 48  | 1,977 |
| 1963 | —   | 5   | 82  | 77  | 111 | 59   | 201  | 600 | 356  | 78  | 1,569 |
| 1964 | —   | 2   | 13  | 119 | 115 | 66   | 79   | 701 | 695  | 56  | 1,846 |
| 1965 | —   | 2   | 61  | 154 | 166 | 115  | 574  | 486 | 639  | 114 | 2,311 |
| 1966 | —   | 3   | 37  | 86  | 163 | 179  | 153  | 567 | 381  | 67  | 1,636 |
| 1967 | —   | 2   | 34  | 58  | 77  | 48   | 6    | 101 | 179  | 18  | 523   |
| 1968 | —   | 14  | 47  | 80  | 144 | 61   | 403  | 119 | 92   | 62  | 1,022 |
| 1969 | —   | 3   | 14  | 67  | 90  | 19   | 38   | 68  | 267  | 53  | 619   |

Salmon are found in all the seven main water courses — Berriedale, Langwell, Dunbeath, Wick, Wester, Thurso and Forss and in Lochs Wester, Watten and Shurrery. On the Thurso River, at Halkirk, is one of the oldest salmon hatcheries in Scotland. Here, a systematic attempt is made to maintain the stocks of salmon. Well over a million eggs are collected annually from the spawning redds and put in the hatchery where a very high percentage of hatch (over 90%) is achieved. After about two and a half months the fry are released in the little burns where they have few competitors or predators. After two years these are called 'smolt' and it is then that the majority migrate to the sea. This attempt at sustaining the stock has been carried a stage further, setting aside the Grassie Loch for the nurture of salmon fry and parr. Here the fry are deposited for two years and so protected that they are able to mature and grow rapidly. When in two years the time comes for them to migrate they are comparatively large and strong. It is possible that this scheme may be extended so that three lochs are similarly used — one for fry, one for one year old parr and one for two years old smolt and a cycle thus established.

Salmon may be fished in the estuaries by fixed drift net from 15th February provided that the salmon are allowed free passage from 12 noon on Saturday to 6 a.m. on Monday. Permission to fish is let to fishermen by the proprietors of the river fishing rights.

### Sea Trout

Sea trout are found in all the above mentioned rivers and the Wester Loch which has short access to the sea. Resembling the salmon in life history the sea trout also assumes its silvery appearance before taking to the sea.

### Brown Trout

The most numerous of our game fish the brown trout, is found in almost all the burns, rivers and lochs of Caithness. Their quality and size vary with the amount of feeding available in their watery homes. They migrate from the streams to the lochs and sometimes to the estuaries but not to the sea.

### Eel

Eels were formerly known in Caithness as "yaas" which was thought by Harvie and Buckley to be a corruption of the Norse "Aal". Eels are still very common but it is clear that their numbers now do not match those of eighty years ago when Norwegian sailors in Wick used to catch them by the barrelful. Our taste for eels has never approached that of the Dutch and Scandinavians and consequently eels have never been fished here for food. They are still quite numerous and may be found almost wherever there is water. The life story of the eel from Sargasso Sea to here and back is now well known and the eel's persistence in its migration is marvellous. This persistence means that it may be found in damp grass away from streams, yet apparently well able to survive.

**Stickleback**

The three-spined stickleback or "bandstickle", the nest-building fish, is found in water-filled quarries and streams all over Caithness. Often caught by children it cannot survive in a jam jar however well fed for it soon uses up the oxygen supply. In a properly set up aquarium, however, it is an interesting subject for study.

**Lamprey**

The book lamprey has been found in the River Wester.

## MARINE FAUNA

Sea shores are the richest of all environments in the variety of game life that they present. Caithness, with a coastline (of roughly 170 km-105 miles) long in proportion to the area of the County, is particularly well endowed with marine fauna. If this environment is extended to the open sea the range of fauna grows astronomically. As fishing is the subject of a separate chapter animals beyond the tides will not be dealt with. It is impossible to deal exhaustively or authoritatively with marine-fauna here but as Caithness is and always has been a seaward looking community no account of its fauna would be complete without mention of the commonest animals found on the shore. Of course much of the Caithness coast offers sheer exposed cliffs to a ceaselessly pounding sea; in such conditions it is difficult for life to establish a foothold. The pebbly beaches are inimical to life — the pebbles endlessly ground against each other by the waves pulverise all organic material. Sandy shores are inhabited by a number of creatures specially adapted to the habitat, such as lobworms, pod razors, cockles, sand gapers and sea mice. Much of the Caithness coast, however, consists of a rocky sloping shore and it is on such a shore, especially where it is sheltered, that marine life is found in profusion.

The normal rocky shore is divided into zones from the High Tide limit to the Low Tide limit according to the dominant type of seaweed that grows there and each zone has its own animals.

At this stage some mention should be made of the two marine mammals which frequent the Caithness coast — The Common Seal and the Atlantic or Grey Seal. Both may be seen round our shores though the Common Seal, as its name suggests, is the more familiar and indeed it breeds on many rocky ledges. The Grey Seal, as far as is known, no longer breeds on the mainland but still does so in sea caves on Stroma. Though the adult Grey Seal is larger than the Common Seal—about 2.75 m (9 ft) long to the Common Seal's 2 m (6 ft 6 in) — it is easy to confuse the cows and immatures of both species even when seen together. Big grey seal bulls are easily picked out because of their size and the Roman Nose profile of the head. Both seals are called 'Silkies' in Caithness and our folklore, in common with that of the Highlands and Islands generally, credits them with supernatural powers enabling them to appear now as human and now as seals. " 'E Silkie Man" a folk tale told in Caithness dialect and centred on a crofter/fisher family of John o'Groats is typical of our seal mythology.

Table 8.

## THE VERTEBRATE FAUNA OF CAITHNESS

### LAND VERTEBRATES

**MAMMALS**

**Ungulates**
Red Deer
Roe Deer
Sika Deer

**Carnivores**
Fox
Badger
Wild Cat
Otter
Stoat
Weasel

**Bats**
Pipistrelle

**Rabbits and Hares**
Rabbit
Brown Hare
Blue Hare

**Insectivores**
Hedgehog
Mole
Common Shrew
Pigmy Shrew
Water Shrew

**Rodents**
Brown Rat
Mouse
Field Vole

**BIRDS**
(See separate chapter)

**AMPHIBIANS**
Frogs
Toads
Newts

**REPTILES**
Adders
Slow Worms
Lizards

### FRESH WATER VERTEBRATES

**FISH**
Salmon
Brown Trout
Sea Trout
Eel
Stickleback
Brook Lamprey

**MAMMALS**
Otter
Ground Vole
Water Shrew

**AMPHIBIANS**
Frogs
Toads
Newts

### SEASHORE VERTEBRATES

**MAMMALS**
Common Seal
Atlantic Seal

**FISH**
Miller's Thumb
Blenny
Stickleback
Pipefish
Fire-bearded Rockling

# CHAPTER 11

# BIRD LIFE

Caithness has long been well known for its fine bird cliffs, but the interior of the County has, in the past, been somewhat neglected by ornithologists. Yet, despite its apparent barrenness, Caithness supports a rich and varied avian fauna. The County lacks many of the small passerines and warblers that enrich the woodlands of the south, but it can claim over a hundred species as regular breeding birds, and many more as winter visitors and passage migrants.

Caithness lies at the extreme northern limit of the breeding range of some species. Members of the tit family are resident, but are not known in Orkney. Among the summer visitors are Swallows, Swifts and Martins, regular breeding species in Caithness, but only the Swallow nests regularly in Orkney. In Shetland, usually, these birds are but passage migrants, though breeding in the more Continental climate of Scandinavia. Conversely, some birds are at the southern limit of their range and are more properly birds of the Arctic. Such birds as Arctic Skua, Common Scoter and Slavonian Grebe are rare breeding birds in Britain and are found nesting only in the north and west of Scotland.

The birds of any region can be divided roughly into two classes; those that breed in the area and those that do not. The breeding birds may be resident and present all the year round, e.g. Blackbirds, Sparrows, and Grouse, or summer visitors, such as Cuckoos, Terns and Willow Warblers. The non-breeding birds are mainly winter visitors or passage migrants, i.e. birds passing through the County to and from their breeding grounds in the north and their southern winter quarters. Stray individuals may turn up in unexpected places from time to time and these are usually termed "wanderers" or "vagrants". There is a good deal of overlap between these divisions and many birds fit into two or more categories. Thus, of the winter visitors, such as the Turnstone, a few birds may stay on into summer instead of going north in the spring with the main flocks. These birds are usually immature and not yet in breeding condition. The solitary Grasshopper Warbler which "reeled" its song by the Thurso River in 1968 is an example of a bird well outside its normal range. These warblers are not usually found north of Inverness and are rare even that far north.

Even the most sedentary of our resident species make limited movements according to food availability, dispersal of young birds, or seasonal changes. Curlews leave their moorland nesting habitats and flock to the coast in winter and in hard weather many duck, such as Mallard, which are normally found on fresh water, take to the sea. Some birds disperse widely after the breeding season: young Herring Gulls may wander up to 320 km (200 miles) away from the nesting area and visitors to the coast such as the Glaucous Gulls from the Arctic are usually young birds in their first winter.

## Migration

This is the great annual movement of whole populations of birds from one area to another and has been a source of interest and speculation from earliest times.

Broadly speaking, migrating species move northwards in spring to their breeding grounds and southwards again in autumn to milder winter quarters. This seasonal movement has produced many explanatory theories and is a most complicated and controversial subject. Many factors are probably involved, including internal physiological changes in the bird itself and external stimuli such as altering daylight hours and temperatures. Migration takes place both by day and by night, even in those species which are normally diurnal, and birds are thought to orientate themselves by the sun and stars to gain their primary direction, as well as making use of landmarks and the relatively stable meteorogical conditions present at these times of the year. Local weather conditions are also of importance and may adversely affect the course and direction of the flight.

The urge to migrate appears to be an inherited rhythm of behaviour. No really satisfactory conclusion has yet been reached to account for some birds migrating while others of similar species do not.

Given fine weather migration takes place over a broad front with the birds often flying at high altitudes. Small birds may fly at heights of up to 900m (3,000 ft) but larger birds, such as geese, have been recorded at heights of 6100m (20,000ft), far beyond the range of binoculars. These birds have been observed from aircraft and picked up on radar screens. This use of radar is a new technique which has greatly increased our knowledge of migration. Under good conditions, therefore, migration flights may pass largely unnoticed, with the birds flying high and direct to their destinations. This is particularly so in spring; in autumn, the numbers are swelled by the young of the year and the passage is more obvious.

Bad weather conditions, such as fog, rain and cross or head winds, can confuse and disorientate the birds and force them down to lower levels to use coast lines or other geographical features as navigational aids. This may have the effect of concentrating the migrants along certain well-marked "migration routes". Flying in bad conditions is exhausting and the birds will often pitch down on any convenient landfall to rest and feed. If this landfall is an island on a migration route, e.g. Fair Isle or the Pentland Skerries, the influx is particularly noticeable and the ground may be swarming with birds. Since the heaviest traffic of migrants seen in Britain is to Scandinavia and the Arctic, bad weather over the North Sea will blow many birds off course. These wind-drifted (and thus probably lost and exhausted) migrants may include the rarities so exciting to ornithologists. A bad year for the birds is usually a good one for the bird-watchers! Such birds as the exotic Hoopoe, Marsh Sandpiper and Harlequin Duck are rarities which have been seen in Caithness in the last ten years.

Of all the passage migrants the geese are the most spectacular: the big skeins of Pink-footed, White-fronted and Grey Lag Geese can be both seen and heard as they cross the County. The Pink-feet are passage migrants only, while the Grey Lag breed in small numbers, and also over-winter. Of the White-fronts, a small number of birds of the Greenland race winter in the County, but the majority go on to west Scotland and Ireland.

## Winter Visitors

The first trickle of autumn migrants really starts in mid-summer with the group of birds known as waders, most of which move on south, and the true winter visitors do not arrive until much later in the year. Turnstone, Purple Sandpipers and Sanderling are some of the common autumn and winter visitors to the shore. Many duck spend the winter on the lochs or around the coast and parties of Long-tailed Duck, together with Wigeon and Goldeneye, are common in some bays. Whooper Swans winter in the County, sometimes in large numbers and are to be seen and heard on suitable lochs. Sometimes, family parties of these swans will rest and feed on farmland.

Two members of the thrush family arrive in winter: the Fieldfare and Redwing. Some of the latter often linger on into spring and may start to nest here in the near future, as they have done lately in other parts of Scotland. Snow Buntings are also fairly common in winter and flocks of these attractive birds may be seen round the stack yards or along the shore. Greenfinches, Chaffinches and Twites, though resident species, all flock in winter and sometimes are joined by visiting Bramblings and Redpolls. Siskins have also been seen in spring and autumn.

A striking feature in winter is the large invasion of Starlings from Scandinavia. Flocks of these birds feed on farmland during the day and gather at sunset in huge roosts consisting of many thousands of birds. The trees in the Square in Thurso are black with Starlings at evening and their noisy squabbling for the best places can be heard above the sound of traffic.

These are the common winter visitors: birds that roam the countryside in flocks, or congregate on open water. There are others that come singly or in small numbers. The Great Northern Diver is a frequent visitor off-shore and the Great Grey Shrike has been seen in some winters. There have been reports of Snowy Owls and this bird may well become a more common visitor now that it has bred in Shetland.

In some autumns there is a curious invasion of certain species of Scandinavian birds which are normally non-migratory. These "irruptions", as they are called, are thought to be due to a build up of population in the breeding areas as a consequence of several successful nesting seasons, thus leading to a shortage of food and territory. This results in mass migration of the immature birds who have a less strong claim to the home ground than the adult birds. Among the most common species prone to this behaviour is the Waxwing which, though usually occurring in small numbers as a passage migrant, also irrupts, as in 1965 and 1966. More recent, has been the irruption of the Greater Spotted Woodpeckers in 1968, when numbers of this normally sedentary bird were seen from Shetland southwards. Many were hard-pressed to find a suitable tree in some localities. Some of these Northern Woodpeckers manage to survive the winter, but most fail to adjust to altered food and environment and after filtering south gradually die out. Another irruptive species is the Crossbill. These continental birds usually arrive earlier in summer and must not be confused with the native Scottish Crossbill.

## Summer Visitors

Of all the summer visitors the most noticeable are the sea birds. Now, the cliffs which have been practically deserted during the winter become alive with birds again. The auks, such as Puffins, Razorbills and Guillemots appear off the coast early in the year, after a winter at sea, and from then on are to be seen near their breeding quarters on the cliffs. Guillemots and Razorbills lay their solitary egg on open ledges on the cliffs; Puffins frequent the grassy slopes nearer the cliff tops, where they excavate a burrow in which to nest.

Another cliff-nesting summer visitor is a small gull, the Kittiwake, which builds a nest of seaweed and grass, cemented with mud and often perched on the most minute ledges. There is a fine colony of these birds below the lighthouse on Dunnet Head.

The other common bird of the cliffs is the Fulmar Petrel, which has spread so spectacularly this century all round the British Isles. It first nested on the Caithness mainland at Dunnet Head in 1905 and is now found everywhere on the cliffs. It has even ousted the Herring Gull from its traditional sites and has spread inland on to buildings. Fulmars can be observed round the cliffs at most times of the year though formerly, as with the other petrels, the breeding areas were deserted in winter.

The Terns, the last of the visiting sea birds, arrive in early May. Caithness has scattered colonies of both Arctic and Common Terns with one small colony of the slightly larger Sandwich Tern. A favourite nesting site for these birds is the open shore where, unfortunately, they are suffering from increasing human disturbance. They no longer nest very successfully on Dunnet Sands (though attempts are still made) but there is some indication that the large colony of Arctic Terns on Stroma is increasing now that the island is depopulated. Terns will also nest on small islets in suitable lochs, often at some distance from the sea.

Mention should be made here of the largest of British sea birds — the Gannet. The nearest breeding station is at Sule Stack, near Sule Skerry, 64 km (40 miles) west of Orkney. In Caithness the birds are frequently seen fishing off shore where they plunge head first into the water, often from considerable heights depending on the swimming depth of the fish which they are pursuing.

The first of the small summer migrants to arrive is the Wheatear, usually in early April, to be followed at the end of the month by the Willow Warbler. By the middle of May most of the other summer visitors have arrived: Sedge Warblers, Swallows, Swifts, Martins, Corncrakes and Cuckoos, though the last bird is not very common in the north of the County. There are usually a few Whitethroats nesting and the Common Redstart, a colourful bird with a brilliant chestnut tail, just enters the County at Langwell.

### Population Changes

Bird populations are never static; changes are constantly taking place, some of which may be obvious while others are scarcely noticeable. These changes may be attributed to natural causes such as climatic variations, failure of food supplies, disease or to human factors — either directly or indirectly. Direct human interference may be by pollution of water, both fresh and salt, and increasing use of the countryside for leisure, as well as by straightforward persecution through indiscriminate egg collecting and shooting. Indirectly, human interference can affect birds by alteration in land usage — such as different farming methods and the erection of buildings.

The agriculture of Caithness is largely pastoral and farming methods have changed less obviously and drastically in the last 50 years than has been the case in the crop-growing areas, where destruction of hedgerows, widespread use of toxic seed dressings and early harvesting have all led to a diminution in bird life. The rise in the human population of Caithness following on the arrival of the Atomic Energy Authority Establishment at Dounreay has meant a growth of buildings and towns and, more seriously from the birds' point of view, increased affluence and leisure, so that hitherto remote parts of the County are becoming accessible to increasing numbers of hill walkers, climbers, sportsmen and bird-watchers. Increased tourism also plays a part, especially where holiday camping sites are situated near beaches and now many of our shore nesting species are suffering from too much disturbance. Excessive and uncontrolled hill burning destroys the habitat of many moorland species and may have had an effect on the declining numbers of grouse.

Caithness has been included in two major bird population explosions affecting the British Isles this century. The Fulmar has already been mentioned as colonising the County from 1905 onwards. Before the turn of the century the main British breeding station of the Fulmar was on St Kilda, where the islanders annually killed large numbers of the birds for food and feathers. Since the island was evacuated in 1930 the number of Fulmars there has obviously increased, but the general population increase of these birds is thought to be due more to a change in fishing techniques than to a direct spread from St Kilda. Deep sea trawlers gut their catch at sea and the opportunist Fulmar takes full advantage of the resulting glut of fish offal to make an easy living.

The other remarkable colonisation of Britain has been by the Collared Dove. Originally an Asian species this dove has spread north-westwards from the Balkans since 1900, first nesting in England in 1955. It arrived in Caithness in 1964/65 and is now a common bird of farms and towns; it nests in gardens and in at least one case, on a sitting-room window sill! The monotonous "Coo-coo-coo" call and destructive habits in gardens are making these otherwise attractive doves far from popular.

Local changes are more difficult to define, but the new Forestry Commission plantations are already attracting small birds such as Finches, Goldcrests and Coal Tits, as well as Long-eared Owls and Woodcock. Unfortunately, they also support a flourishing Woodpigeon population.

On the debit side, Caithness has suffered the general decline in Raptors, i.e. hawks, falcons and eagles, that has occurred throughout the British Isles. The Peregrine Falcon used to nest on the cliffs, but has not done so successfully for some years and is now a rare bird in the County. The Golden Eagle has attempted to breed in west Caithness but, as elsewhere, has been much persecuted. The Hen Harrier is not uncommonly seen in winter but is a very rare breeding bird. Sparrow Hawks and Merlins are both scarce and the only plentiful hawk is the Kestrel, whose numbers seem to be on the increase. This decline in birds of prey is partly due to direct disturbance and destruction by man through egg collecting, shooting the birds as "vermin," and the use of certain toxic chemicals (used in modern farming) which accumulate in the bodies of the birds and render their eggs infertile. Particularly deadly were the aldrin-based sheep-dips which the birds absorbed into their bodies when feeding on carrion; these are now forbidden by law. All "Birds of Prey" are now protected. But despite this—and the fact that modern research has shown such birds are not responsible for the decline in game birds—they are still severely persecuted.

Another bird whose numbers have declined is the Lapwing. This decrease is explained by two factors: the collecting of eggs and alteration in farming methods. Since the Lapwing is a bird of the farmlands and rarely nests on the open moor, outwintered cattle who may trample on the eggs, and increased mechanisation, have both had a detrimental effect. It should be emphasised here that under the Protection of Birds Act of 1947 it is an offence to take the eggs of any wild bird, except under special licence. This Act has become particularly important following the severe winter of 1964 which destroyed so much wild life.

Today, conservation is a most important part of ornithology, as it covers the status of all wild birds throughout the country. In an attempt to preserve our natural heritage, it seeks to control those species that are adjudged to be pests and to protect those that are in danger of extermination.

## SOME OF THE BREEDING BIRDS OF CAITHNESS

**LOCAL: This means the bird is found where the habitat is suitable.**

| NAME | DIALECT NAME | STATUS |
|---|---|---|
| Red-throated Diver | Ramgoose | Local |
| Little Grebe | | Very Local |
| Slavonian Grebe | | Rare |
| Fulmar | Mallimack | Very common |
| Cormorant | Scarf | A few scattered cliff colonies |
| Shag | Scarf | Common |
| Grey Heron | | Rare — a cliff nesting species in Caithness |
| Grey Lag Goose | | Rare |
| Mute Swan | | Fairly common and increasing |
| Shelduck | | Common but local |
| Mallard | Wild Duck | Common |
| Teal | | Common |
| Wigeon | | Scarce as breeding bird |
| Shoveler | | Scarce |
| Tufted Duck | | Scarce |
| Eider Duck | | Local |
| Common Scoter | Black Duck | Rare |
| Red-breasted Merganser | | Common |
| Sparrow Hawk | | Rare |
| Hen Harrier | Blue Hawk | Rare |
| Peregrine | | Formerly common — now very rare |
| Merlin | | Decreasing |
| Kestrel | | Common |
| Red Grouse | | Common |
| Black Grouse | Black Cock | Very local |
| Partridge | | Widespread but not common |
| Pheasant | | Present on estates |
| Water Rail | | Local |
| Corncrake | | Formerly common, but now decreasing |
| Moorhen | | Common |
| Coot | | Common |
| Oystercatcher | Sea Pie | Common |
| Ringed Plover | Sand Lairag | Common |
| Golden Plover | Rainy Birds | Common |
| Lapwing | Shochad | Common |
| Dunlin | Plover's Page | Common |
| Redshank | Peter Redlegs | Very Common |
| Greenshank, | Stiltie | Very local |
| Common Sandpiper | Willie Beebs, Willie-Weet-Feet | Widespread |
| Curlew | Faap | Very Common |
| Snipe | | Common |
| Arctic Skua | Scootie Allen | Very rare. A few scattered colonies |
| Black-headed Gull | | Abundant |
| Lesser Black-backed Gull | | Local |
| Herring Gull | Skorrie | Abundant |
| Greater Black-backed Gull | | Common |
| Common Gull | Hill Mae | Common |

| | | |
|---|---|---|
| Kittiwake | Kittag<br>Kittifake | Many large cliff<br>colonies |
| Sandwich Tern | | Summer visitors<br>fluctuating numbers |
| Common Tern | Picktarnie | Summer visitor<br>widespread |
| Arctic Tern | | Summer visitor<br>widespread |
| Razorbill | Borray | Cliff nester — common |
| Guillemot | Okie, Awpie,<br>Paamar Scarf | Several large cliff<br>colonies |
| Black Guillemot | Tystie | Common |
| Puffin | Tammie,<br>Sea Cockie, Cootrie | Scattered cliff<br>colonies |
| Woodpigeon | Woody | Common |
| Rock Dove | Rocky | Common along coast |
| Collared Dove | | Becoming common |
| Cuckoo | | Widespread, but not<br>common |
| Long-eared Owl | | Local |
| Short-eared Owl | | Scarce |
| Tawny Owl | | Local |
| Swift | | Very local |
| Sky Lark | Lairag | Abundant |
| Sand Martin | | Very local |
| Swallow | Witchag | Fairly common |
| House Martin | | Fairly common |
| Meadow Pipit | Titlark, Teetlan | Abundant |
| Rock Pipit | | Common |
| Grey Wagtail | | Rare |
| Pied White/Wagtail | Willie Wagtail | Common |
| Dipper | | Local |
| Wren | | Common |
| Dunnock | | Common |
| Sedge Warbler | | Summer visitor — local |
| Whitethroat | | Summer visitor — scarce |
| Willow Warbler | | Summer visitor — common |
| Goldcrest | | Local, but widespread |
| Whinchat | | Very local |
| Stonechat | Jeckiebeet | Fairly common |
| Wheatear | Stonechecker | Common |
| Common Redstart | | Rare |
| Robin | Redbreast | Common |
| Ring Ouzel | | Very local |
| Blackbird | Black Jock | Common |
| Song Thrush | Mavis, Mavie | Common |
| Coal Tit | | Rare |
| Blue Tit | | Fairly common |
| Great Tit | | Very scarce |
| Tree Creeper | | Local, but widespread |
| Corn Bunting | Thistlecock Lairag,<br>Boltie Lairag | Very local |
| Yellow Bunting | Yellow Yite,<br>Yellow Yarling | Common |
| Reed Bunting | | Common |
| Chaffinch | Shilfie | Common |
| Greenfinch | Green Lintie | Common |
| Twite | Heather Lintie | Common |
| Linnet | Rose Lintie | Scarce |

| House Sparrow | Spreug | Abundant |
| Starling | Stirler | Abundant |

| Jackdaw | | | Common |
| Rook | | | Common |
| Hooded Crow | } "Crows" { | Common |
| Raven | | | Fairly common |

In their own interest, some birds have not been included in this list.

## SOME WINTER VISITORS

Great Northern Diver
Grey Lag Goose
White-fronted Goose
Whooper Swan
Wigeon
Pochard
Tufted Duck
Long-tailed Duck
Waxwing
Redwing
Brambling

Goldeneye
Turnstone
Purple Sandpiper
Dunlin
Sanderling
Iceland Gull
Glaucous Gull
Great Grey Shrike
Fieldfare — "Feltie"
Snowbunting — "Shaffle"
Redpoll

H

# PART II

# *Historical*

# CHAPTER 12

# THE EARLY INHABITANTS

Archaeologists divide the long period of time before written records were kept into three stages which, from the materials principally used for cutting tools, are generally known as the Stone, Bronze and Iron Ages. To some extent these terms are misleading, Though bronze implements were not introduced into, for example, Caithness until many centuries after men using stone tools had settled here, the use of stone implements continued into the Iron Age and in some parts of the Hebrides has come down to times within living memory. The terms are also misleading for another reason: Caithness was settled by man much later than more southerly parts of Western Europe, so that by the time a way of life had been introduced into the area its original character was changing and clear distinctions between, for example, the later Stone Age settlers and the Early Bronze Age arrivals, are not easily made.

The Stone Age covers a very long period. Indeed, it seems to comprise about 95% of human history and it too has been subdivided into two main parts, the Palaeolithic, or Old Stone Age, and the Neolithic, or New Stone Age, with a third, transitional period, called the Mesolithic, or Middle Stone Age, tucked in between them as an afterthought.

The Old Stone Age is contemporaneous with the geological period known as the Pleistocene and with the last Ice Ages in northern latitudes. During this period men lived in caves with now-extinct animals such as the mammoth and the woolly rhinoceros, but Scotland was covered in ice for most of the time and there is no evidence at all of their presence in Caithness, though a site at Inchnadamph in Sutherland has yielded evidence of the presence of a hunting party.

It was only when the ice melted that small bands of colonists began to move north to settle the area. These were nomadic squatters, living in coastal caves and in rough shelters among the brushwood around lochs and along river banks. Their way of life was at the Mesolithic stage of culture: they knew nothing of farming and had no metal implements, but lived by collecting, hunting and fishing. The remains of their meals of fish, birds and small animals (caught using harpoon and spears made by embedding small pieces of flint—"microliths"— in bone or wooden shafts), and of shell-fish, are found in middens in many parts of Scotland. A Mesolithic settlement was identified at Keiss during work last century by Laing and Huxley. Its probable date is rather late, indicating that this nomadic strand-looping way of life persisted among some inhabitants of Caithness long after a more permanent settlement pattern had been established by later farming communities. The most extensively studied Mesolithic sites in Scotland are at Oban, and it is common to speak of all similar sites in the north as belonging to the Obanian way of life. Mesolithic settlements in the north have not been dated, but one in Wigtownshire has been shown by radio-carbon methods to date from well before 4000 B.C., so perhaps that is a reasonable date for the first arrival of settlers in this area. It is difficult to speculate on the numbers of immigrants who could support themselves at the Mesolithic standard of living in Caithness; a suggestion that the population of the whole of Scotland did not exceed a few hundreds would seem to be reasonable.

The next prehistoric period is distinguished from all that had gone before, by one of the greatest economic and technological revolutions in human history, a revolution that transformed the way of life from an opportunist, food-gathering level to a more settled one in which farming and animal husbandry gave man some measure of control of his food supply. This Neolithic way of life began in the Near East about 10,000 years ago with the cultivation of barley and wheat and the breeding of cattle, sheep and pigs. Slowly the revolution spread across Europe and arrived in Britain, probably via Spain and Western France in the last centuries before 3000 B.C. By this time, the land bridge which, in Palaeolithic and early Mesolithic times, had joined Britain to Europe had been severed with the formation of the English Channel and these new settlers arrived by sea in simple dug-out boats. By this means they were able to penetrate northwards to the Shetlands. They have left impressive evidence of their presence in the Chambered Tombs, of which there are remains of 67 in Caithness.

These tombs belong to a large class conventionally termed "megalithic" (Greek: great stone) which has a wide distribution throughout Western Europe, and seems to have been derived from a rock-cut tomb tradition in the Aegean area.

Examination of the less-ruinous examples shows that they were constructed of dry masonry which often incorporates large uprights (known as orthostats) and cover-slabs (lintels). They were built to contain successive burials and therefore have an entrance passage which is generally very low and narrow for easy closure, giving access to the actual chamber itself. The tomb was then artificially put underground by covering it with a mound of earth or a cairn of stones. The covering is never simply a heap of earth or stone: it always has a regular shape and its boundaries were originally defined by a kerb or low wall. The shapes of the cairns and the designs of the chambers are many and there is no clear correlation between the two. Several types of cairns are to be seen in the Caithness examples: at Yarrows (ND 304432), Shebster (ND 013653 and ND 014654) and Camster (ND 260442) are long cairns with "horns" (Fig. 11), all of them over 60m (200 ft) in length and containing in some cases an estimated 3050 metric tonnes (3000 tons) of material, whilst at Camster (ND 260440), (Fig. 11), (Ham ND 235738) and Shebster (ND 013646) are simple circular cairns. A kind of hybrid plan, the short horned cairn, effectively a circular cairn with horns is to be seen at Ormiegill (ND 332429) and Garrywhin (ND 313411). Where chamber details are to be seen, many of the Caithness tombs seem to have contained "tripartite Camster chambers" in which a roughly oval chamber is divided into three sections by two pairs of orthostats. The first section to be reached from the entrance passage generally had the same low lintelled roofline as the passage, and the other two sections were roofed by corbelling — a technique by which each course of masonry is allowed to project a little over the one below it — until the roof opening was sufficiently small to be closed by large lintel slabs. This type of chamber is designated after that in Camster round cairn (Fig. 11) which probably ranks as the finest chambered tomb on the British mainland.

The burial rites seem to have varied and evidence of both inhumation and

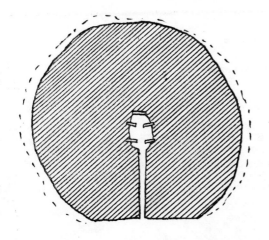

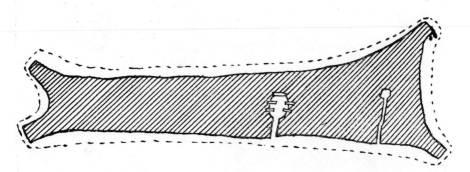

**Figure 11.   Plan of the Grey Cairns of Camster (round and long horned cairns)**

(NOTE:   Re-excavation of these cairns, conducted during the past decade by R. Ritchie and by J.X.W.P. Corcoran, has shown that the above plans, based on Joseph Anderson's original site plans, are incorrect in certain details. Revised plans have not yet been published.)

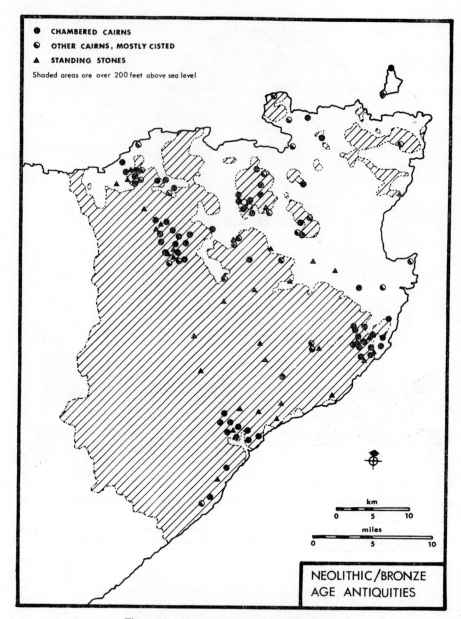

CHAMBERED CAIRNS

OTHER CAIRNS, MOSTLY CISTED

STANDING STONES

Shaded areas are over 200 feet above sea level

km
0    5    10

miles
0    5    10

NEOLITHIC/BRONZE
AGE ANTIQUITIES

**Figure 12.  Neolithic/Bronze Age antiquities**

cremation have been found. Though the tombs cannot be taken as an indication of religious beliefs as we would know them, the effort required to construct them shows evidence of some recognition of the significance of death — perhaps of a contrast between the transience of life and the apparent permanence of death — and it has been suggested that the returning of the dead to an underground chamber, often, in inhumations, lying in a foetal position, might be evidence of worship of an earth mother goddess. As farmers at a primitive stage of development, these peoples would be only too conscious of their dependence on the earth.

Most of the evidence of the mode of living of the Neolithic tomb builders has disappeared, but two groups of stone dwellings of the period have survived in Orkney. In Caithness and more southerly parts of Britain, where wood was more readily available than in the northern Isles, the dwellings would probably have been of timber construction, but no complete plan of such a house has yet been found. The Orkney dwellings, at Skara Brae and Rinyo, were of roughly rectangular plan with rounded corners, roofed by corbelling and drift-wood to leave a large central smoke-hole. Each hut had a stone-kerbed fireplace, beds which could be filled with heather and animal skins, and shelves and storage places. Bones found on the Orkney sites show that cattle and sheep (of the type still found on Soay, St Kilda) were kept. Barley was grown; there is no clear evidence of it from excavations of the Orkney houses, but imprints of barley grains have been found on pottery from chambered tombs. Pottery which is often found in tombs, was at first crude, resembling leather vessels with rounded bases but later some decoration was used. Clothing was probably mainly of animal skins, though the art of weaving was introduced into Britain in Neolithic times. From the distribution of chambered tombs (Fig. 12) it is clear that in Caithness the Neolithic farmers lived on well-drained ground on the shoulders of hills overlooking the straths which at the time would be heavily wooded with birch, alder and pine making settlement there impossible in the absence of axes suitable for tree-felling.

The dating of the chambered tombs is not clear, principally because they continued in use for several hundreds of years. Recent radio-carbon dates for similar tombs in Ireland suggest various dates between 3200 and 2500 B.C., and one must see construction of at least some of the Caithness tombs as commencing before 2500 B.C. with evidence from pottery finds of continuing use for over a thousand years.

While the Neolithic culture was still flourishing, new waves of immigrants, some of whom knew the use of bronze, began to reach the area. Though they brought about no significant change in the way of life, burial finds permit the new arrivals to be distinguished from the Neolithic peoples; the skulls of the latter were long-headed whereas those of the newcomers were round-headed. (In quantitative terms, a long-headed skull has a maximum breadth equal to 0.7 of its length from forehead to crown, a round-headed skull has breadth equal to about 0.8 of its length).

The Early Bronze Age peoples appear to have been more warlike than their Neolithic predecessors, but there is no evidence that their settlement in the area was anything but peaceful. In their remains, imported materials are very frequent and implements of flint (rather than stone) became much more common. With no native flint in the area, many of these implements were imported, ready made, principally from 'factories' in Ireland. Though the use of bronze was known to these people, items made from it are found in only about 5% of burials which have been dated to Early Bronze Age times on the evidence of characteristic pottery forms ("beakers", leading to the name "Beaker Folk" for the first arrivals).

Early Bronze Age burials are always found in round cairns in southern Britain, and some writers have suggested that the round chambered cairns of Caithness were built by Neolithic/Bronze Age peoples towards the end of the tomb-building period. Tomb finds from these cairns usually consist of bits of pottery, animal bones, small domestic implements of bone or stone, and small leaf or lozenge-shaped flint arrowheads, but in one Caithness example beads of a jet necklace have been reported. (The jet might have been imported from Brora).

The dominant remains of the early Bronze Age, however, are the standing stone settings, typified for many people by Stonehenge but represented in Caithness by numerous monuments of varied layout. It has long been recognised that standing stones represent some form of ceremonial site, and it has often been suggested that sun-worship was the principal form of ceremony. Even the roughest of datings, however, must eliminate any possibility of a connection with Druidical rites contemporaneous with the Roman period in southern Britain. The date discrepancy is at least fifteen hundred years, though, of course, this does not preclude the possibility of later use of pre-existing and, by then ruinous, Bronze Age ceremonial sites by the Iron Age Druids.

Recent work by Professor Alexander Thom has gone some way to defining the original purpose of the settings. In the course of detailed surveys of several hundreds of settings, Thom has been able to show quite remarkable similarities in construction and layout. Firstly, it is apparent that the stone settings throughout Britain have been laid out using a "yard-stick" which is about 83 cm (2.72 ft) in length; this unit, previously noted from careful surveys of chambered tombs on the continent of Europe, is now generally known as the "megalithic yard". Further, he has shown that the so-called "circular" settings are not infrequently either flattened or pointed and are laid out in a manner indicating that the erectors knew the property of a right-angled triangle now known as Pythagoras' Theorem. Finally, he has shown that taking compass sitings using either lines drawn from stone to stone across settings, or lines drawn from an outlier to stones in an array, or lines drawn from an isolated stone to geographical features on the eastern horizon, defines a group of sunrise directions which divide the year into sixteen "months" each 22, 23, or 24 days in length. This suggests the idea of a year-long calendar of ceremonials, though actual sun-worship may not have been the principal motive.

These conclusions about the form and purpose of the stone settings are disturbing, for it had not previously been suggested that primitive farming communities of about 1850 B.C. were sufficiently advanced for complicated astronomical observations to be a feature of their lives. Thom has pointed out, however, that the "know-how" involved could be simply transmitted; a "megalithic yard-stick" is easily carried around and the method of laying out and using the setting need be known to few. He suggests that a new local setting of stones could be synchronised with already established settings farther south by using bonfires; the May Day Beltane fires of medieval Britain and the Bonfire Night fires of more recent times, both of which fall close to a stonesetting calendar date lying midway between an equinox and a solstice, might represent folk memories of synchronisation dates.

There is some evidence from elsewhere in Britain (e.g. The Ring of Brodgar in Orkney) that the stone settings represent late developments of already existing ceremonial sites known generally as "henges" — enclosures of the order of 60 m (200 ft) in diameter surrounded by a ditch which in turn is surrounded by a bank. (The construction of a ditch inside a bank precludes the possibility that the henges had any defensive purpose). There is no Continental parallel for the stone settings found in Britain, but it must be noted that the Bronze Age settlers arrived here to find a still flourishing megalithic building tradition; calendar sites elsewhere in Europe may have been set with wooden posts.

The most impressive stone setting in Caithness is the truncated oval at Achavanich (ND 188417), but the most interesting are the stone rows which are almost unique to the County. The best array, of 200 earthfast boulders arranged in 22 nearly parallel rows, is at Mid Clyth (ND 204384). Others are at Upper Dounreay (ND 012659), Garrywhin (ND 313413) and Dirlot (ND 124488). Outside Caithness, there are other examples of stone rows in the far south-west on Dartmoor, and a comparison with stone alignments at Carnac in Brittany might be made. There are pairs of standing stones at the Loch of Yarrows (ND 316432) and at Latheron (ND 200337), and single monoliths at Reay (ND 973651), Ben Dorrery (ND 066550), Watten (ND 245544) and the Hill of Rangag (ND 176448). There is a ruinous "circle" at Guidebest (ND 181351) and another at Broubster (ND 048608).

About 1500 B.C. there occurred a noticeable change in pottery styles. Beakers which have been found in association with earlier burials were replaced by very ornate, often impractical, containers known as "food-vessels" (from a supposed association with the need to supply the dead with sustenance for the journey to an after life). There was also a change in burial customs and the dead were no longer interred in chambered tombs which must have become disused from about this time. Burials became individual ones in cists — small chambers from about 60 cm x 40 cm (24 in. x 16 in.) to about 150 cm x 110 cm (60 in. x 45 in.) in area made by setting four upright slabs in a hole about 40 cm (16 in.) deep, with a capstone for a cover. There are remains of a cist burial near the most northerly stone in the Achavanich setting mentioned above and two cists were found beneath a 12 m (40 ft.) diameter cairn on Warth Hill (ND 371698).

From this period, 1500-1000 B.C. are thought to date the mysterious cup-and-ring marked stones, found in many parts of Britain and suggested by some to be star maps and by others to be maps showing trade routes. Some Caithness examples are to be seen in a private museum at Auckengill (ND 368637); each takes the form of a boulder with cups, 3 cm-10 cm (1.3 in.-4 in.) in diameter, pecked into one face. The "rings" would be narrow grooves surrounding the cups but there are no signs of these on the Caithness boulders.

Another change in burial custom took place about 1000 B.C. when cremation rites finally ousted inhumation, and ashes and cremated bones were, from this time on, buried in large pots up to 50 cm (20 in.) in height, known as cinerary urns. An urn burial was found as a secondary interment in the chambered cairn at Yarrows (ND 305434).

The finds of food vessels and of cinerary urns in Caithness have been relatively few, though it is not clear whether this is indicative that the area remained "backward" in not accepting new customs, or that the population was small. There are few remains of the dwellings of the Bronze Age period to provide evidence, and it is not until late Bronze Age times, round about 500 B.C., that any significant remains of settlement are to be found anywhere in Scotland. These were still on the well-drained shoulders of hills, typically between the 200 and 500 foot contours in most of the rest of northern Britain, but perhaps a little lower in this extreme northerly area, with some settlement on sandy coastal areas. Throughout this long period, however, the way of life must have continued much as it was when farming and stockraising were first introduced in Neolithic times. To some extent it must have been a largely nomadic existence with agriculture as a minor part of the economy and little really permanent settlement, and under these circumstances the population probably remained small.

About 600 B.C. there is some evidence of a change in climate, and wetter and cooler conditions seem to have become more prevalent. The resulting vegetation change on the higher ground with a rapid build-up of peat would have tended to drive the hill farmers down to lower altitudes which until this time had been covered in woodland of birch, alder and pine. The movement to lower lying ground would have been impossible, had it not been for the introduction of iron tools by the arrival of the Celtic Iron Age immigants from north-western Europe at just about this time. Their arrival and the settlement of the fertile straths marks the prelude to the age of the brochs which is the subject of the next chapter.

## APPENDIX: IMPORTANT SITES IN CAITHNESS: NEOLITHIC/BRONZE AGE
### (See Fig. 12)

NOTE:   Mention of a site does not imply right of access. Five of the sites in the list are in
the ownership of the Ministry of Public Buildings and Works and are open to
inspection at all times. These are listed as numbers 4, 5, 9, 14 and 16. Permission to
visit other sites should be sought in advance.

1. **Achavanich** Standing Stones (ND 188417)
      Set in the form of a truncated oval, open to the south-east, the Achavanich setting
measures 68.6 m x 30.5 m (225 ft x 100 ft). It may originally have had about sixty stones set
at about 2.5 m (8 ft) apart, but about twenty are now missing though there is no evidence
that the open end of the setting was ever closed. Each thick slab of flagstone stands
about 1.5 m (5 ft) high. There is a cist near the most northerly stone of the setting.

2. **Ben Dorrery** Standing Stone (ND 066550)
      One of several isolated stones in the area, this one stands at about the 180 m (600 ft),
contour on the east side of Ben Dorrery.

3. **Broubster** Standing Stones (ND 048608)
      On a moorland ridge between the township of Broubster (now deserted) and Loch
Calder stands this setting of which only nine of the original thirty two stones remain.
Standing 2.7 m (9 ft) apart, the stones are set in an open-ended truncated oval (c.f. Achavanich) measuring 42.7 m x 27.5 m (140 ft x 90 ft). The stone at the north-eastern end of
the setting is the largest. There is a 2.1 m (7 ft) high outlier to the south-west.

4. **Camster Long** Chambered Cairn (ND 260442)
      This long horned cairn, one of the largest in Britain, covers an area 61 m x 20 m (200
ft x 65 ft). The main chamber is reached by a passage leading in from the long east side
and is of tripartite Camster type. However, the roof is missing. There is a minor chamber
nearer to the eastern horn.

5. **Camster Round** Chambered Cairn (ND 260440)
      This is a round cairn, 15.4m (55 ft) in diameter and 3.6 m (12 ft) in height. The passage
just over 6 m (20 ft) long leads in from the south-east and has side walls interrupted by
four opposed pairs of slabs in the manner of door jambs. The roughly oval chamber is
divided into three parts by orthostats. One part nearest the passage is roofed by lintels,
but the other two have a corbelled roof (in which a roof-light has now been incorporated).

6. **Dirlot** Stone Rows (ND 124488)
      Fragmentary remains of about 20 rows of small stones now overgrown by moorland
still remain. The site is difficult to find.

7. **Dorrery** Chambered Cairn (ND 075554)
      Remains of a chambered cairn is situated 400 m (440 yards) north-by-east of Dorrery
Lodge. Now only a turf-covered stony mound 12.7 m (42 ft) in diameter and 1.5 m (5 ft)
in height remains. Projecting slabs outline the passage and tri-partite Camster-type
chamber.

8. **Earl's Cairn** Chambered Cairn (ND 263697)
      Situated 3.6 km (2¼ miles) south-west of Mey is a round cairn with a tri-partite Cam-
ster-type chamber.

9. **Garrywhin** Chambered Cairn (ND 313411)
      This is a ruinous short-horned cairn, but details of the structure can be distinguished
The chamber, entered from the south is in two parts, an outer small one and an inner,
almost circular, compartment.

10. **Garrywhin** Stone Rows (ND 313413)
      This consists of an array of six rows each of about eight stones, radiating south-west
down a slope. The longest row is about 60 m (200 ft) long. The array lies about 180 m
(200 yards) to the north-north-east of the chambered cairn.

11. **Guidebest** Standing Stones (ND 181351)
      Close by the left bank of the Burn of Latheronwheel are the remains of a more or
less circular setting of which seven stones now remain. The overall diameter is about
58 m (190 ft) and the tallest stone is just under 1.5 m (5 ft) high.

12. **Hill of Rangag** Standing Stone (ND 176448)
      Close to the Causewaymire is a standing stone 2.75 m (9 ft) in height.

13. **Loch of Yarrows** Standing Stones (ND 316432)

Two pillars 5.6 m (18.5 ft) apart stand prominently on a ridge overlooking the Loch of Yarrows. They are clearly visible from the A9 road.

14. **Mid Clyth** Stone Rows (ND 294384)

This is the most important and most impressive monument of its type and consists of an array of 22 rows each with an average of eight stones. It is signposted "Hill of Many Stones" from the A9 road.

15. **Ormiegill** Chambered Cairn (ND 332429)

This ruinous short horned cairn covers an area of about 23 m x 21 m (75 ft x 70 ft). The chamber of the tri-partite Camster type is entered by a passage from the south.

16. **Shebster** Chambered Cairns (ND 013653; ND 014654)

Two long horned cairns may be seen on the summit of Cnoc Freiceadain or Ward Hill. Both are turf covered.

17. **Upper Dounreay** Stone Rows (ND 012659)

This consists of an array of about 100 stones in 13 rows.

18. **Warth Hill** Cairn with Cists (ND 371698)

This is a cairn of about 12 m (40 ft) diameter which originally enclosed two cists both of which on excavation contained crouched skeletons.

19. **Watten** Standing Stone (ND 244544)

To the north of the main road on the Wick side of Watten bridge is a single upright pillar.

20. **Yarrows** Chambered Cairn (ND 304432)

This long horned cairn is 73 m (240 ft) in length with a width of 28 m (92 ft) across the eastern horns and 16 m (53 ft) across the western horns. The tri-partite Camster-type chamber is entered by a passage from the east where the horns and facade were found on excavation to be defined by double lines of boulders; the rest of the cairn was outlined by single stones. A second chambered cairn nearby (ND 305434) has been heavily plundered.

# CHAPTER 13

# THE AGE OF THE BROCHS

Brochs, popularly — but incorrectly — known as Pictish Towers or Pict's Houses, belong to a family of defensive structures of the Iron Age period in northern Scotland. Though Iron Age forts of varied designs are widely scattered throughout north-western Europe, brochs are principally to be found only in Skye, Ross and Cromarty, Sutherland, Caithness, Orkney and Shetland, with a dozen or so south of the Great Glen. Of the five or six hundred broch sites recorded in the literature, there are about 110 in Caithness with identifiable remains and records refer to a further 35 reputed sites on which the remains are too slight for positive identification.

The Iron Age colonists whose descendants built the brochs seem to have begun to arrive in the area in the 6th century B.C. Prior to their arrival, as we have seen in the last chapter, the land had been settled by stock-raising farming communities, descendants of the Neolithic/Bronze Age peoples who had been moving into the area for over 2000 years and of whose early settlement there was widespread evidence in the long-disused chambered tombs and standing stones which dot the upland areas. Until the use of iron implements became known in the area, settlement was principally confined to the upland areas where remains of late Bronze Age farmsteads — the foundations of circular huts and piles of stones cleared from arable plots — are often to be found on the shoulders of hills.

The climatic change which began in the 7th century B.C. and which, by 600 B.C., had set complex folk migrations into motion all over north-western Europe, forced the abandonment of the hill farms and some settlements were moved to well-drained ground at lower altitudes. The extensive settlement of hut circles on the sandy outwash at Invernaver (NC 699613) in Sutherland may date from this period, though there is little evidence in Caithness of similar movements.

The migrations of Iron Age peoples into Britain from the Rhineland began in the 6th century B.C. and by 500 B.C. some of these peoples had reached as far north as Shetland. At first the Iron Age colonists lived peacefully alongside the aboriginal inhabitants of the area, the latter benefiting from the introduction of iron axes and hoes which permitted clearance of the scrubland and woodland vegetation of the straths and the coastal plains.

The homesteads of these early Iron Age settlers are difficult to find, and it has been suggested that many of them lay on sites where, for defensive purposes, they were later replaced by brochs. There exist in Caithness, however, homesteads, known locally as "wags", which are basically round stone-walled houses with attached above-ground oblong chambers, and which have been tentatively ascribed to the early (pre-broch) Iron Age. Two examples are to be seen at Forse (ND 204352) and Langwell (ND 102218).

For the next few hundred years, more colonists moved into the area each year and more land was cleared for farming, and, as the number of settlers swelled, the demand for the better land became intense. At this time the number of immigrants into Britain was reaching a peak as many tribes in north-western Europe were forced to seek new land either because their homelands were becoming overpopulated or because the increasing power of Rome was displacing frontier tribes.

So it became necessary to defend the land from the predations of newcomers and the first of the various defensive structures we normally associate with the Iron Age were laid out. In Caithness, the best examples of early Iron Age defensive works are the hill-forts, such as "Bualie Oscar" or Ben Freiceadain (ND 059558), Garrywhin (ND 314414) and "Cnoc na Ratha" or Shurrery (ND 053577), and the promontory forts, such as Holborn Head (ND 108715) and St John's Point (ND 310752). In all of these, the main structural work takes the form of massive embankments, taking advantage of any natural features offered by the site, such as the chasms on Holborn Head or the outcrops round the summit of Ben Freiceadain. On less obviously defensive sites, the defensive works would probably take the form of ditches and embankments surrounding the settlements, and evidence from excavations in Orkney and Shetland suggests that the outer defensive works which surround the remains of many brochs — there are good examples in Caithness at Bruan (ND 310394), Ousdale (ND 072188), Rangag (ND 180417), Skirza (ND 394684), Thing's Va (ND 081683), Westerdale (ND 133510) and Loch of Yarrows (ND 308435) — may represent early attempts to defend the sites.

It would seem, however, that the broch site ditches, with little advantage in most cases from natural features, proved inadequate and some more solid defensive structure became necessary. The structure evolved was the broch.

For many years, these structures have excited the attention of archaeologists, both professional and amateur, but no clear picture of how and why they were developed has emerged until the last ten years or so. The best preserved of all brochs is that at Mousa (HU 457236) in Shetland, and from it, and a comparison with more ruinous examples elsewhere, it is possible to give a general description of a broch tower as it might have been.

A broch was a tower, up to about 12 m (40 ft) or so in height (Fig. 13). The wall was very thick at the base — a typical example might be 4.5 m (15 ft) thick — surrounding a central open courtyard about 9 m (30 ft) in diameter. The only passage through the wall from the outside to the courtyard was at ground level and generally took the form of a tunnel of the order of 1 m (3.25 ft) in width and perhaps a little over a metre in height. Upright slabs projecting from the passage walls would act as door-checks, jambs against which a door could be placed to seal the passage and prevent entry; most brochs have a single set of door checks but others, such as Ousdale and Thing's Va, have two sets.

The outer surface of the broch wall was smooth and tapered inwards a little — this is often called "showing a batter" — but probably became vertical again near the top. The inner wall had a less obvious batter but had several openings through it from passages running within the wall. The wall itself was more or less solid for the first 3 m (10 ft) up from ground level though small intramural chambers with corbelled roofs are often found at ground level; when these open from the inner courtyard they are usually regarded as storage chambers, and when they open from the entrance passage they are often, but

(A. Luciani)

PLATE 14. *Prehistoric stone setting, Achavanich.*

(R. Stewart)

PLATE 15. *A broch, Ousdale.*

PLATE 16.　*Prehistoric chambered cairns (round and long), Camster.*

PLATE 17.　*Prehistoric stone rows at "Hill o' Many Stanes", Clyth.*

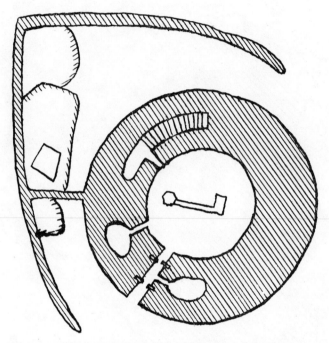

Figure 13.   Plan of Ousdale Broch, with L-shaped defensive structure

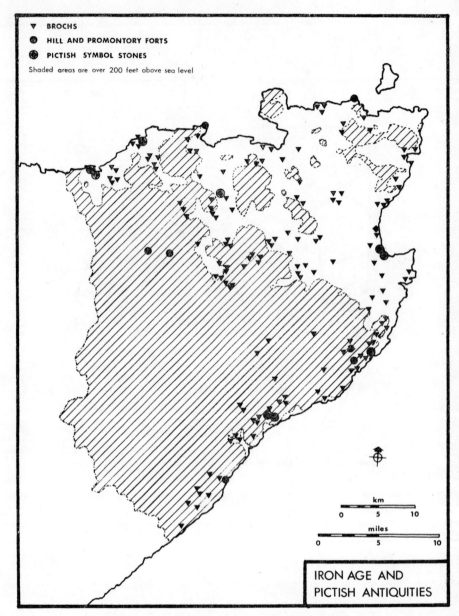

**Figure 14.    Sites of Iron Age and Pictish Antiquites**

probably incorrectly, called "guard chambers". (There are good examples of both types at Ousdale). Higher up, the wall is hollow, the inner and outer skins being linked together at intervals of about 2 m (6.45 ft) in height by flat lintels. Making the wall hollow served three purposes:

(a) It lightened the weight on the foundations, reducing the risk of collapse of a structure which, after all, was built by drystone techniques without mortar;

(b) It permitted a tower of as much as 12 m (40 ft) or more in height to be erected without scaffolding, for the builders could stand in the hollow to build the inner and outer skins, placing the flat lintels across to link the two walls as the tower went up in height; and, finally,

(c) It permitted a staircase to be spiralled up inside the wall to give access to the top of the completed tower and, via the passageways within the walls, to the openings overlooking the courtyard floor. These staircases in brochs show great similarities in that they always spiral clockwise and invariably start about a quarter to a half way round the courtyard to the left as one enters from the entrance passage.

The other important features of the broch structures are the scarcements or ledges of projecting stones which run around the wall overlooking the court-yard. Only one Caithness broch, Ousdale, still remains intact to sufficient height to show a scarcement.

Surrounding the broch tower, generally within the outer defences, are the foundations of small circular huts. These are particularly well developed at Nybster (ND 370632) and Yarrows (ND 308435). (Visitors to Nybster broch should note that the site shows considerable ornamentation of relatively modern origin). Early excavations of brochs were unable to distinguish the the relative ages of the broch tower and the extramural settlement, and it was frequently suggested that the tower was no more than a refuge for the villagers when danger threatened. Iron implements and finds in brochs of bits of glass of a character usually associated with the Romano-Celtic period in southern Britain, suggested that the nature of the danger might have been associated with the slave-trading activities of the Romans and their subjected peoples.

More recent work in Orkney and Shetland has shown, however, that the extra-mural settlements are generally later in date than the broch tower itself. Further, careful examination of the courtyards of brochs shows the presence of fireplaces, fresh-water wells and drainage systems, and of post holes in which wooden pillars would support wooden floors resting on the scarcements project-ing from the face of the inner wall. These suggest that brochs were designed for more permanent occupation and in recent years, following the work of John Hamilton at Clickhimin in Shetland, it has become necessary to look upon a broch as a kind of "block of multi-storey flats" of the Iron Age, providing accom-modation on the floors in its courtyard for a family group of perhaps 30-35 people. (Access to the floors could be obtained either by means of ladders or via the intra-mural stairway and the larger openings through the inner wall; the smaller of the openings on the inner wall play no part in this; they simply permit stress relief and accommodate any slumping which might occur in the struc-ture after completion).

The origin of the structures is less clear but a derivation from the forts and duns of Ireland and western Scotland has been tentatively suggested. Generally, these structures enclose a much larger courtyard area than do the brochs but, in these too, recent excavations suggest that wooden floors were often built around the inside of the wall. Hamilton's work suggests that the broch was derived from these by a process of increasing the height, possibly as a defensive response to the use of fire spears by attackers, who aimed to set the wooden structures alight and so to force the defenders out into the open. A necessary corollary of increasing the height of a drystone structure is that the overall diameter must be reduced if the risk of collapse is to be avoided. The effect of reducing the diameter is to make the broch eminently suitable for erection within the early Iron Age ringwall surrounding a settlement. Hamilton has suggested that the development of the broch took place in Orkney from whence its construction spread to Shetland and to the mainland of northern Britain. That Orkney was a centre of influence at this period is evidenced by the fact that the Roman fleet of Claudius concluded a non-aggression treaty with Orcadian chieftains in 43 A.D.

The brochs might have served a purpose in defending territory from attackers who came principally by sea. A distribution map of broch sites (Fig. 14) shows a heavy concentration along the coastal strips and up the fertile straths. If, indeed, the attackers did come by sea, then a broch distribution map might give a misleading impression of the pattern of settlement, for communities well into the hinterland might not require to take extreme defensive measures. Assuming an average broch community of about 30 persons, then, if all the brochs were simultaneously occupied, an assumption which may not in fact be justified, the total population living in the brochs would only be about 4000. If to this, a further 1000 is added to allow for hill-fort and promontory fort dwellers and for those living on marginal land well away from the coasts and straths, a total population of about 5000 would seem to be a generous estimate.

Then, in the years following 150 A.D., the political climate seems to have improved. This might be associated with the stabilization of the frontier between the Roman province of Britannia and Northern Britain by the building and manning of Hadrian's Wall and, for a short time, of the Antonine Wall, so preventing the incursion of further settlers into the north. It is suggested that the broch-dwellers, no longer needing their towers for defence, spared themselves the trouble of upkeep by dismantling them and using the stone to build the extramural settlements of small circular huts previously noted.

Throughout the whole of this Iron Age period the people had pursued a stock-raising and agricultural pattern of life. Implements found in brochs are those associated with animal husbandry, the working of the land and domestic pursuits such as weaving, pottery and basket-making. There is little to suggest that the broch dwellers were particularly war-like in outlook and their towers seem to have been purely defensive in character. The principal advantage gained from the introduction of iron implements is that they permitted movement of settlements to new areas — a change which is reflected in the pattern of farming in Caithness today, for many of the recorded broch sites lie on or close to what is still recognised as pasturage and arable land.

Thus, the age of the brochs, besides giving the County some of its most interesting archaeological remains, was the first step in the establishment of today's settlement pattern.

Then, in the 4th century A.D., by which time the brochs were in ruins, the area came under Pictish influence. This is further considered in the following chapter.

## APPENDIX—IMPORTANT SITES IN CATHNESS: IRON AGE
### (See Fig. 14)

NOTE:   Mention of a site does not imply right of public access. Where it is necessary to cross
cultivated or pastoral land, prior permission must be sought.

1. **Ben Freiceadain** Hill Fort (ND 059558)
   This is the most northerly hill-fort of any size on the British mainland. It covers an
area about 275 m x 143 m (900 ft x 470 ft) within a single wall about 3.6 m (12 ft) thick.
The entrance is to the west-north-west and is delineated by upright slabs. There is a ruinous
Neolithic/Bronze Age cairn, two thousand years older than the fort, on the summit.

2. **Bruan** Broch (ND 310394)
   A site much plundered as a source of building stone, it now remains as a turf-covered
stony mound about 3 m (10 ft) in height. There is evidence of an earlier defence work in
the form of a ditch with a wall on its inner lip surrounding the broch. The wall is best seen
to the west of the broch.

3. **Forse** Homestead ("Wag") (ND 204352)
   Here are the very dilapidated remains of a circular enclosure 13.7 m (45 ft) in diameter
with a wall 1.2 m (4 ft) thick. There are remains of other structures around and within the
enclosure. A perimeter bank of turf enclosing an oval area 38 m x 30.5 m (125 ft x 100 ft)
seems to have surrounded the homestead.

4. **Garrywhin** Hill Fort (ND 314414)
   Occupies an area about 180 m (590 ft) in length and up to 60 m (200 ft) in width on a
ridge near Loch Watenan. It is surrounded by boggy tracks on all sides but the north,
at which side the entrance through the 2.5 m (8 ft) thick wall is delineated by upright slabs
to give the most impressive example in northern Scotland.

5. **Holborn Head** Promontory Fort (ND 108715)
   The fort is formed by a broad wall across the promontory. Natural fissures and
chasms have been used to good effect in arranging the wall layout.

6. **Keiss** Broch (ND 353611)
   One of a number of brochs in the area, this one is most easily reached by walking
northwards along the foreshore from Keiss Harbour. A 3.6 m (12 ft) thick wall encloses
a 10.6 m (35 ft) diameter courtyard. There are post-broch extra-mural settlements and
there is much evidence of later re-use of the courtyard.

7. **Langwell** Homestead ("Wag") (ND 102218)
   A circular wall, 1.8 m (6 ft) thick, surrounds an 8.2m (27 ft) diameter courtyard. Of
the two side-by-side passages through the wall, one gives access from the outside while the
other leads to a contiguous galleried structure, roughly oblong in shape but with rounded
ends, measuring 14.6 m x 4.25 m (48 ft x 14 ft). The galleried structure is divided into two,
and one half has three upright pillars of stone set on either side of its long axis so dividing
it into a long central passage with two side aisles. The central passage and side aisles
were roofed by slabs resting on the pillars and on the perimeter wall. This type of
structure strongly resembles earth-houses (or souterrains) of the Pictish north-east of
Scotland.

8. **Ousdale** Broch (ND 072188)—Fig. 13
   This broch, the best surviving one in the County, stands above Ousdale burn about
midway between the A9 road and the sea. The site is defended to the east by the steep
descent to the burn and on other sides by a wall 2.5 m (8 ft) thick. The wall of the broch
is 4.3 m (14 ft) thick enclosing an 8.5 m (28 ft) diameter courtyard. The entrance has two
· sets of door checks between which is the access port to a mural chamber. A second mural
chamber opens from the courtyard. Both chambers have corbelled roofs. The stairway
starts from the courtyard to the north. A scarcement (ledge) for internal flooring can still
be seen near the top of the inner wall. There has been some recent, out-of-character, re-
building of the inner face of the wall near the entrance passage.

9. **St John's Point** Promontory Fort (ND 310752)
   This is the most northerly promontory fort on the mainland, formed by a ditch with

a 3 m (10 ft) high rampart on the inner lip and a slight upcast mound on the outer lip. The rampart is, in all, about 180 m (600 ft) in length and cuts off an area of about 4 hectares (10 acres).

### 10. Shurrery Hill Fort (ND 053577)

It occupies Cnoc na Ratha about 1.6 km (1 mile) to the north of the fort at Ben Freiceadain (No. 1). A wall of stone slabs about 2 m (7 ft) thick encloses an area of about 91.5 m x 70 m (300 ft x 230 ft). There are two entrances, both lined with slabs. There is a secondary enclosure about 9 m (30 ft) in diameter formed by a wall about 2 m (7 ft) thick against the outer wall on the south-east .

### 11. Skirza Broch (ND 394684)

This broch occupies the neck of a narrow promontory. There is an outer ditch and embankment. The broch wall is about 4.3 m (14 ft) thick enclosing a rather small courtyard only 6.6 m (22 ft) in diameter. The entrance, from the seaward side, has door checks. There are extensive post-broch structures both inside and outside the broch wall.

### 12. Thing's Va Broch (ND 081683)

A broch situated within a ditch about 9 m (30 ft) wide and 1.2 m to 2.5 m (4 ft to 8 ft) in depth, enclosing a mound about 33 m (110 ft) across, on which the broch stood about 5.5 m to 6 m (18 ft to 20 ft) from the inner lip. The broch entrance passage enters from the south-east with two sets of door-checks. Stones projecting from the mound suggest a wall thickness of about 4.6 m (15 ft) with a courtyard diameter of 9.3 m (30 ft).

### 13. Westerdale Broch (ND 133510)

A large uneven mound covers the broch as well as the outworks and secondary structures. The broch wall was about 3.7 m (12 ft) in thickness and enclosed a courtyard 8.5 m (28 ft) in diameter. The ditch which surrounds the site may originally have been a moat filled from the Thurso River.

### 14. Yarrows Broch (ND 308435)

This broch occupies an easily defensible promontory in the Loch of Yarrows. It shows evidence of preliminary defensive ditching of the neck of the promontory. The site has numerous hut enclosures surrounding the broch tower which, when excavated in 1866-7 by Joseph Anderson, could not be dated. Recent views of broch development would suggest these to form a village of the immediate post-broch period.

# CHAPTER 14

# THE PICTS

In her book on "The Picts" Dr Isobel Henderson says that virtually no Pictish records have survived and modern scholars can still not provide neat answers to such basic questions as: Who were they? What language did they speak? What did they call themselves? What happened to them after the Scots took over? Nevertheless, the work of Dr Henderson, Dr Wainwright and others has added a great deal to our knowledge of these early people. it is known, for example, that the name PICTI, given by classical writers from the late 3rd century A.D. to the tribes north of the Antonine Wall, had no racial content but was simply a convenient name to describe the tribes of mixed origin and language who inhabited this area. Although we have no reliable historical evidence, traditions concerning the origin of the Picts are preserved by ancient writers. Wainwright says that these stories cannot be accepted as historical statements, but they are interesting for the unanimity with which they locate the Picts in the North of Scotland.

The bulk of the Pictish populace was probably of native Bronze Age, or very early Iron Age descent, speaking a language which was not Celtic, perhaps not even Indo-European — the language developed in prehistoric times, probably in Central Asia, from which most European and Central Asian languages have evolved. A much smaller group, possibly the ruling classes, were of late Iron Age origin, entering what is now Scotland in the 1st century B.C. as a result of Roman pressure in Gaul and southern Britain.

It was believed that the Iron Age invaders who settled north of the Moray Firth and in the northern isles were of a different, though related, 'culture' from the Iron Age invaders who settled between the Firth of Forth and Moray Firth. The characteristic structure of the northern invaders was thought to be the broch, while the southern invaders favoured the vitrified or stone, timber-laced fort, but it has been shown by MacKie (1967) that the gritty pottery and arte-facts found in vitrified forts go back to the 7th century B.C., perhaps to the late 8th century; that is, the late Bronze Age. MacKie (1965) had also suggested that brochs first appeared in the Western Isles and subsequently spread to the far north, including Caithness. He envisaged a static population, settled from Caithness to the Forth/Clyde Valley, which had been formed in the 8th or 7th centuries B.C. by an amalgamation of natives and Continental immigrants, and which ultimately became known as the Picts.

No vitrified forts have as yet been identified in Caithness, but more than a hundred brochs are known, many of them on the fertile straths and coastal lands. In the past they were commonly known as Picts' castles or houses but it is now agreed that they cannot be called Pictish for they belong to a period before the emergence of the historical Picts and are not even found exclusively in districts which later comprised part of the historical kingdom of the Picts.

The broch builders were, however, in all probability the ancestors of at least some element of the Pictish population.

In the 4th century A.D. the Picts were acting together and, moreover, in alliance with the Scots. The high water mark of this unity, it is said, was the great raid of A.D. 367 when Picts, Scots, Franks and Saxons attacked southern Britain simultaneously. In the late 4th century Marcellinus wrote of the Picts as comprising two peoples. Bede tells how Columba preached to "the provinces of the northern Picts", while Ninian a long time before had converted "the southern Picts". Historians are uncertain if Bede's words should be taken as evidence for the division of the Picts into two political groups, the north and the south, during the period A.D. 400 to 600, or even until 735, for Bede writes in the present tense. It is open to question whether the use of northern and southern is merely a geographical reference.

By the middle of the 6th century we have a truly historical king of the Picts —Bridei (or Brude), son of Maelchon. Adomnan, the 9th Abbot of Iona, writing towards the end of the 7th century described Columba's visit to Brude's fortress capital. This fortress has not yet been identified, but it is believed that it stood on the site of the vitrified fort at Craig Phadrig, near Inverness. Bede implies that Brude was the powerful king of all the Picts, both on the mainland and on the northern isles, for the regulus or local ruler of the Orkneys was in attendance at Brude's court, Orcadians were held as hostages, and at Columba's request Brude instructed the Orkney chiefs to afford safe conduct to Cormack and other priests in northern waters. The close of Brude's reign about 584 A.D. is held to mark the end of the importance of the north in Pictish affairs. Later kings certainly seem to have been based in the south. The growing strength of the Scots in the west, and the increasing menace of the Angles in the south, provide ample justification for such a change.

In 685 A.D. the Picts under Bridei (or Brude), son of Bili, were strong enough to defeat the Angles of Northumbria at Nechtansmere (now Dunnichen in Angus). This Brude is the first Pictish king since Brude McMaelchon to have caught the attention of foreign chroniclers; in the Irish Annals it is recorded that he led a raid on the Orkneys in 682, which resulted in much devastation. It has been recently suggested that the raid was associated with the Norse occupation of the northern isles. A siege of Dunbaitte is interpreted by Skene as a reference to Brude's activities at Dunbeath, Caithness, but this is guesswork.

Place-names afford no more evidence of the Pictish presence in Caithness than the written record. More than three hundred names with the element PIT have been counted in the north-east of Scotland (e.g. Pittenweem and Pitlochry) and it is known that this element embodies a Pictish word meaning farm or steading, but these place-names are found only in an area extending from south-east Sutherland to the Forth, the districts where vitrified forts are found, and are quite unknown in Caithness. Professor Jackson, writing in "The Problem of the Picts", suggests that in the main Pictish area the Celtic-speaking Iron Age invaders mingled with the Bronze Age natives, adopting some of their tribal names and even, to some extent, their language. In the far north and west the situation was somewhat different; here the invaders left remarkably few traces of P-Celtic names—the early form of Celtic used by these people. Subsequent repopulation by Celtic and Norse-speaking peoples may account for this in part, but Professor Jackson believes that the contrast is sufficiently striking to suggest that the immigrants of the north and west gave up their

Celtic speech almost entirely, adopting the non-Indo-European speech of the Bronze Age natives.

One relic found in Caithness which is indisputably Pictish is the symbol stone. At least ten such stones have been discovered in Caithness (see Appendix A). The symbols, thirty-five in number, are as enigmatic as the Picts themselves. They never occur singly and are usually in groups of four or five, but, in the case of the Ulbster Stone, no less than eight are found. Some combinations never occur; for example, a crescent may be crossed with a V-shaped rod; but never with a Z-rod. The double disc may be crossed with a V-rod, but never with a Z-rod. Boldly incised animals are frequently found with the symbols — the salmon, serpent, eagle, duck, goose, hound, bull, stag, bear, deer, horse and highly stylised creatures known as the hippocampus and elephant. Most of the symbols are abstract designs, but some represent real objects, although so stylised as to bear little resemblance to the originals. Two or three are recognisable — the comb, mirror and case, broken sword, etc. It is now accepted that symbol stones are artistically and symbolically non-Christian.

The oldest class of symbol stone is that with symbols incised more or less upon unshaped boulders and is thought to date from A.D. 650. The second class of stone is more carefully dressed and its symbols are carved in relief, often richly decorated with Celtic design ornamental spirals, and are accompanied by a Christian cross of Celtic design, similarly enriched. The division in time between Class I and Class II stones is said to mark the conversion of the Picts to Christianity — an event of disputed date in southern Pictland, but probably around 600 A.D. in northern Pictland, with eventual extension to Caithness and the northern isles. Certainly the Norsemen found priests among the Picts when they colonised the north about the year 800 A.D. Class III stones bear crosses but no symbols.

Two of the Caithness symbol stones have ogam inscriptions. This system of writing is composed of strokes or notches arranged in combinations along a stem line. Henderson says that the great majority of inscriptions in Pictland appear to be in the language of the Bronze Age natives, although written, for the most part, in the Irish ogam alphabet. The variety of ogam used is said to suggest a date about the 8th century and, as one inscription is found on a Class I stone, it follows that these stones were still erected in Caithness in the 8th century.

Symbol stones in the far north — that is, in Sutherland and Caithness — have been found almost without exception on the coastal plain, but immediately south of Sutherland the picture changes and stones are usually found on inland sites. Large numbers have come from old burial grounds or have been found beside early churches, so there is a strong supposition that they were individual headstones.

One writer suggests that the symbol stones are the personal monuments of the Celtic-speaking ruling class using a simple but widely-known code to represent the clan and status of the dead. The animals, it is suggested, indicate his clan or family grouping and the symbols his personal status (e.g. sub-king) or occupation (e.g. warrior, metal-worker or priest). Another writer has shown that the V-and Z-shaped rods are in fact broken arrows, and he suggests that these and the broken sword are symbols of a dead warrior. Wainwright (1955) comments that although these symbol stones often include figures of Pictish warriors, huntsmen and priests revealing in minute detail their dress, ornaments, arms and equipment, no-one has yet attempted to assemble this very full and varied body of easily accessible evidence. Pottery impressions show that they were farmers and that they had turned to the cultivation of oats.

Less easy to date are the simple incised crosses found on rough boulders at Mid-Clyth, Latheron, Clach-na-Caplaich, Skinnet and elsewhere in the County. One opinion is that the two Mid-Clyth crosses are pre-Norse, and therefore contemporary with the elaborate Class III stones, but the rest are probably 10th or 11th century.

The Picts had long been Christian when the Norsemen colonised Caithness and the northern isles, for they recognised the existence of both Picts and priests in a number of place-names. In the isles we find Pettadale (O.N. "*Petta-dalr*," valley of the Picts), Petester (O.N. "*Petta saeter*", sheiling of the Picts) and Pentland Firth. Priests are remembered by Papa Stour (O.N. "*Papi*", a priest, and "*storr*", big; hence, big island of the Priests), Papa Skerry (Rock of the Priests) and in Caithness Papigoe (Inlet of the Priests). Mackinlay mentions two early saints who may have been Picts. One, St Fergus, reputedly converted the "barbarous inhabitants" of Caithness and the parish church of Halkirk was probably dedicated to him, as it was anciently known as St Fergus Parish. He was probably "Fergustus, Episcopus Scotiae Pictus" who attended a council in Rome in 721.

He was also patron saint of Wick. The other saint was St Drostan or Trostan, who is said to have been a nephew of St Columba but is not mentioned in the family genealogies, nor by Adomnan. Mackinlay says that his name may be Pictish and that chapels were dedicated to him at Westfield, Brabster, Olrig and probably at Gills.

## APPENDIX

### List of Pictish Symbol Stones in Caithness

| Found at | Description | Reference |
|---|---|---|
| Ackergill<br>ND 348549 | Notched rectangle. | PSAS, LX 179 |
| Ackergill<br>ND 348549 | Fish, decorated rectangle.<br>ogam inscription. | PSAS, LX, 179<br>IMC, No. 587 |
| Birkle Hill<br>ND 583338 | Mirror, triple oval. | PSAS, XXIX, 272<br>IMC, No. 577 |
| Sandside<br>ND 969655 | Triple oval, mirror and<br>mirror case. | ECMS, III, 29-30<br>IMC, No. 407 |
| Crosskirk<br>ND 024702 | Crescent and V-rod, horse<br>shoe. | ECMS, III, 30<br>IMC, No. 405 |
| Latheron<br>ND 198334 | Crescent and V-rod. | PSAS, XCII, 40 |
| Ulbster<br>? | Equal-armed cross, animals,<br>men, serpent, flower, horse<br>and colt. Plain Latin cross,<br>elephant, fish, crescent and<br>V-rod, double disc, hippo-<br>campus, crescents linked by<br>circle. | ECMS, III, 33-35<br>IMC, No. 444<br>PSAS, XCII, 55 |
| Skinnet<br>ND 131621 | Cross in relief, serpents,<br>horses, Cross with inter-<br>lacing triple ovals,<br>crescent and V-rod. | ECMS, III, 30-33<br>IMC, No. 445<br>PSAS, XCII, 55 |
| Latheron<br>? | Fish, bird, decorated rect-<br>angle, horsemen, ogam,<br>inscription. | IMC, No. 299<br>PSAS, XXXVIII,<br>534 |
| Reay<br>NC 967648 | Interlaced cross, bull,<br>hound and other animals. | PSAS, LXXXIV,<br>218 |

| | |
|---|---|
| PSAS | Proceedings of the Society of Antiquaries of Scotland. |
| IMC | Inventory of Monuments and Structures in Caithness. |
| ECMS | Early Christian Monuments of Scotland. |

# CHAPTER 15

# THE VIKINGS

The Viking influence in Caithness extended over a period of a little over 350 years, from about 875 AD when the northern part of the mainland was conquered by the Norse Earl of Orkney, Sigurd I and Thorstein the Red, making Sigurd the first Earl of Orkney and Caithness, to 1231 AD when John the last of the Norse Earls was ignominiously murdered in a Thurso cellar.

This period differs from the periods discussed in the last three chapters because for the first time the names of individuals are recorded in the pages of history. And for this reason it is tempting to see the Norse period as the age of the Vikings, the age of the bold warriors whose exploits have been immortalised in the Sagas. But it was in the era of Norse settlement that the distribution of population, which had moved in the previous thousand years from the well-drained hillsides to the straths and coastal plain, finally took up something like its present form as boatload after boatload of anonymous settlers, forced out of Scandinavia by what we would now call a population explosion, established themselves as farmers.

Of course, the first arrivals were Vikings en route to plunder the rich monasteries of Northumbria. It has been suggested that the first Norse settlers arrived in Caithness in the year 863 AD but it is probable that the existence of rich farmlands in the area had been known to marauding Viking bands for more than a century before that date.

The first Norse Earl, Sigurd, who finally annexed Caithness to his Orkney Earldom, was the uncle of Rollo, and hence an ancestor of William the Conqueror. Then for three centuries the pages of the sagas ring with the names of Thorfinn, Arnfinn, Sweyn, Ljot and Skuli, Sigurd the Stout, Harald, and scores of other heroes and villians giving the impression that Caithness was indisputably part of the Norse world. But this was never so. The Norsemen never managed to establish either their language or their udal laws in Caithness. The County was always a crossroads, an area in which the Norse and Scottish worlds were to meet, sometimes amicably, sometimes in battle.

Thus in the year 950 AD, a dispute about succession to the earldom between two brothers, Ljot and Skuli, found Ljot's claim to the title supported by the King of Norway and Skuli's by the King of Scotland. In the contest which resulted, Skuli was assisted by a Celtic chieftain from Sutherland, but in a battle at Dale, Skuli was slain and Ljot became the undisputed Earl. Skuli's former ally, the Celtic chieftain, sought revenge, however, and Ljot was slain at a later battle at Toftingal. Ljot's widow, Ranghilde, married Arnfinn, also a brother to Ljot and Skuli, but murdered him at Murkle so ending the claims of the brothers to the Earldom.

The close contacts between the Norse and Scottish spheres of influence are to be seen more clearly in the early 11th century, when Sigurd II, sometimes called Sigurd the Stout, became Earl of Orkney and Caithness. Sigurd was a Norseman, but his second wife was daughter of King Malcolm II of Scotland. During his lifetime the earldom was converted to Christianity by Olaf Tryggveson, and yet Sigurd was to die in 1014 AD at the battle of Clontarf, fighting on the pagan side.

Sigurd left four sons, Summorlid, Brusi, Einar and Thorfinn, the latter sometimes known as Thorfinn the Mighty. Thorfinn became Earl of Caithness with his maternal grandfather's agreement, while Sigurd's other three sons divided up the sovereignty of the Northern Isles between them. When Malcolm died in 1034 AD the succession to the Scottish throne was disputed and Thorfinn refused to pay any further tribute to the Scottish king. He was therefore supplanted as Scottish-supported Earl of Caithness by a Celtic chieftain, Moddan of the Dales. Thorfinn's ally, Thorkel Fostri, however, destroyed Moddan in Thurso by setting fire to his house and killing him as he tried to escape. Thorfinn thus became accepted as Earl of Orkney and Caithness, and made a pilgrimage to Rome to be absolved of all his sins by the Pope. On his return he founded the church on Birsay in which after his death in 1064 he was interred.

For much of the period of Norse influence, Caithness was ruled, not directly by the Earl, but by governors. One of the eleventh century governors, Olaus Rolfi, found himself in dispute with Frakirk, widow of a Strathnaver chieftain. Having decided to destroy Olaus, Frakirk sent her grandson to attack him at Duncansby where Olaus and his followers were celebrating Yuletide. Olaus died when his house was set on fire. His wife, Asleif, and sons, Sweyn and Gunni, were away and thus escaped Olaus' fate, but hearing of the attack they sought refuge in Orkney. Sweyn Asliefson later became a noted pirate with a refuge castle at Lambaborg (Bucholie) and was responsible in one of his exploits for abducting his one time friend Earl Paul and forcing the succession of his nephew Harald Maddadson. With Sweyn behind him, Harald Maddadson's pretentious behaviour soon excited the annoyance of the Norwegian king, Eyestein, who in 1151 AD succeeded in seizing Harald in his ship in Thurso bay and forced him to ransom himself with three merks of gold. (Sweyn at the time was away on one of his piratical exploits; on one of these he got revenge on Frakirk, burning her in her house — obviously a fashionable way of settling a dispute).

Harald Maddadson also found himself in dispute with the Scottish king, William the Lion, who in retaliation gave part of Caithness to another Harald, generally known as Harald (or Harold) the Younger. The two Haralds met in battle in 1196 AD on Clardon Hill and though the actual site of the battle is not known, Harald's Tower near Thurso (built by Sir John Sinclair and for many years a mausoleum of the Sinclair family) reputedly stands on the spot where Harald the Younger was killed in the battle.

Harald Maddadson's next act in defiance of King William was to land at Scrabster with the aim of proving his right to the Earldom. The people of Thurso had given allegiance to King William, and John, second Bishop of Caithness, whose castle was at Burnside near Scrabster, went to meet Harald to try to intercede on their behalf. Harald, however, was not to be treated with and allowed one of his followers, Lomberd, to cut out the Bishop's tongue. Harald then over-ran the whole of Caithness. Hearing of this, and of the fate of the unfortunate Bishop, King William came to Caithness with an army to be met by Harald's army at Ousdale. Harald, however, noticing that he had fewer troops than the king, sued for peace. The King merely exacted a fine and generously re-instated him in the earldom. Harald died in 1206, aged 73, and was succeeded by his son John.

In John's time, another bishop, Adam, was barbarously put to death in his palace at Halkirk in 1222 AD. He had exacted very heavy tithes on his tenants — in particular, a tax on butter — and a group of them took the opportunity of an annual fair at Braal to bring their grievances to Earl John's notice. The earl is reputed to have been irritated by the bishop's tenants and to have said: "The devil take the bishop and his butter; you may roast him, if you please!" Three hundred tenants, led by two sons of Simon Harbister, from Harpsdale, did just that. Again the Scottish king, this time Alexander II, came north to avenge the bishop's death.

Adam was succeeded as bishop by the most distinguished of all of them, Gilbert Murray (Moray). His appointment to Caithness from a post as Archdeacon of Moray seems to have been a consequence of the high esteem in which he was held by the Scottish King. (The unfortunate Adam, his predecessor, came to Caithness from a position as Abbot of Melrose, also with the Scottish King's support). Bishop Gilbert is said to have built a church in Thurso and it has been suggested that the semi-circular apsidal end of Old St Peter's (now known as the Forss vault) represents the sole remaining part of this church. He supposedly translated the Psalms into Gaelic, which would seem to imply that this was the language of many of the people in his episcopacy, but his main influence was in moving the seat of the bishopric to Dornoch. Later, King Alexander II made Bishop Gilbert his Treasurer for the north. He died on April 1st, 1245 AD and was later sanctified, the anniversary of his death now being St Gilbert's Day.

From these episodes it is fairly clear why the Norse influence in Caithness was so much less significant than it was in Orkney and Shetland. The Norse Earls, for all but the first few decades of the period, were never in undisputed control of the County, and when John, whose casual remark had led to Bishop Adam's death, was murdered in a Thurso cellar by a band of malcontents from Orkney in the year 1231 AD, all Norse pretence to succession to the earldom was effectively at an end. This event took place thirty-two years before the Battle of Largs which historians customarily mark as the end of Scandinavian rule in the north. For the next hundred years there were to be Norse pretenders to the earldom, but never did they get the approval of both the Scottish and Norwegian kings which had been enjoyed by most of their predecessors. Finally in 1331 AD the earldom passed to the Anglo-Norman Henry St Clair (or Sinclair) of Roslin to whose descendants it has passed ever since.

There are few surviving archaeological remains of the Norse period in Caithness, though finds of burials and of houses have been reported from Reay and Freswick. Some signs of the Norse settlement at Freswick are still to be seen but removal of sand for agricultural purposes is a constant hazard to the site. Of Sweyn Asliefson's castle at Bucholie naught remains, the structures now to be seen on the site being of later date, but the castle of Old Wick and, possibly, Braal Castle are simple towers which appear to be of Norse period date. The church at Crosskirk, St Mary's, is a twelfth century building and must have been built in Norse times though its close resemblance to Irish churches of the period would seem to be further evidence of strong influences from the south. Of the Norse castle in Thurso there are no remains: only the street name Castlegreen recalls its existence.

But if the Norsemen left few material remains and if their language and laws have had little influence on Caithness dialect and custom, the memorials of the Norse period are easily found on our maps. From the pages of the Sagas, there appear, in the 350 years of Norse influence, a few dozen named individuals, some of whose doings have been recounted above. And yet, the number of Norse peoples to come to Caithness must be counted in thousands. The County abounds in place names of Norse origin. This is not the place to discuss this topic in any detail but a quick look at a map will show that the whole north-east of Caithness has settlement place names of Norse origin, while the area close to the County march with Sutherland has some Norse geographical place names but most names are of Gaelic origin (see chapter 26). Elements to look out for are -ster (old Norse: *stathr* = farm settlement) and -bster (old Norse: *bolstathr*=farm) in the settlement area. There are also several names based on -setter (old Norse: *setr* = homestead, not to be confused with *saetr* = mountain pasture; mountain pastures or shielings in Caithness generally have the Gaelic *-airigh* ending, e.g. Lieurary). The ending -wick (old Norse: *vik*=bay) occurs widely, and gave the present County town its name. The origin of the name Thurso is in dispute; the only postulated origin which is almost certainly incorrect is that most commonly believed; that it comes from Thor's -aa=Thor's river. This is unlikely as the Norsemen called the Thurso river, Skinandi (=the shining one), a name now recalled as Skinnet. Two other suggested origins are Thor's haugr (=Thor's mound) and Thjor's -aa (=bull river, a name suggested by the appearance of Tarvedun, apparently debased Celtic for bull-fort, on Ptolemy's map of Britain in the second century AD).

Thus we have a picture of the whole of the presently populated parts of Caithness, settled by Norse farmers and there is some evidence that Thurso in Norse times was a seaport shipping grain back to the Scandinavian homeland. Caithness has sometimes been called the granary of Scandinavia.

Of course, it is well-known that Norse penetration of the Scottish mainland extended much farther than the County march with Sutherland, but it is in that region that Norse names take on a geographical bias—the ending—dale (old Norse: *dalr* =valley) occurs at Helmsdale, Ousdale, Berriedale, Navidale, Armadale, Westerdale and, possibly, fused with Gaelic elements, at Achvarasdal—suggesting exploration but not settlement.

In previous accounts of the Norse period in Caithness there has been too much emphasis on the Viking sagas, too much attention to the exploits of a few colourful individuals. What the sagas do show, as the excerpts recounted in this chapter indicate, is that Norse influence in Caithness was never undisputed and that Scottish and Scandinavian forces were always at work. The evidence of place names, however, suggests the settlement of the County by peaceful farming communities, probably co-existing with the earlier inhabitants, the well-known drive and energy of the Norsemen permitting the opening up of new areas for cultivation. At times, the lives of these people must have been disturbed by the feuds and forays recounted in the sagas, but there is no support for a view of the Norse period as one of war and rampage. The events which are recorded could hardly have taken up more than a few years of the 350-year period. There is no reason to suppose that, for the rest of the time, life was not peaceful and undisturbed. The Norse longhouse, with its large living room and byre all under the one roof, has, after all, much in common with the croft and byre.

# CHAPTER 16

# FROM THE VIKINGS TO THE "FORTY FIVE"

**Families, Feuds and Wars**

In 1379 Sir Henry St Clair was granted the Earldom of Orkney by King Haco. One of Henry's successors, William, surrendered Orkney to the Crown in 1455 and was compensated with the Earldom of Caithness.

For the ensuing 200 years Caithness knew little but trouble and bloodshed through the feudal rivalries of the Sinclairs, Gunns, Keiths, Sutherlands, Mackays, and others.

One of the most prominent families of the 14th century was that of Cheyne. The last male of the line, Reginald, was a substantial landowner who held half of Caithness. He was a signatory of the Declaration of Arbroath in 1320. On Cheyne's death, his daughter married John de Keith, son of the Marischal of Scotland. Thus, on Cheyne's death the Keiths gained a foothold in Caithness, their stronghold being Ackergill Tower.

The Clan Gunn who initially held Castle Gunn and Halberry Castle, Clyth, later resided in the hilly country bordering Caithness and Sutherland. Their neighbours, the Mackays of Strathnaver, made many marauding forays into Caithness. In 1426 during one of these raids a battle took place between the two clans at Harpsdale, near Halkirk.

Twelve years later the Keiths and Mackays linked forces and defeated the Gunns at Tannach Moor, near Wick. The most treacherous incident in these clan feuds occurred about the middle of the 15th century (so the story goes), when a party of Keiths surprised the Gunns at prayer in the Chapel of St Tears, between Castle Girnigoe and Ackergill Tower. Only five of the Gunns survived. Lawlessness was so rife that the King in 1611 referred to the "inciville and barbarous behaviour of the most part of oure subjectis in Caithness."

A particularly disastrous episode in Caithness and Scottish history was James IV's fateful journey to Flodden. William, Earl of Caithness, set off on a Monday to assist James IV with an army of some 300 men clad in green. The Caithness contingent was wiped out and their fate had such an effect on the County that for a long time afterwards no Sinclair would cross the Ord on a Monday. Andrew Stewart, Bishop of Caithness, was also slain in the battle.

Earl William was succeeded by his son, John, who in 1529 set off on a military venture to Orkney to re-instate a relative who had been expelled. Earl John and his 500 men were all slain at the Battle of Summerdale — the last pitched battle on Orcadian soil.

A well-known figure who visited Caithness in 1591 was the Earl of Bothwell who had been married to Mary, Queen of Scots. Bothwell was no doubt grateful to Earl George who was Chancellor of the jury which acquitted Bothwell of being implicated in the murder of Darnley. This Earl George was responsible for a hideous crime. Having fallen out with his son, John, he lured

PLATE 19. *Ice House. Mey.*

(A. Luciani)

PLATE 18. *Prehistoric standing stone, Rangag.*

(A. Luciani)

(A. Luciani)

PLATE 20.   *St Mary's, a 12th century chapel at Crosskirk, Forss.*

(A. Luciani)

PLATE 21.   *Old St Peter's Church, Thurso.*

him into his castle at Girnigoe where he was thrown into a dungeon, dying in torment six years later.

The next Earl, also George, was frequently at loggerheads with the Earl of Sutherland, who on one occasion, sallied into Caithness and plundered Latheron parish. This foray was called the 'Creach Iarn' — the harrying of Latheron. Sutherland's next raid was in 1588 when he ravaged a large part of Caithness and burnt the town of Wick, sparing only the church. This episode was long remembered as 'Latha na creach more' — the day of the great spoil.

Yet another piece of military folly happened in 1612 when Colonel George Sinclair, a soldier of fortune, raised 900 mercenaries and crossed to Norway to fight for the King of Sweden. However, the mercenaries were ambushed by the Norwegians in a narrow pass and the slaughter was so appalling that only a handful of the 900 returned.

In 1651 Cromwell's troops came to Caithness and stayed for 3-4 years, their principal stronghold being Ackergill Tower.

George, the 6th Earl of Caithness, was forced to sell his estates to Campbell of Glenorchy. On George's death, Campbell assumed the title, although his claim was bitterly opposed by Sinclair of Keiss. Campbell was most unpopular in Caithness and so many difficulties were put in the way of his agents that he decided to teach the Caithness folk a sharp lesson. In 1680 he marched north with a force of 700 men. The Sinclairs who had gathered at Wick marched to meet him at Altimarlach, 4.8 km (3 miles) from the mouth of the Wick river. And so, the last clan battle fought on Scottish soil ended disastrously for the Sinclairs. On the way to Altimarlach Glenorchy's piper composed the well-known tune, "The Campbells are Coming."

## The Church

Many early churches were dedicated to the Celtic missionaries. Later Roman Catholic dedications, mainly to Saints, were often built on pre-existing sites to eradicate memories of the earlier Celtic church.

The Bishop's See was the 'The Land of Cat' which consisted of the modern counties of Caithness and Sutherland. The church held a vast amount of real estate throughout the diocese in the form of lands and fishing — both salt and fresh water. These lands were at Scrabster, Lythmore, Stemster, Dorrery (which was used as a shieling) and Scotscalder. On Braehour Burn the Bishops had built a mill for their tenants. Moreover, in each parish of the diocese the Church exacted a tenth part (tiend) of all oats, bere, hay, etc., raised by tenants of non-church lands.

Some of the early churches are historically and architecturally worthy of mention. Certainly the oldest ecclesiastical structure remaining in the County is St Mary's Chapel. Crosskirk (ND 025701) which may date from the 12th century. It consists of a nave and chancel, now both roofless. Interiorly, the nave measures 5.49 m (17 ft 10 in) east-west by 3.35 m (10 ft 11 in) north-south. It is entered by a flat-headed doorway with inclining jambs. The architecture has strong similarities to chapels constructed in Ireland at this time.

The Church of Old St Peter's, Thurso (ND 120686) must have been a handsome building with its striking window. In outline the Church is cruciform, measuring 24 m (79 ft) east-west and 25 m (82 ft) north-south across the transepts. The apsidal cell, which resembles that of St Margaret's Chapel in Edinburgh Castle, may be of 12th century construction. Certainly, dedication of the

J

Church to St Peter suggests an early date of construction. Undoubtedly, the present shape and transepts belong to the 16th and 17th centuries.

Some 3.2 km (2 miles) west of John O'Groats is Canisbay Church (ND 343728) whose original structure may date from the 15th century although there is reference to a church in this area as far back as 1222. Its oblong structure, some 25.6 m by 7.3 m (84 ft by 24 ft) along the south and north transepts, has been much altered over the centuries. The tower in the centre of the west front is the feature most indicative of a pre-Reformation date. The Church appears to have been dedicated to St Drostan. The Rev. John Morrison, author of some of the best known paraphrases, taught at a number of schools in Caithness before becoming minister at this church.

Dunnet Church (ND 220712) strongly resembles that of Canisbay, but has no transepts. The round-arched doorway in the north wall with its broad splay down from the jambs and the staircase are indicative of a pre-Reformation construction. Pont, who produced the first map of Scotland was minister here in the early part of the 17th century.

In the north-east corner of Reay churchyard (ND 969648) are the reconstructed remains of part of the old Church of Reay which is said to be dedicated to St Colman. The interior measures 4.9 m by 3.6 m (16 ft 2 in by 11 ft 8 in). On the end wall to the right of the entrance is a panel bearing the date 1691 and showing the Munro arms of the eagle's head.

Following the Reformation the Roman Catholic Bishop, Stewart, who accepted Presbyterianism, was commissioned in 1563 by the General Assembly to "plant Kirks" in the County. By 1574 there were eight ministers and 16 "readers" with occasional "exhorters" in the diocese.

In 1581 the Church in Caithness was divided into synods and presbyteries. The Presbytery consisted of the parishes of Wick, Halkirk, Skinnet, Reay, Bower, Watten, Olrig, Canisbay, Latheron, Dunnet, Farr and Ardurness. But allegiance to the old established religion was still strong. Early in the 17th century the Privy Council notes with dismay that the Catholic religion still has a strong foothold in Caithness. Following the Restoration of the Monarchy after Cromwell's time, Episcopacy returned to Caithness in 1670.

Two Caithness men who signed the National Covenant of 1638 were John, Master of Berriedale and Sir James Sinclair of Murkle. The latter even raised a body of men to help in the struggle.

In 1650 the Marquis of Montrose having raised the Royal Standard, sailed from Orkney to the Bay of Sannick, Duncansby, with a large band of German and Danish mercenaries. On his way south he attacked and took Dunbeath Castle. Montrose ordered the Caithness clergy to sign in favour of Episcopacy; all but one, the clergyman at Watten/Bower obeyed. Episcopacy was reinstated until the last Bishop of Caithness, Andrew Wood, was ejected following the Act abolishing the Prelacy in 1689.

The slowness of the Protestant faith coming to Caithness may have been partly due to the apathy of the landowners who either favoured Catholicism (e.g. the Earl of Caithness) or had little interest in religious matters. Congregations, too, do not seem to have been well disposed to change and open resentment was often shown to incoming Presbyterian ministers.

Certainly in the early part of the 18th century a minister's life in Caithness was an arduous and dangerous one. The Rev. Alexander Pope, Reay, armed himself with a cudgel as protection against "semi-barbarous" elements in his flock. Apparently he used the cudgel with much vigour and telling effect!

Worshippers at this time and during the preceding centuries must have stood crowded on the church's earthen floor or sat on "creepies" (stools) which they brought with them. The morning service commonly began at 10 a.m., lasted 2-2½ hours and was followed by an afternoon service. In rural areas it was common that a church bell would ring early in the morning to awake people for church. For this purpose the bell-tower at Latheron (ND 201338) was constructed, as the bell of the local church could not carry the sound a long distance because of the configuration of the land. The bell-tower consists of a detachable belfrey 7.3 m (24 ft) high and 2.1 m (7 ft) square and was probably built about the end of the 17th century. The bell was removed from the tower in 1825.

Elders of the Kirk session were very watchful over their flocks and placed considerable restraint on the people. Those found "guilty" at Kirk Session meetings had to do penance by rebukings, fines, occupying the stool of repentance, appearing in sackcloth before the congregation, wearing a paper hood with the victim's "crime" written on it, standing at the pillory, or standing bare-legged in a tub of cold water. Sometimes the Church was over-zealous in meting out punishment; e.g. the Rev. Brodie of Latheron Church was suspended for nine months because he slit a man's ear with a razor, for stealing!

A compassionate work of the Church over a long period of time was in helping the large number of vagrants in the County. Their numbers sometimes rose to alarming proportions. The poor, who were legally allowed to beg, wore little stamps of lead round their necks, but were only permitted to beg within their own parishes. Each month the Kirk-Session allocated an allowance to such unfortunate paupers, money commonly being raised by donations to the 'Poor Box'.

**Education**

Illiteracy was so common in Caithness in the 16th century that even some of the nobility could not write.

Most of the landowners paid little attention to the education of their tenants, so that by the beginning of the 18th century few people were literate. A Presbytery minute of 1727 says that of 1600 people who had 'come of age', 1500 could speak Gaelic only, and a mere five could read. Gaelic at this time was the principal language in most parishes except Bower, Canisbay, Dunnet and Olrig.

There were no schools in Wick and Thurso until 1706 and any building was regarded as suitable accommodation — even the steeple of Dunnet Church was used as a school-room! At this time it was common for men to take up positions as schoolteachers while preparing for the ministry. Teachers were paid meagre salaries and frequently received their remuneration in kind. The first woman teacher in Caithness, Miss Elspet Johnson, was appointed to Weydale in 1718 at a salary of £1.30 per annum! As part of their contract teachers might live with a pupil's parents and they often acted in other capacities, e.g. clerks, to supplement their income.

Children had long distances to travel, usually on foot and over rough tracks. The school week was commonly six days and hours of attendance could be from 7 a.m. to 6 p.m.

## Agriculture

As early as the 14th century Caithness was important for grain, Thurso having a considerable trade with the Scandinavian and Baltic lands. The fact that the weights and measures of Caithness were made the Standards of Scotland in David II's reign indicates the commercial importance of the County at this time.

The chief drawbacks to agricultural advancement were open farmland (which necessitated herding of animals during the crop-growing season), over-cropping (there was no rotation), lack of drainage and insecurity of tenure.

The oldest method of farming about which any detail is known in Caithness, was "run-rig", whereby the arable land was divided into strips or rigs some 6 m to 12 m (20 ft to 40 ft) wide with waste-land between.

These strips were reallocated from time to time. Outwith this 'infield' was the 'outfield' or grazing area of common land.

According to Donaldson, land on the Mey estate was divided into penny-land ( =4.8 hectares =12 acres), half-pennyland, farthingland and octos. Smaller tenants had holdings of some two farthinglands ( =2.4 hectares =6 acres). Most tenants seem to have had cows, oxen and horses. Grain-growing, particularly bere and oats, was the predominant agricultural interest, with stock-rearing on the uplands which were mainly common land, e.g. the Latheron area. There was a considerable surplus of grain and buyers used to send ships mainly to Staxigoe and Thurso to carry the cargoes south. At these two ports large storehouses were erected. In a good year some 2,540,000 kg (2,500 tons) might be shipped.

Maintaining livestock over the winter period posed quite a problem as root crops were unknown. Sheep as well as cattle were taken indoors. Straw was used as a winter keep with perhaps a few sheaves for the horses — which were exported from Orkney to Caithness. Many animals, then, had to be sold or slaughtered before the onset of winter. By spring the retained cattle were almost starving. Sheep were small in stature, of poor quality and with short-haired fleeces. Lambs were separated when very young from the ewes so that the household could obtain milk.

Lairds usually rented the land directly to tenants. The 'tacksman' — an intermediary between tenant and laird — who was so common in the Highlands, seems to be less in evidence in Caithness. The tenant held his land by paying rent to the laird in kind (e.g. bere, meal, oatmeal, hens, geese, eggs, calves, pigs, peats, etc.) as well as money. From his bowman the laird received a regular supply of butter and cheese in addition to rent in money. Lowest in the social order was the cottar who was a poorly paid servant with a tiny holding of perhaps 0.6 hectares (1½ acres). Quite a common method used by lairds for distributing land was the 'wadset' — whereby the owner could sell land but had the right of redemption at any time.

By the early 18th century hay was available and so more animals could be kept over winter. Salt was in great demand for preserving meat; probably some of it was obtained from the salt-pans at the mouth of the Brora River.

Until the 18th century the plough used was a primitive construction known as the "thrapple plough". The plough's beam was nearly the same length as the modern plough with a sole and mould boards of wood. To effectively turn the soil this cumbersome plough required the efforts of three people and a few beasts of burden; their conjoined efforts ploughed a mere 0.1 hectares (¼ acre) per day.

To fertilise the land people applied seaweed, compost, manure, old thatch and lime, which was used from an early date. Lime was taken from Stroma to the mainland of Caithness. It was also obtained from Reay and from many lochs in the County where marl had accumulated (see Chapter 5).

The burning of kelp to make alkali was certainly established in Caithness early in the 18th century. It was burned in shallow pits, fused into a compact mass and was then shipped south.

Grain was separated from the straw by using a 'flail' — a staff hinged by leather to a handle. Oats would then be winnowed in hand riddles or on hill tops known as "shilling hills", or in barns so constructed that the wind would pass through — e.g. the barn at Lhaid Haye, Dunbeath (ND 175307).

Most of the tenants and cottars had to work exceptionally long hours. From March to October they would work from 4 a.m. till 7 p.m. with two one-hour breaks. In winter and slack months peat was dug and taken home on horseback.

## Social Conditions

The early houses were built of sods or stone reinforced with clay, the roofs being of turf, sometimes overlaid with straw. The thatch was held down by straw ropes ("simmons"). Later, flags were used as a roofing material, tiles not being introduced until the mid 17th century. Holes in the walls of houses were stuffed with straw or moss. In the centre of the earth floor was a peat-burning fire whose reek escaped through a hole in the roof, which, in foul weather, was plugged by bracken. From the 'rantle-tree' above the fire hung the cooking utensils.

The house was divided into two sections, a 'firehouse and cellar' — a 'but and ben'. Humans, livestock and poultry shared the same door, the byre being separated from the livingroom by a partition of flagstones.

When the early type of house which lodged both men and beast was departed from, cattle were transferred to a separate building ,which was usually built on to the dwelling house, with a passage between the two.

Inside the houses, the atmosphere was dim with an ever-present pall of peat reek which stained the skin a brown colour and made it very leathery. Light was obtained from the peat fire or some small windows, often just a skylight. Seldom used was the primitive light of a wick stuck in a container, perhaps of fat. Decayed firtree roots, mostly dug up from the moss and impregnated with resin, were used as torches.

A later development was the making of candles from animal fat.

Furnishings were sparse and of simple design. A typical cottage would have stools, a table, rough cupboards built into the wall and a 'dresser' made of flagstones. A heather 'besom' (brush) was used for sweeping.

The earliest beds were stone recesses filled with straw, heather or sheep-skins. Overhead protections were then added to safeguard the sleeper from falling soot. From this piece of improvisation probably evolved the 'box-bed'.

The gentry were dressed in splendid finery whether they could afford it or not. However, the typical garment worn at this time by the mass of men was the belted plaid — the kilt was unknown until the 18th century. Underneath the plaid a coarse woollen shirt was worn. Women wore a plaid of the same material.

An interesting social account of the County was given by John Elder of

Caithness who, c. 1542, made a map of Scotland and forwarded it to Henry VIII. The map has been lost but the letter is still in the British Museum. In his letter Elder says " . . . for boithe somer and wynter (except where the froest is mooste vehemente) goynge alwaies bair leggide and bair footide, our delite and pleasure is not only in huntynge of redd deir, wolfes, foxes and graies, whereof we abound and have greate plentie." . . . "The delicatt gentillmen of Scotland call us Redshanks."

Wool was spun on the distaff and spindle; the spinning wheel came at a much later date.

Footwear, rarely worn, was known as 'rillins' — untanned horse or cow hide strapped round the foot with thongs, the hairy side outward.

Although food was monotonous, most people received adequate sustenance apart from the major famines of 1634 and 1671 when crops failed because of heavy rain. During these famines people killed their dogs for food and many died from starvation before Government help arrived. On the whole, people here seem to have been better off than most of their northern neighbours as few of the famines that scourged the Highlands influenced Caithness. Elder's account and Donaldson's evidence in the Mey Papers suggest this. Moreover, Caithness seems to have been the only place north of Inverness with enough surplus food to maintain Cromwell's troops.

Oatmeal and bere were the stuff of life, and were often given to servants as a considerable part of their income, as coins were few and often foreign. Moreover, Scottish coins were all called in after the Union in 1707. From oatmeal was made porridge, gruel and oatcakes. This diet was usually accompanied by milk obtained from the ewe, goat or cow with butter and cheese in the summer. Fish added some variety to the fare, but to the cotter and many tenants, meat was a luxury they could not afford. A popular dish, introduced in the late 17th century, was 'kail'. No fork or knife was used at a meal, only the wooden or horned spoon. Plates were usually of wood; no earthenware articles appeared until the latter part of the 17th century.

The drudgery of life was often lightened by boisterous social occasions. There were fairs, country dances, weddings and funerals. A Caithness funeral was merrier than many an English wedding! On such occasions large quantities of the favourite beverage, ale, were dispensed and smuggling of the other alchoholic beverages was rife.

The common ailments of the time were ague and rheumatism. Healing was mainly in the hands of apothecaries whose favourite cure was 'blood-letting' by means of leeches. Many of the prescriptions they concocted resembled the contents of the witches' cauldron in Macbeth!

Yet many of the old women appear to have had a useful knowledge of the value of herbs as medicines; they called them "healing bladies". One type of application called 'trets' consisted of strips of cotton dipped in animal fat, hung up to dry and stored for future use as poultices. Such dressings were soon covered in mould but had healing properties probably contained in the penicillin-like mould.

In view of the many primitive and doubtful medical skills available to them, small wonder the supernatural was often invoked. Charms were worn for protection and the rowan-tree was the symbol for warding off evil. There was a common fear of the 'changeling' child and the 'uncanny eye'. By the early 17th century witchcraft was looked on with horror, and the Church was most zealous in dealing with 'suspects'.

## The Towns
### Wick

In 1503 Wick, then a tiny settlement, was made the seat of the Sheriff Court. When made a Royal Burgh by James VI in 1589 Wick was a small village of thatched houses. Such a Royal Burgh was a privileged community granted rights by the monarch to help it develop trade. From 1589 to 1707 Wick sent its own Commissioner to the Scottish Parliament.

In 1656 Wick had no vessels while Thurso had two sloops of 30,000 kg (30 tons) each. Wick's population at this time must have been some 600 people. The town had 10 merchants, 6 tailors, 5 weavers, 4 smiths, 5 shoemakers, 4 coopers and 4 glovers. Moreover, the burgh records for 1660 show a great variety of goods in the town's trading: bere, trees, beef, mutton, pork, butter, cheese, cloth, wool, tallow, hides, ale, 'aqua vity', mill stones, grave stones, and free stones.

The burghers of Wick and Thurso had a virtual monopoly of commerce. A man could become a burgher by heredity, purchase, or marriage. Burgher's daughters were always at a premium! Non-burghers were called 'unfreemen' and had no say in how the town was governed.

After the 1707 Union fishing fell into decline; only from the two towns was it a full-time occupation.

### Thurso

The historian Torfaeus called Thurso 'oppidum Cathnesiae' — the town of Caithness. In 1633 Thurso was made a free burgh of barony by Charles I (which gave it commercial privileges more limited in scope and diversity than those of the Royal Burgh).

In the Middle Ages Thurso had an important trade with the continent and for nearly two centuries it was the chief seat of the Sheriff Court. By the mid-17th century Thurso had a considerable export of meal, beef, pork, skins, hides, oil, tallow, and fish. Its main imports were timber, iron, salt and wine.

On the north side of Shore Street a part of 17th century Thurso remains in the form of a circular turret standing out in the centre of the housing frontage.

## Transport

The principal means of transport during the period under consideration was by horse. Not a single road existed in the County and this meant that Caithness by land was virtually isolated from the south, communication being much easier by sea. Exports and imports were carried principally through the ports of Thurso and Staxigoe, commodities such as grain and meal being taken to the ports on pack horses. The horses carried a wooden saddle called a "clibber" and baskets of wicker work (crubbans), or straw bags (cazies) were fastened to the saddle. Each of these containers held a quantity of 130 kg (2 bolls). The horses went in single file, the halter of each tied to the tail of the one in front. Women also acted as beasts of burden and carried heavy wicker baskets on their backs.

The earliest form of public transport was supplied by "currors" or foot-runners who carried letters, money or articles of value. The last of them, David Allan, died in Halkirk in 1797.

Drove roads do not seem to have become significant until the 17th century, when drovers from the north would converge on Spittal before moving south. There was also a popular drove track from Reay to the south, via Altnabreac.

1726-37 was a time of road building in the Highlands under the direction of General Wade. The old road bridges over the Reisgill and Latheronwheel burns are said to belong to this period. Prior to this date burns and rivers were crossed by a ford with a ferry service crossing the Thurso river near its mouth. The '15 rebellion had stimulated the growth of communication links; the '45 was just around the corner.

# CHAPTER 17

# SINCE THE "FORTY FIVE"

In Caithness, no less than in the rest of Scotland, the Forty-Five may truly be regarded as a watershed in history. This is true for many reasons, political, social and economic, so closely intertwined as to be inseparable. It is no light matter to be the losing side in a civil war, and the Highlands had suffered that supreme misfortune. History books have always been willing enough to relate the atrocities that immediately followed defeat, but thereafter a long silence ensued. The sufferings of the Highlanders in the two hundred years that followed were kept discreetly quiet, and during the terrible Clearance period no person of standing in public life made any sustained protest on their behalf, such as, for instance, Wilberforce made on behalf of slaves in distant lands. The ruthless driving out of Highlanders from their own land was permitted and aided by law.

At first sight it may seem that too much is being made of the matter in a chapter purporting to deal with Caithness, but inevitably Caithness was, and continues to be, deeply affected by events in its immediate neighbourhood. Not that Caithness **wanted** to be involved in the Forty-Five. Few counties in Scotland could have been less involved. True, the lairds were Jacobite in sentiment, and loyally drank toasts to the Stewart cause, but, although there was some oddly suspicious behaviour, most of them took good care to do no more than to express their sentiments, except to pay part of the land tax to a party of rebels who scoured Caithness for recruits. There seem to have been two exceptions, Sinclair of Geise and the Laird of Dunn. The former, and four of his tenants, were the only Caithness men arrested for complicity in the rebellion. The Laird of Dunn also intended to pay more than lip service to the cause; he instructed his factor, Finlayson, to assemble his tenants and their oldest sons to march to the Hill of Spittal. The women, however, took action; they hid the men in peat stacks and under corn sheaves, and themselves took over the ploughing. The Laird was so mortified that he shot himself, whereupon the men re-emerged and life returned to normal.

This is an illuminating story. Many of the Highland prisoners of the Forty-Five pleaded in their defence that they had been forced into service by their chiefs, but the Dunn story clearly indicates a very different relationship between laird and tenant, certainly not that close bond of kinship, blood and loyalty of the Highland clan.

In the circumstances, the time-wasting prudence of the Caithness lairds paid dividends. The County was spared the attentions of Cumberland and his underlings. It was not, however, spared the effects of the legislation that followed. The abolition of the heritable jurisdictions operated in favour of justice ultimately, but the conversion of clan chiefs into landowners who held the land as their personal property opened the way to the fearful abuses that followed.

The new landlords had tasted the sweetness of gracious living in London, but gracious living requires money, and less than fifty years after Culloden they realised how they could raise the money — out of their estates. The Napoleonic Wars had created a demand for wool for uniforms, and meat, so why not turn these Highland valleys and grazings into sheep farms? There was only one snag — the Highland people lived there. That presented no great difficulty. All that was necessary was legal notice to quit, presented by the Sheriff-Officer. If the people proved recalcitrant, troops could be, and were, called in to enforce the law. And so, over a period of ninety odd years, the Highlands were systematically drained of their people, with the utmost ruthlessness, in circumstances like those of war.

Somewhere it has been remarked that not the least of the tragedy was that the Highlanders, many of whom were undoubtedly living in conditions of great poverty, often of starvation, were driven out at the very time when their prospects were improving. The Agricultural Revolution was in full swing farther south, but owing to the inevitable time lag and the depressed situation following the 'Forty-Five', it had not then penetrated the Highlands and was not allowed to.

Now, although Caithness had managed to keep clear of the troubles of the 'Forty-Five', it could not avoid the Clearances, and it is one of the grim ironies of history that Sir John Sinclair, one of the very few lairds who was genuinely interested in the welfare of his tenants, was actually an early evictor. He knew of the great performance of the new, improved Cheviot or mountain sheep, of the much finer wool and the heavier carcass, and he was anxious to try them out on his estate so that he could, from personal knowledge, recommend their introduction to his tenants. But he needed somewhere to try out the experiment, and for this he selected Langwell, a valley in the south of Caithness. But Langwell had people in it, eighty-six families. They could, however, be accommodated elsewhere, and the great experiment tried out. And they were, at Badbea, a hilly, precipitous area, north of the Ord, right on the edge of a great wall of cliffs.

### Social Conditions

At this point it becomes necessary to turn back to consider the actual living conditions in Caithness during the second half of the 18th century.

There were, of course, very different living conditions among the various social classes of Caithness at this period. At the upper end of the scale, were the lairds, who were **in,** but not **of** the County. According to Donaldson's "Caithness in the 18th century", the Caithness lairds, the majority of them Sinclairs, lived in splendid isolation, remote from tacksmen and tenants. They were a little, closed community, who enjoyed one another's hospitality and kept in close touch with each other. They could, after all, commandeer the services of a tenant to walk across Caithness to deliver a letter to a friend. They spoke excellent English and were devoted Episcopalians. They lived the life of Jane Eyre's Rochester and his circle. With rents in kind and the grain crops of Caithness for income, and with almost unlimited right to call on the services of their tenants, they fared very well indeed.

At the other end of the scale is the picture of their tenants painted by Pennant, in 1779. Life was very primitive. The women were beasts of burden, even carrying dung in baskets (cassies) on their backs. "The common people here are kept in great servitude, and most of their time is given to their lairds, an invincible impediment to the prosperity of the country."

One writer, after giving minute details, observed that some of these services which had been converted to money rent were still being exacted as formerly. He thought that legislation was needed to abolish such practices.

Housing conditions were grim. The windowless houses were built either of stone for about 1 m (3 ft), and then feal (turf), or, in many cases, entirely of turf. The roof was supported by tree trunks which reached from the ground, meeting to form an inverted V. The roof itself was formed of divots, thatched with heather or rushes. The fire was in the middle of the floor, and a hole was left in the roof, not directly above it, in case heavy rain might extinguish the fire, but rather to a side. The livestock shared the house quite freely; cattle were in a partition beyond, separated only by a low flag division with a straw mat for a kind of door, while pigs, hens and smaller creatures mingled freely with the people. On the other side of the kitchen was the sleeping quarters, the cellar. At first the bed was merely a shakedown of heather with sheepskin coverings, but later the box bed, a wooden bed with a ceiling and doors, was introduced. Except for firelight, the place was dark and foul. Robert Dick, in 1830 wrote, "Many of the poor people never saw the sun until they came out and sat down at the end of their cots."

Joiner-made furniture hardly existed. Caithness flagstone made do for dresser and table. Crockery was non-existent. Wooden bowls and horn spoons were the eating utensils. Flat stones served as plates.

Their food consisted mainly of some form of oat meal or bere meal — brose, porridge brochen, sowens and 'burstins'. (See Chapter 28). They got, however, some of the butter and cheese they made in summertime.

However, the position of Caithness on the seaboard, near rich fishing grounds, made a considerable difference to life. Although fishing was not carried on commercially until the last decade of the century, fishing for the family was an old-established habit and the majority of Caithness folk were able to have either fresh or dried fish for a considerable part of the year, and in very hard times they eked out with limpets and 'wilks' (periwinkles). After all, seven of the ten parishes border the sea, and even the inland ones, Watten, Bower and Halkirk are not far from it, and have rivers and lochs themselves. Moreover, there would be an occasional treat of pork or mutton. "Canisbay had an abundance of swine." They also had vegetable gardens containing cabbage and sybots (small onions).

Ale throughout the year, and milk when the cows were milking — there would be little or none in winter — were the beverages.

The fare was sufficient, but must have been rather monotonous. However, and this is most important, **Caithness people did not suffer from hunger.**

According to the appendix to Calder's "History of Caithness," the dress of the lower order of both sexes was very plain, consisting entirely of woollen stuffs of home manufacture. The men wore coats, vests and breeches of black or hodden gray. The women wore plain drugget (a coarse woollen material). Older women wore scarlet plaid; some managed a blue short gown with red sleeves.

"The woollen stuff of home manufacture" was, later in the century, made by itinerant tailors, who stayed in the home of the customer until the job was done. Travelling shoemakers followed. The farmer, who did the tanning himself, provided the cloth and the leather, Presumably the brogues of tanned leather, costing 8p to 13p (1/6 to 2/6), were their best. For working purposes they wore "rillins", untanned leather boots tied with thongs, with the hairy side outwards. Very large numbers of people went barefoot for a considerable part of the year, some, particularly young people, all the time.

By the last decades of the century, however, linen was an established industry, and linen underwear was coming into use. Several writers in the Old Statistical Account assert that rheumatism had been unknown in the County before the wearing of linen began. It is worth recalling that the body of a man found in a Lyth moss (he was believed to have been a fugitive of the '45 period) was clad completely in two sets of woollen clothing, now in the Museum of Antiquities in Edinburgh.

On the face of things, Caithness seemed almost entirely in the Middle Ages until the advent of the Improvers and the Agricultural Revolution. Yet it was not entirely so. It had always managed to grow good crops of oats and bere, and the position of the people was not quite so hopeless as the above account would suggest. Donaldson observed from the Mey papers that it was possible for a tenant to move from one estate to another. He noted another unexpected point — the Mey tenants were sufficiently literate to conduct their business affairs.

Momentous changes, however, were on the way. Tea appears in the gentry's accounts in 1754, and whisky is mentioned in the Wick records in 1758. By 1776 there were between eighty and ninety stills in the County, and both the Old and the New Statistical Accounts make constant reference to excessive drinking. It had quickly become a serious social problem.

1754 was the year of yet another revolution — the introduction of the potato. At first the new vegetable was confined to the gardens of the gentry, but larger numbers of the people began to cultivate it, and by the time of the Old Statistical Account potatoes are mentioned regularly as one of the crops.

1767 was yet another landmark in our history, for in that year the herring fishing started, and although it was not an immediate success, it was definitely established by 1790. Thus within less than forty years the staple dinner of the great majority of Caithness folk for well over a century was being produced: tatties and herring, followed by a cup of tea. A complete revolution in eating habits had been established.

Let us, then, take a look at Caithness as it must have appeared about 1780: low-lying, bleak and treeless, with no roads, only some fearfully potholed tracks. The majority of the houses were hovels. The only cheerful sight on the landscape would be excellent crops of bere and rather less excellent ones of oats. A fair number of small black cattle, garrons (small, sturdy, native horses) and small, coarse-woolled sheep of many colours herded by children or women on the commons. The laird's house would be rather different — a rather low, two-storied house with crow-stepped gables and heavy slate roof. His garden would be enclosed and fairly well stocked.

The towns were little better — small, dirty places; thatched houses with no water or sanitation, peat stacks in most cases and a byre attached, for the townsfolk had their cattle and their pigs too. In both Wick and Thurso townspeople had livestock within the burgh boundaries until well on in this century. Donald Grant, in "Old Thurso," records the efforts, usually unavailing, of the authorities in Thurso to keep livestock under control and to keep the town a bit cleaner. The files of the "John O'Groat Journal" show that the sale of dung was at one time a source of revenue to Wick, which sorely needed it!

Apart from the great stores where grain and meal were kept for shipping at Thurso and Staxigoe (the latter is still in use for other storage purposes), the only buildings of interest and dignity were a few churches, e.g. Thurso's beautiful Old St Peter's, the pre-Reformation churches of Canisbay and Dunnet, and Reay Church built in 1739.

Not the least important difference, two hundred years ago, was that there was not a single harbour round the coast of Caithness; there was no harbour between Cromarty and Stromness.

Change, however, was on the way, and was in fact taking place quite rapidly. Despite the poor roads it is recorded in the Old Statistical Account for Halkirk that there were 220 carts of different sizes. The Dunnet record makes the same point. There was a manufactory for them in Thurso in 1797, employing thirteen wrights and four blacksmiths.

It is worth while noting here how events and developments elsewhere were influencing Caithness. Regarding Reay in the Old Statistical Account, it is noted that in 1773 several families had emigrated to North America. But the American War of Independence broke out and Reay furnished the greater part of two companies of Fencibles during that war. In 1788 "some poor people and one or two reduced families went to the cotton mills in Lanark and Stanley."

Dunnet found another outlet for its unemployed. The writer noted a great disproportion between the sexes (males 645, females 754) owing to the number that enlisted with different recruiting parties during the American War; a great many had gone to sea, others to Hudson's Bay, and yet others south.

Sir John Sinclair found something different in Thurso; Caithnessmen were by then showing less inclination to go to the army, although they made excellent soldiers, but during and after the Napoleonic wars they had been going into the navy, for which they had previously shown little inclination. Could the press gang have made the difference? Extremely interesting press gang tales even yet are current, and Neil Gunn specifically refers to them in "The Silver Darlings."

The Canisbay men became soldiers, and the Rev. Dr Morrison credits them with "a more enlarged knowledge of their country and a more extensive acquaintance and correspondence with one another than obtain among the peasantry of any other part of Great Britain." This is in line with Donaldson's remarks about the degree of literacy in Mey. It is worth noting that one of the Canisbay soldiers, a Mowat from Freswick, settled in Canada and became the father of Sir Oliver Mowat, one of the great advocates of the union of Canada into a Dominion, and later Prime Minister of Ontario.

## THE IMPROVERS

The name of Sir John Sinclair, born in 1754, the year of the introduction of tea and potatoes, is justly associated with improvement in agriculture, but he was not the first improver in Caithness. That honour is sometimes credited to Sheriff Traill, owner of Olrig, but from the Old Statistical Account it would appear that his father, the Rev. George Traill of Hobbister, has probably a greater title. It was he who erected a lint-mill, a barley-mill, and a corn-mill, and also a threshing machine, all, excepting the lint-mill, moved by one wheel and driven by the same stream. His son, the Sheriff, was a resident laird, and his name shines in our history, for he carried out improvements which today give Castletown and Olrig a special appearance, and he had regard to his tenants while doing so.

He started the flagstone industry — the beautiful Regency streets recently built in the south needed good pavements — and thus had an alternative industry close at hand to offer those who were displaced by the union of very small crofts into larger holdings, and it was noted that he would not evict a widow.

It is abundantly clear then from the Old Statistical Account that Caithness desperately needed improvement, but that improvement on a considerable scale was already in train, and giving good results, which brings back us to the extraordinary case of Sir John Sinclair.

John Prebble, in "The Highland Clearances" has this to say of him: "He was probably the only Scot of his age who used the word 'improvement' objectively. Had he been listened to, had his example been copied, the half-century of evictions, burnings, riots and exile that followed might have been avoided. It was the kindly old man's tragedy that he brought the Great Sheep north for the benefit of his people, but was unable to prevent others from using it to oust theirs."

It does not seem to occur to 'improvers' of any age, 'planners', we would call them now, that the kindest thing that can be done to most people is to leave them alone to get on with their own business, if it is a legitimate one, however much better the improver thinks it can be done! Sir John needed ground to experiment with his sheep, and he wanted it done on a fairly large scale, so Langwell was 'cleared' and its people sent to break in Badbea. From the planner's point of view the move made sense. The herring fishing was rising fast — men could be absorbed into it. Agricultural improvement was the fashion of the day: draining, ditching, enclosing, building. There was need for farm servants, labourers, and all kinds of skilled men. And there were the armed forces; the French in 1792 were an ugly proposition! There would be no lack of work for the evicted Langwell tenants.

The Langwell tenants, however, did not seem to see things in quite the same light. Driven from a sheltered inland valley they do not seem to have enjoyed their eyries near the cliffs of Badbea. Tradition has it that the weaver had to tether his children to prevent them from being blown over the rock. Ulitmately, but not for two generations or so, not until after Holy John had left a light to guide the fishermen home by night while he prayed for them, they betook themselves to New Zealand, and Badbea returned to desolation.

The sheep, however, flourished and became one of the great assets of modern Caithness, the North Country Cheviot.

Sir John did not set the example — that had been done two years earlier in Ross-shire. He made what he regarded as reasonable provision for the evicted; he allowed them to settle on another part of his estate. There is evidence that he repented the terrible blunder, for blunder it proved to be, but he could not undo it. Lairds all over the Highlands saw the possibilities of wealth from sheep, and the Clearances gathered momentum.

## THE CLEARANCES

As Caithness Clearances were not attended by the atrocities committed elsewhere, particularly in Sutherland and Ross-shire, they have been little publicised, but they took place, nevertheless. In addition to the Langwell valley, Brubster, Shurrery and Shebster (all in the parish of Reay), were also cleared (192 families). There were evictions to make way for the farm of Noss near Wick. Some families were evicted from the Ha' Green of Duncansby and went to Stroma. The New Statistical Account (1841), without using the actual word "clearance" refers to other clearances, in Watten, for instance; and the Rev. Charles Thompson of Wick spoke out clearly on the matter.

Nevertheless, when that has been said, it must be allowed that the Caithness Lairds came considerably better out of the whole cruel business than most others in the Highlands. Elsewhere the people were driven out wholesale, without any warning or any provision for their welfare. Many settled in Caithness and a considerable number of the present inhabitants of the County are descended from these refugees. Temple Sinclair, of Lybster, practically started Lybster on its career as a fishing village in order to provide a livelihood for the evicted.

The New Statistical Account throws a great deal of light on the position.

Gaelic had been on the decline in Latheron, but "the importation of several colonies of Highlanders from the heights of Kildonan and other parts of Sutherlandshire about twenty years earlier" had given it a boost. There was a sharp dividing line between Gaelic and English — the Burn of East Clyth. "On the eastern side of it scarcely a word of Gaelic was either spoken or understood, and on the west side, English shared the same fate."

The New Statistical Account was written in 1840, some forty-five to fifty years after the Old One, and the following extract from the account of Latheron just referred to shows how marked the advance in housing conditions had been. "The old hovels are fast disappearing and neat substantial houses, having vents or chimney tops in one or both ends, are occupying their places." The people were cleaner and neater, and in danger of dressing beyond their means. The Caithness love of dress seems to have bothered quite a few of the gentlemen who wrote the accounts, both Old and New. "The ordinary food consists of oat and bear (sic) meal, potatoes and fish of various kinds, of which there is usually an abundant supply." In the latter article few parishes are possessed of equal advantages, for, "in addition to the opportunities of obtaining white fish of excellent quality when the weather is moderate, each family lays in a regular stock of from one to three barrels of cured herring, according to the number of persons of which it consists. This, with potatoes, milk and a moderate quantity of bread, together with a little animal food occasionally, forms a wholesome and nourishing diet, at all seasons."

That paragraph sums up living conditions in rural Caithness until the outbreak of the First World War.

Before proceeding further, one curious and constantly recurring item of the second Account is worthy of comment. The minister's stipend and the teacher's salary were paid in kind — so many chalders of oatmeal and bere. There was usually a cash allowance, £10 or under, for communion elements. One must assume that very little specie was current at the time. And Scots measures were used; chalders, bolls, mutchkins and chopins.

To return, however, to the account of Latheron. There is a paragraph in that same article which introduces something very unusual in Caithness history — crop failure, for three successive years previous to 1840. The writer observes that the hardship was borne passively; there was no riot, robbery or bloodshed. "To behold 7000 people suffering under the most distressing destitution for three successive years, many families without a handful of meal in their houses for weeks together, others satisfied with a little water-gruel once a day, and still nothing but quietness and submission prevailing, what a triumph for that sound

Scriptural education to which they are early habituated, and consequent religious principle of which it seldom fails to be productive." It evidently did not occur to the Rev. Mr Davidson that the submissive spirit of a starving people might be due to other causes, to a broken spirit and want of hope. He noted with satisfaction their strict Sabbath observance and church going.

Like nearly all the writers in both Accounts he comments on the heavy drinking. He attributes the suppression of smuggling and illicit distilling to the activities of a "gauger" called M'Mahon, whose name was a terror to all Caithness, but from the number of convictions for illicit distilling after the date of publication (1841) one suspects that Mr M'Mahon was not as successful as Mr Davidson was led to believe.

To revert to the subject of the influx of Clearance victims. Caithness was ready and willing to receive them, for the County was entering on its boom century. The herring fishing was established and expanding as fast as men and boats could be found. As the subject is being dealt with in another chapter, it is not necessary to enter into detail here, except to mention its far-reaching economic significance to the north.

### Crofter-Fishermen

It was a basic assumption that a croft did not in itself provide a full livelihood. The croft provided a house, milk and meal, eggs, vegetables and maybe pork, but the rest of a man's livelihood had to come from some other source, and for many a crofter-family on the seaboard parishes that extra income came from, or was related to, the sea.

The crofter-fisherman depended on the fishing for money for his rent, and there was a cottage industry attached to it, the making of nets, first from hemp, and later, from cotton. All over the countryside women made these nets, and carried them to Wick, where the ropes were put on them. Later, women worked in networks set up in Wick, for the herring fishing involved many ancillary industries.

Let us then, before departing from the subject, survey the crofter-fisherman's year. During the winter he ploughed, and maybe mended nets at night. If he had a very small croft he would have only one horse, and work with a neighbour similarly situated, for a pair of horses was needed for the plough. If he had a bigger place, he might manage to keep a pair himself. Garrons, or garron crosses, were still preferred on crofts to the mighty, gluttonous, oat-eating Clydesdale of the big farms. He ploughed and cleaned the ground for his root crops, sowed his seed, "set" (planted) his potatoes, attended to the lambing of his small flock of sheep, in some areas went to the lobster fishing for a short time (lobster fishing was another development of the 1790's), cut his peats, sowed his turnips, went to the herring fishing, came home, carted his peats if his wife and family had not already done so, cut his corn with the scythe (the reaper, the "back-delivery", came much later), while his wife and/or children lifted and bound it, secured the harvest, lifted the potatoes, and then either went to the Yarmouth fishing which lasted till early December, or in some cases went labouring to the big farms or any building construction works on hand.

It should be observed that skilled craftsmen, such as weavers, carpenters, masons and so on nearly all had a small patch of land (a "dellin") small enough to be delved. They also went to the fishing, an activity which zealous improvers thought ridiculous.

(A. Luciani)

PLATE 22.   *Old Caithness croft, Lhaid Haye, Dunbeath.*

(A. Luciani)

PLATE 23.   *Old 18th century bridge (now removed) and new bridge at Halkirk.*

(A. Luciani)

PLATE 24.   *The only working grain mill in Caithness, at Huna.*

(R. Stewart)

PLATE 25.   *Memorial at Badbea, Ousdale, commemorating the people of this Clearance Settlement.*

There was one class of skilled craftsmen whose achievements even yet are of importance — the boat carpenters of Stroma and John Banks of Duncansby. So superb was their modelling and their craftsmanship that many of their yawls, larch on oak, are still in service after a hundred years, and, says an enthusiastic owner, will last another hundred if properly looked after. The tradition is that when a Stroma carpenter got an order for a boat he went to the woodyard, studied the timber there, selected a trunk suitable for the size of his boat, measured it, allowing for waste in cutting and then gave instructions for sawing. He kept it for a year to make sure it was properly seasoned, and built for £1 per 30.5 cm (1 ft) of keel, including oars and masts. Sails were extra, usually made by an old sailor. These boats varied in length from 3.7 m to 5.5 m (12 ft to 18 ft) of keel.

Crofters, of course, were not farmers — mostly they were allowed to cultivate only the second rate land which it was scarcely worth while for big farmers to bother with, unless for rough pasture.

It was a corollary of the Clearances and the improving movement that land should be in big units, and so, on fertile land, small tenants were evicted to make way for big farms. Eight tenants, for example, were evicted to make way for the farm of Stainland, near Thurso. Later, other factors entered into the composition of farms; when the various Reform Acts were passed, land units were formed by the usual eviction method to make up a place with a sufficient rent to qualify the tenant for a vote. A vote was important.

Land was paying, paying so well that it was profitable for owners of large estates in other parts of the country, both England and Scotland, to buy Caithness estates. It is quite remarkable to observe the names of new landowners in the New Statistical Account.

Thus was introduced a factor which has been so detrimental to Caithness development, the absentee landlord. The New Statistical Account is full of complaints about non-resident heritors. The writer on Canisbay in 1840 complained of the almost total lack of development in the parish for this very reason.

It must be realised that these absentee landlords not only did not interest themselves in the development of their estates (that was left to the hated factors) but they bled the area white. Tenants were rack-rented without mercy; bitter tales even yet are current of evictions of people to make way for those who offered higher rents. The crofting areas had their full quota of neighbours who would offer a higher rent for a man's land. And the rents were spent outwith Scotland.

We have passed from Statistical Accounts into a new source of information — newspapers. With the increasing prosperity brought by the herring fishing and the steadily increasing literacy rate, newspapers came into being, the "John O' Groat Journal" in 1836, and the "Northern Ensign" in 1850. The latter, long since defunct, deserves more than passing mention for the valiant fight it put up for the sorely tried people of the north.

It reported meetings, it gave figures of rents for estates, for different years, and it was not the only newspaper to champion the cause. The Highlanders too, such as were left of them, began to realise the virtue of uniting to fight for themselves. They formed the Highland Land League; they sent their most gifted speakers to the cities in the south of Scotland where some of their evicted kinsmen had settled and made good. English newspapers began to report the

K

scandals of the Highlands. In 1882 the Liverpool "Daily Post" published an article on the subject; it noted that the agricultural rental of the Clyth estate which had been £2,925 in 1862-3 was then £4,325, and that, despite an alleged agricultural depression.

Under mounting pressure, Gladstone appointed a Crofters' Commission to investigate the situation. The Commissioners personally went round the area to see what was going on. One woman, on seeing them inspect the land, thought it was the factor preparing to raise the rent yet again. One of the Commissioners however, remarked "Poor land, mistress, poor land," and the rent was reduced! By an odd twist of fate, Gladstone was out of office by the time the Commission reported but Lord Salisbury, the Tory Prime Minister, accepted their findings and passed the Crofter's Holdings Act, which guaranteed security of tenure and compensation for improvements. It had been one of the bitterest grievances that a tenant who broke out more land was certain to have his rent increased and might even be evicted in favour of someone who would offer a higher rent.

And so, in 1886, a hundred and forty years after Culloden, some measure of protection was at last afforded the Highlanders.

Thereafter, many palliatives were tried to ease the problems of the crofters, none of them very successful. One, however, must rank as of prime importance. A Highlands and Islands Medical Services Board was set up, which organised a subsidised medical service for the area. The scheme worked well; for generations now there has been an effective medical service in the area — one that folk could afford. It was the prototype of others, including the National Health Service.

It may seem that too much space has been devoted to land grievances, but the matter was of far more than local importance. The dispossessed people who did not emigrate went in search of work to the industrial areas, where, as un-skilled labour in the days before Trade Union power, they were used to reduce the wages of skilled men. The Clearances and land troubles of Scotland as well as of Ireland contributed in no small measure to the industrial misery and squalor of Glasgow and south-west. They also contributed to the rise of the United States and Canada.

Yet 19th century Caithness was far from being a land of unrelieved gloom; it was, for many people, a place of refuge, a place where work could be obtained. The herring fishing had developed into an almost full-time job and the herring fleet followed the shoals round the fishing grounds, e.g. the west coast and the Yarmouth fishing. There was net-making, rope-making, coopering, shipping and carting. One farmer put forward the theory that the big farms round Wick owe much of their fertility to the amount of herring guts and horse dung that was carted on to them.

Another point that is apt to be forgotten is that the days of mass-production and ready-made goods had not yet arrived; milliners, dressmakers and tailors were still employed by shops, which were small factories as well as retail shops. Country districts had tailors, dressmakers, shoemakers, weavers, carpenters, blacksmiths, joiners, masons and other skilled men. Where one or two great basic industries were flourishing, there was also urgent need for these others.

And Caithness had yet another industry which needed a huge labour force — the flagstone industry. Traill shipped his first consignment in 1825, and the venture proved such a success that the village of Castletown and the harbour of Castlehill were built for the industry. Other quarries soon opened and for nearly a century proved a source of employment. At its height it employed about 1,000 men.

It must have been a century of quarrying, not only of flagstone, but also of building material. The fishing industry meant an enormous amount of building at Pulteneytown, Lybster, Keiss, and innumerable harbours. Wick has reason to be grateful to Sir John Sinclair, who, among his numerous activities, was one of the moving spirits of the British Fisheries Society, and one of the leading lights in developing the fisheries. He had much to do with the building of the first harbour, in 1810.

There was also a great burst of energy in farm building, not only houses and steadings, but dykes, for observant people will notice that there are many types of farm fencing in Caithness: built walls, flagstone fences, wire fences and hedges. An Orkney man named Louttit spent his life building the stone dykes round Keiss Mains — "The Square."

There was another less publicised form of quarrying — the quarrying done by crofters to build their own houses and steadings. Very often a man opened a quarry on his own croft.

The evolution of the crofter's house is a story in itself. From the miserable hovels described earlier he moved to a stone cottage with windows and chimneys. Such a house, most often built by communal labour, was sometimes built in two stages, beginning with a kitchen and closet. The closet end usually had a feal gable, to be removed when, at a later and more affluent period in life, an extra room was added. Thus the traditional croft house, a thatched cottage with a "but and ben" and a closet, came into being. Sometimes it was all built at the same time. If a mason was employed, he got £7 for the job. The earliest of these houses had clay for mortar; it was many decades later before lime was used.

These houses at first had no ceilings, but by the end of the century house-proud folk were fixing up cotton and/or paper ceilings to hide the divots. At a later stage wooden ceilings were put up. The kitchen had an open fire, and there was usually a grate in the ben end. They had flagstone floors, but some "uppish" people later on put wooden floors in their ben end. The vast majority were still thatched. It was a sign of considerable affluence if a man could afford a slate roof. The first slated roof in the parish of Canisbay belonged to the factor. The cottage is now a roofless ruin beside the Mill of Mey.

Furniture and furnishings had also come within the reach of ordinary folk. A new house would have a box bed, or maybe two built in back to back, the backs thus forming a partition between the kitchen and the closet. In the kitchen there would be a dresser (sideboard) with an aumbry, a huge plate rack at the back. Crockery was by now common and supplies were augmented from the usual source, the sea. Caithness sea-faring men seemed to have had a passion for bringing home bonnie china and dishes, and surely some of these treasures must still survive in some houses, too beautiful ever to be used. The men who shipped the herring to the Baltic brought home other gifts—amber jewellery for their womenfolk. With even a little prosperity had come the desire for, and the means to provide, a little grace and beauty.

Actually, by the end of the 19th century the kitchen of a well-doing fisherman or crofter-fisherman, with a house-proud wife, was a pleasant and comely place. With its cheerful open fire, either a clock on the mantlepiece or a "wag-at-the-wa", a wooden rocking chair, a spinning wheel, three or four plain wooden chairs, a meal-kist, a table, a dresser, papered walls and some sort of picture or text on the walls, a rag mat in front of the fire, and, of course, a box bed, it was an attractive home. The "room" or "ben end" would have an iron bed with brass knobs, a table, and maybe some chairs with seats upholstered with horse hair.

This might be described as the upper end of the scale for working folk, but not all crofters, fishermen or other working people reached that stage quickly, and there was one class who had little opportunity to do so — the farm servants. Here we must pause and consider another aspect of the Caithness scene, life on the big farms.

The big farmers of the County in the 19th century were a master race, in every sense of the word. In some cases they were incomers, brought in by the 'improvers', often necessarily, to introduce new methods. For the same reason south country farm servants were introduced, and there were also the shepherds who came in with the sheep. The farmers lived in commodious farm houses, while their servants lived in bothies, in much harder conditions than the crofters. The shepherds were the aristocrats of farm service; they got good cottages and fair terms. The farmers, however, with a few honourable exceptions, observed the employers' code of the period, to get as much work for as little pay as possible.

But the extraordinary diversity of quality of Caithness soil has actually led to an almost equal diversity of the social structure. Big continuous stretches of fertile land meant big farms (except the few that were broken up into holdings after the First World War). There are, however, smaller pockets of fertile land and much marginal land, which "smaller" men could break in, or move into, and so on, on an increasing scale. The result was that until fairly recently it was possible for a shrewd, capable, hardworking man to start in a small way, move in time to a bigger place and so on up the scale until he reached farm status, something that was much more difficult in counties that were mostly fertile and so laid out in big farms. This graduated scale did allow a limited number of native Caithnessians and Clearance descendants to make good on the land, and thus farming in Caithness is less rigidly stratified than in many other counties.

As the 19th century drew on the herring fishing reached its peak about the sixties and Pulteneytown, or "Poltney", to give it its familiar name, developed rapidly; men left other jobs and became full-time fishermen. Some of the crofter fishermen, however, retained their crofts and there used to be a plough-ing match at Thrumster where a "Skippers Cup" was awarded, only skippers being eligible to compete! Even yet, some of the fishing families retain the crofts in which their Clearance ancestors settled. Fishing, however, tended to become a full-time occupation and men moved to Pulteneytown or one of the fishing villages to pursue it, but many crofter-fishermen continued their dual existence until well on into the 20th century.

Before we leave the topic of the sea, it is desirable to add a paragraph about another little-known activity of the period — piloting. During the 19th century, when America was rising fast, a great volume of shipping passed through the Pentland Firth. These were the days of sail, of course, and it was necessary to engage a local pilot to take ships through. The rewards were high — three guineas for a fee — and very often salt meat and duty-free drink and tobacco were added to the fee. Ships coming from America signalled for a pilot long before they approached Dunnet Head, at the western end of the Firth — it was said that some of the more resourceful boats would linger out at sea watching for them — and ships going west signalled or "flagged" as they rounded Noss Head, to get a pilot before they reached the eastern end, Duncansby Head and the Pentland Skerries. There was keen competition for a ship and men would strip their shirts off and pull like mad to win. So keen were they on the job that a whole community left Nybster, north of Keiss, and settled at Ackergill, where the name "Pilots' Row" still commemorates them.

The winner of the race, for two or three boats would race for a ship, had usually two courses open to him when he had boarded the vessel. Either, he could send his own small boat, with its two-man crew, back home and trust to be landed on the other coast by the ship's boat after the Firth had been cleared. He then walked 32 km to 40 km (20 miles to 25 miles) home. West-bound ships used to land their pilot at Thurso. Or, the pilot could take his own crew aboard, let the ship tow his boat, and then he and his crew regained their own boat after the ship was in safe waters. It was an exciting, and could be a dangerous, game, and several boats were lost. If bad weather prevailed, the ship sometimes could not land the pilot and had to take him on to her port of destination. There were men known as "Savannah" and "Quebec". Tradition has it that "Quebec" reached there wearing slippers; he had not had time to put on his boots! If the herring fishing was the Caithness epic, piloting was certainly its saga.

The advent of steam gradually put an end to piloting, and most of these restless, hardy adventurers left the piloting districts, often to emigrate.

There was another occasional asset — wrecks. Here it must be made plain that there is no suggestion of deliberate wrecking. On the contrary, Caithness had, and still has, a very proud record of saving life. But natural hazards on a dangerous coast and the poor condition of many well-insured old ships did make wrecks a fairly common occurrence. Far more often than not they were horrible tragedies, with no benefit to anyone, and Caithnessmen themselves were often the victims. But occasionally there was a windfall. During the early days of the Free Kirk, when that communion had a big building problem, a cargo of timber was wrecked on the east coast, near Latheron, and bought by a zealous Free Kirk man, for cheap timber for the new kirks. The "Ohio" at Auckingill stocked many a householder with crockery for a lifetime, and the "Thyra" near Duncansby Head provided linen. One valuable side-line was timber for houses — many reconstructed houses on the north-east corner incorporated ships' timber in its structure. Occasionally, too, there was a salvage award, bringing valuable extra cash to the salvers, that little bit of unobtainable capital which could give a man a considerable "lift". But these cases apart, and they were very few, wrecks were a source of sorrow, not of profit, to Caithness.

References have been made occasionally both to emigration and immigration; that was one of the extraordinary features of the 19th century. There was a steady flow of settlers into Caithness, to the quarries, to the herring fishing, and to farm service, but at the same time there was a steady flow outwards, mostly to the Dominions and the United States.

It is interesting to note the effect, even yet, of the Clearances and the evictions on the attitude of the majority of Caithness men. They developed a passionate, even irrational, hatred of the gentry and the well-to-do. Few Caithness men, except maybe gardeners, would feel themselves honourably employed if they worked as personal servants for them. They emigrated, they went to whaling, they went to sea in the hardest of conditions, they persisted in going to the herring fishing even when its decline was obvious; they worked for a pittance in industrial cities, but they would not work for their oppressors or their descendants, even if innocent of wrong-doing. The women could not afford to indulge these sentiments; many of them had to become domestic servants, but the herring fishing offered them a tough alternative as herring gutters.

In the last decades of the century the boom was over; the herring fishing was in decline. The main cause was the gradual disappearance of the great herring shoals, but for a long time Caithness just could not believe it. Emigration stepped up. By the beginning of this century another industry was in trouble, the flagstone one. Increased freights were cutting profits and later developments in the use of concrete were almost to finish it.

The decline had not fully manifested itself when the First World War broke out, but that terrible tragedy and its early aftermath, the financial collapse of Germany, may be said to have administered the coup-de-grace to Wick, or at least to its staple industry. For Wick refused to die; it switched to white-fishing, and is still an important fishing port, but white fishing does not provide ancillary industries as the older one did. However, the setting up of one or two new industries in Wick and the new development site may provide a replacement for these losses. Thurso, its coasting trade and flagstone polishing gone, declined into little more than a beautiful village.

Rural Caithness suffered terribly. There seemed nothing for the survivors to come back to, and there was yet another rush of emigration, and the more marginal crofts began to assume that dreary aspect of decay which now marks some of the countryside.

### The Tinkers

One must not, in any account of this County, omit reference to one class of its people, the tinkers, believed by some to be descendants of the oldest of all Caithness races. Their history is curious, and tragic.

Up till about fifty years ago they had a definite place in our economy: they were the tinsmiths, the men who made the pails for milking and carrying water; they also made skellads (water-jugs shaped like a saucepan, with a long handle) and jugs. They used to live in caves round the shore, or in tents, but they travelled the country in summer time. They also sold dishes and other odds and ends and bought old clothes and rags. They worked, and they begged, and were recognised as "characters" by the countryside. But the introduction of enamel, and later the arrival of Woolworth's, killed their trade, and they became unemployed. At the same time developments in farming cut out their occasional employment as farm labourers. They still do some itinerant trading, mainly in vans, and some of them have set up as scrap merchants, but many of them are unemployed.

They are not "travellers" any more, to use the modern euphemism. Caithness long ago housed them in Council houses, but assimilation among the ordinary population has been slow, although there are occasional successful cases. Most of them are, in fact, a serious problem at the time of writing.

### Religion

Caithness was well to the fore in the troubles that overtook the kirk. But before launching into the main theme, it is worth recording a pleasant tale of gratitude. There was a cholera epidemic in Wick in 1832, and a very kindly person in that terrible spell was the Roman Catholic priest, Father Lovi, who attended all sufferers, indifferent to his personal danger. His loving kindness so moved the townsfolk that they gave the site for a chapel for him (St Joachim's Church) and, with a few exceptions, there has been little anti-Catholic bigotry in Wick.

Church relations are an extremely complicated tale, and the present writer cannot hope to unravel them, but it is fitting to return to our starting point — the adherence of the lairds to the Episcopal Church. Caithness had actually been slow to adopt the Presbyterian system, but by the 1830's it was well established. Now, the ruling class from whom Members of Parliament were then drawn were Anglicans, or Episcopalians, who were used to the idea that the landlord, or heritor, as the Scots called him, was entitled to present the clergyman to the parish. The practice came to be increasingly resented in Scotland, however, and there were very scandalous scenes at these forcible inductions. The induction scene in Galt's "Annals of the Parish" might well have been derived from an almost identical episode in Canisbay.

By 1843 the majority of Scots decided to sever their connection with the Established Church and form the Free Church of Scotland, the famous movement known as the Disruption.

It is impossible in an age which is indifferent to, or sceptical of, religion to convey the spirit of the times. There was genuine spiritual feeling in the movement but at the present time one cannot help feeling that the Disruption provided an outlet for many frustrations which were not fundamentally religious, and here it is time to consider their leaders.

Frequent reference has been made in this chapter to the Statistical Accounts, both of which were largely compiled by clergymen. A good deal of the personality of the writers comes through. We see a scholarly, shrewd, intelligent and observant band of men, with wide interests. Their interests had to be wide, for the Church was responsible for education and poor relief. It was these men who led their people out into the wilderness. The vast majority of Caithness congregations went "out" but the Canisbay minister, at the instance of his wife, it is said, remained in the Established Church and such was his personal popularity that a considerable section of the congregation remained with him. It is probably to this that we owe the preservation of that ancient building.

The lairds in some cases put every possible obstacle in the way of the seceders, who had to hold open-air services, but gradually resistance was worn down and the new manses and kirks were built entirely by voluntary subscription.

There was, however, no **doctrinal** dispute between the various Presbyterian bodies and later the majority of the Free Church decided to unite with another considerable body, the United Presbyterians, thus forming the United Free Church. This was opposed, however, by a minority of the Free Church, and again there was a gross misunderstanding of Scottish affairs in London — the award of the property of the majority of the Free Church to a minority! Special legislation had to be passed to rectify the situation. But the United Free Church had to build again. There was less bitterness in the last big union, that of the United Free Church with the Auld Kirk. The Parish of Latheron seems to have specialised in these schisms. One old Lybster lady used to boast that she had contributed to the building of three churches!

Other bodies are represented in the County too: Congregationalists, the Salvation Army and the oldest Baptist congregation in Scotland, at Keiss. The influx of people to Dounreay has considerably strengthened some of these bodies, particularly the Roman Catholic and Episcopal persuasions. Fortunately, they seem to have acquired the knack of living in neighbourly charity, or is it indifference?

### General

To return to secular affairs. The Second World War in some ways affected Caithness less than the First, despite the fact there were aerodromes and that many troops were stationed here. There were far fewer Caithness men killed in it, although this time civilians were killed, in Wick and at John O'Groats.

Things were not quite like the situation after the First War; there were fewer emigrants this time, because there were far fewer to go. This time another John Sinclair (now Lord Lieutenant) did something; he was the moving spirit in the Thurso Fish-selling Company which brought a fair number of boats to Scrabster, now also an important fishing port.

Yet the prospects looked poor until the establishment of an experimental nuclear reactor at Dounreay and the advent of the "Atomics." Although Dounreay contributed enormously to the prosperity of the County, an unpleasant feeling of fairy gold persists. For Dounreay is in Caithness, but not of it. It is not based on natural assets, and it is dependent over-much on government policy.

Modern developments have brought curious and unexpected results in the County. With modern standards of housing and amenities, better roads and a water supply (it was the first County in Scotland to supply the rural areas as well as the towns), electricity, motor transport and generous grants of all kinds to boost the once neglected countryside, things look worse than ever. Stroma, home of noted fishermen and boat-carpenters, is deserted; elsewhere, land wrested from the heather is going to rushes, not even reverting to its former wild beauty of heather. Possibly the most potent reason is the dearth of women. For country girls now find work in Wick or Thurso, where they have already been compelled to go to school. Every morning by car or bus they travel to the towns and quite eligible country bachelors, with good prospects, can scarcely find wives. Not the big farmers though; they can!

Dounreay, too, has caused a serious distortion of life throughout the countryside. Men and women living over 48 km (30 miles) away leave home before seven in the morning not returning home till after six, by which time they are too tired to take any part in the life of their own area, which is increasingly becoming a dormitory for them.

Another serious problem for Caithness is transport charges. One might say that it is only now that Caithness is feeling the full effect of the Clearances. Trains and buses running through the vast empty stretches of the Highlands just cannot pay, and the north is in serious danger of losing vital communications because Sutherland is empty. Developments at Invergordon will certainly not help this situation.

Yet it is not necessary to despair. There is a good deal of resilience in the County, and perhaps with judicious assistance from the Highland Development Board, a new Caithness may emerge, different outwardly, but retaining some of its finer qualities, its former ability to face formidable material difficulties, and its cheerful good humour, sometimes sardonic, sometimes kindly.

CHAPTER 18

# THE CASTLES OF CAITHNESS

The castles of Caithness, like all Scottish castles, are the most romantic man-made features of our landscape, dominating all others. The history of the stone-built castle begins during the 12th century with feudalism — the system by which responsibility for local government and ownership of land went hand in hand.

## THE NORSE CASTLES

During the Norman infiltration of southern Scotland, under the rule of the early kings of the Canmore dynasty, Caithness still lay under the subjection of Norway, ruled by the Norse earls of Orcadia, a province stretching from Shetland to the Dornoch Firth. The earliest Caithness castles — as distinct from the much earlier brochs — were undoubtedly built by these Norse invaders. The architecture of these early Norse structures was in fact closely allied to that of their Norman cousins, although much smaller and less sophisticated. Usually built on a rocky and inaccessible position on a pensinsula only large enough to contain the building and its defences, and with a sheer drop to the waves perhaps 30 m (100 ft) below, their keeps were small, unvaulted, rectangular in form and three or four storeys in height.

### Thurso

Strange to say, however, one of the earliest mentioned Caithness castles was not on a site of this kind but situated well in from the sea, at Ormlie, Thurso. The Orkneyinga Saga tells how, shortly after 1136, Earl Rognvald — the builder of St Magnus Cathedral — "having rode from Berriedale with a large retinue" held a conference at Thurso Castle, with his co-ruler Earl Harold, as a result of which the two earls were reconciled. Again, in 1196 it is recorded that William, King of Scots, having gathered a great army, sent it to Thurso, the town of Earl Harold (the Wicked), and destroyed his castle there. Although nothing now remains of the castle (which should not be confused with the much later Thurso-East) it is on record that in 1612 it was the seat of Sir John Sinclair of Greenland and Rattar.

### Bucholie

The other two main Norse settlements in Caithness about the middle of the 12th century, in addition to Thurso, were Freswick and Wick, and they too seem to have been protected and dominated by powerful castles. At Freswick the great castle of Lambaborg is first mentioned as the stronghold of Sweyn Asliefson, the celebrated Norse pirate whose exploits fill many pages of the Orkneyinga Saga. He is the reputed ancestor of the Caithness Swansons. It was the Mowats who, having received a charter of the lands of Freswick from King Robert the Bruce, brought the present name of Bucholie with them from

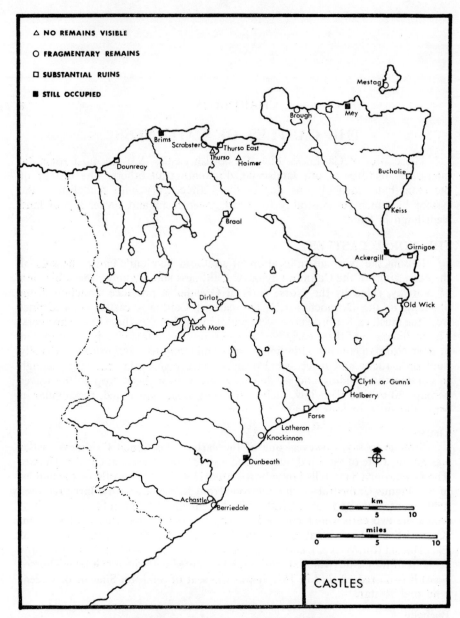

Figure 15.   Sites of the Castles of Caithness

their estate in Aberdeenshire. They remained in possession until 1661 when it was sold to Sinclair of Rattar.

Built upon a peninsular rock joined by a narrow neck of land — which had been cut through by a trench 1.8 m (7 ft) wide and 2.7 m (9 ft) deep, obviously spanned originally by a wooden movable bridge — the main keep rose from the edge of the trench. A passage from the doorway facing the land leads right through the keep to a long narrow courtyard beyond, with a range of buildings on each side of it. An unusual feature of the architecture is that the outer walls were built with an external batter.

The keep was small, measuring some 4.3 m (14 ft) by 6 m (20 ft) with walls 1.2 m (4 ft) thick at basement but narrowing as a result of the batter to about 0.8 m (2½ ft). The ground floor and second floor had been vaulted, while the intermediate floor had been supported on joists. From this one must assume that the structure was extensively altered during the centuries of Mowat occupation.

### Oldwick

Oldwick castle, near Wick, is a building of very great antiquity going far back into the Norse occupation era, although, unlike the castles of Thurso and Bucholie, there is no documentary evidence to support this statement. In the Sagas there is frequent mention of Wick, apparently a very important place and often visited by the great leading personages of the Norse ruling hierarchy, including Earl Rognvald. It must be assumed they stayed at Oldwick.

Situated on a tongue of land with a steep geo on each side, it is a huge, unshapely mass forming an excellent landmark far out at sea. The roofless keep still stands to a height of three storeys and is a rectangular block of very rude masonry measuring some 7.3 m by 4.9 m (24 ft by 16¼ ft), with walls about 2.1 m (7 ft) in thickness at the base, narrowing as they go upward to form ledges on which the floor joists rested. The entrance, as is often the case with early castles, was at first floor level and presumably was reached by an outside stair. The windows are small and narrow, being merely observation loops. Down the centre of the pensinsula, beyond the keep, runs a long narrow passage with fragments of buildings on each side of it. A broad ditch cuts off the castle site from the mainland.

In the recorded history of Oldwick we find that in the 14th century it was one of the many strongholds of Sir Reginald de Cheyne. He held large estates in Caithness by virtue of a charter granted by King David II, confirming the right that he (Reginald) already possessed these lands by his marriage to one of the two grand-daughters and co-heiresses of John, 24th Earl of Caithness of the Norse line. One of Sir Reginald's daughters and co-heiresses carried the property to the Sutherlands of Duffus and it later passed again through an heiress to the Oliphant family. Sold by them in 1606 to the Earl of Caithness, it was acquired by Glenorchy in 1676 and from that family it passed by sale to the Dunbars of Hempriggs. They were the direct representatives of the Sutherlands of Duffus, of Sir Reginald de Cheyne and his wife, and of the ancient earls of the Norse line who had almost certainly built it eight centuries ago.

### Forse

On the east coast of Caithness are two other ancient castles which were also part of the heritage brought to Sir Reginald de Cheyne by his marriage with the grand-daughter of Earl John. The sites of both are as impressive and awesome as those already described.

At Forse Castle a considerable portion of walling remains; its architecture and masonry so closely resemble that of Oldwick in every detail that its Norse origin can hardly be in doubt. On Sir Reginald's death Forse passed to his daughter Mariot and to her descendants, the Keiths. About 1408, Kenneth Sutherland, younger son of the 5th Earl of Sutherland, married the heiress of Keith of Forse, and thereafter seventeen successive lairds of Forse held the estate until recent times. In 1771 the 14th Sutherland of Forse, while losing in law his claim to the Sutherland Earldom, was adjudged heir-male of the Sutherland line and Chief of the clan Sutherland.

### Berriedale

The castle of Berriedale, the other Cheyne stronghold, passed along with Oldwick to the Sutherlands of Duffus. Its lairds were also lairds of Oldwick, until it was sold to the Earl of Caithness. Sold by Glenorchy, along with other Caithness estates, it was acquired by a branch of the Sutherlands of Forse, being finally sold by them in 1775. The remains are only fragmentary but the whole plan seems to be very similar to the others, except that at Berriedale traces of an enclosing wall of enceinte are visible.

### Castle Gunn

On forbidding and desolate sites on the rocky east coast at Clyth are the fragmentary remains of two castles closely associated with the clan Gunn. The older, Castle Gunn, or Clyth Castle the earliest seat of the clan, is almost inaccessible. Romantic and tragic traditions of an early Gunn chieftain and his Danish princess bride are associated with it.

### Halberry

Castle Gunn appears to have been superseded by Halberry, 1.6 km (1 mile) to the south. There, in the 15th century, George Gunn, Crowner or Coroner of Caithness, ruled in great feudal splendour. He was 7th chief in direct descent from Gunni Olafson, the founder, but following his death as a result of a bitter feud with the Keiths of Ackergill, his eldest son removed the headquarters of the clan to Kildonan and Halberry fell into decay.

### Brough

On a long rocky promontory near Brough, Dunnet are the foundations of a castle which by its situation may well be of Norse origin, but nothing whatsoever is known about it.

### Mestag

A similar origin may be assumed for Castle Mestag on the island of Stroma. Occupying the whole summit of a detached stack about 4.3 m (14 ft) out from the cliffs, it could only have been reached by a bridge. Concerning it, history is again silent.

### Braal

The ancient castle of Braal, known to be of Norse origin (although perhaps not in quite its present form) is a striking contrast to the others. Beautifully situated among woods on the banks of the River Thurso at Halkirk, it is the best preserved of the Norse strongholds. It was the principal seat of John, 24th Earl of Caithness (1206-1231). It has many architectural characteristics of Old-wick, but is larger and has more sophisticated adornments although of the same rectangular form with walls 2.5 m to 3 m (8 ft to 10 ft) thick. Originally known as Brathwell, it was in 1375 granted by Robert II to his son David, Earl of Strathearn, along with the Earldom of Caithness, which at that time was in abeyance. In 1450, James II bestowed Braal, again with the Earldom, on the High Admiral of Scotland, Sir George Crichton who, it is believed, had already inherited Dunbeath Castle from his mother. On Sir George's death in 1455, the Earldom was restored to the heir of the ancient line, William Sinclair. The Sinclair earls held Braal until the usurpation by Glenorchy in 1676. It was after-wards acquired by and is still held by the Sinclairs of Ulbster, a junior branch of the ancient line.

## Dunbeath

Two extremely old castles in the County are still inhabited, although no exact confirmation of their date of erection can be established. These are Dun-beath Castle and Ackergill Tower.

Dunbeath Castle stands on the same kind of rocky peninsula so often used by our early castle builders, but the architecture with its elongated oblong plan and vaulted ground floor puts it firmly into the 13th or 14th century. In a castle continuously occupied throughout the centuries and thereby often altered to meet changing requirement, it is difficult to access its character, but certainly a substantial part of its fabric goes back to or beyond 1428, the earliest recorded date. The first recorded owners are the Sutherlands, believed to be of the Dun-robin family. Then followed, it is thought by heirship, the Crichtons. By charter from James IV the castle passed to the family of Innes and thence by marriage of an Innes heiress to a younger son of the second Sinclair Earl. With this family, and afterwards with another branch of the Sinclairs, it remained until quite recent times.

## Ackergill

With no natural defences Ackergill Tower, unlike Dunbeath, stands on a low shore close by the sea, although originally it was almost certainly sur-rounded by a moat and defensive walling. Much of the main tower remains un-altered from medieval times, but the top floor and battlements are new. The tower measures 14.6 m by 10.4 m (48 ft by 34 ft) is 20.7 m (68 ft) and five storeys high, with walls some 3 m (9-10 ft) thick. The two lower floors are vaulted. A straight stair in the thickness of the wall goes upward to the great hall, with its minstrels' gallery; another flight of spiral steps takes one up to the top of the tower. This ancient tower with its mural chambers, its turrets, its deep well and its two dove-cots, plus the fact that it is one of the oldest inhabited houses in the north of Scotland, make it a most interesting place.

The lands of Ackergill were presumably part of the ancient Norse heritage which came to Sir Reginald de Cheyne through his wife. She and her sister inherited half of Caithness between them, the other half going to Magnus, the heir-male and next (the 25th) Earl. From Cheyne it descended through a daughter to the Keiths who held it until early in the 17th century, when it passed into the hands of the Earl of Caithness.

It was acquired from the usurping Glenorchy family by the Dunbars of Hempriggs in 1699. The tower was greatly added to and embellished by them about the middle of last century, the old keep being finely incorporated without losing its character.

### Dirlot
The most picturesque position of any of our Caithness castles must be that of Dirlot. Built on top of a high and very steep rock rising from the edge of the River Thurso, some 4.8 km (3 miles) downstream from Loch More, only fragments now remain. The keep was small, the interior being only 5.5 m by 3 m (18 ft by 10 ft), with walls 2 m (6½ ft) thick. It is believed to be yet another of the castles of de Cheyne and was afterwards in turn, held by the Gunns, Sutherlands and MacKays. The history of Caithness is sprinkled with stirring episodes centred round this ancient and isolated stronghold.

### Loch More Castle
Calder in his "History of Caithness" mentions a castle or hunting lodge built by de Cheyne at the point where the River Thurso flows from Loch More. No vestige of it now remains.

### Achastle
Yet another castle of this same period of the 14th-15th century, is Achastle. It would appear to have been a large keep with dimensions of 21.3 m by 13.1 m (70 ft by 43 ft) situated on a high ridge at the point where the waters of the Langwell and Berriedale meet. Protected by the steep banks of these rivers on two sides, it was further enflanked on the unprotected sides by a broad deep ditch. Cordiner, writing about 1788, mentions two square towers joined by a curtain wall. These have now gone. It is said to have been built and held for a long time by the family of Sutherland, a branch of the Dunrobin family, but no history of any kind seems to have survived.

### Scrabster
Into this period, too, comes the Castle of Scrabster, anciently Scrabestoun, which during the whole period of its occupation was the seat of the bishops of Caithness. Only fragments remain on the site, situated on the low rocky shore halfway between Thurso and Scrabster. The castle dates from before 1328, but nothing is known of its architecture, although Cordiner states that the walls were strongly built and defensible and that there appeared to be mural apartments.

### Knockinnon
Knockinnon Castle, Dunbeath, is the only fortified structure answering to the description of a castle of enceinte. This was a style of architecture which had its heyday in the 13th century. In such a castle a great curtain wall surrounded the whole area and within it the great tower rose, usually at the corner farthest away from the fortified gatehouse. Somewhere along the massive wall may have been, in separate buildings, the chapel, bakehouse, kitchens, smithy, stores, retainers' barracks, etc. A typical example of such a castle is Urquhart, Inverness, but the best known one is Edinburgh. The buildings and curtain wall together constitute the castle.

Tradition has it that the erection of Knockinnon Castle was begun by William, 2nd Sinclair Earl of Caithness who, having been called away to join in the invasion of England, fell at Flodden, and so the castle was never finished. The situation is one of the most commanding and strategic in the County, as it dominates the approaches from the south. Only the bare foundations of the various buildings and the wall can now be seen.

### Girnigoe

The great stronghold of Girnigoe Castle, the most spectacular ruin in the north of Scotland, was the last of our castles (with the possible exception of Keiss) to be built on a precipitous cliff. Erected sometime between 1476 and 1496 by William, the 2nd Sinclair Earl, it was at the time completely impregnable. The peninsula on which it stands had been cut away from the mainland not only at the neck but again half way along by a great ditch. On the edge of the second trench the keep rose to three or four storeys, with one wing behind on the sea side, and behind that again, a courtyard with outbuildings.

In front, between the ditches, was the outer ward of Girnigoe with a strong gatehouse and a long vaulted pend with a portcullis opening from the main drawbridge. Over, behind and around these entrance buildings was erected in 1606 the new and very fine architectural addition, known as Castle Sinclair. Another drawbridge over the second moat connected the two parts of Girnigoe. The basement of the older part with its two dungeons — one containing a deep well — was vaulted, as was the entire ground storey. However, the upper floors were made of wood. A fine oriel window, now fallen into the sea, adorned the great hall on the first floor. A stone stair descended to sea level from a chamber some distance behind the castle.

Girnigoe remained the seat of five successive earls, passing ultimately to Glenorchy. Besieged by the rightful heir, about 1690, it was taken and partially destroyed by (for the first time in Caithness) the use of firearms or artillery. Since that time it has been allowed to fall into decay. The ownership returned to the Earls in recent years and it is listed in Debrett's "Peerage" as the official seat of the Earldom.

## L AND Z PLAN CASTLES

In the development of the Scottish castle during the 15th and 16th centuries, as firearms came into use, the castle builders added a wing or a "jamb" to a corner of the main keep, so that from gun loops in the main buildings and in the wing fire could be directed along the whole castle front. And so was introduced the L-plan castle. Later castles were given added or even all round protection by two wings at diagonal corners so that the castle defenders could cover the castle approaches in every direction. This is the Z plan. At the same time the towers were built higher to give extra room and often the "jambs," ending in turrets, were of equal height with the main building.

### Keiss

Such a castle was Keiss. This tall slim tower is a modified form of the Z plan owing to the restricted site on which it stands, jutting out slightly towards the sea on the edge of a cliff. The two diagonally opposite towers are small, one of them containing the stair. Only the basement was vaulted. All the upper floors, the stairway and a large section of wall, including the entrance, are gone.

The castle dates from about the end of the 16th century, although the site might previously have been a fortified one, for tradition has "a fortalice of Raddar" there in ancient times. The castle was a property of the Earls of Caithness. From Glenorchy it passed to the Sinclairs of Dunbeath, one of whom, Sir William Sinclair, founded the Baptist Church in Caithness.

### Mey

The now-royal castle of Mey is a typical Z plan castle of the 16th century. More modern additions down the years have not destroyed its character, as the original structure can easily be determined. There is vaulting on the ground floor and also above the main staircase. Jutting towers, corbelled turrets, a great hall 12.2 m by 5.5 m (40 ft by 18 ft), a kitchen fireplace 3.7 m (12½ ft) wide by 1.8 m (6 ft) in depth, numerous gun holes on the ground and first floors, a wealth of decorative detail, plus the fact that it is still inhabited — and by a royal personage — makes it one of the most interesting residences in the north.

Built between 1566 and 1572 by George, 4th Earl of Caithness, it was granted by him to his second son William, but on this son's early death he conferred it on the next son George, who founded the baronetical family of Sinclair of Mey. In 1789, the Mey family, on the extinction of the elder line, succeeded to the Earldom and the castle was the seat of the Earldom for the next hundred years.

### Latheron

A 2.1 m (7 ft) thick fragment of wall on a steep bank of the Latheron burn, a short distance from the public road, marks the site of Latheron Castle. The greater part of the building, although ruinous, was standing in 1726. No history is known, but the estate was a possession of the Sinclair family, cadets of Mey, as early as 1635. Presumably the castle was built and occupied by them.

### Dounreay

On the north coast of Caithness, about 6.4 km (4 miles) apart, are two late 16th century castles, Dounreay and Brims, both of L plan architecture. Dounreay is considered to be a perfect example of a Scottish laird's castle of that time. The only vaulting is over the staircase, which rises from the doorway in the re-entrant angle around which shot-holes pierce the walls. Now roofless and ruinous, there is still much of interest to be seen. It was occupied up to the latter half of the 19th century. Once church lands, Dounreay passed first to the Sinclairs of Dunbeath and later to the Earls of Caithness. It is now within the compound of the United Kingdom Atomic Energy Authority's establishment.

### Brims

Brims Castle, also a Sinclair seat, stands on the cliffs where the Brims burn flows into the sea. The keep is rectangular, with a tower containing a newel stair attached at one corner. It is three storeys high over a vaulted basement, with one room on each floor. An interesting old gateway, with mouldings, opens on to a courtyard. The castle has been long used as part of the farmhouses.

### Thurso-East

Near Thurso were two 17th century castles, both seats of the Sinclair family. At Thurso-East the original castle was built by the 6th Sinclair Earl,

PLATE 26. *Sinclair and Girnigoe Castles near Wick.*

(A. Luciani)

PLATE 27. *The Castle of Mey.*

(A. Luicani)

falling into the hands of Glenorchy after Sinclair's death. It was destroyed by Sinclair of Keiss, the rightful heir, during the struggle to assert his claims. Passing then to the Sinclairs of Ulbster, a splendid new castle rose on the site, but it is now partially dismantled.

### Haimer

Haimer Castle, no longer in existence, was built by Alexander, the 9th Earl, whose landed patrimony was Murkle. It is said that he moved his place of residence to a more inland site as the notorious pirate, Gow, whom he had offended, had bombarded his house there. Haimer proved only just out of range of Gow's guns, for it is said that a cannon ball landed at Broynach nearby. A square tower consisting of some eight or nine rooms, the castle was abandoned after its builder's death in 1765.

To tell the whole story of the castles of Caithness would require many volumes. The families who built and occupied them played a full part in the unfolding history of our County. It is a story of strife and warfare, feuds and forays, intermingled with brave and stirring deeds; patriotism and high ideals are intermixed with bitter jealousies and dark and dreadful crimes. The castles tell a story of the gradual turning to a more peaceful way of living, for, existing as they have through all the recorded history of our County, they have seen and show in their stones the transition of one century to the next. They will most certainly be with us yet for a very long time to come.

L

## ORDNANCE SURVEY MAP REFERENCES TO THE CASTLES OF CAITHNESS

| Castle | O.S. Reference |
|---|---|
| Achastle | ND 116227 |
| Ackergill | ND 353547 |
| Berriedale | ND 121224 |
| Braal | ND 136600 |
| Brims | ND 043710 |
| Brough | ND 228741 |
| Bucholie (Lambaborg) | ND 382658 |
| Dirlot | ND 126487 |
| Dounreay | ND 983670 |
| Dunbeath | ND 158283 |
| Forss | ND 224338 |
| Girnigoe | ND 378549 |
| Gunn (Clyth) | ND 308386 |
| Haimer | ND 142672 |
| Halberry | ND 302378 |
| Keiss | ND 357616 |
| Knockinnon | ND 181315 |
| Latheron | ND 199334 |
| Loch More | ND 083461 |
| Mestag | ND 340764 |
| Mey | ND 289739 |
| Oldwick | ND 370489 |
| Scrabster | ND 107692 |
| Thurso East | ND 124689 |
| Thurso (Ormlie) | ND 112681 |

CHAPTER 19

# A CENTURY OF EDUCATION IN CAITHNESS

Prior to the passing of the 1872 Education Act the statutory system of education in Scotland had been prescribed by two Acts of Parliament. One, in 1696, decreed that a school be established in every parish, that the heritors (landed proprietors) provide a "commodious house" for a school and that they settle a salary of 100 to 200 merks on a schoolmaster. One writer later remarked, "Never was there a wiser law, and never was a law more studiously disregarded"; it was not until 1773 that the heritors of Reay were forced to accept their responsibility for educating the young. The second Act, in 1803, raised the minimum salary to 300 merks, and the maximum to 400 merks (£22.22). Provision was made for the revision of salaries every 25 years "where necessary" and heritors were now obliged to provide a schoolhouse of two rooms, including a kitchen, for the teacher. Heritors were also permitted to divide large parishes by establishing 'side' schools. These schools were similar to parish schools but the heritors were not obliged to provide accommodation for the teacher of the 'side' school.

In 1824 an Act authorised the creation of new ecclesiastical parishes in over-crowded cities and in remote districts. A further Act, in 1838 extended the parochial system to these "quoad sacra" parishes. As these new schools were supported by Parliamentary grants they were known as 'parliamentary' schools.

When a Royal Commission was appointed in 1864 to inquire into education in Scotland, it found a statutory system of parochial, side and parliamentary schools "established by law and maintained by local assessment." It also found a supplementary system which in practice furnished more than two-thirds of the education in country districts and almost all of it in towns. It is reported that a mere 1,035 schools out of 4,450 constituted the entire national system of education. Unfortunately, no reports on Caithness schools were included in the Commission's report.

An important, though as yet neglected, source of information concerning the geography and social history of Caithness is the series of Parish Names Books compiled between 1870 and 1872 by the Ordnance Survey in connection with the first series of O.S. maps. These volumes, fifteen in number, contain detailed descriptions of buildings in town and country, antiquities, geographical features, etc. 79 schools (see Appendix A) are mentioned; the descriptions are sometimes sketchy but they provide a unique record of schools in the County on the eve of the passing of the 1872 Education Act.

Space does not permit analysis of educational provision in the County at that time but two examples may suffice to show the variety of schools to be found. Thurso is credited with four schools. The oldest, the Benevolent Institution in Rose Street, was built in 1856. It was said to be supported by charity and to cater for girls "who learned skills to make them suitable wives for working

163

**Figure 16. Brubster School**

men." The Parish School, transferred in 1870 from the market place (near the present Salvation Army Hall), stood in a field on the outskirts of the town, but a road — to be called Castle Street — was already being led in. The largest and most popular school, the Free Church School in Duncan Street, was also a new school, having moved from Manson's Lane in 1868. The fourth establishment, the Miller Institution, was built in 1862 by a local benefactor, Alexander Miller. The subjects offered were English, Mathematics, Latin, Greek and French, at a cost of £0.33½ a quarter session.

Four other schools existed at this time but were not listed by the Ordnance Survey, presumably because the buildings were used for other purposes. Two were exclusive schools for "young ladies" — Miss Edmonstone's in Olrig Street and Mrs Russell's in Campbell Street. They charged £1.05 per quarter for instruction in English and French. A Miss Keith taught in an adventure (a private venture) school in Campbell Street and in the Bethel at the Fisherbiggins Adam Mackay ran a day school for fisher lads.

The landward area of Thurso Parish was served by schools at Forss, Weydale and Janetstown. Forss School, erected about 1825 by the Society in Scotland for the Propagation of Christian Knowledge (S.S.P.C.K.) was supported by grants from the church, school fees and £6 from Sinclair of Forss in lieu of "cow pasture," thus giving its teacher £65 per annum. Weydale, rebuilt in 1872 by Sir Tollemache Sinclair for his tenants, brought its young teacher only £10 plus "children's pence". Janetstown too had a new school, built in 1867 to accommodate 60 children, but its roll soon reached 84.

Wick Parish School, built in 1869 on the Kirkhill, and still standing, had an average attendance of 140. Its upper part was used as a school and the ground floor was used as a teacher's dwelling. With a population of almost 13,000 in the parish, it was fortunate that the Free Church erected two schools in town and three more in the landward area. One Free Church School, in Stafford Lane, had an average attendance of 180: the Ordnance Survey reports that the underpart was used as a store. The second Free Church School stood at the corner of Macrae and Kinnaird Streets. The largest school in town was Pulteneytown Academy, built in 1839 by the British Fisheries Society and attended by more than 300 boys and girls. Two "ragged" schools for pauper children are recorded. One still stands in a lane off High Street and is described as "a private building rented and permanently used as a school for poor children." The other "ragged" school was in Miller Street at its junction with Telford Street.

The Free Church maintained schools at Bilbster, at Bruan — still standing to the north of the old church — and one at Staxigoe, the latter not being listed by the Ordnance Survey. A report dated 1867 states that the Free Church School at Staxigoe had been vacant for some years — presumably it had not re-opened when the surveyors visited the area early in 1870.

The S.S.P.C.K. had a school at Thrumster as early as 1730 but it was later transferred to Ulbster, and in 1866 it was again moved — this time to Sarclet. The school was visited in 1868 by a Society inspector who commended the teacher, John Tulloch, for his enterprise in having a wooden floor installed but noted disapprovingly that the school was used for Volunteer drills and Balls. The S.S.P.C.K. also maintained a school at Staxigoe. Like many schools along the coast this school was noted for its teaching of navigation. A newspaper report for 1865 states, "A remarkably well-executed chart from England to Cape Verde Islands has been made by one of the pupils of Mr Brass's navigation class at Staxigoe. It is admirably finished in colours with an ornamental border of the flags of all nations." Two schools are mentioned at Stirkoke in 1841: a General Assembly School and a Female School of Industry, where girls were taught useful domestic arts. Only the Assembly School was still functioning in 1870.

The Education Act of 1872 saw the transfer of all parochial, General Assembly and S.S.P.C.K. schools to the newly elected Parish School Boards. The Boards' main function was the provision of elementary education (now compulsory for all children aged 5 to 13) and to meet the cost of providing schools, staff, equipment, etc., they were empowered to raise a local rate. Under section 27 of the Act the new Boards had a duty to ascertain the educational requirements of their districts and to provide additional schools if they were found necessary. Unfortunately, only three sets of School Board minutes have survived in Caithness: those of Halkirk and Thurso are complete but the first volume of the Bower minutes, covering the period 1873-1888, has been lost.

The new Boards took up their duties with enthusiasm. Halkirk School Board opened a school at Scotscalder in 1875 (closing the Calder and Olgrinmore schools). It enlarged the Parish School (renamed the North School, the Free Church School being called the South School), rebuilt Lieurary School in 1876 and in the following year built a school at Spittal. As Watten School Board had moved its school from Dunn to Lanergill, less than 3.2 km (2 miles) from the school at Toftingall, Halkirk School Board tried to obtain a site nearer Banniskirk but this was refused by the proprietor and a site at Spittal was chosen instead. Thurso School Board built a new school at Forss and extended Weydale, the Parish School (renamed Castle Street Public School) and Janetstown School. In agreement with Olrig School Board, it extended Murkle School to provide accommodation for children from the Clardon district of Thurso.

Other Boards were equally busy. Bower School Board built a new school at Bower in 1875, closing both the Free Church and the old Parish Schools, Lyth and Stanstill Schools were enlarged and a new school built at Stemster in 1877. Dunnet School Board found itself with more schools than it required but was unable to agree which school should be closed. Consequently, it continued all its schools, including an infant school at Scarfskerry, until 1879 when the Board agreed to build a central school at Crossroads, closing Brough, Barrock, Rattar and Scarfskerry Schools. At Castletown, Olrig School Board used the Traill Hall as a school until a new one was built in 1875, at which time the Free Church School probably closed. It was also decided to extend the school at Tain.

Canisbay School Board had more schools than was considered necessary and the Free Church, Slickly and Freswick Subscription Schools were closed. A new school was required at Aukingill, but as it served the Keiss area its erection was undertaken by the Keiss School Board. Its first teacher, when its opened in 1876, was the father of James Maxton, the socialist M.P. A new school was built at Keiss in 1875 and the Parliamentary, Society and Free Church Schools were closed.

Wick School Board was faced with the task of replacing or enlarging all of its schools. The Free Church School in Stafford Lane (called the North School after 1872) had been criticised in 1867 when a local paper reported, "It is certainly most shameful for the greatest congregation in the North of Scotland to leave the young packed and nearly suffocated for want of room and air." The introduction of compulsory education worsened the situation and the Board had to build a new school in Girnigoe street in 1876. Pulteneytown Academy and the Free Church School in Pulteneytown (known as the South School) were extended in 1875. The former Parish School was not suitable for extension but continued in use until 1895.

The landward areas were now the responsibility of the Wick Landward School Board and this body reported, "Staxigoe and Stirkoke Schools are in good condition. Janetstown, Bilbster, Tannach, Thrumster, Staxigoe Society, and Louisburgh Private and Adventure Schools are indifferent. Reiss is bad and Bruan requires repair." Reiss School closed when Killimster was opened. New schools were built at Whaligoe and Tannach in 1875 and Wick West Banks opened in 1877.

Watten School Board replaced Dunn School with a more suitably sited school at Lanergill in 1876. Gersa was replaced in the same year and the Free Church School at Watten closed. Presumably the present Watten School was built at this time.

Latheron School Board closed Ramscraig School in 1876 following complaints by the inspector that the roof admitted rain freely, that the walls were neither lathed nor plastered, and large chinks at the door and windows admitted rain and wind. The teacher and children were transferred to new premises at Borgue. A new school at Achavanich in 1876 led to the closing of Rangag and Osclay Schools. Houstry, Buoltach, Swiney and Newlands Schools were replaced after complaints about the lack of accommodation. For example, the Newlands teacher, James Cuthbert, wrote in his log book:

11.1.1876   "122 Present. Difficult to keep order. School crowded — standing room only."

18.2.1876   "School crowded almost to suffocation. Had windows down. Difficult to keep order. Scholars got half delirious before 4 o'clock."

The opening of a new school at Newlands in 1877, saw the closure of the small school at Roster, now a mere mound of rubble beside the road. The Free Church School at Lybster was extended in 1877; a new school was built at Dunbeath in 1878, and the Torbeg, Dunbeath Female and the Latheron Free Church Schools closed. An "interim" school is recorded at Berriedale in 1877 but the log book does not begin until 1893. Ousdale, possibly the smallest school in Scotland, is first mentioned in 1899 but it may be older as the early log books have been lost. Finally, the upland districts of Reay Parish were supplied with schools: Dounreay in 1879, Brubster and Brawlbin in 1893.

An attempt to introduce some unity into the primary school curriculum was made with the code of 1892 which instituted the Merit Certificate. This certificate was intended as a leaving certificate to be awarded at the end of the compulsory period of schooling, that is at 13 years of age. In 1898 its function was changed so that the Merit Certificate became the dividing line between primary and secondary education. To meet the needs of such pupils as were likely to remain at school up to 16 — and whose aim was a commercial rather than a professional career — Higher Grade Departments were set up. Five such departments were eventually set up in Caithness at Castletown, Halkirk, Lybster, Thurso and Wick. One further change should be noted: in November 1918, the County replaced the parish as the unit of educational administration.

In the early 1920's there were still 68 schools (see Appendix B) in the County. Today there are only 28, including new schools recently completed at

Hillhead (Wick), Pennyland and Mountpleasant (Thurso). The closure of schools was most rapid in the period 1960-69 when twenty schools were closed.

The cause of the decline is a complex one but the key factor is undoubtedly rural depopulation. The coastal parishes once supported a crofting-fishing economy but the centralisation of the herring industry on Wick, followed by the gradual collapse of herring fishing, led to serious depopulation. Now, the derelict cottage is a characteristic feature of this area where, in 1949, 420 ruins were counted. The parishes of Thurso, Olrig and Halkirk had flourishing flagstone industries but these too declined in the years before the first World War. In recent years, however, the most important factor has been the increasing process of amalgamation and mechanisation of agricultural holdings. All parishes have suffered from depopulation, but Latheron lost more than 75% of its people and three other parishes (Canisbay, Dunnet and Halkirk) lost more than 60% in the period 1861-1961. The effect on school rolls has been disastrous. For example, Newlands School had a roll of 141 in 1882, this fell to 70 in 1911 and by 1950 it was only 12. The school closed in 1959.

The siting of the Atomic Energy Authority's establishment at Dounreay in 1956 led to a total population increase of 4,660 by 1961 and a further 887 by 1966; yet, 15 schools were closed during these 10 years. The increase in population has not been uniform throughout the County. Several parishes, notably Latheron, continue to decline. Dounreay has, in fact, accelerated the process of depopulation by offering workers better housing, wages and working conditions than were normally obtainable on the land. One further factor was that the Education Act of 1946 made attendance at a secondary school compulsory for all pupils over the age of 12. Prior to 1946 it was not uncommon for rural children to receive all of their education in the local primary school. The effect of this legislation has been to deplete school rolls even further, in some cases making them no longer viable.

As early as 1935 it was proposed to close the Higher Grade Department of Castletown School. Following protests by parents the motion was overturned, but the respite was only temporary, for the Higher Grade was withdrawn sometime in 1938. All three rural secondary schools (Halkirk, Castletown and Lybster) were officially graded as Junior Secondary Schools in 1946. In December 1966, the Education Committee decided to close the secondary departments of these three schools "on educational grounds". The decision was naturally opposed, but the Committee's proposal was strengthened by the Scottish Education Department's recommendation that secondary education should be organised along comprehensive lines — necessitating the centralisation of secondary education on Wick and Thurso and so the secondary departments were closed at the end of June 1967.

In recent years the Education Committee has rebuilt or extended Reay, Watten and Crossroad Schools to serve as district schools. These attractive buildings provide accommodation for local children and also children from neighbouring schools. Children were transferred from Dounreay to Reay, from Gersa to Watten, and from Mey to the new school at Crossroads. Similar extensions are planned elsewhere in the County; six schools: Janetstown, Spittal, Murkle, Dunnet, Stemster and Latheron are stated to have "no long-term future." If the trend continues there may ultimately be no schools outwith the towns and larger villages.

The old log-books throw light on many long forgotten practices; e.g., the game of 'knotty'. The reader may remember Don Manson's plaint:

> "Ye never hear o' knottie noo,
> 'E game is never seen,
> An' yet we played it everyday
> Upon the village green . . .
>
> 'E crofters 'gainst 'e villagers
> At dinner time we'd play
> An' up an' doon 'e green we'd race
> Till 'e bell called us away."

The Lybster log-book records one instance, in October 1875, when the bell did not call the pupils away. The teacher writes,

"In the afternoon . . . several boys who continued playing their game of notty half an hour after the hour of opening, were shut out and for the remainder of the day hindered the work inside by noisy demonstrations outside."

Next day the demonstrators were punished.

It is clear that the punishment was summary and severe. One teacher records in March, 1875, that four boys were late for school. "Gave each of them about a dozen 'palmies' which they bore with Christian patience." Another country schoolmaster confides in 1878, "I find that corporal punishment improves the preparation of lessons by girls in Standard V."

Conditions were often uncomfortable for teacher and pupils. The teacher at Newlands complains in October, 1873, that the Latheron School Board had not yet provided fuel and adds, "Had recourse to the primitive 'carry a peat' system which is troublesome and disagreeable." A few days later he admits that it generally meant they had no fire at all and, in January, 1875, he had to tell his pupils to bring 2d each per quarter. This practice, known as 'fuel money', continued throughout the County until 1889 when it was abolished. The same teacher reported seven broken panes early in November, 1876, but no action was taken and, on the 1st December, he writes, "Had to light candles again. Panes not mended yet and we have to keep a shutter on." On the 7th he says, "Candles burning all day, school being so dark."

Teachers until 1906 served a five-year apprenticeship as pupil-teachers, at the end of which period they either obtained employment as assistant teacher or were admitted as Queen's Scholars to a training college. Candidates for posts as pupil teachers were required to provide proof of their worthiness and the log-book of Crossroads Schools contains two interesting examples of such certificates.

13.8.1880　"I hereby certify that David Budge, aged 15 years, is not at present subject to any ailment likely to interfere with the Profession of Teacher."

Dr D. S., Dunnet.

"I hereby certify that David Budge and Jessie Malcolm, candidates for the offices of pupil-teachers, are of excellent character, and have been carefully trained by their parents who are well known for sobriety, integrity, industry and consistent Christian conduct."

Apprenticeship usually began at the age of 13 years, and the pupil-teachers received instruction from the headmaster from 9 to 10 a.m. and from 4 to 4.30 p.m., the intervening period being given over to teaching practice, usually with the infant classes — a practice deplored by the Inspectors. Salary for the first year was £10, and this was increased yearly by £2.50 to give a maximum of £20 in the final year.

At the beginning of the period under review the country schoolmaster had a salary of about £60. Forty years later, in 1914, it had risen to £100 and today a headmaster in a rural school earns some £1,900, reflecting the increased cost of living rather than public recognition of his worth!

In the early 1860's Caithness teachers formed an association "to promote the general interests of teachers and to raise the status of education in the county." Quarterly meetings were held in the inn at Dunn to discuss topics such as "Music as a branch of Education" and "Grammar"; the session ended with dinner and was regarded as a social event. In November, 1874, Caithness teachers, alarmed by the activities of some Parish School Boards, formed a local association of the Educational Institute of Scotland with the aims of studying teaching methods, legislation affecting the interests of education teachers, and the proceedings of School Boards which were considered to be prejudicial to the cause of education or oppressive on teachers. Relations between teachers and School Boards were not always good, and teachers were often subject to pressure from the Board or individual members — resistance could mean dismissal. One poignant entry in a County log book says, "Bade farewell to MEY Public School. Very sorry parting with my scholars. Advice to new teacher. NB: Walk not in the footsteps of thy predecessor. Outward walk and conversation referred to — not school duties". In two instances (Watten in 1905, and Keiss in 1917) the E.I.S. was successful in having the local School Board boycotted. Relations are now very good and Caithness County Council was among the first in Scotland to invite teachers to serve on the Education Committee and co-operation between teachers and employers can hardly be improved.

## APPENDIX A
## SCHOOLS LISTED BY ORDNANCE SURVEY (1870-1872)

| Parish | School | Built | Teacher | Map Ref. |
|---|---|---|---|---|
| Bower | Barrock Assembly | c.1841 | J. Steven | ND 292631 |
| | Bower Parish | r.1820 | A. McInnes | ND 238621 |
| | Bower Free Church | | J. Murray | ND 231605 |
| | Stanstill Society | | | ND 279596 |
| | Stemster Subscription | | J. Esplin | ND 174625 |
| Canisbay | Aukingill Subscription | c.1870 | J. Geddes | ND 368637 |
| | Canisbay Free Church | | | ND 347721 |
| | Canisbay Parish | r.1866 | J. Sutherland | ND 348722 |
| | Freswick Proprietor's | | | ND 369678 |
| | Freswick Assembly | c.1841 | B. Baikie | ND 379684 |
| | Duncansby Assembly | c.1841 | J. Mann | ND 383725 |
| | Mey Society | r.1867 | D. Paterson | ND 286726 |
| | Slickly Female Assembly | | Miss Murray | ND 302667 |
| | Stroma Society | r.1860 | G. Stalker | ND 354773 |
| Dunnet | Barrock Free Church | c.1850 | N. Elder | ND 258714 |
| | Brough Proprietor's | | G. Sinclair | ND 224734 |
| | Dunnet Parish | r.1864 | R. Campbell | ND 223715 |
| | Dunnet Sessional | c.1820 | Mrs Baikie | ND 219712 |
| | Greenland Free Church | 1866 | W. Whyte | ND 253666 |
| | Rattar Assembly | 1839 | E. Paterson | ND 258722 |
| Halkirk | Calder Free Church | | | ND 093594 |
| | Halkirk Parish | 1836 | D. Meiklejohn | ND 133594 |
| | Halkirk Free Church | 1850 | Miss Auld | ND 132592 |
| | Harpsdale Free Church | 1841 | W. Bain | ND 130546 |
| | Lieurary Assembly | | J. Carson | ND 065635 |
| | Olgrinmore Proprietor's | 1858 | | ND 100541 |
| | Toftingall Assembly | 1846 | A. Purdie | ND 168545? |
| | Westerdale Free Church | 1860 | | ND 128516 |
| Keiss | Keiss Parliamentary | c.1838 | A. Morrison | ND 344620 |
| | Keiss Society | | Miss Gould | ? |
| | Keiss Free Church | | Mr Banks | ND 348613 |
| Latheron | Berriedale Proprietor's | | A. Cameron | ? |
| | Braemore Proprietor's | | | ND 074303 |
| | Buoltach Free Church | | | ND 176351 |
| | Dunbeath Parliamentary | 1849 | Mr Fernie | ND 159295 |
| | Dunbeath Female Subscription | | Miss Smith | ND 155294 |
| | Houstry Free Church | | | ND 154351 |
| | Latheron Free Church | | | ND 198337 |
| | Latheron Parish | 1861 | W, Mackay | ND 199336 |
| | Lybster Free Church | c.1848 | J. Kinnaird | ND 251375 |
| | Newlands Free Church | | R. Gunn | ND 263376 |
| | Osclay Subscription | | J. Sutherland | ND 220391 |
| | Ramscraig Subscription | | Mr Mackay | ND 140267 |
| | Rangag Subscription | | | ND 179441 |
| | Roster Subscription | | J. Gair | ND 262398 |
| | Swiney Free Church | | Mr Georgeson | ND 232368 |
| | Torbeg Free Church | | | ND 167305 |
| | Lybster Subscription | | J. Robertson | ND 251375 |
| Olrig | Castletown Parish | | E. Cameron | ND 196674 |
| | Castletown Female Prop. | c.1840 | Miss Lockhart | ND 195679 |
| | Castletown Infant Prop. | c.1840 | Miss Mackay | ND 195678 |
| | Castletown Free Church | 1843 | Mrs Riach | ND 196679 |
| | Murkle Free Church | c.1850 | W. Swanson | ND 155682 |
| | Tain Free Church | c.1850 | A. Sinclair | ND 128665 |
| Reay | Reay Parish | r.c.1860 | J. Gunn | ND 969649 |
| | Shebster Free Church | 1849 | E. Matheson | ND 025640 |

| Thurso | Forss Assembly | c.1825 | Mr Glass | ND 046690 |
| | Janetstown Side | r.1867 | T. Smith | ND 083654 |
| | Weydale Proprietor's | r.1872 | R. Brims | ND 146646 |
| (Burgh) | Miller Institution | 1862 | Mr Waters | ND 115681 |
| | Benevolent Institution | 1856 | Miss Harley | ND 115685 |
| | Thurso Parish | r.1870 | T. Meikle | ND 114685 |
| | Thurso Free Church | r.1868 | W. Docherty | ND 114685 |
| Watten | Dunn Free Church | 1835 | W. Meiklejohn | ND 201568 |
| | Gersa Free Church | | A. Sutherland | ND 260575 |
| | Watten Parish | r.1867 | J. Taylor | ND 238620 |
| | Watten Free Church | | J. Mackay | ND 229606 |
| Wick | Bilbster Free Church | | Mr Sutherland | ND 293523 |
| | Bruan Free Church | | Mr Waters | ND 313395 |
| | Reiss Adventure | | D. Mackenzie | ND 334547 |
| | Staxigoe Society | | C. Brass | ND 383523 |
| | Stirkoke Assembly | c.1840 | | ND 322497 |
| | Sarclet Society | c.1866 | J. Tulloch | ND 341445 |
| (Burgh) | Wick Free Church | | G. Gunn | ND 364507 |
| | Pulteneytown Free Church | | A. Sinclair | ND 366502 |
| | Wick Ragged School | | Miss Forbes | ND 363511 |
| | Wick Ragged School | | | ND 364508 |
| | Wick Parish | r.1869 | D. Nicolson | ND 362514 |
| | Pulteneytown Academy | 1839 | | ND 364506 |

## LEGEND
r. rebuilt
c. about
r.c. rebuilt about

## APPENDIX B
### SCHOOLS IN CAITHNESS - 1924

| Parish | School | Teacher | Map Ref. |
| --- | --- | --- | --- |
| Olrig | Murkle | A. G. McIntosh | ND 155682 |
| | Castletown Higher Grade | A. S. Robertson | ND 196675 |
| | Tain | Mrs Dickson | ND 218664 |
| | Durran | Miss Cameron | ND 186636 |
| Reay | Reay | Peter Muir | ND 970650 |
| | Dounreay | Miss Lobban | ND 018665 |
| | Shurrery | Miss McLeod | ? |
| | Shebster | Miss Duchart | ND 010640 |
| | Brawlbin | Miss Mowat | ND 073634 |
| Watten | Watten | Andrew Malloch | ND 241545 |
| | Lanergill | J. A. Sutherland | ND 196548 |
| | Gersa | T. D. Bathgate | ND 259575 |
| Thurso | Miller Institution | A. R. Murison | ND 114681 |
| | West Public | A. R. Murison | ND 114684 |
| | Forss | Miss Hamilton | ND 046690 |
| | Weydale | Mrs Shearer | ND 146646 |
| Bower | Bower | Miss Bain | ND 237621 |
| | Barrock | John Young | ND 292631 |
| | Stemster | W. R. Mackay | ND 175609 |
| | Stanstill | Miss Flett | ND 279596 |
| | Gillock | Miss Slater | ND 210597 |
| Canisbay | Canisbay | T. B. Taylor | ND 348722 |
| | Freswick | Mrs J. Sutherland | ND 380684 |
| | John O'Groats | Arthur Brown | ND 383725 |
| | Stroma | Miss Taylor | ND 354773 |

|          |                       |                     |           |
|----------|-----------------------|---------------------|-----------|
|          | Brabster              | Miss Macdonald      | ND 316692 |
|          | Aukingill             | Miss Nicolson       | ND 368636 |
|          | Mey                   | T. S. Towers        | ND 287728 |
| Dunnet   | Dunnet                | R. C. Moir          | ND 222715 |
|          | Crossroads            | J. H. Taylor        | ND 245728 |
|          | Greenland             | G. Manson           | ND 253666 |
| Halkirk  | Halkirk Higher Grade  | W. Black            | ND 133594 |
|          | Spittal               | R. L. Brown         | ND 169537 |
|          | Westerdale            | Miss Mackay         | ND 128516 |
|          | Harpsdale             | Mrs Farquhar        | ND 130546 |
|          | Scotscalder           | Miss Sutherland     | ND 096564 |
|          | Lieurary              | J. Mackenzie        | ND 065636 |
|          | Altnabreac            | Miss Coutts         | ND 004456 |
|          | Banniskirk            | Miss Mowat          | ND 156583 |
|          | Glutt                 | Vacant              | ND 000368 |
|          | Backlass              | Miss Sutherland     | ND 081424 |
|          | Dalnawillan           | Miss Chrystall      | ND 030408 |
| Keiss    | Keiss                 | J. H. C. Sutherland | ND 348611 |
| Latheron | Bruan                 | W. Falconer         | ND 325417 |
|          | Newlands              | Miss Sinclair       | ND 263379 |
|          | Lybster Higher Grade  | David Campbell      | ND 247357 |
|          | Swiney                | W. Mackay           | ND 232372 |
|          | Achavanich            | Mrs Campbell        | ND 180427 |
|          | Houstry               | Miss Millar         | ND 153345 |
|          | Braemore              | Miss McEwan         | ND 074303 |
|          | Latheron              | H. Mackay           | ND 200336 |
|          | Buoltach              | Miss Shearer        | ND 172347 |
|          | Dunbeath              | D. Forbes           | ND 159295 |
|          | Borgue                | Miss McLean         | ND 131247 |
|          | Berriedale            | Miss Georgeson      | ND 121228 |
|          | Ousdale               | Mrs Urquhart        | ND 075204 |
|          | Camster               | Mrs Mackay          | ND 263414 |
| Wick     | Wick High School      | A. Robertson        | ND 361504 |
|          | Pulteneytown Academy  | D. Sutherland       | ND 364506 |
|          | North Public          | G. Millikin         | ND 365511 |
|          | South Public          | W. Smith            | ND 367503 |
|          | Ackergill             | Miss Baikie         | ND 354535 |
|          | Bilbster              | Miss Grant          | ND 294523 |
|          | Killimster            | Mrs Skinner         | ND 328553 |
|          | Staxigoe              | A. Hume             | ND 383523 |
|          | Tannach               | Mrs Henderson       | ND 323479 |
|          | Thrumster             | W. Neilson          | ND 341445 |
|          | Whaligoe              | Mrs Mason           | ND 324416 |

# PART III

# *General*

(R. Roberts)

PLATE 28.  *The gorge at Dirlot on Thurso River.*

(A. Luciani)

PLATE 29.  *The attractive dell at Berriedale.*

(R. Stewart)

PLATE 30.  *North Country Cheviot sheep at Thurso Mart.*

(R. Stewart)

PLATE 31.  *Model of "Fifie" fishing boat.*

# CHAPTER 20

# AGRICULTURE

Long before many counties in Scotland which have since gained a reputation for their farming enterprises, Caithness had a system of farming that not only produced sufficient food for its inhabitants but also a surplus, which was exported to other parts of the country as well as to Scandinavia.

According to Donaldson, Thurso was already a port of no little importance as early as the 14th century and was involved quite considerably in the grain trade with Norway, Sweden and Denmark. What is perhaps even more surprising is that these crops were produced in an area not really conducive to the growing of arable crops both from a soil and a climatic point of view. Thus two important features of Caithness agriculture became clearly manifested: one, the natural fertility of the soil in certain parts of the County, and two, the ardour, diligence and ability with which the people toiled on the land, a point which is still very much in evidence today.

Three distinct eras can clearly be seen when examining the farming systems which have been employed from the earliest times until the present day. Firstly, there were the very primitive forms of agriculture culminating in the "run-rig" system, which was only superceded in the 19th century as a result of the change over to a method of farming dependent upon the use of the Five Course Rotation, which forms the basis of most rotations used in Caithness at present. This meant that turnips and grass seed mixtures took their turn along with oats and barley in the rotation and in 1902 grass and clover ousted oats as the principal crop of Caithness, a position it had held for many centuries. Thus, during the last hundred years Caithness has become an area noted for its production of store cattle and sheep rather than a County with a superabundance of grain. One of the reasons for the falling off in the growing of cereals was that the Government was importing large quantities of cheap grain into Britain.

### History of Agriculture in Caithness Before 1750

Being situated in the furthermost north-east tip of the mainland of Great Britain, Caithness appears to have been divorced from the rest of the mainland in certain aspects, which, however, did not really hamper its progress until perhaps the mid 19th century. Land communications were very bad owing to the complete absence of roads and the difficulties created by the mountains of Sutherland to the west and the Ord of Caithness to the south; hence, sea travel was an easier way of transacting business with areas farther south. A secondary effect of this partial isolation was that Gaelic in some parishes was not the mother tongue but, instead, English with a strong local Scots dialect was the commonly used language. Because of the comparatively easy sea passage from countries such as Norway and Sweden, there is abundant evidence to show that Caithness was much more influenced in its development by the frequent inva-

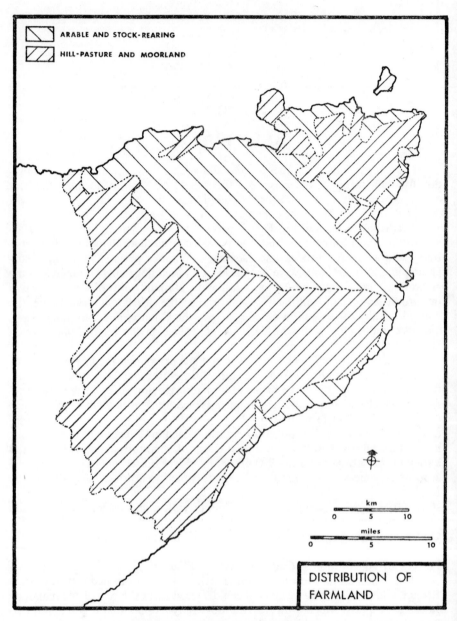

ARABLE AND STOCK-REARING

HILL-PASTURE AND MOORLAND

km

0    5    10

miles

0    5    10

DISTRIBUTION OF FARMLAND

Figure 17.  Distribution of Farmland

sions of Norsemen than it was by people from other countries of Scotland.

The "visits" which these foreigners made from time to time and the duration of their stay varied greatly, but one direct result of their journeys was the transporting back of considerable quantities of farm produce. A certain amount of inter-marrying took place between the Norse people and the Caithnessians and hence the links between parts of Scandinavia and Caithness became very strong. By the 14th century the production of oats and bere (hardy, small, four-row barley) was quite extensive and trading with these parts was well established. Hence, Caithness, although remote geographically, had established itself as a place of some commercial importance at an early date.

## The Primitive Farmers

From an early time the land worked by the tenant farmers was divided into an "infield" and an "outfield". The former was on the best ground and it received all the available manure, being cultivated on the "run-rig" system. Here, each farmer was allocated strips, or ridges, of ground scattered among those of his neighbours in an effort to give the fairest distribution of good and poor land. As the ridges were reallocated by lot each year, it was impossible to carry out any improvements on the part of the individual tenants. The outfield was rough pasture for cattle and sheep and received no other manure than the droppings of the animals which grazed upon it. Occasionally, part of it was ploughed up and cropped for a year or two, so long as it produced any worthwhile harvest, and was then allowed to return to rough pasture, while another portion was taken into cultivation.

The "infield" was sown with successive crops of oats and bere, until such time as the yields were so low or the field so over-run with weeds and rushes that the crops failed; then, after a year's fallow, the same succession of crops was repeated. Because of the normally cold late spring, it was often well into May before the seed was harrowed in. At the beginning of the 17th century there were three varieties of oats commonly grown in the County — White, Grey and Black. The first did not do well on the poorish windswept soil and the head was liable to "shake" whereas the black oat stood the wind better and, along with common bere, was the crop most commonly sown. The average return for Scotland at that time was little more than twofold whereas in Caithness oats gave fivefold and bere, sevenfold returns. Liberal dressings of seaweed, composted manures and lime would seem to be the reason for these high yields. It was common practice in Canisbay to build layers of seaweed, farmyard manure and sods into a heap and after it had lain for some months to apply this compost to the soil. Frequently, seaweed was used by itself, normally being applied in the autumn so that it had a chance to begin to rot down and release plant foods by sowing time. Lime was in common use by the 17th century and a lime-kiln was built on Mey Estate in 1741 as limestone was abundant on the estate. Limestone was transported from Stroma to Canisbay and sold in bolls; 3.5p (8d) per boll being a common price at that time. These local supplies, however, were insufficient for the needs of the whole County and lime was brought to Caithness in the ships that came to take away grain.

It is reported by Donaldson that food was cheap in the early 18th century and lairds in Caithness could live better on 1000 merks (£55.55) than their counterparts in the south could on four times as much! In public taverns food was given away free — only the liquor being charged for; thus the profit from the sale of the latter must have been good. When crops failed in certain years during the 17th and 18th centuries many cases of starvation and hardship were recorded in the counties of Sutherland, Ross and Cromarty, Inverness and Moray. Badly affected tenants, who were unable to pay their rents were evicted and many cattle perished. But, strangely enough, little is recorded in Caithness in anything like the same degree of severity due largely to the superior type of farming at that time practised.

## The Early Implements

It was as well that the great majority of people earned their living from the land, as the farm implements and the methods used were quite poor; thus the large labour force was invaluable. At the beginning of the 17th century the "thrapple" plough (drawn by four or six garrons or oxen, or a combination of the two) was in common use. It was entirely made of wood except for an iron coulter and share. This implement cost about 20p (4/-) and required three people to operate it — one to hold it on a straight course, one to press his whole weight and strength on the middle of the beam to keep the plough in the soil, and the driver, usually a woman, who walked backwards between the two foremost beasts. This plough was replaced by the two-horse plough near the end of the 18th century but it was felt that the older, heavier plough pulverised the soil better. Harrows were merely heavy pieces of wood with long wooden pegs or metal nails driven through them.

## Mode of Transportation

The main means of transporting materials was in "crubbans" — wicker baskets, one being slung on either side of a garron from a wooden saddle called a "clibber". Bags made of straw (cazies) were used to hold grain, each being capable of taking half a boll, approximately 32 kg (70 lb). When transporting large quantities the horses were tied head and tail and it was commonplace to find forty or fifty of these animals taking grain to the large store-houses at Thurso and Staxigoe. The time involved in this type of work must have been great as the rate of travel was slow and so boats were used wherever possible along the coast-line. Dung and seaweed were also taken to the fields in "crubbans" which in many cases were carried on the backs of women and not on those of the garrons!

## Conditions of the Common People

The houses of the common people served as an abode for their domestic animals as well as for themselves. They resembled the "but and ben" of other parts of Scotland at that time but were called a "firehouse and a cellar" in Caithness. A common door, usually the only wooden part of the building, served for all the entrants, the livestock going to one end and the people to the other. A low turf partition divided the sections of the building but normally the dogs, hens, pigs and smaller domestic animals, attracted by the heat of the peat fire, lived with the family. At one end of the house stood the barn and kiln; in front of it sprawled the midden and behind it was the walled-in patch of ground or garden, which was, near the end of the century, to become important for growing potatoes and kail, two useful additions to the monotonous diet of bere meal and oatmeal.

The houses of the better classes had an extra room for visitors, originally referred to as the "cellar" (later the "shaummer" or "chamber"). It would have been the fore-runner of the "bothy" or hostel which was to become such an important feature of farm life in Scotland during the latter part of the 19th century and first half of the 20th century.

The level of feeding of the ordinary tenant farmer and his family was low, having brose or porridge for breakfast, boiled kale and beremeal cakes at mid-day and brose for supper. The introduction of potatoes into Caithness around 1750 made an improvement, especially in years when there was a bad grain harvest. The people who lived round the coast could supplement their diet with fish and over the County as a whole the standard of living was much higher than that enjoyed by their equals in many parts of Scotland. Milk from the native cows was always plentiful and after the introduction of turnips in the mid 18th century there was not the same need to slaughter so many of their animals and salt the meat, most of which was exported in barrels. This was mainly shipped to Leith along with skins, hides, feathers, tallow, oil, hams, pork and geese.

### Landowners — Tenants — Cottars

These were the three classes of people who were involved in farming the land. The landowners had their own farm or "home-farm" as it was commonly called, situated on the best land. The tenant farmers had their small strips of ground for which they paid rent in the form of grain and so many days labour on the landlord's farm. Rents were not paid in cash normally until the 18th century and even then payments in kind were more common as very little money was in circulation. The cottars had a poorer existence than the tenant farmers as the better of the latter were sometimes able to afford one or two servants and so the cottars lived quite frugally on their crofts, which were sometimes barely able to produce sufficient oats and bere to maintain the cottar families. The rent was paid mainly by the cottars labouring on the home farm, augmented occasionally by a little grain. The cottars greatly outnumbered the tenant farmers and thus formed the main work force in the County. The duties required of both tenants and cottars included weeding, cutting down the grain, gathering, threshing, kilning, milling and transporting the grain to the ships. As the 18th century progressed prices and wages rose, while services rendered remained the same, and thus both tenant and cottar felt the pinch as they had to pay in services at the current high rate wages. Hence the lairds secured the benefit of the increase, which was equal in fact to a rise in rent. During this period a farm servant could earn a cash wage of around £1.42 (28/6) per annum, and if he was ambitious enough acquire a farm of 2.4-4 hectares (6-10 acres) with some out-run at a rent of £3.50 to £5.00 per annum. This sum included 4 oxen, a plough, harrows and a garron. Upon setting up house it was customary for him to go "thugging" among his neighbours i.e. requesting contributions of seed oats and bere to enable him to carry out his first sowing.

### Time of Reform

During the middle decades of the 18th century a wind of change had begun to blow through agriculture in Caithness just as it had done in England and in the central areas of Scotland a number of years earlier. This was partly due to the increased need of food for the rapidly increasing population in many of the new towns which were springing up as a result of the Industrial Revolution.

However, it was the mid 19th century before the changes became clearly visible.

It is useful here to assess the importance of Caithness as a centre of international trade at the beginning of the 18th century as this prestige was very soon to disappear because of both internal and external pressures. Shetland at that time had virtually no contact with Caithness, as it was wholly dependent on its herring trade with Holland, Germany and Denmark. The only cultivated ground was narrow strips round the ragged coast-line, which grew a little grain. In Orkney, the people were crofters primarily, who had fishing as a subsidiary occupation. In certain years there was a surplus of grain which found its way usually to Shetland but at other times oats were imported from Caithness as the exposed situation of the land made cereal growing very difficult. Grass has always grown well in the moister climate of Orkney and we find references to an interesting trade, which existed then between Caithness and Orkney. For most of the 18th and the early part of the 19th centuries Caithness procured its horses from Orkney, where horse-breeding was a flourishing business. Colts were imported from Caithness and other parts of the mainland and reared for two to three years before being sold back. The district of Reay, which is hilly by nature was not suited to grain growing; nor were Canisbay, Olrig and Dunnet. These areas became noted for the rearing of cattle and goats and sent quite a number of colts annually from Huna to Orkney, a reasonably short and quick passage on the strong tides of the Pentland Firth.

Caithness on the other hand was predominantly a grain growing area and vied with Banffshire for the honour of producing oats and barley next in importance to the Lothians. Thurso and Staxigoe traded constantly with important continental ports such as Bergen, Hamburg, Gothenburg as well as Leith, Aberdeen and Inverness. Strangely enough, none of the ships, which plied between these ports belonged to people in Caithness; instead, the owners came mainly from the three Scottish ports just mentioned. Large quantities of oatmeal were also sent to Ireland, the Western Isles and Sutherland. Salt, coal, iron and bottles were commodities taken to Caithness by the ships coming to pick up grain. The bottles were no doubt for the immense quantities of whisky produced at that time as well as for the wines, which came from France and Spain in barrels.

It was well known that the main industry in both Thurso and Wick for a great many years was the salting of meat and hides. The burgh regulations of Thurso around 1700 contained the proviso that all carcasses of cattle and sheep brought to market should be accompanied by their hides, skins and tallow and that the beef or mutton was not to be minced, cut or spoilt. The beef was mainly sent to the naval victualling contractors at Inverness.

### Agriculture in Caithness after 1750

As is to be expected in an industry so dependent on natural phenomena such as soils and climatic conditions, the changes that took place were very gradual but slowly and surely a better system of farming found its way onto the Caithness farms. Perhaps these improvements can be attributed to the activities of one man, who had a great deal of foresight and helped to promote new ideas in England and Scotland as well as in his native Caithness. This was Sir John Sinclair of Ulbster, who, by his own endeavours, established the Board of Agriculture in 1793 and became its first president. He wished to know more about the new ways of farming and corresponded with prominent farmers of the time not only in this country but also on the continent. As a result he acquired a great deal of valuable information, which he arranged and published in his "Code of Agriculture." Sir John demonstrated on his own estate what could be done in improving waste land by proper drainage and the cultivation of the old arable land by a new rotational system of crops, which included turnips and rotation grass for the first time. Perhaps the best thing he did was to grant long-term leases upon liberal terms to hard-working tenants. This meant that tenant farmers could put a lot into the ground physically and financially without the former fears of being evicted.

As a direct result of the founding of the Board of Agriculture, statistics have now been kept for more than one hundred years and it is possible to refer to actual figures when discussing individual topics. Various chapters in this book deal thoroughly with subjects closely related to agriculture and hence it will be necessary only to draw attention to factors specifically concerned with farming in Caithness.

### Natural Features

Being comparatively low-lying most of the good land lies below 90 m (300 ft) above sea level with practically no arable ground above 150 m (500 ft). The highest ground occurs in the west and south-west, where Caithness borders Sutherland. The good arable areas in Caithness are found at various places along the coast-line and in the broad belt, which follows a line from Wick to Thurso through Watten, flanking the two rivers for a large part of the way. The underlying flagstone, coming within inches of the surface in places, has set the Caithness farmer difficult problems as regards drainage.

Being open on two sides to the sea has influenced the climate to a great extent and cool, temperate conditions have been the result. The low mid-summer temperatures and the short summer nights, which produce a small daily range of temperatures, have limited the selection of crops which can be profitably grown. Although not so cold as other places in Britain in winter, the low angle of the sun at that time of year and the short day produce a long winter. The cold easterly winds in March, and sometimes in May, retard the flush of new grass, and so the growing season is cut short.

The mean annual rainfall is not excessive at 760 mm (30 in) in the east to over 1,015 mm (40 in) in the higher western areas, but, in a cool climate with low evaporation and poor drainage, acid conditions are found in many areas, as seen in the large stretches of peat. This, however, is partly counteracted by the naturally high lime content of much of the underlying rock. The amounts of rain and snow seem to be fairly evenly distributed throughout the seasons although the early months of the year tend to be drier because of the prevailing south-east winds at that time, and wetter weather from late summer onwards very often hampers harvesting operations.

### Land Use

Regular statistics for agriculture were not often taken until 1866, and the first available figures are those for 1868, as shown in Table 9 depicting how the land is divided. Apart from the years 1868 and 1968 all the others used for comparative purposes in the various tables have been selected at random.

From these figures it is seen that the total area of the County has twice decreased, The first fall is partly due to a change in the County boundary and

Table 9.   AGRICULTURAL LAND IN CAITHNESS

| YEAR | TOTAL AREA | | TOTAL AREA IN AGRICULTURE | |
|---|---|---|---|---|
| | HECTARES | ACRES | HECTARES | ACRES |
| 1868 | 184,092 | 455,708 | | |
| 1895 | 180,574 | 446,017 | 138,004 | 340,871 |
| 1921 | 177,665 | 438,833 | 136,772 | 337,826 |
| 1938 | 177,665 | 438,833 | 168,904 | 417,194 |
| 1944 | 177,665 | 438,833 | 162,824 | 402,175 |
| 1949 | 177,665 | 438,833 | 163,746 | 404,454 |
| 1955 | 177,665 | 438,833 | 157,259 | 388,430 |
| 1968 | 17,7665 | 438,833 | 163,066 | 402,772 |

*(No rough grazing figure was available)*

the second one is accounted for by the exclusion of the surface area of inland water. The notable increase of the "total area in agriculture" was between 1921 and 1938 (see Table 9). From that year (1938) the statistics deal with deer forests **capable** of being used for grazing, whereas previously they had included only deer forests **used** for grazing. In 1959 the conditions were further amended so as to include **all** deer forests, whether grazed or not and this added 3,237 hectares (8,000 acres) making a total of 130,704 hectares (323,000 acres) of rough grazing in that year.

### Types of Farming

Apart from the crofting areas, which occur chiefly round the coast, Caithness is a County devoted to the rearing of beef cattle and sheep, utilising a large proportion of the arable land products in the process. Store cattle and lambs are sold to the fattening area farther south, although many lambs and older sheep are fattened up locally.

The importance of crofting is shown by the fact that 51% of the holdings in 1955 were of less than 6 hectares (15 acres) and this was only a slight decrease from the total in 1896. However, changes have taken place in the relative importance of the different kinds of holdings — many crofts have been abandoned or worked along with larger holdings and a number of large arable farms have been divided into smaller units of 12-40 hectares (30-100 acres); thus, there has been a decline in the number of the smaller holdings from 0.4-12 hectares (1-30 acres) and also the larger farms of over 61 hectares (150 acres). This is clearly shown in Table 10. The large and medium-sized farms are found naturally on the best arable ground with the crofts occupying the less productive land.

Between 1955 and 1968 the size groups of the frequency distribution have been altered and we find that the total number of holdings in 1968 is now 1612, showing a significant decrease in the number of the very small units with a consequent increase in the larger-sized units.

### Arable Land

This is chiefly found on the shelly boulder clay, consisting mainly of good strong clays and loams.

The typical Caithness Five Course Rotation of Oats, Turnips, Oats, Hay

**Table 10. FREQUENCY DISTRIBUTION OF HOLDINGS IN CAITHNESS (IN AREA GROUPINGS)**

| Year | Hectares / Acres | 0.4-2 / 1-5 | 2-6 / 5-15 | 6-12 / 15-30 | 12-20 / 30-50 | 20-30 / 50-75 | 30-40 / 75-100 | 40-61 / 100-150 | 61-121 / 150-300 | 121+ / 300+ | Total |
|------|------|------|------|------|------|------|------|------|------|------|------|
| | | | | Size Groups — | | | | | | | |
| 1868 | | — | | — | | — | | — | | — | — |
| 1896 | | 669 | | 1,597 | | 201 | | 159 | | 68 | 2,694 |
| 1921 | | 547 | 968 | 492 | 228 | 174 | 87 | 79 | 101 | 51 | 2,727 |
| 1938 | | 430 | 877 | 456 | 235 | 211 | 108 | 92 | 87 | 44 | 2,540 |
| 1944 | | 439 | 861 | 443 | 235 | 218 | 100 | 88 | 82 | 31 | 2,497 |
| 1949 | | 436 | 856 | 421 | 245 | 221 | 99 | 90 | 80 | 33 | 2,481 |
| 1955 | | 420 | 822 | 445 | 227 | 208 | 112 | 92 | 82 | 31 | 2,439 |

| Year | Hectares / Acres | 2-4 / 5-10 | 4-10 / 10-25 | 10-20 / 25-50 | 20-50 / 50-125 | | 51-101' / 125-250 | 101+ / 250+ | Total |
|------|------|------|------|------|------|------|------|------|------|
| | | | | Size Groups | | | | | |
| 1968 | | 154 | 167 | 325 | 223 | 351 | 187 | 205 | 1,612 |

and Pasture is based on the system of alternate husbandry and is still used in many parts of the County today with perhaps the addition of one or two year's extra grass and barley often replacing the second grain crop with an occasional second successive crop of oats before the roots. With a big reduction in the acreage of the latter, as is clearly shown in Table 11, and a substantial increase in rotation grass, many farmers have disregarded the standard rotation and now grow cereals for two or three years before putting the field in grass for three or four years, and then repeating the programme. As a result, hay and silage have taken the place of turnips and swedes as the main winter stockfeed.

In 1960 there was a redefinition of rotation and permanent grasses, taking a simple age criterion in the new division, namely, over or under seven years. This probably slightly exaggerated the trend towards temporary grasses.

The relatively stable acreage of arable land including rotation grass has been due to the combination of arable ground with the rearing of cattle and sheep. This prevented the disastrous fall in the arable area, which occurred in many parts of Britain after 1870 as a result of imported grain. A rise of over 75 per cent in rotation grass since 1868 and a fall in practically all other crops has been the result of increased cost of production, particularly in the growing of turnips and swedes, and a decrease in the number of older court-fed bullocks because the public have a preference for light-weight beef. And so we see there is a relationship between the increase of arable grass and the number of sheep and cattle as shown in Table 12.

Cereal crops, with oats more popular than barley, were the principal sown crops until rotation grass took over the leading role at the beginning of the 20th century. The extent of cereal growing in the 19th century may be judged from the following figures. Calder reckoned that there were at least 80 to 90 stills in Caithness around 1780 and each used 100-150 bolls of barley (6350-9525 kg) in the distilling of whisky. Prior to the making of spirits, ale was the great beverage of the common people and Calder reports that 1949 bolls (60,250 kg) of malt were brewed into ale in 1668. In fact a brewing and distilling company was established in the Parish of Reay in 1697. As heavy duty was placed on whisky the amount of bere grown was greatly reduced and the way was open for oats to become the largest crop. It was estimated that 80,000

Table 11.　AREAS OF CROPS, GRASS AND ROUGH GRAZING

| CROPS | | YEARS | | | | | | | |
|---|---|---|---|---|---|---|---|---|---|
| | | 1868 | 1895 | 1921 | 1938 | 1944 | 1949 | 1955 | 1968 |
| CEREALS | Hectares | 13,689 | 14,349 | 13,374 | 9,405 | 11,736 | 10,149 | 9,424 | 8,366 |
| | Acres | 33,812 | 35,442 | 32,034 | 22,984 | 28,987 | 25,067 | 23,278 | 20,663 |
| ROOTS | Hectares | 5,990 | 6,733 | 5,183 | 3,809 | 3,718 | 3,543 | 3,366 | 1,688 |
| | Acres | 14,796 | 15,631 | 12,802 | 9,409 | 9,183 | 8,751 | 8,313 | 4,169 |
| ROTATION GRASS | Hectares | 11,017 | 12,044 | 14,601 | 17,674 | 14,229 | 15,534 | 15,636 | 19,544 |
| | Acres | 27,211 | 29,748 | 36,066 | 43,654 | 35,135 | 38,370 | 38,622 | 48,299 |
| PERMANENT GRASS | Hectares | 8,624 | 11,577 | 10,159 | 10,218 | 7,010 | 8,529 | 9,104 | 7,725 |
| | Acres | 21,302 | 28,596 | 25,983 | 25,237 | 17,314 | 21,066 | 22,487 | 19,080 |
| TOTAL AREA UNDER CROPS AND GRASS | Hectares | 40,169 | 44,545 | 43,467 | 41,269 | 37,130 | 37,992 | 37,935 | 37,656 |
| | Acres | 99,217 | 110,026 | 107,363 | 101,934 | 91,710 | 93,841 | 93,699 | 93,011 |
| ROUGH GRAZING | Hectares | n.a. | 93,460 | 93,305 | 127,636 | 125,694 | 125,714 | 108,393 | 125,349 |
| | Acres | n.a. | 230,845 | 230,463 | 315,260 | 310,465 | 310,513 | 294,731 | 309,613 |

bolls (5,079,360 kg) were produced at the beginning of the 19th century and as much as 25,000 bolls (1,587,300 kg) were exported. From about 1960 there has been a swing back in favour of barley growing as a result of it being used largely for feeding to stock and also because of the newer short-strawed varieties being able to make use of the increased fertiliser applications which would in most cases cause oats to lodge.

The areas devoted to turnips and swedes have declined, principally due to the big labour requirements of such crops and the added popularity of silage. However, where they are grown, the yields and quality are first class as the crop seems to suit local conditions.

Potatoes became popular with the crofter as it effected a change in his all too monotonous diet, but today only sufficient is grown for local requirements. Small quantities of other crops such as rape, cabbage and tares are sometimes grown. An interesting point is that the bare fallow has now disappeared although 70.8 hectares (175 acres) were recorded as late as 1937.

Permanent pasture occupies much less land now than it did at the beginning of the 20th century and as a whole much less of it is now used to provide hay, as the rotation grass mixtures are selected and chosen with an eye to their hay-producing capacity during the first year and hence heavier yields of better feeding value are produced.

Rough grazings accounted for 70.5% of the total area of Caithness in 1968 and recent increases may be due to the abandonment of marginal improved land, especially on small crofts. Normally sheep can be grazed here; although some areas are only of value for a limited time during the summer, others can carry cattle especially if improved land is adjoining. Four distinct types are found: **Heather Moors** which occupy much of Caithness and where drainage is adequate can carry extensive flocks of sheep. There may be competition from deer, grouse and hares; **Grass Moors** where, in the absence of strong acid conditions, grass grows in contrast to heather and sheep do well; **Peat Bogs and Mosses,** which are of no commercial value; and lastly, **Sandy Links Grazings,** which produce very little in dry summers but are useful for autumn and winter use, as drainage creates no problems.

In tilling the soil the Caithness farmer has not been slow to try new methods which were to benefit himself, and many of the improvements have been the direct result of his practical knowledge allied to his shrewdness. As an example of this we find fertilisers being applied freely by the end of the 19th century. The most commonly used ones are superphosphate, bone flour, bone meal, dissolved bones, basic slag, sulphate of ammonia, nitrate of soda and kainit. Hence we see that three plant foods, Nitrogen, Phosphorus and Potassium, which have become so commonly referred to as N, P and K are not so new in Caithness. The greatest emphasis, it seems, at that time, was on phosphates, which still are applied in large amounts in the County to produce good returns. The value of lime had long been recognised.

### Livestock

The small native black cattle, which roamed over most of the County from early times were only outnumbered by sheep after the beginning of the 19th century. From Table 12 it is evident that their increase was quite fantastic. The swing from grain production to arable grass leys had a lot to do with this.

## Sheep

From the early 1920's the numbers rose rapidly, until they reached a peak of 246,630 in 1939, since which time the sheep population has remained remarkably constant. At the present time there may be a slight falling off in sheep numbers in favour of an increase in beef cattle as returns from the latter appear to leave the farmer a better margin of profit.

Sheep are very numerous all over the County except in those parts of the higher western areas which are boggy and unsuitable. The greatest density of numbers is on the better land utilising the rotation grass with the help of rough pasture during summer. The North Country Cheviot, introduced into Caithness, at Langwell, by Sir John Sinclair at the end of the 18th century, is by far the most popular breed today, having completely ousted the smaller, native black-faced Kerry sheep. Some Scotch Blackfaces are found but only on the harder, wetter areas of the west. When crossed with a Border Leicester ram, the Cheviot ewe produces Half-bred lambs, which are much in demand by farmers from the arable districts of the south.

Lambs from the arable farms are normally sold fat from summer till the following spring, when they are termed hoggs. Those not fattened and the lambs from the hill farms, which cannot easily carry stock through the winter, are sold at the lamb sales which take place regularly from August to November.

The wool clip is an important source of income and although no spinning of wool and weaving of cloth is done in the County today, wool from Caithness sheep is regarded as being of a high quality. This may be the result of crossing with the Merino sheep, which Sir John Sinclair took to Langwell in 1821.

The stock-carrying capacity on the moorland farms of Caithness is approximately 100 ewes per 405 hectares (1000) acres). Thus, a sheep farm of 2025 hectares (5000 acres) would produce about 907 kg (2000 lb) of wool, 5442 kg (12,000 lb) of lamb mutton in store condition and 100 "cast" five year old breeding ewes sold to low-ground farms for breeding half-bred lambs. In addition, out-wintered cattle are grazed and so the moorland areas provide a considerable reservoir of stock for lowland arable farms and are of great economic importance to agriculture in Caithness.

## Cattle

Caithness has earned the reputation of breeding and rearing good beef animals. The growing of good grass and turnips has had a lot to do with this

### Table 12
### NUMBERS OF LIVESTOCK AND TRACTORS IN CAITHNESS

| YEAR | CATTLE | | SHEEP | PIGS | WORKING | TRACTORS |
| | DAIRY | BEEF | | | HORSES | |
|------|-------|------|-------|------|---------|----------|
| 1868 | | 21,226 | 96,295 | 1,707 | N.A. | — |
| 1895 | | 21,646 | 108,621 | 1,806 | 4,274 | — |
| 1921 | | 19,525 | 134,611 | 1,869 | 3,985 | — |
| 1938 | 8,302 | 12,444 | 242,929 | 2,082 | 3,148 | — |
| 1944 | 7,371 | 16,212 | 222,404 | 1,740 | 2,565 | 360 |
| 1949 | 6,018 | 20,731 | 225,824 | 2,107 | 1,876 | 447 |
| 1955 | 4,155 | 24,321 | 221,786 | 4,377 | 914 | 1007 |
| 1968 | 2,732 | 35,844 | 235,457 | 1,470 | 42x | 1432ø |

x December 1965 was the last recorded figure
ø February 1967 was the nearest statistic available

as has the cooler climate which encourages a vigorous and early growth of hair. The original black cattle of the County were improved by crossing with West Highland (Kyloe) bulls from Argyllshire for the lowland farms. Bulls were taken from Skye for the hill farms and so during the 18th century the Kyloe was becoming dominant. However, the Shorthorn was beginning to make its mark and by 1850 its crosses predominated at a time when the Aberdeen Angus breed was practically unknown in Caithness. The progress of the "black-poll" was extremely rapid as it produced a quality calf when mated with the Shorthorn Cow. The latter had the mothering qualities to give its offspring a good start in life, while the black bull produced a short blocky-type animal which was relatively light in the bone and fattened easily. The white face of the Hereford as a cross with the Aberdeen-Angus is becoming more popular but the good black calves still command a higher average price in the sale ring.

Traditionally, calving took place in the spring, so that by the time grass became plentiful the calves would be big enough to make use of it, and along with the milk received from their dams the rates of growth were very satisfactory. By the time of the calf sales in the autumn these animals had developed into strong, sturdy stores. Recently, the smaller calves have been overwintered and sold in April when they have made good prices, which has more than compensated for the extra cost involved in bringing them through the winter.

Scour in calves born inside during the winter months has necessitated other changes and many herds now calve either wholly or partly outside in the autumn, with the remainder after February or March, so that no calving takes place inside.

From Table 12 it will be noticed that the numbers of beef cattle have nearly trebled since 1938 whereas dairy cattle have declined by the same proportion. The main reason for this is that Caithness is too far from the large town populations and only requires sufficient milk for local needs. Approximately 11,375 litres (2,500 gallons) are produced daily during the winter months but this increases to 20,460 litres (4,500 gallons) in the summer time; hence the bulk of the milk is produced cheaply from the abundant grass. The daily requirements for the County are about 8,182 litres (1,800 gallons) at the height of the demand in summer, any surplus being previously made into cream and sent south for churning into butter. However, an extension to the cheese factory at Wick will use all this extra production and more, so that there may well be a market for more milk in future years.

### Pigs

In an area best suited to the growing of grass and fodder crops and being too distant from a big population, pigs have not become the important animal enterprise that they have in other parts of Scotland. In fact, they are regarded chiefly as a side-line in Caithness at present. The yearly figures remain remarkably constant except for the fluctuations which we get in the familiar pig cycle varying from four to eight years. 1955 was a good example of a peak in production but it levelled out again by 1968.

### Poultry

Here again the distance from markets together with the lack of shelter and cold damp weather have never really encouraged large-scale poultry enterprises in Caithness but small flocks kept in deep litter houses have been more than sufficient for local needs in recent years. A figure of 47,000 (approximately) was recorded in 1885 and it increased to around 130,000 by 1937. Ducks, turkeys and geese are also kept in fairly small numbers.

### Horses and Tractors

The one-time very popular Clydesdale has disappeared almost completely and statistics were no longer recorded after December 1955. The introduction of vehicular power in the form of tractors, which could do the same job in a fraction of the time, was the reason why the horses fell from favour. Numbers fell slightly during the 1930's, receiving a boost during the Second World War due to the scarcity of fuel, but the increase in tractors after the end of the hostilities has gone on until a relatively high figure was recorded in 1967.

Machines, too, have increased at an alarming rate due in some part to the extra power supplied by the tractor. It is interesting to note that the binder, both tractor and horse-powered models, which took the place of the old reaper, is itself being replaced by combines, all in the space of about fifty to sixty years.

### Labour

The gradual decrease in the number of working horses has been accompanied by a decrease in the number of people employed to work on the land. In recent years the reduction in farm staffs has been exceptionally great so that in many places there is a scarcity of labour. Two main factors may be to blame for this: the absence of a five-day week as in other industries, and the competition of higher wages in other jobs which do not involve working outside in all weathers. The decision to site the Dounreay Establishment in the west of the County may be partly to blame for the drift from the land, but on the other hand, this establishment has provided work for the crofter, who has still time to work the land in his spare time. In many cases the extra money may have saved the croft from going back to rough pasture.

Table 13 gives a breakdown of the labour employed in Caithness but unfortunately the totals do not include those farmers' sons who are classed as self-employed and so the numbers are not a true reflection of the total number of people engaged in practical agriculture in the County. With the small numbers of young people coming into farming, Caithness could very easily become an area mainly of family farms.

Table 13. **NUMBER OF WORKERS EMPLOYED IN AGRICULTURAL HOLDINGS OF MORE THAN 0.40 HECTARE (1 ACRE) IN SIZE**

| YEAR | REGULAR WORKERS | | | | | | |
| | MALE | | WOMEN AND GIRLS | TOTAL | PART-TIME | CASUAL | TOTAL |
| | under 21 | over 21 | | | | | |
| 1921 | 435 | 972 | 572 | 1,979 | 573 | | 2,552 |
| 1938 | 287 | 962 | 375 | 1,624 | 281 | | 1,905 |
| 1944 | 1059 | | 302 | 1,361 | 288 | | 1,649 |
| 1949 | 224 | 887 | 277 | 1,388 | 259 | | 1,647 |
| 1955Ø | 219 | 746 | 144 | 1,109 | 153 | 166 | 1,428 |
| 1968 | 50 | 391 | 39 | 477 | 56 | 93 | 626 |

Ø  Since 1955 the figures are slightly different because of the change in the Agricultural Wages Regulations, the age of twenty being adopted as a class boundary.

## AGRICULTURAL SOCIETIES AND ASSOCIATIONS

Caithness has not lagged behind other parts of Scotland in supporting organisations which are concerned with farming.

In 1830 the Caithness Agricultural Society was founded and continues to flourish. The Society was set up to bring about the improvement of agriculture and rural industries in the County and this it has done over the years by holding an Annual County Show in Wick and in Thurso in alternate years, by conducting experiments with and by holding competitions of, all kinds of crops, grain, live-stock, etc. The Annual County Show is a shop-window of the livestock of Caithness and provides those interested with an opportunity of seeing the largest and finest display of North Country Cheviot Sheep in the United Kingdom.

At first the Society also sought to secure parliamentary action in support of agriculture but this role has gradually declined with the development of the National Farmers' Union of Scotland, founded nationally in 1914 and in Caithness in July 1918. With a membership of over 700, the Caithness Area of the N.F.U. of Scotland is one of the most active and strongly supported in the country and its voice is heard and listened to wherever matters affecting the hills and uplands are being discussed. Since January 1964, the setting up of Caithness Livestock Breeders Ltd., a farmers' co-operative registered under the Industrial and Provident Societies Acts, has had an influence on the traditional trading and marketing arrangements of Caithness farmers. Its objects can be said to be directly concerned with the commercial interests of farmers whereas the other bodies mentioned are, perhaps, more concerned with the political and legal framework within which farmers operate. The Caithness Grassland Society meets regularly and as its name implies is primarily concerned with the production and utilisation of grass.

Last, but by no means least, is the important connection which Caithness has with the Scottish Association of Young Farmers' Clubs. The Junior Agricultural Club movement began in the United States of America in 1899 and their 4-H Club activities soon became known internationally. The club movement had its initiation in Scotland in 1923, actually in Caithness, due to the enthusiasm of three people — Mr John Robson of Lynegar, Watten, who became the first President; Mr John Sutherland, the local headmaster, who was the first club Leader and Mr Alexander Black, the County Advisor of the College of Agriculture in Thurso, who became the first secretary — under the auspices and rules of the "Daily Mail" International Federation of Young Farmers Clubs. The forementioned paper was responsible for introducing the Young Farmers' Club movement into Britain in 1921, the first club being at Hemyock in Devon.

Agriculture has always been the largest single industry in Caithness, as it has also been throughout Great Britain as a whole and it seems very unlikely that this is going to change in this northern farming County. However, certain factors may alter the present agricultural policies, the main one being whether the U.K. becomes a member of the E.E.C. (Common Market) in the near future. However, at present, the level of subsidies and guarantee, payments, etc. which are made known in the Annual Price Review have a more direct bearing on the individual farmer, but given a fair return for his input of energy, knowledge and capital Caithness should retain its high reputation in agricultural circles.

# CHAPTER 21

# WOODLAND

Caithness has the lowest percentage of woodland of any county in Great Britain, except Zetland. The main reason for this is the severe exposure to weather which the County experiences, lying as it does in the northern corner of Scotland and having little topographical shelter. At the end of the last ice age alder and willow, followed by birch, rowan, hazel and Scots pine colonised the bare mineral soils left by the receding ice. Gradually, however, because the climate was becoming wetter, and as the land is relatively low-lying and poorly drained, peat began accumulating and killed most of the tree cover, except in the better drained soil bordering burns and rivers. Where peat has been removed by natural erosion or for burning, tree stumps are sometimes exposed. These stumps may be 4,000-9,000 years old, having grown before the peat became too deep and finally choked them.

Until as recently as 200 years ago all straths in the parishes of Latheron and Halkirk had scrub woods of birch with alder, hazel, rowan and willow (Henderson). No Scots pine is recorded as being natural in Caithness at this time. However, it is possible that it may have been cut out for building and burning long before this time. Planted woods, too, were very scarce in the County, except for 342 hectares (848 acres) of plantations in the two straths at Berriedale. These yielded large-sized timber about 1760. This particular area is mountainous with deep valleys and hence local shelter, which is not typical of the rest of the county, is obtained.

All the scrub woods in the County were repeatedly and heavily cut for firewood and the bark of the trees was used for tanning shoe leather. What larger-sized timber remained was cut for house building and for making plough beams and crubbans (for carrying oats or peat on horses' backs).

These woods were also used for sheltering cattle; such animals would have prevented any regrowth occurring by eating self-sown seedlings and sucker shoots from cut stumps. In the 18th century it was recorded that these wooded straths supported more cattle, as the grass began growing earlier in spring and was more luxuriant than in non-wooded straths. On the other hand, more cattle died from disease in wooded straths.

About 1792, European larch and Scots pine were planted at Langwell but they have now been mostly cut down or windthrown. A few smaller plantations were established in other parts of the County during the ensuing century but, even so, the total area covered by trees in 1947 was under 810 hectares (2,000 acres) of which less than 20% was considered suitable for economic management; in no other county did this figure fall below 50%.

Following the acquisition of Rumster Farm near Lybster the Forestry Commission started planting in Caithness in 1948. At about the same time the Research Division of the Forestry Commission began establishing pilot

PLATE 32. *Wick Harbour a century ago.*

(John O'Groat Journal)

(A. Luciani)

PLATE 33.   *Shore Street, Thurso.*

(A. Luciani)

PLATE 34.   *Scrabster Harbour, with Dunnet Head in background.*

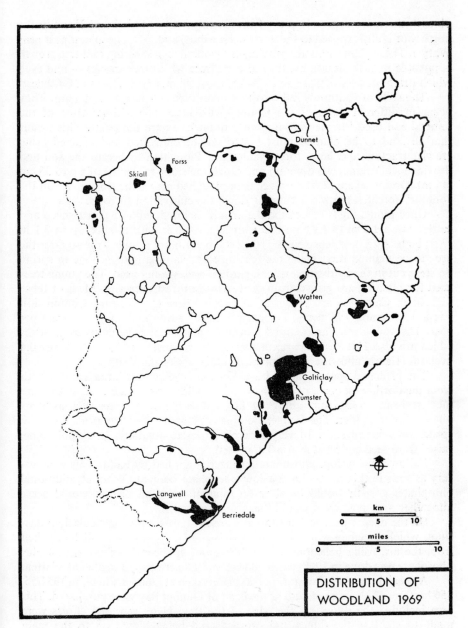

**Figure 18. Distribution of Woodland**

N

plots in the more exposed parts of the County; *a*) at Skiall and Forss in the north (both fully exposed to the north-west winds) and, *b*) on deep, flat peat near Watten. These plantations are proving most valuable in showing that tree growth is possible in such situations; they also indicate which tree species — and even which strains of a particular species — are most suited to conditions in Caithness.

The soils of Caithness fall into two main types — peat and mineral. They occur in different parts of the County with little intermixing. Most of the mineral soil used for planting is poorly drained, as are the peats. This means that all land to be planted must first of all be cultivated and drained using crawler tractors and large forestry ploughs. Ploughing to aerate the soil and provide local drainage is done up and down the slope to depths of up to 35 cm (14 in). Drains 60 cm (2 ft) deep are then ploughed across the slope just "off the contour" to catch the water running down the cultivation furrows.

Once ploughing is completed the area is enclosed, either against sheep and cattle with a 1.2 m (4 ft) high fence, or against deer with a fence up to 2.1 m (7 ft) high. As a deer fence costs £600-£800 per 1.6 km (1 mile), the squarer the area to be planted the smaller the fencing cost. Planting is then done in spring on steps cut in the cultivation ridges, garden spades being used. The young trees used for planting are grown from seed sown in forest nurseries. Most of those planted in Caithness are grown at Dornoch where the Forestry Commission has a 17 hectares (43 acres) nursery producing seven million young trees per year. The young trees are planted 2 m (6 ft) apart along the cultivation ridges which are also 2 m (6 ft) apart; this spacing gives just over 1,000 trees per 0.4 hectares (1 acre) allowing for unplanted ridges, racks and drains.

The principal species planted are Lodgepole pine and Sitka spruce, both from the north-west coast of North America. These species are used as they are more resistant to exposure and grow faster than the native trees such as Scots pine, birch and alder. The Lodgepole pine is planted mainly on peat, the Sitka spruce on mineral soils. In very severely exposed situations Lodgepole pine, raised from seed collected in Alaska, is used.

Following planting, phosphate fertilizer is applied by hand. This is necessary as soils in this region have a low phosphate content. Without additional phosphate, growth would be slow on mineral soils; on peat it would cease altogether and most trees would die.

On the deeper peats other nutrients are in short supply, particularly potassium, which together with subsequent dressings of phosphate will be applied from the air, using helicopters. The first aerial application of potassium plus phosphate was done in 1968, when 28 hectares (68 acres) were treated at Watten.

A special type of afforestation was undertaken at Dunnet where, in 1954/55, 356 hectares (879 acres) of land at the head of Dunnet Bay were purchased. This area included the dunes on the edge of the Bay. Here, repeated efforts were made to stabilise the dunes and prevent sand being blown on to the main Castletown-Dunnet road. This was done by erecting artificial hedges of brushwood across "blow-outs" (areas of severe wind erosion). These hedges soon became covered by small dunes and similar hedges were erected on top of the old ones. This process was repeated several times over the years until dunes up to 6 m (20 ft) high were created. To the leeward of the hedges loose sand was covered by Scots pine tops taken from thinnings in the Black Isle, Balblair and Dornoch Forests and young trees were planted through this "thatch". Corsican pine was the species planted initially but it was not able to resist the blast. Subsequently, mountain pine from the Pyrenees was found to be the most suitable species. (This area has now been sold to the County Council).

At present, the total area planted by the Forestry Commission in Caithness is 1,215 hectares (3,000 acres) of which 850 hectares (2,100 acres) are at Rumster, which now includes Golticlay. The remainder is scattered over most of the County as relatively small blocks which, in addition to timber, provide shelter for farm animals. The current annual planting programme is 170 hectares (420 acres) which is more than the total coniferous woodland that existed in the County before 1948. There is no limit set for the total area to be afforested in Caithness, although there are obviously areas where afforestation would be impossible or undesirable, such as on rich agricultural ground, peatland with a badly broken surface, peatland which is too soft for tractors to cross, hill tops where exposure is too severe for tree growth, and areas which are too small to justify fencing.

Private landowners have done some planting during the last 20 years to produce shelter blocks, replace felled woodland or in the case of Welbeck Estates at Berriedale, to create coniferous plantations primarily for timber production. The total area of private woodland in Caithness is difficult to estimate but it is probably some 770 hectares (1,900 acres) of which only about half seems capable of economic management.

State and private woodland, including scrub, will amount to about 1985 hectares (4,900 acres) which is still only 1 % of the total land area of the County (see fig. 18). Nevertheless, the effect on the landscape is already becoming noticeable. As well as producing timber, woodland encourages wild life of all types — mammals, birds, insects and plants — and by so doing, increases the amenity value of the countryside. Young coniferous plantations, once the tree canopy has closed, kill most of the ground vegetation. However, where the vegetation survives such as on rock outcrops, burnsides, roads and failed patches, there is generally a wider range of plants which are also more luxuriant than those found on the open hill, where periodic burning produces a fire climax vegetation dominated by heather and deer grass.

# CHAPTER 22

# THE FISHING INDUSTRY

### Herring

The rise of the herring fishing in Caithness was associated with the Sutherland clearances and subsequent migration of the surplus agricultural population.

The people moved to the coast from the sheltered glens and straths of the Highlands and had to break in virgin soil and cultivate marginal land. In the initial period of breaking in these crofts they had to supplement their diet by fishing and by the time the boom in the herring industry occurred these crofter-fisherman already had the necessary elementary skills.

In the early 17th century the Government, motivated by a desire to undermine Dutch sea-power, began to encourage the growth of fishing.

The County was fortunate in the respect that some of the best inshore fishing grounds in the world were off its east coast. In late summer and autumn dense shoals of mature fat herrings congregated close inshore, well within reach of the smallest boats.

The Free British Fishery Society was founded in 1750 and introduced the bounty system of subsidies to encourage the growth of the Fishery. An annual bounty of £1.50 per 1,016 kg (30/- per ton) was awarded on all decked vessels of 20,320 kg (20 tons) and upwards engaged in the herring fishing plus 5p (1/-) per barrel of herring cured.

In 1786 the powers of the Society were extended to include the building of "towns, villages, harbours, quays, piers and fishing stations in the Highlands and Islands of North Britain". This it was stated "would greatly contribute to the improvement of the Fisheries, Agriculture, Manufactures, and other useful objects in that part of Britain."

In 1797 the bounty was increased to 10p (2/-) a barrel. 1808 saw the appointment of the Commissioners of British Fisheries and in 1815 the bounty was increased to 20p (4/-) per barrel.

From that time the Fishery increased by leaps and bounds to reach a maximum at the end of the 19th century.

The foundation of the Wick herring fishery was laid in 1767 when John Sutherland of Wester, John Anderson of Wick and Alexander Miller of Staxigoe fitted out two small sloops and operated from Staxigoe, which had the better anchorage and landing facilities. However, difficulties were encountered and through some formality they failed to qualify for the bounty. The next year only one sloop set out but this time she gained the bounty.

Although 363 barrels of herring were exported in 1782 little further progress was made until the Incorporation of the British Fishery Society in 1786. From then onwards, with the encouragement of this Society, the herring fishing increased annually.

Such were the prospects for the fishing that a completely new village was planned and laid out by a Captain Brodie in 1788. It lay 6.4 km (4 miles) south of Wick at the head of a sheltered creek or 'clett' and was known as 'Sarclet' or 'Brodie's Town'.

By 1790 the catch had increased to 13,000 barrels and 32 small sloops were fishing. Next year there were 44 sloops and by 1795, 200 boats were fishing from Wick.

Encouraged by the rising catch and the numbers employed, the British Fishery Society acquired a large space of ground on the south side of Wick bay for the establishment of a fishing village and in 1808 laid out feus and started, under the direction of the famous engineer Telford, the construction of a harbour. This village, called Pulteneytown after the chairman of the Fishery Commission, Sir William Pulteney, was settled by crofters and fishers from the surrounding villages. Many of its street names are those of Telford's friends.

In 1810 the inner harbour was completed, having cost £16,000. This led to a phenomenal increase in trade. By this time the herring fishing was being pursued in the summer months from the districts of Dunbeath, Lybster, and Clyth.

A few weeks before the Battle of Waterloo the Government raised the bounty to 20p (4/-) per barrel. This marked the beginning of a boom so great that Pulteney Harbour became inadequate and the building of an outer harbour was begun in 1824.

In 1835 there were 830 boats, by 1851 the number had risen to 1000, and in 1862 the fishery reached its peak with 1122 boats fishing from Wick.

Since distance from markets and poor transport facilities precluded the supplying of a large market for fresh herring, cured herring was the mainstay of the industry. This was not perishable and gradually more of the cured article was exported. The Scottish herring industry was at this time the greatest in Europe. During the season every creek and inlet presented a most animated scene, every level space being covered with thousands and thousands of barrels, interspersed with the busy scene of delivery, of gutting and packing and all the bustle and detail attendant on the cure.

During the mid 19th century the typical herring boat was about 9 m (30 ft) long and undecked, offering no protection to the fishermen from wind and waves. They were mostly locally built, each district having its own distinctive shape and design, most famous of all being the Fifie (with a straight stern) and the Zulu with its sloping stern.

At this time the nets used to catch herring were made from hemp. The weaving of a single net could occupy a whole winter for one man.

The introduction of ready-made cotton nets, which were finer and more efficient, led to a vast increase in catching power. Bigger and better boats were built. Oars gave way to sail and a winch — an 'Iron Man' — powered by hand, was introduced to reduce the labour of hauling larger fleets of nets.

The fishing reached its peak during the 1860's. Catches of 80 to 100 crans were not unknown. The number of boats engaged in the trade is almost unbelievable. Around 1840 the number of boats operating was — Wick 760, Clyth 70, Lybster 100, Swiney (Achastle) 10, Forse 32, Latheronwheel 35 and Dunbeath 76. In Latheron Parish, at this time, the number of people employed in herring fishing was:

1321 fishermen
106 coopers
937 packers (women)
178 labourers
50 fish curers

Each summer season the local crews were supplemented by hired men from Lewis and Harris, hundreds of whom, all Gaelic-speaking, arrived in July. They were generally accommodated in the homes of their employers and in weather unsuitable for fishing might be found assisting with the harvest.

These people were engaged for the season on a share-of-the-catch basis. A man lucky enough to be engaged immediately on his arrival might be seen busily engaged on making ready his employer's craft for sea; the man not so lucky sat around twiting (whittling) a piece of wood — the recognised sign that he was unemployed.

Most of these Western Islanders were deeply religious men and were regular attenders at Church Services conducted specially for them in their own language by the local Free Church ministers. Even at sea it was not unusual for them to engage in the singing of psalms, followed by prayers, after they had shot the nets.

The introduction of the steam drifter around the turn of the century led to a decline at the smaller ports, since they could not accommodate the size of vessel now engaged in the fishing. Herring fishing became an all year round occupation with drifters and large motor boats making an annual autumn voyage to Yarmouth. Accompanying them went curers, coopers, gutters and packers.

## The Seine-Net

"What do you do with all the rope?" is a question frequently asked by the visitor viewing a seine-net boat.

Perhaps few realise just how much rope there is. The modern seine-netter of the type using the Caithness ports of Wick, Scrabster and Lybster will carry from 1500 m to 3000 m (4920 ft to 9840 ft) of rope, divided into two lengths, one on each side of the vessel. When the vessel is operating, the gear in the water consists, in essentials, of nothing more than two long ropes and a cone-shaped net. The gear is laid on the sea bed in a roughly triangular pattern. As the boat moves ahead and the ropes are hauled slowly on board the net moves forward, closing gradually, but held open for a time by the friction of the ropes on the sea-bottom and their resistance to the water. Fish are herded by the closing ropes into the path of the net and if all goes according to plan they are swept up by the 'wings' of the net and gathered into the cone-shaped bag.

First tried out in Denmark in the 1850s, this method of fishing for white fish proved so successful that it is now in use in all parts of the world.

The great advantage of the seine-net is that it can be used all the year round. Boats do not have to leave their home port, as with the herring catches. Crews are paid on a share system and since the greater the catch the bigger the pay, the incentive to work is high.

The first vessels belonging to Wick to fish by this method were steam drifters driven from the herring fishing for economic reasons in the 1930s. They did not, however, land their catches in the County but at Grimsby where the market was more suited to their produce. "Zoe", "Fairy Hill", "Drift

Fisher", "Morven Hill", and "The Pearl", are all well-remembered names of herring-drifters whose owners pioneered seine-netting.

The vigour with which seine-net fishing had flourished from Scrabster since the Second World War is largely due to the initiative and drive of one man — John Sinclair, now Lord Lieutenant of Caithness.

However, since the steam-powered drifters used so much coal as to make their fuel costs uneconomic, motor power was found more suitable and now all seine-net vessels are diesel-powered.

Among electronic aids fitted are echo-sounders, used for locating fish and determining the nature of the sea-bottom. The Decca Navigator, which is used to fix the vessel's position, is of particular importance. With its aid the position of rocks and wrecks on the sea-bed can be plotted and avoided.

Seine-netting which was largely a 'chuck-it and chance it' method, taken on land marks, before the 1950s, had become a precision method of fishing, the introduction of these aids enabling a skipper to place his gear right up against or in among obstacles where fish sometimes abound.

Five days in the week, weather permitting, a fleet of some 40 boats set out from the three seine-net harbours in the County (Wick, Scrabster and Lybster) usually long before dawn, although in summer it is sometimes necessary to fish during the night.

Each vessel's destination will depend on the whim of its individual skipper. He may head straight for a spot of his own fancy, he may spend some time searching different grounds using his echo-sounding devices to detect traces of shoals of fish, or he may make up his mind from information he gleans from his radio, listening to the conversation of other skippers.

Fish shoals can move quickly and a ground which is quite productive one day can be completely bare the next. The ability to locate the shoal, and after finding it, to catch fish, is the measure of a skipper's success.

On finding traces of fish the skipper will decide to shoot his gear.

His first considerations will be the nature of the bottom and how much rope can be paid out. The general rule is 'more rope more fish', but many grounds are restricted by the presence of snags on the sea-bottom. The skipper must use his knowledge of the sea-bed to avoid these since ringing in a 'fastener' means a spoiled haul with a chance of damaging or even losing a valuable net.

He must also take into consideration the strength and direction of the tide. Seine-net gear is reckoned to be most effective when towed against the tide, but in some areas near the Pentland Firth tides are so strong that it becomes impossible to tow against them and so the gear must be set to be towed in the same direction as the tide.

First, a marker buoy attached to one end of the warp (rope) is placed in the water. Then the vessel steams away at full speed paying out rope until the desired amount has been 'shot'. The net is put over, followed by an equal amount of rope, the whole forming a roughly triangular shape.

Picking up the marker buoy the boat moves slowly ahead while both ropes are winched in. At first the net does not move much but the ropes begin to shepherd fish into its path. As the warps become straighter the speed of the net increases and fish pass down its bag into the cod-end. When the ropes have come together the net is closed and has ceased to fish, and it is then a case of bringing the net on board as quickly as possible so that another haul can begin. The operation will be repeated perhaps six to eight times per day.

This method is worked successfully by Caithness boats on grounds ranging from the northern half of the Moray Firth to Cape Wrath, Sule Skerry and all around the Orkney Islands.

Individual hauls containing up to 250 boxes of cod have been known but a more common average would be some 255 kg (5 cwt) of fish, generally cod or haddock, although flatfish and skate are also caught.

Auctions are held daily at both Wick and Scrabster.

### Table 14
#### Number of Seine-Net Boats and Value of the Catch

|        | Boats | Kilos     | (Cwt)   | £       |
|--------|-------|-----------|---------|---------|
| 1947   | 56    | 5,474,411 | 107,764 | 254,279 |
| 1957   | 50    | 7,224,007 | 142,197 | 394,944 |
| 1962   | 43    | 4,266,133 | 83,979  | 307,061 |
| 1967   | 41    | 4,812,640 | 94,737  | 385,126 |
| 1968   | 36    | 5,511,012 | 110,453 | 430,816 |

## Shell Fishing

As early as 1793 attempts were made to catch lobsters commercially. Although they were found to be plentiful and easily caught, the fishing was not a success since lobsters must be marketed alive and a large proportion of the catch died while being transported south by sailing vessel.

Only after the opening of the railway was it possible for lobsters to be sent to London alive and since that time every small harbour along both east and north coasts of the County has had small boats engaged in catching lobsters.

Now a pond has been opened at Scrabster for keeping lobsters alive until they are needed. They are then sent south, sometimes by plane, to London or even to the Continental markets of Paris and Amsterdam.

### Table 15.   Shell-fish values

| Year | £      |
|------|--------|
| 1947 | 15,501 |
| 1957 | 15,878 |
| 1962 | 21,870 |
| 1967 | 30,469 |
| 1968 | 51,701 |

## Line-Fishing

During late autumn and winter, when the 'Highlandmen' had gone home it was the practice to haul the larger boats well up clear of the sea, where they were safe from the winter storms. Two crews might then join together to man a smaller boat, which was more easily handled in bad weather, and engage in line-fishing, which must have been one of the most difficult methods of earning a living it is possible to imagine.

The line used to catch haddocks was known as the 'small' line. This was a long cotton line with hooks attached to it by 'snoods' made from plaited horse-hair. These hooks were baited with mussels or limpets.

For best results a line had to be shot in the dark in the morning so as to be in position when the fish were inclined to feed at the first of day. So men had to launch their boats in the middle of the night, row and sail their way to the grounds, shoot and haul their lines, make their way back to shore, land their catch and then turn to and bait the line again ready for next morning. Good old days indeed! For cod a heavier line, known as the 'great' line was used.

Another method was the hand-line or 'ripper.' for catching cod and saithe. This consisted of a line long enough to reach the bottom of the sea, with a lead weight fitted with polished hooks at the end. The line jerked up and down in imitation of the movements of a small fish and was a very successful method of catching cod.

Although the small line is no longer used in the County, occasional use is made of the great line to catch halibut. Wick and Scrabster still have their fleets of small boats using these hand lines.

## General

The greatest change in the public's taste for fish has been the reduction in demand for the salt herring. Not long ago, it was a staple diet. Many people in the County will recall being served four or five times a week with "tatties and herring".

Ling and cod used to be salted in spring and stored for the following winter. Before modern transport gave easy access to southern markets, salmon was commonly consumed.

In the heyday of line fishing both plaice and lemon-sole was regarded as dirty fish, fit only for use as bait. Nowadays, both are highly prized for food.

Some of the cod being landed at Caithness is shipped south to England, processed into fish fingers, packaged and returned to the County!

The distance of the County from the main centres of population has always been a drawback to the development of the fishing. Transport costs are high and this is reflected in the price returned to the fisherman. Hope for the future would seem to lie in the establishment of fish processing plants within the County, which would create employment and reduce the cost of transport.

Caithness is also unfortunate in its lack of really good harbours. Scrabster is the only harbour in the County which is accessible at all times. On the east coast both Wick and Lybster can be dangerous to enter with onshore winds, and in the event of a sudden gale, boats can be forced to run as far as Cromarty for shelter. This lack of a safe refuge has always been a source of difficulty for the fisherman. In 1848 thirty-seven men and forty-one boats were lost in one morning while trying to enter Wick in a south-easterly gale.

Attempts to make Wick Harbour safer have been foiled by the sea. In 1872 Stevenson's breakwater was destroyed and in 1877 a new pier was washed away.

This year (1970) fishermen have again been agitating to have something done to improve accessibility to Wick Harbour and reduce the element of risk while entering the harbour during onshore winds. As the incidence of easterly wind seems to be increasing, the need for action assumes a greater urgency.

# CHAPTER 23

# OTHER CAITHNESS INDUSTRIES

By no stretch of imagination could Caithness be termed an industrial County; yet it has been, and still is, famous for some of its products which are justly appreciated over the Ord and indeed over the seas.

Caithness did not undergo a sudden industrialisation two hundred years ago, as did Central Scotland, at the time of the Industrial Revolution, for the industries of the County were not dependent on coal. Certain industries have sprung up, flourished and died out again; some of these have recently been revived while others have maintained their position over the years. If it were possible to think of Caithness in terms of an industrial revolution then perhaps this event is only now about to take place, with the guarantee of a plentiful supply of electricity generated at hand from the nuclear reactors at Dounreay.

Caithness industries fall mainly into two classes — the Export industries and the Service industries — although a third industry, Tourism, which may be considered as a little of both, is becoming increasingly important to the prosperity of the County.

## The Flagstone Industry

The most famous of all exports from Caithness has undoubtedly been paving stones, the term 'Caithness flagstone' being known in the building trade throughout the world. The fact that much of the County rests on a layer of hard grey rock which splits readily into large thin flat pieces or flags must not have escaped the notice of the early inhabitants of our County, but this digging and splitting of stone did not achieve the status of an industry until about 1825. The genius behind this transformation was the Sheriff of the County, James Traill of Rattar, who was born in 1758 and died in 1847. He lived in the House of Castlehill at Castletown. The first shipment of flagstones left the little harbour there in 1825, although it is recorded that in the summer of 1793 several cargoes of stone were shipped to Aberdeen from Castlehill. Traill had the harbour enlarged and a bogie track laid to the nearby quarries. By 1840 there were over 100 workers and the annual shipment was 27,870 m² (300,000 ft²).

In a matter of 15 years the population of Castletown had doubled, and even today a few of the original quarry workers' houses still stand along the north side of the long main street, the old bings of stone rubble standing behind them. In the 1830's more quarries were opened up in various parts of the County, among them Holborn Head and Weydale. By 1837, stone dressing yards had been introduced, this work being concentrated on both sides of the river mouth at Thurso where the harbour and brickworks are today. At first, the stones were shaped into squares and rectangles by hand-saws but in a short time steam saws and polishers were introduced. Most of the stone was shipped from Castletown, Thurso and Scrabster while there was also some trade, through Wick, to all the principal cities of Britain and to many places in Europe and even North America. Sometimes the flags were the main cargo; at other times they acted as ballast for returning colliers.

At the turn of the century the average annual output was over 162,570,000 kg (16,000 tons), valued at about £23,000, the industry then employing over 500 men. These statistics show that at that time Caithness rated second only to Aberdeenshire, with its granite industry, as a quarrying County. Caithness flagstones were used for paving the London Docks and indeed a part of the Strand was similarly paved. Station platforms, harbours and the entrance halls of large public buildings are other instances of the use of this type of stone. In the County itself the stone was a universal structural material being used for paving, fencing, building and roofing. In an early sales booklet the following commendation occurs: "In addition to its great strength and durability, the stone is generally so close in grain as to be impervious to moisture. It resists the action of severe frost and it does not scale or become slippery".

The industry began to decline after the 1914-18 war, when the costs of transport and labour began to rise, and also as a result of the introduction of concrete pavements and paving blocks. By 1939, in Edinburgh for instance, the cost of flagstone was 12/6d per m² (yd²) as against the price of a non-slip paving block of 4/6d per m² (yd²). By the 1939-45 war the industry had turned a full circle in that once more only a few farmers and landowners quarried flags for paving and fencing.

In 1949, however, the industry was revived when Spittal Quarry was re-opened. This quarry produces high-quality flagstones with the aid of two diamond slitting saws and two polishing machines. The same company also reopened Achanarras Quarry which now produces building stone and a few fine slates. Many County Council houses and other buildings have masonry facings of this most attractive rust-coloured stone. In the last three or four years a small market has been found for table tops of Spittal flag polished and oiled to a beautiful charcoal-grey colour, and for fireplaces made of cut blocks from Achanarras stone. So it may be said that once again Caithness is exporting flagstone.

### Other Quarrying Operations

Building stone, a soft sandstone, easily hewn and shaped, yellow or reddish in colour, was quarried on the Dunnet peninsula. Millstones were produced at one time in a yard at the top of Dunnet Head.

Roadstone is now chiefly obtained from Bower Quarry although, until about ten years ago, a hard type of road metal was quarried on the west side of Reay. There are various sand and gravel pits, the largest being at Dalemore. Dry marl is a powdery earth, containing almost 50% lime, used for agricultural purposes. During the 19th century it was dredged from a few lochs in the west of the County and its use revived during and after the 1939-45 war; until the 1950's it was being dredged from Loch Lieurary. It is allowed to weather for a few months before use.

Shell sand is also used as farm lime and was worked extensively until a few years ago on the shore just east of John o' Groats. In 1947 2,032,127 kg (2000 tons) were removed and 80% of this was used within the County. By the 1950's large deposits of limestone were being worked near Ullapool making the winning of local materials uneconomic.

A deposit of coarse marine shells, obtained from the same area as the shell sand, was collected and taken to a factory at the South Head in Wick where it was processed and sent to England as poultry grit, at an average rate of 203,212 kg (200 tons) per week. This plant commenced operation in 1943 and closed in 1950 when it became uneconomic owing to rising costs of both labour and transport.

According to an old record, about 101,606 kg (100 tons) of kelp was produced from seaweed in the Canisbay area in the late 1700's.

An inferior quality 'coal' which has never been mined, is found at Halkirk and Barrogill.

## Textile Industry

In days gone by, this was essentially a home industry. It was quite the custom for a gentleman to buy, or even make, a spinning wheel as a wedding present for his bride who would then spin and knit garments for the family. Some homes were also able to afford a loom of simple construction.

Weaving was an industry of some importance in the 18th century although it has sadly declined at the present time. The first Statistical Account mentions that in Thurso alone there were 73 weavers employed in weaving of coarse woollens and linen. At that time most of the wool was imported from Leith and Inverness. Flax was also largely imported, dressed and spun in the County and exported again mostly as yarn. Only two larger mills survived to carry on the production of woollen materials, i.e. Harrow Mill in Wick, near to where the present Glass Factory is situated, and the Stirkoke Mill. The latter shows an interesting development in motive power. The mill when founded in 1877 was powered entirely by a water wheel. This was superceded by a paraffin/oil engine and it in turn by a gas plant and engine. At the time the mill was closed in 1961 the power was supplied by a large diesel engine. The maximum staff of 16 men and women made woollen yarn and some tweeds, but mostly blankets, and during the 1914-18 War supplied large quantities of blankets to the Army. Prior to 1939 most of the raw wool was obtained locally, but latterly about 50% was taken from the south. Before the mill closed, 227 kg (500 lb) of raw wool were used per month, 75% of the output was yarn and the rest, blankets.

In 1947 a Stocking Knitting Factory was opened in a vacant building at Wick Airport making Argyll hose, mainly for export. The wool was sent to Wick from Leicester and the completed items returned there for finishing and packing. Over 50 women were employed until this enterprise closed down in 1952. Shortly afterwards it was resuscitated in the town centre where it continues to function.

Straw plaiting, another export industry worthy of mention, was at its zenith in the early 1800's. It is recorded that upwards of 200 women in the County plaited straw. The hanks of plait were sent to Luton for fabrication into items both useful and ornamental, e.g. hats and baskets.

The development of plastics has in many cases led to the replacement of the traditional textiles. In 1959 a Plastics Factory was established in Halkirk in the Old School buildings. Work commenced with a staff of 6; a number which has now risen to 25 (4 men and 21 women). The factory is a branch of the parent factory at Corsham in Wiltshire. It fabricates a range of items from PVC sheeting, the original intention being to supply protective clothing for use at Dounreay. However, Halkirk-made plastic clothing, toys, etc. are now used all over the country.

### Brewing and Distilling

Brewing and distilling was once a relatively important industry in Caithness although it is doubtful if the County ever came near to Orkney in the amount of small-scale private brewing that took place. The First Statistical Account advocates the encouragement of brewing "to lessen the consumption of spirits and to supercede the importation of London porter". There were breweries in Wick and Thurso, the latter now a furniture store at the Riverside.

In the 18th century a number of small private stills existed, particularly in the Watten area. With the introduction, in 1823, of legislation which made distilling legal on the payment of a licence, distilleries were set up in Thurso, Halkirk and Wick. Wulf Burn distillery was situated on the burn which flows into the sea between Thurso and Scrabster. It commenced operation about 1826 but now no trace of it remains. At Gerston, near Halkirk, there existed a relatively large distillery on the bank of the Thurso river just above the present farm of that name. Some buildings of this distillery are still extant as farm out-buildings. 'Gerston', particularly in the 1860's, was a whisky of some merit; indeed testimonials state that it was a favourite with prominent politicians of the time, among them Sir Robert Peel. Between Halkirk Bridge and Gerston, on the same bank of the river, was yet another distillery — the 'Ben Morven' — which was built in the latter years of the last century, and although the complex of buildings was probably the largest of all the distilleries in the County, its production of spirit was intermittent. It closed down during the 1914-18 War, and although attempts were made to revive it, was finally dismantled in the 1920's and some of the stones used for building in Thurso. The only building that remains, part of the still house, is now a private dwelling.

The Pulteneytown Distillery in Wick has also had an interrupted history, with a break of 25 years, during which time some of the buildings were converted into a meal mill.

The Distillery was founded in 1826 by James Henderson who had been making whisky in a small pot still distillery farther inland for 30 years previously. Most of the barley was shipped in from Aberdeenshire and the water supply, so important to any distillery, came from Loch Hempriggs. The whisky was made by the traditional method — malting, drying over peat, grinding, mashing, fermenting and distilling. By the end of the century, Pulteney was producing over 363,680 litres (80,000 gallons) of whisky per year. The distillery, which is one of the oldest in the north, remained in the hands of the same family until 1920 when it was taken over by a Dundee firm who were superceded three years later by a famous Perth company. It was closed down in 1926 during a time of great national unrest and depression. A move to reopen the plant was stifled by the onset of the 1939-45 War, and it was not until 1951 that the "barley bree" began to flow again. In 1955 the Distillery was taken over by its present owners, a large Canadian-based concern, who set about a complete modernisation. The malt floor and kiln were demolished and arrangements made to obtain the malt from an associate company who specialise in this part of the process. It is imported in bulk from Kirkcaldy and fed into three large bins or 'deposits' as they are called. The old wooden fermentation vessels were replaced by four stainless steel vessels of 25,457 litres (5,600 gallons) capacity each. The stills were reconditioned and in place of the roaring coal fire underneath, steam jackets were installed and the steam supplied from an oil-fired boiler.

Today, the demand for Pulteney whisky is at an all-time high and the five bonded warehouses, covering an area of 2.02 hectares (5 acres), are capable of storing no less than 8,182,730 litres (1,800,000 proof gallons). The Distillery boasts one of the most up-to-date warehouses in the trade with special steel racking to allow the casks to be stored nine high, whereas they were formerly stored two or three high, resting on each other. Almost all of the spirit goes south for blending into some very famous proprietary brands, but a little is retained and sold locally as "Old Pulteney". The present output is in excess of 36,368 litres (8,000 gallons) per week, and the number employed is 16.

### Cheese-Making

One of the most recent Caithness industries was started in the old railway station in Lybster. Cheese-making may well come under the general heading of agriculture, and indeed as a farmhouse product this is so, but with the construction of a factory it may well be termed an industry. This company was started in 1964 by four local men as an aid to the unemployment situation. In 1965 a Danish cheese technologist joined the staff and production was increased. A limited Company was formed in 1967 when the turnover was £7,000 p.a. This rose to £34,000 in 1969 and reached £60,000 in 1970 when the Company moved into a modern factory in Wick. At present twenty people are employed. 60% or so of the product, three semi-soft cheeses, is exported to Canada, U.S.A., South Africa, Japan and many other countries.

### Glass Factory

This recently-started and rapidly-expanding industry with its trademark "CG" has put the name of Caithness in the forefront of delicate and artistic modern glassware. In 1959, a local Laird who was perturbed at the possibility of an increase in unemployment after the construction at Dounreay had been completed, set out to find an industry which would produce high-quality goods, find a ready market and yet be so small and light as to make transport a not too expensive item. A glass factory amply fulfilled all his requirements and after months of consultation it was agreed that a factory could be built at a cost of £50,000. Within a short time a public company was floated, and in 1960 work commenced. A technologist and designer were brought in along with several glassblowers from various European glass-blowing centres who trained a number of local apprentices in the skills of hand-blown glass. The company had fluctuating fortunes in the early days, but in 1966 it came under new management and that year sales topped £100,000.

The training officer is of Spanish ancestry, and with 40 years' experience in the industry is recognised to be one of the two best paperweight-makers in the world. There is also a first-class designer and a team of five engravers using the old 15th century method of glass engraving. The total number of employees is 90 and so successful is the company that a new subsidiary factory was set up last year in Oban.

Although there is an inexhaustible supply of sand in Caithness it contains detrimental impurities and consequently sand is imported, by road, from Loch

Aline in Argyll. This sand is graded, dried, mixed with soda and various other materials including off-cuts from the previous production, and melted in a clay pot in one of the seven oil-fired furnaces, at a temperature of 1450°C(2642°F). When the glass is ready the top surface is scraped to prevent the glassblowers from gathering any volatiles. The next process, of marrying balls of coloured and clear glass before blowing in a mould to a predetermined shape, makes the product different from almost all other British glassmakers. The glass is carefully cooled in a furnace with a moving conveyor hearth, finished off, graded, inspected and packed. In addition to this being a most skilful process it is also very spectacular, and this year over 50,000 tourists visited the factory.

## Small Industries

It is difficult to define precisely the word 'industry'. One very reliable dictionary states, "any productive occupation, especially one in which considerable numbers of people are employed". However, as Caithness is a County with a relatively small population the above definition should be interpreted loosely, and mention must be made of several small industries.

At the turn of the century there were book-binders in both Thurso and Wick, and at the present time there is a book printer and publisher in Thurso. Prior to the 1914-18 War, sound oak furniture was produced in Wick, pieces of which now make goodly prices on the collector's market, and the work of a Wick copper-smith whose speciality was copper kettles, is also of interest to collectors. Between the Wars, a very fine woodcarving business existed in Castletown; by the 1950's however it had practically closed down. A recording studio in Wick has produced a number of splendid records over the past six years, some of these featuring the famous Wick Scottish Dance Band.

## Service Industries

These industries which cater for the needs of the inhabitants of the County, often tend to be overlooked in any account such as this chapter. They are, of course, of the utmost importance to us all and it is invidious to place them in any order of precedence.

There is no traditional 'brickworks' in the County, there being no workable deposits of clay, but there is a busy factory making concrete blocks, situated at the river mouth in Thurso, which has been a going-concern for some years now, and a younger plant of the same type in Halkirk which is only three years old. There is also a pre-cast concrete works in Thurso.

Both Wick and Thurso housed gasworks dating from the middle of the last century, which in the last two years have been closed down and the consumer supplied with propane-type gas from large 'bottles'. This new-type gas is distributed from the old premises.

The printing works in Wick, in addition to doing general printing, produces the 'John o'Groat Journal', first published in 1836, the main weekly newspaper for this part of the North of Scotland, and the 'Caithness Courier', a Thurso-based paper which has also passed its 100th anniversary.

One laundry, functioning in Wick, provides dyeing and dry-cleaning services, and together with a similar concern which closed in 1963, did a considerable postal trade with Orkney and Sutherland.

Engineering services are provided by an engineering works at the Harbour in Wick, doing mainly marine engineering repairs and some automobile work, and by the Millbank foundry in Thurso — a development from a mill-wright's shop. Until 1960 there existed a relic of former years, a cupola furnace for making cast iron. The First Statistical Account notes the existence of a cart and plough works in Thurso, employing four smiths and 13 wrights. Nowadays the two engineering works have practically taken over from the many blacksmiths' forges that were once so popular as social centres.

A relatively small number of boats are being built in the County at the present time, one of the remaining boat builders having moved to Ross-shire four years ago; but in 1840 the Wick shipyard had two vessels on the stocks, and twelve small boat-building yards were in operation. Until 1947, a small yard built dual-purpose seine-net and fishing drifters of up to 61,100 kg (60 tons) displacement, at a rate of approximately two per year. The boats used to be launched directly into the Wick river, but with the construction of the new harbour bridge in 1937 these had to be taken on rollers and launched into the inner harbour. With the interest shown by the Authorities increasing, and more encouragement in the form of loans for building new boats being given, one may well hope to see an expansion of the ship-building industry in Wick.

## Mills

For centuries the main source of power for Caithness industry has been provided by harnessing the plentiful supplies of water in the County. The earliest known water mill in Britain is the horizontal wheel or vertical shaft type, which has been called the Greek, Norse, Click or Clack Mill.

This type of mill has probably been in use over a period of some 3000 years. The horizontal wheel which is fitted with wooden blades is connected directly to the upper millstone by a vertical shaft. Grain is fed into a hole in the centre of the upper millstone from a hopper through a tray. Attached to the tray by a piece of string is a small stone that rests on the upper mill stone which, when rotating, pulls the small stone and shakes the tray, causing the grain to fall into the hole in the mill stone. A variation on this method, found in Orkney, involves the use of a projection on the upper mill stone which strikes the tray each time the stone rotates producing a clicking sound and hence the name 'Click' or 'Clack' Mill.

Click Mills have been found in many countries; in Britain, mills in working condition are located only in Orkney and Shetland where at least 500 were in use. They are known to exist in Ireland, the Isle of Man, the Western Islands and Sutherland. It seems reasonable to suppose that they were built in Caithness, but no definite evidence of one has yet been found. The Click Mill usually measured some 6 m by 4 m (20 ft by 13 ft) with a wheel rather less than 1 m (3 ft) diameter and up to 10 cm (4 in) in thickness. It is strange that no evidence can be found in the County of the existence of this primitive type of mill, although it is almost certain that such mills existed. They may have been superceded long ago by a more efficient type of wheel or, as has been suggested, the landlords built larger mills and made the tenants use these in preference to their own home-made types.

The earliest vertical wheel mills were known as "undershot wheels", having a flow of water impinging upon the lower buckets of the wheel. Later developments included the "breast wheel" and the "overshot wheel".

In 1759 John Smeaton, an eminent Yorkshire civil engineer, showed that the overshot wheel had an efficiency of about three times that of the undershot wheel.

PLATE 35. *John O' Groats, showing the last house and the hotel.*

PLATE 36. *Reay village and Dounreay Experimental Reactor Establishment.*

(R. M. Sharpe)

PLATE 37.  *Aerial view of Wick.*

Most of the waterwheels in Caithness are of the overshot type, where it is the weight of the water in the buckets which causes the wheel to rotate. There are, however, examples of other types of wheels to be found.

Many of the mills in the County were made in Thurso Foundry where between 1810-1910, 20 people were employed. Here, wheels of up to 4.5 m (15 ft) diameter were built.

At Huna, where there may have been a mill from at least 1600 A.D., is found the only working mill in Caithness. The present mill, rebuilt in 1902, has an overshot wheel of 3.5 m (11½ft) diameter and runs at 18 rev/min, giving 350 rev/min at the mill stone. The castings for the mill were made in the Wick Foundry.

The ruin of a most interesting mill is situated at Crosskirk on the very mouth of the Forss river. This was a snuff-mill and worked intermittently for over 100 years. It is thought to have operated illegally for at least a part of this time when the tobacco required for the product was smuggled from passing French and Dutch ships.

One might think that the strong winds encountered in Caithness would have made windmills an attractive source of power but the winds are very often too strong and variable in direction to be used to a large extent although a number of places used small two-blade rotors to produce domestic electricity. Of these machines only two or three are still in running order.

### The Spinning Wheel

About the year 1800 the horizontal spinning wheel was replaced by the upright wheel, which was popularly known in the north as the 'Caithness' wheel.

Spinning wheels were originally used to spin woollen yarn, but it was to the linen trade that they owed their universal popularity in the 18th and 19th centuries.

Captain Henderson notes in 1812 that there are three flax mills in Caithness (which at this time had several lint mills and a large bleachfield at Thurso, where flax was finished in "the highest style").

Flax was grown in many parts of Caithness and the County seems to have been a good area for the industry to develop. It seems likely, however, that spinning for local manufacturers died out about 1840 and so, once more, the spinning wheel reverted to the role of making wool for private use.

### Nuclear Industry

If flagstone quarrying was the main industry and source of employment in Caithness in the 19th Century, then surely the United Kingdom Atomic Energy Authority's Establishment at Dounreay fulfils this role in the 20th Century.

The decision to build an Atomic Energy Establishment at Dounreay was taken in 1953 and construction work commenced in March 1955. Many factors influenced the choice of the Dounreay site: it was situated on the coast and almost at sea level; there were plentiful supplies of fresh water; communications by land, sea and air were good; and there already existed an almost brand new aerodrome comprising hangars and other buildings, roads and other essential services.

The complex, which comprised a Fast Breeder Reactor and a Materials

O

Testing Reactor, fuel element fabrication and chemical processing plants, was to all intents and purposes complete by the end of 1958 at a cost of some £28.5 million pounds. During the construction stage approximately 3000 men were employed, half of whom were local. The total running staff is now of the order of 2000, again about half of these have been recruited locally.

The Dounreay Fast Reactor (DFR) in its 41 m (135 ft) diameter steel sphere has become not only a landmark for miles around but somewhat of a symbol of the Atomic Energy industry. In the heart of the reactor heat is generated which is conducted away to heat exchangers by the ingenious use of liquid metal coolant. In the heat exchanger the hot metal converts water to steam which in turn drives a conventional turbine connected to an alternator where the electricity is produced. Electrical output when the reactor is running has reached 14 megawatts and since this is a good deal more than the site's requirements the power is "exported" to the grid of the North of Scotland Hydro Electric Board thereby supplying up to one half of the power required by the entire North of Scotland. This is the first instance of a fast reactor supplying power for public use. The main task of DFR however is to provide a facility for experiments in fast reactor systems and many irradiation experiments can be carried out in the core. Countries throughout the world pay to have experiments put into the heart of the reactor.

The Dounreay Materials Testing Reactor (DMTR) was the first major reactor in Scotland and began to operate (became critical) in May 1958. It was widely used as an irradiation facility for experimental work until closed down in 1969 when the tasks for which it was built had been accomplished. The fuel for this reactor and for DFR is made at Dounreay, the MTR type of fuel being exported to many different countries.

The Prototype Fast Reactor (PFR) is being constructed on a site a little to the west of the DFR. This massive reactor complex represents a half-way stage between the DFR and a large commercial fast reactor. It is designed to have an output of some 250 megawatts while the next stage (CFR) will produce at least 1000 megawatts. The building of PFR was sanctioned in February 1966 and work is now well forward. It is due to be completed in 1972 and should be producing full power a year later. This power will also be fed into the electrical grid system, special overhead transmission lines having been erected for this purpose.

It is impossible, adequately, to explain the Dounreay project in a few paragraphs. The best way to gain an understanding of the Dounreay Experimental Reactor Establishment is to visit the Dounreay Exhibition housed in the Control Tower of the original airfield. The exhibition, opened in June 1960 by the late Sir Hugh Fraser, then Chairman of the Scottish Tourist Board, attracted in its first five years almost 70,000 visitors from every corner of the world. It is open from May to September and is a 'must' for summer tourists.

**Tourism**

Until very recently tourism was something which just happened. Exiled Caithnessians returned to their homeland for summer holidays and visitors from the south came for fishing, shooting, and stalking. Now money, time and labour are being spent in trying to attract tourists to the County. Information centres are provided by the new Tourist Organisation which is actively engaged in persuading visitors to come to the North. In former years many tourists visited the West but there was a tendency to by-pass the Northern Counties. The scope of the 'bed and breakfast' type of hospitality has been widened greatly and hoteliers are being encouraged to increase their capacity. New sports of sea-angling and sand-yachting are now well established, the former from Scrabster and Wick and the latter on Dunnet Beach where there is usually no lack of wind. More effort is being made to publicise such events as the County Show, the various Gala Weeks and the Highland Games at Dunbeath and Halkirk. The Caithness Glass Factory is visited by many tourists each year as is the Atomic Energy Authority Exhibition at Dounreay.

With the number of tourists increasing yearly, a market has been found for the products of many small craft industries, among them shell-craft, enamel, mink and pebble jewellery, horn-work, painting and sketching, and knitting. The speed with which this type of commerce is increasing is a tribute to the ingenuity of the Caithnessians.

The financial restrictions on foreign travel have in some measure helped tourism in Caithness but there is little doubt that, as the speed of the "rat race" increases and the resorts in the south become more overcrowded, a large number of peace-seeking people will head for the north. Tourism as a Caithness industry is only in its infancy and presents a challenge to us all.

# CHAPTER 24

# COMMUNICATIONS

### Sea

From early times in Caithness the main method of communication would have been by sea. The first colonisers no doubt arrived by this mode of transport. In the 8th and 9th centuries the Vikings sailed their longships into Wick, Thurso, Freswick and Lybster, establishing the first strong trading link with a continental country. When Caithness became absorbed into the Kingdom of Scotland, sea links with the main ports of eastern Scotland were created. By the Middle Ages there was a trans-North Sea traffic from Caithness to the Baltic Lands and the Low Countries. Later, Thurso became a port of call for emigrant ships to North America.

Following the introduction of the coach service from the south in 1819 a mail service was begun between Huna and St Margaret's Hope in South Ronaldsay.

With the advent of steam propulsion, regular services were operated between Leith, Wick and the Northern Isles. This service was fortnightly in 1833, weekly in 1836 and twice weekly by 1860. The first regular mail service between Scrabster and Stromness was started in 1856 by W. Stranger with the paddle steamer 'Royal Mail'. In 1869 the mail service was acquired by G. Robertson using a screw steamer 'The Express'. The Highland Railway Company took over the service in 1877, using the S.S. 'John O'Groat', but relinquished the contract in 1882 to the North of Scotland Steam Navigation Co. Ltd. They, after operating the 'St Olaf' until 1892, introduced the 'St Ola' which carried out sterling service until 1950, when it was replaced by the present ship bearing the same name.

The Leith service was suspended during the 1939-45 War. An attempt to revive a weekly cargo from Wick-Leith was made in 1955, but it was withdrawn after a few months.

### Road

Over the centuries three natural breaks through the bogland and hills fringing the Caithness-Sutherland border became established as natural routeways.

The most southerly of these routeways crossed the Ord at the foot of the Ord burn, wound along the cliffs to Ousdale and ran inland, crossing the Langwell about a mile upstream and the Berriedale Water at Millery. From there it traversed the heights behind Borgue and Ramscraigs, crossing Dunbeath Water below Milton and then following close upon the coast to Wick.

In the centre of the County march was a natural pass by the foot of Ben Griam and Ben Alisky via Strathmore and Harpsdale to Halkirk. This was a commonly used "bolt-hole" for the Gunns and McIvors during their forays into Caithness. Many a bloody encounter occurred along its length!

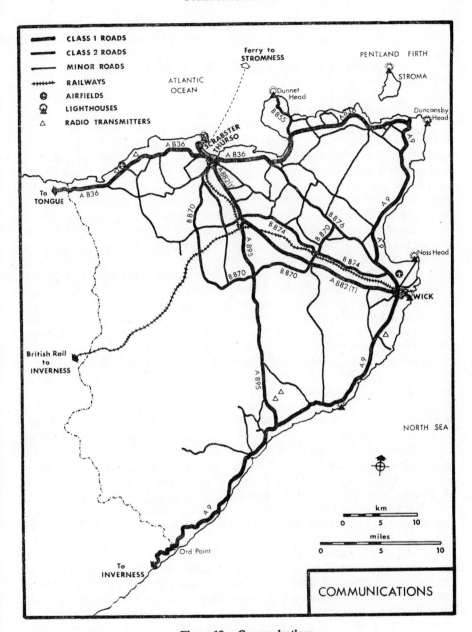

**Figure 19. Communications**

The third routeway ran along the north coast where the open country from Melvich to the east offered a natural and easy link between Strathnaver and Thurso.

In the middle of the 18th Century roads were still almost non-existent, but some progress had been made towards the extension of General Wade's military road network. A map, published in 1776, shows an extension of this road network throughout the County.

The following is a description of the principal routeways in Caithness, as indicated by the 1776 map. An east coast road from Sutherland entered Caithness by a ford near the sea and followed the cliffs to Ousdale, crossing the Langwell and Berriedale Rivers over two bridges which were in use until a few years ago. From here it ran close by the sea, crossing Dunbeath Water near the site of the swing bridge by the harbour. The old bridges near Latheronwheel harbour and the Reisgill Burn mark its former course. Passing through Lybster at the Cross, the road pushed north to Hillhead and Mavsey, thereafter following mainly the course of the present road to Wick. From the County town the route went out by Robert Street, turning left at the Old Toll House (since demolished), past Westerseat Farm to near Lochshell, then following what is now the present road by Sibster, Watten Mains, Tister, Durran and Haimer, entering Thurso near Mount Pleasant. A road (more or less along existing lines) from Thurso - Dunnet - Canisbay - John O'Groats - Keiss, linked up with the main Wick-Thurso road at Lochshell. About the year 1790 Sir John Sinclair, by mustering all his tenants, constructed a new route over the Causewaymire from Georgemas to Latheron. The original 'road' over this boggy track had left the coast at Knockinnon and followed the Smerral valley before rejoining the route followed by Sir John's new road near Rangag.

In 1801 Telford, the greatest road builder of his age, visited Caithness as part of his survey of roads in the Northern Highlands. Anticipating the potential of the fishing industry, Telford stressed the need for a deep water port at Wick and improved road communications with the south. By 1803 he had completed plans for a harbour, a three-arch bridge across the Wick River and the layout of a new town. He also directed the survey of new roads across the Ord up to Wick and from Wick across to Thurso.

Work began on the Wick scheme in 1806, the bridge being opened the following year. The Wick-Thurso road was completed in 1813 and the coast road three years later. New bridges were constructed over the Dunbeath river and the burns at Reisgill, Latheronwheel and the Ord.

During the next 25 years many estate tracks were taken over and improved by the local authorities. This policy, which has continued to the present time, has given Caithness a network of roads whose quality and density have surprised many a tourist.

In 1819, three years after the completion of the coast road, the mail coach service was extended from Inverness to Thurso, the termini being the Caledonian Hotel, Inverness and the Royal Hotel, Thurso. A weekly service was provided leaving Inverness each Monday morning at 6.15 and arriving in Thurso at noon on Wednesday. The return journey began from Thurso on Thursday at 6.00 p.m., arriving in Inverness at mid-day on Saturday. Staging inns were built along the route at regular intervals of some 19 km (12 miles). In Caithness these stops were at Berriedale, Lybster, Wick and Thura. This service continued until the opening of the railway, the last coach leaving Thurso on 1st August, 1873.

The railway did not immediately secure the contract for carrying mails· For some time after the opening of the line mails were carried by the "Mail Fly" — a fast, light, two-horse trap. Moreover, coaches still operated on internal routes. The Royal Hotel, Thurso, operated a service to Bettyhill and John O'Groats. A. Sinclair and Co., Wick and the Portland Arms, Lybster, had rival services between Wick and Dunbeath.

The first motor coach services were introduced in 1915 by Robertson and Waters, operating from Wick to Helmsdale and Wick to John O'Groats. These services were greatly extended during the 1920's and by 1930 it was possible to travel by motor bus from Thurso to London.

## Rail

Following the extension of the railway up to Helmsdale, a Caithness Railway Company was formed to provide a line between Wick and Thurso with a link to the south.

The laying of the line between the Caithness towns would be a relatively simple task, but linkage with the south would provide a much more intricate and costly problem. A survey (initiated by the Duke of Sutherland) undertaken in 1864, reported that it was financially impracticable to take a line across the deep water cuts at the Ord, Berriedale, Dunbeath and Latheronwheel. It recommended, instead, a line following the Helmsdale and Kildonan Valleys to Forsinard, then by Ballach Bridge to Altnabreac. From here, the two alternatives suggested were:

1. By the south of Dorrery to near Spittal Hill, there to unite with a cross line from Wick to Thurso at a point 10.8 km (6¾ miles) from Thurso.
2. Across country by Loch More and the Achavanich Valley to Latheron, thence to Wick.

The survey recommended the first alternative, from which could be built two branch lines — from the west end of Loch Watten to Castletown 10.4 km (6½ miles) and from Wick to Lybster 21.3 km (13¼ miles).

The joint boards of the Caithness and Sutherland Railway Companies commissioned in 1866 a further survey which considered three possible routes:

1. From Forsinard the line would run via Altnabreac, Strathmore, Dale, and south of Mybster Inn to Dunn, with a junction to the already authorised railway between Wick and Thurso. From this junction 16.5 km (10¼ miles) from Wick and 18.5 km (11½ miles) from Thurso a branch line would run to Castletown.
2. A line, as above, would be laid to Wick, a branch going to Thurso from near Loch Sletill or Altnabreac.
3. From Ballach Bridge a line would wind by Loch Dhu and Rangag down to the coast at Latheron and then on to Wick.

In 1871 the new Sutherland and Caithness Railway Company authorised a route suggested in the survey of 1864. The line was opened for traffic in 1874, with stations at Altnabreac, Scotscalder, Halkirk, Georgemas, Bower, Watten and Wick, with a branch line from Georgemas to Thurso having an intermediary stop at Hoy.

The idea of a branch line to Castletown was abandoned, but in 1899, authorisation was given for a 21.3 km (13¼ mile) branch to Lybster. The line was opened in 1903, with intermediate stops at Thrumster, Ulbster, Clyth and

Occumster. This was the last line to be built in the north and the first to be closed, in 1943.

### Wireless Station

In 1910 Wick wireless station was built and operated by the Admiralty; in 1920 it was taken over by the General Post Office.

### Post Office and Telegraph Services

The Post Office extended its telegraphic service into the County in 1868; within a year it had linked Wick and Thurso with the south. Local crofters found a side benefit from this service in the use of the telegraph poles as staking points for their cattle as they grazed by the roadside!

### Air

In 1931 Captain Fresson, an ex-R.A.F. pilot, visited Wick with an 'Air Circus', giving 25p (5/-) hops from a field on Barnyards Farm, Wick.

While in the town he was asked to fly two passengers to Kirkwall; during the trip he conceived the idea of an air service across the Pentland Firth. This plan (which would also include a service south to Inverness) was enthusiastically supported by all the Councils concerned.

The inaugural flight from Inverness to Kirkwall was made on the 8th May, 1933. The following year, an Aberdeen-Wick-Kirkwall service was introduced.

In 1934 a Company, Highland Airways Ltd., was formed, with Captain Fresson as Managing Director.

In 1934, a rival company, Allied Airways, Ltd., introduced a service from Aberdeen to Thurso and Kirkwall.

Four years later the Transport Board, arbitrating between the rival companies, allocated the Aberdeen-Thurso-Kirkwall-Shetland service to Allied Airways Ltd., while the Inverness-Wick-Kirkwall-Shetland service was to be operated by Scottish Airways Ltd., with whom Highland Airways had amalgamated. The latter company also operated a service from Kirkwall to the islands of Stronsay, Shapinsay and North Ronaldsay. In 1938 an emergency landing field was laid out in Stroma.

All these services proved a great success and a social boon to the North. Only the inter-island service in the Orkneys was dropped during the War years. In 1945 it was planned to reintroduce the pre-war services, Stroma to be included in the Orkney North Isles run. However, with the nationalisation of all passenger air services, the new board decided against the inter-island air link and further decided to introduce larger aircraft into the northern area. In 1968 a private company, "Loganair", obtained a licence to re-open the Orkney Isles services. The success of this venture may be a pointer as to how transport links in the Highlands can be speedily and efficiently improved.

# CHAPTER 25

# POPULATION STATISTICS

The County of Caithness, with a total area of 177,590 hectares (438,833 acres) has an overall population density of approximately 0.4 persons per hectare (0.1 per acre).

The County can be divided into three zones for the study of population distribution. These consist of the burghs of Wick with a population density of 2.5 persons per hectare (6.4 per acre), and Thurso with a population density of 3.8 persons per hectare (9.0 per acre). The third zone comprises the landward area i.e., the non-urban parts of the County. This landward area is sub-divided into five regions which also form the District Council areas. These are the:

(1) Western District: of Halkirk, Reay, and Thurso areas.
(2) Southern District: of Berriedale, Clyth, Dunbeath, and Lybster areas.
(3) Eastern District: of Keiss, Watten, and Wick areas.
(4) Northern District: of Canisbay and Dunnet areas.
(5) Central District: of Bower, Castletown, and Olrig areas.

In only one of these areas — Central — does the population density reach the County average.

Census records have been kept at decennial intervals since 1801, with the exception of the year 1941 when the incidence of the World War prevented a count being taken. The figures for those 150 years show that the population grew from 22,609 in 1801, to a maximum of 41,111 in 1861, then decreased at varying speeds until in 1951 the count was almost identical with that of 1801. Since 1951 the impact of new industry has reversed this trend so that the 1961 census showed an increase of 4,500 persons in the County.

Table 16 shows the figures obtained at each census since 1801 in respect of the total number of people in the County. However, owing to re-arrangement of the burgh boundaries and to changes in the legislative system which caused the term 'Parliamentary Burgh' to disappear, the census figures relating to Wick during the 19th century are not easily clarified.

The union between the burghs of Wick and Pulteneytown in 1902 further complicates the entries for the Burgh of Wick. To minimise these discrepancies the figures quoted for Wick from 1841 to 1911 are those for the Parliamentary Burgh, while those quoted since that date are for the (Joint) Municipal Burgh.

From Table 16 it can be seen that a steady increase in County population was maintained from 1801 for a period of some 60 years; then, during the next 80 years a reverse current lowered the figure to its original level. However, since then, an increase of nearly 2% per annum has been noted in the census of 1961 and in the intercensal survey of 1966.

The population of Wick had been almost constantly twice that of Thurso until a remarkable change was recorded in the period 1951 to 1966, when Thurso

217

trebled its population to over 9,000. Wick, whilst increasing its total slightly over the same period, suffered to a certain extent from the tendency of workers at the Dounreay Atomic Establishment to 'migrate' to Thurso; hence, Wick's increase in population was not nearly as dramatic as that of its counterpart.

The growth of the towns also had its effect on the landward population, for, as was common throughout Britain, the rural dwellers moved to the urban areas in significant numbers. This tendency is reflected in the total landward area figure dropping by approximately 2,000 persons per decade.

One factor contributing to this decline is the present complete depopulation of the Island of Stroma. In 1951 the island maintained 111 persons; then, within a decade the inhabitants numbered only 12. Now, only a ghost island remains.

The graph shown in figure 22 illustrates the changing pattern. An analysis of the statistics shows that, of the total County population there were, in 1961, seven persons aged 95 years or over (5 female, and 2 male), and that only one of those seven lived in a town. At the opposite end of the scale there were 2,807 children under five years of age divided almost equally between the sexes, (1405 males to 1402 females).

Overall, the male population slightly outnumbers the female (13,760 to 13,610): but in the 20-30 age group single men outnumber single women by a ratio of over 2:1 (1012 : 475).

The record of birthplaces shows that 2,317 Caithness residents were born outwith Scotland and that a further 238 persons were born outside the British Isles — 113 in Commonwealth countries, 24 in Colonies or Protectorates and 101 in foreign countries or at sea.

(The figures quoted in this chapter are based on those obtained by the Registrar General in complete censuses of the County and on the estimates obtained in the intercensal survey of 10 per cent of the County, which was taken in 1966).

Table 16.  POPULATION STATISTICS 1801-1966

| YEAR | WHOLE COUNTY | WICK INC. PULTENEYTOWN | THURSO | LANDWARD AREA |
|------|--------------|------------------------|--------|---------------|
| 1801 | 22,609 | | | |
| 1811 | 23,419 | | | |
| 1821 | 29,181 | | | |
| 1831 | 34,529 | | | |
| 1841 | 36,343 | 5,522 | 2,510 | 28,311 |
| 1851 | 38,709 | 6,722 | 2,908 | 29,079 |
| 1861 | 41,111 | 7,505 | 3,426 | 30,180 |
| 1871 | 39,992 | 8,145 | 3,622 | 28,225 |
| 1881 | 38,865 | 8,053 | 4,055 | 26,757 |
| 1891 | 37,177 | 8,512 | 3,936 | 24,729 |
| 1901 | 33,870 | 7,911 | 3,723 | 22,136 |
| 1911 | 32,010 | 8,674 | 3,355 | 20,081 |
| 1921 | 28,285 | 8,115 | 3,039 | 17,131 |
| 1931 | 25,656 | 7,548 | 3,007 | 15,101 |
| 1951 | 22,710 | 7,161 | 3,249 | 12,300 |
| 1961 | 27,370 | 7,399 | 8,037 | 11,934 |
| 1966 | 28,257 | 7,418 | 9,012 | 11,827 |

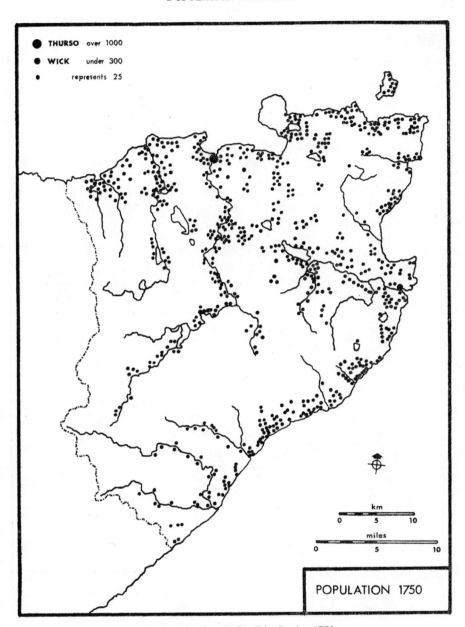

**Figure 20.   Population Distribution 1750**

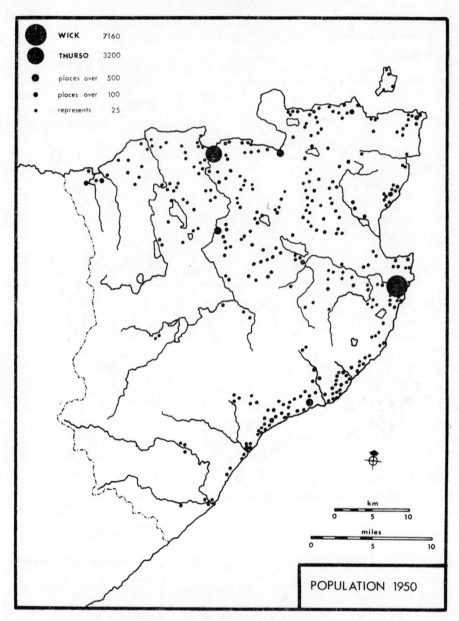

**Figure 21.  Population Distribution 1950**

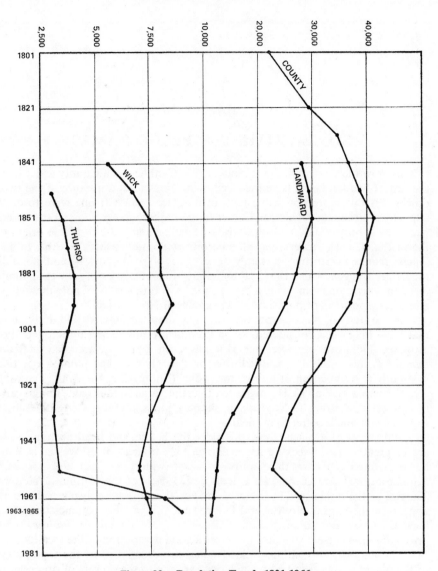

**Figure 22. Population Trends 1801-1966**

# CHAPTER 26

# SOME CAITHNESS PLACE NAMES

By now the reader will have realised that Caithness is a County apart from the rest of Scotland — it is neither Celtic nor Norse, but a mixture of the two; nowhere is this more noticeable than in its place names. If one were to draw a line from Brims through Loch Calder to the Latheron area, most of the names with Gaelic roots would be to the west of this line and those of Norse origin to the east of it. This, however, is still an arbitrary division, as it is possible to find Gaelic names in Stroma; certainly *sgeir bhan* — white rock — and possibly the *Geo of Gougan*, where the great amount of foam during stormy weather may justify a derivation from *gogan* a cog, a milk pail. It is worthy of note that nearly all the larger centres of population have names of Norse origin.

In the study of place-names there are few simple certainties and derivations that have long been considered beyond doubt are now being questioned. For instance, Thingswa on Scrabster Hill has been generally accepted as from *things'vollr* (assembly field). But Professor Per Thorson has pointed out that in no other combination of 'thing' and 'vollr' (Thingvellir, Dingwall, Tynwald, etc.) is there a medial 's'. He suggested that the name should read 'thing-svath, assembly slope', from O.N. *svath*, a slippery place, a slope. Certainly 'slope' suits the site much better than 'field'.

Old forms of a place-name, the older the better, and local pronunciation are of great value in seeking its meaning. An earlier form of Wester is Was-buster, from O.N. *vass*, the genitive of *vatn* (water; a loch) and *bolstathr*, a homestead. There is, or was, a loch beside each of the Caithness Westers. Thus we get the 'homestead by the loch' and not 'the more westerly place'. Holborn appears in old maps as Hobrun and Hobron and this was the pronunciation of the local fishermen not so long ago. This leads more directly to *ha-brun* (high brow) than the present spelling, and gives a good description of the locality.

The majority of Caithness place-names are descriptive of the topography of the places in question and we must pay tribute to the powers of observation and to the imagination of the people who bestowed the names. Each tiny feature of the landscape had its own name and it is to be regretted that so many of them have been lost over the years. (A place may even have two names, depending on who is looking at it and from what viewpoint. On the coast near Brims there are a number of small caves at the foot of the rock face. To fishermen passing at sea they look like a row of shop doors and to them they are known as 'The Shoppies'. To the landsmen of the district who look down on them from above they are known as 'The Green Doors' because of the green slime all about them.) Even the fairly modern field names such as 'Labour in Vain' and 'Scrape Misery' tell their tale, although they may lack glamour.

A number of names have an interesting legend attached to them to explain how these names were given but care must be taken with them. Too often folk etymology has been at work; the story has been put together to suit the older name. A few such names and legends are given later in this chapter.

Historians do not agree on the origin of the name 'Caithness'. An early map by Ptolemy ascribed to this area the name Cornavii — the folk of the horn or promontory. Legend says that Cruithne, King of the Picts divided his kingdom of Alban (Scotland) into seven parts for his seven sons and Cat, the youngest, was given Cait. '*Ness*' means a 'headland' in Norse and so Catness — Cat's Headland. In Norse, '*kati*' is a 'small ship' and local pronunciation for the County is Kaitness. Moreover, the Norse regarding Cat's tribe as Picts and the old name for the Pentland Firth is Pictland Firth. The only certain fact seems to be that the name 'Caithness' in one form or another has existed for a very long time.

Lynegar farm ('*lyn*' — flax and '*akr*' — field) near Watten is a reminder of the days when linen was produced in the County.

To the west of Holborn Head is a rocky promontory known as Falcon Craig. Tradition has it that peregrine falcons which nested here (as they did until a few years ago) were given by the laird as presents or sold throughout Scotland for training purposes. Indeed, it is believed that the kings of Scotland obtained their falcons from this site.

Scarf Craig near Holborn Head and Scarfskerry derive from 'scarf' the local name for a shag or cormorant; these locations are favourite nesting places of the birds, hence Scarfskerry — the rock of the Scarfs.

Gallowhill field, to the west of Pennyland Farm, Thurso, is reputedly the site where in 1222 the assassins of Bishop Adam were hanged by King Alexander when he visited Thurso to avenge the murder.

Opposite the lodge at Thurso East farm is Company Field so called from stage coach days when the Royal Mail Company rented the field for their horses.

Dunnet Head is a fairly recent name. On old maps the name varies from Quincnap and Quinnieknap to Whindyknap. The only possible derivation appears to be the Norse *kvernan*, a quern. Perhaps people believed the headland looked quern-shaped from the sea.

The Atomic Energy Authority's Establishment at Dounreay is sometimes referred to as 'Downreay' — down from the village of Reay; a more likely origin of the word is from the Gaelic *dun* — a fort, thus the 'fort of Reay.'

The Burn of Cloisters near Murkle reminds us that here was the site of one of the largest nunneries in the north, while Spittal is situated close to where the hospital of St. Magnus was built as a haven for weary travellers.

A curious name, the Tails of Watten, is found on Watten Mains Estate. Here, the fields have been squared off leaving tails as untidy pieces of land down by the loch side.

Bowermadden (Norse *bur* — a storehouse) was the storehouse of Earl Moddam, one of King Duncan's generals who was slain here in 1042.

The Calder district is partly in the Norse and partly in the Gaelic sector of the County, hence North Calder and Scotscalder.

Scotland's Haven may have been so named as it is the part of the Scottish mainland nearest to the Orkneys. The nearby chapel of St. John, on the headland of the same name, was built on the point on an enclosure. The Gaelic *Lainn*, an enclosure, and *sgot*, which implies the triangular corner of a square, give *Sgot Lann*, perhaps a more likely origin for Scotland's Haven.

Pulteneytown, now part of Wick, was founded by the British Fisheries Society in 1808 and named after Sir William Pulteney.

Some place names have interesting legends:

**Achcomhairle** — Field of the Counsel. When it was proposed to transfer the Jamesmas Market from Spittal Hill to Georgemas Hill, the men of Spittal met here to consider what steps to take to retain the market. (G. *achadh*, a field; *comhairle*, counsel).

**Clach Seasaimh** — The halt stone. The story goes that a man was bringing back to the Dalnawillan area a child who had been attending school at the coast. It was bitter weather and the child was tied to the man's back in a plaid. At this stone on the top of a small hill the man halted for a rest and found, when he examined the child, that it was dead of exposure. A cairn now marks the spot. (G. *clach*, a stone; *seasamh*, standing).

**Achadh Beathaig** — Sophia's field. This is said to have been the first field in Strathmore to be cultivated. Sophia was the daughter of Gunn the Crowner. (G. *achadh*, a field; *Beathag*, Sophia).

**Poll an Damh** — The pool of the ox or stag. In this case the Damh was a man who was given the title of Ox because of his strength. He quarrelled with his master over unpaid wages and the master instigated his death in this pool of Thurso River. (G. *Poll*, pool; *damh*, ox or stag).

**Loch nam Fear** — Loch of the men. Two men named Calder were killed beside this loch by a man Bain. Under cover of darkness he carried their bodies to his home in Dalnawillan and buried them beneath his byre floor. (G. *fear*, a man).

The following are a few elements that appear regularly in farm names:

O.N. *bólstathr* (*ból*, a place for penning cattle; *stathr*, an abode) became a farm name. When the meaning of O.N. names began to be lost many such long names were shortened. *Bolstathr* > *buster* (with a few examples of bist, best, bust, bost) > *bster* (where the first element was one syllable and the 'b' could be pronounced) > *ster* (where 'b' was difficult to pronounce or where the first syllable ended in 'm' which assimilated the 'b').

    **Stemster**—Stone homestead (O.N. *Stein*, stone, nb > mb regularly.)

    **Scrabster** — The homestead at the edge. (O.N. *skara*, genitive of *skör*, an edge)

O.N. *baer* or *byr* was originally a farm name and later a district name. It appears today as by, bay, bae, bea, bie, etc.

    **Duncansby** — Dungal's settlement.

O.N. *skali*, originally a shed or hut and later a hall, is commonly found as *skaill*.

O.N. *garthr*, a yard or enclosure, is found as -garth, -gar, -grah, -grow.

    **Raggra**, the corner enclosure (O.N. *rá*, a corner)

    **Hestigrow**, the horse pen (O.N. *hestr*, a horse)

    **Whitegar**, the white enclosure (O.N. *hvítr*, white)

O.N. *setr*, an abode, is often found as -side. An earlier form of **Sandside** was Sandset, the dwelling by the sand. *Setr* is sometimes difficult to differentiate from *saetr*, hill pasture.

O.N. *kví*, originally a pen for sheep, appears as quoy and is usually found on the outskirts of early settlements.

    **Quoynee** — The new *quoy* or farm (O.N. *ný*, new)

O.N. *völlr*, a field, appears today as well, wall, field, wa, etc.

    **Filoway**, the dirty field (O.N. *fúll*, dirty).

    **Langwell**, the long field (O.N. *langa-völlr*)

G. *achadh*, a field, appears as *ach-, acha-, achi-, achie-, achu-*, etc.

    **Achalone** — Field of the damp meadow (G. *lon*, a damp meadow).

    **Achinavish** — Field of fairies. Originally Achnahavish (G. *aibheis*, place of fairies).

    **Achnamine** — Peat moss field (G. *moine*, peat moss)

G. *airigh*, a sheiling, this was borrowed into Norse as 'erg'.

    **Garvary** — The rough sheiling (G. *garbh*, rough)

G. *baile*, a town, a village, a farm town.

    **Balcladaich** — The shore town (G. *cladach*, shore).

    **Ballachly** — The burial place township (G. *claidh*, genitive of *cladha*, burial place)

G. *bard*, a field.

    **Bardnaheich** — Horses' field (G. *each*, a horse).

    **Bardintulloch** — The tulloch field (G. *tulach*, a hillock or mound)

G. *buaile*, a fold for cattle, appears as *bul-, bual-, boul-, bal-*, etc.

PLATE 38.  *Aerial view of Thurso.*

(R. M. Sharpe)

(A. Luciani)

PLATE 39. *St. Ola at Scrabster*

(I. Fulton)

PLATE 40 *Traditional and Fibre-glass seine netters, Lybster*

**Buldoo** — The black fold (G. *dubh*, black).
**Bulno** — The new fold (G. *nodha* or *nuadh*, new)
G. *dail*, a field. Can be distinguished from O.N. *dalr*, a dale, by the fact that as a rule the qualifying part comes first in Norse and last in Gaelic.
   **Daluachar** — The rushy field (G. *luachair*, rushes).
   **Dalganachan** — The sandy field (G. *gainmheach*, sand).

## THE FOLLOWING IS A SELECTED LIST OF PLACE NAMES IN THE COUNTY

**Achimenach:** the middle field. G. *achadh*, field; *meadhonach*, middle.
**Ackergill:** O.N. *akkeri-kill*, anchorage inlet.
**Altnabreac:** burn of the trout. G. *allt*, burn; *breac*, trout.
**Assery:** O.N. *Asgrim's erg*, Asgrim's sheiling. *Asgrim > Aski; erg* is a loan word from G. *airigh*, sheiling.
**Auckingill:** O.N. *Hákonar-gil*, Hakon's gill. *Gil* is a deep narrow ravine.
**Balantsionnach:** the fox's township. G. *baile*, township; *sionnach*, fox.
**Balintra:** the shore town. G. *traigh*, shore.
**Bardnaclavan:** the field of the buzzard. G. *bard*, field; *clamhan*, buzzard.
**Barrogil:** gill of the borg. O.N. *borgar-gil; borg* means a round hill or a place of fortification.
**Berriedale:** rocky ground dale. O.N. *berg*, rock; *dalr*, dale. Possibly Icelandic *bjarg*, rocks or precipices.
**Birklehill:** hill of the birches. O.N. *birki*, birch tree. A map of 1772 says "here is heath and birches".
**Borgie:** the dome-shaped hill or the fortified place, depending on the locality.
**Bower:** O.N. *búr*, a storehouse.
**Braal:** the broad field. O.N. *breithr*, broad; *völlr*, a field.
**Brims:** O.N. *brim*, surf, or perhaps *brim-nes*, surf point.
**Bruan:** O.N. *brún*, brow or brea.
**Brubster:** the bridge homestead. O.N. *brú*, a bridge; *bólstathr*, homestead.
**Buckies:** O.N. *bakki*, a ridge, with English plural.
**Buldoo:** black fold. G. *buaile*, a fold; *dubh*, black.
**Buleney:** fold of the damp meadows. G. *buaile*, a fold; *leanaidhe*, of damp meadows.
**Buolfruich:** fold of the heather. G. *fraoch*, heather.
**Calder:** the Saga gives *Kálfadalr*, calf dale, but it is possible that this should be O.N. *kaladalr*, cold dale, preserved in Gaelic as *Caladal*.
**Camster:** the crest homestead. O.N. *kambr*, crest; *bolstathr*, homestead.
**Canisbay:** (1222 *Canenisbi*). There is some difference of opinion as to the derivation and the following suggestions have been put forward:
   O.N. *Konungs-baer*, kings' settlement. *Conan's býr*, Conan's farm (Conan assumed to have been an early Celtic chief).
   *Kennends-baer*, cleric's farm. Canan's settlement (a Canan family is mentioned in the Book of Deer and one of them may have founded a church in Caithness).
**Carnavagry:** cairn of the place of toads. G. *carn*, a cairn; *magraidh*, a place of toads (*magan*, a toad).
**Castletown:** the castle comes from the earlier Castlehill but it is doubtful if there ever was a castle there. The Shelly Hillock, an ancient kitchen midden, could have been mistaken for the ruins of an old stronghold.
**Causeymire:** the deep moor. O.N. *kjós*, deep; *myrr*, moorland.
**Clow, The:** G. *clobha*, a pair of tongs. The shape of the burn course here suggests the top of a pair of tongs.
**Clyth:** O.N. *hlíth*, a slope.
**Cogle or Cogill:** O.N. *kóf-gil*, misty ravine.
**Comlifoot:** meadow at the cairn. O.N. *kuml*, a burial cairn; *fit*, a meadow beside water. The cairn is no longer there.
**Corbiegeo:** O.N. *korpa-gjá*, raven geo.
**Corsback:** O.N. *kross bakki*, ridge or bank of the cross.
**Crask:** G. *crasg*, a crossing place in the hills.
**Dalnaha:** G. *dail na h-ath*, field of the ford. The ford crosses Strathmore Water.
**Dalnawillan:** G. *dail na mhuileinn*, field of the mill. Above it is Loch a' Mhuileinn, the loch that supplied water power to the mill.

P

**Dounreay:** (1539 Dunra) the fortified place, remains of a broch. G. *dun*, a fort; *rath*, a circular fortified place.

**Drumhollistan:** the ridge of the holy stone. G. *druim*, a ridge; O.N. *helga-stein*, a holy stone. The 'Split Stone' is sometimes taken as the stone in question but there is nothing to support this apart from the fact that the Split Stone was important enough to serve as the boundary mark between Caithness and Strathnaver.

**Dunbeath:** the birch hill. G. *dun*, a hill; *beithe*, birch tree.

**Durran:** the soft strip. O.N. *dý*, a bog; *rein*, a strip of land. The Loch of Durran has been drained but the ground it covered is still very soft.

**Dwarwick:** the dwarf's or demon's bay. O.N. *dvergr*, dwarf or demon; *vík*, a bay.

**Earneymillock:** the eagle's hillock. O.N. *arnr*, a sea-eagle.

**Eas Gluta:** the Glutt waterfall. G. *eas*, waterfall; *glut*, a bite, a hollowed place in the hills.

**Elf-Mire:** O.N. *álf-mýrr*, elf-mire. Elf stones (arrowheads) are said to have been found here.

**Fasgeo:** Probably *Fasa-gjá*, Fasi's geo, but may be from O.N. *fárs*, dangerous (*fárs>fás*).

**Feith Gamhna:** the stirk's mire. G. *feith*, mire; *gamnha*, the genitive of *gamhain*, a stirk.

**Fierciegeo:** a noisy geo when the tide is flowing. Local pronunciation favours O.N. *thursa-gjá*, giant's geo (*thurs>furs*).

**Flex:** O.N. *fles*, a green spot on a hillside.

**Forse, Forss:** O.N. *fors*, a waterfall.

**Framside:** farthest out farm. O.N. *fram*, farthest out or up; *setr*, a homestead.

**Freswick:** appears in the Sagas as Trathsvik and Thrasvik. This may be a Norse rendering of a Gaelic name containing G. *traghad*, genitive of *traigh*, a beach. The sand-beach creek. Or it may be a man's name—Thrasi's creek.

**Geise:** the gushing water (as the burn passes through a narrow channel and over a fall), O.N. *gjósa*, to gush.

**Gloop, The:** a deep hole. O.N. *gloppa*, a big hole. A recess at the bottom of the Gloop in Stroma was known as the Malt Barn from the amount of illicit distilling that went on in it.

**Geodh nan Fitheach:** the raven's geo. G. *geodha*, a geo; *fitheach*, a raven.

**Georgemas:** named from the market held on nearby Sordale Hill on St George's Day. It was transferred from Spittal Hill c. 1827 where it was held on St James's Day and known as the Jamesmas.

**Gerston:** (1591 Greistane) by metathesis from 'grey stone'.

**Gillock:** O.N. *gil*, a gully or small ravine, with diminutive *-ock*.

**Haimer:** probably O.N. *heimr*, a residence.

**Halkirk:** O.N. *há-kirkja*, high church. Named from the abbey church, originally at Skinnet and later at Halkirk.

**Hallum:** O.N. *helg-heimr*, holy homestead, i.e. a farm with a sanctuary. (*helg-heimr>hel-eim*).

**Halsary:** O.N. *hals*, a slack in the hills; *erg*, a shieling (from G. *airigh*). Shieling in the slack of the hill.

**Ham:** probably O.N. *hamn*, a haven, but *hvammr*, a small valley, would also suit.

**Harrow:** O.N. *hörgr*, a heathen place of worship.

**Howe:** O.N. *haugr*, a mound. These were built for various purposes, usually burial or sacrificial.

**Huna:** O.N. *Huna-á*, Huni's burn.

**Inkstack:** O.N. *eng-stegi*, pasture on a steep ascent.

**Inshag:** G. *innis*, cattle pasture, with diminutive *-ag*.

**Iresgeo:** O.N. *eyrr*, gravel beach; *gjá*, geo.

**Ishnamolt:** G. *innis nam mult*, pasture ground of wethers.

**Jubigill:** O.N. *djúpa-gil*, deep ravine.

**Knockglass:** G. *cnoc*, a hillock; *glas*, green. The green mound.

**Keiss:** O.N. *keis*, a rounded ridge.

**Kilpheddir:** G. *kill Pheadair*, Peter's church.

**Knapperfield:** O.N. *knapper*, a knob (or *napr*, cold); *völlr*, a field.

**Laid, Lhaid:** G. *leathad*, a slope.

**Langaton:** O.N. *langa-tangi*, long tongue or spit of land.

**Lathach nam Poiteag:** the mire of the potholes. These holes, now distorted by weathering, were made by tenants digging for resinous fir roots to be used as fuel or for light.

**Latheron:** There is some discussion on this name but G. *lathair roin*, presence of the seal or seal-calf, seems to fit fairly well. It was a place favoured by seals.

**Lieurary:** O.N. *ljóra-erg*, a shieling (hut) with a vent or chimney. The root is O.N. *ljos*, light, from which come G. *luidhear*, chimney, vent.

**Lorg an Fhamhair:** the giant's footstep. An artificial, well-cut footmark in an outcrop of rock on Portnellan. The local legend attributes it to a giant but such features were usually associated with the installation in office of a local chief. G. *lorg*, footstep; *famhair*, a giant.

**Lucifer Moss:** so named from the amount of sulphur in its peat.

**Lybster:** again there is discussion on this name but the Gaelic form Liabost suggests an earlier O.N. *hlíthar-bólstathr*, homestead on the slope.

**Lyberry:** O.N. *lýra-berg* or Icelandic *Lý-berg*, pollock (lythe) rock.

**Markwell:** O.N. *mark-völlr*, boundary field.

**Mestag, Castle:** O.N. *ma-stakkr*, sea-mew stack. Ruins of a building on this detached stack are associated with Sweyn and it is sometimes called 'The Robber's Castle'.

**Methow:** O.N. *mith*, middle; *haugr*, mound. The middle mound.

**Mey:** G. *magh*, a plain.

**Miralea:** the local pronunciation of this stream is Mirnaloo. G. *meur nan laogh*, the calves' branch or streamlet. Beside it is **Meur nam bo**, the cow's streamlet.

**Morven:** G. *mor bheinn*, big mountain.

**Murkle:** O.N. *myrk-hóll*, dark hill.

**Mybster:** O.N. *mýri-bólstathr*, moorland homestead.

**Oldwick:** G. *allt*, a precipice (primary meaning); O.N. *vik*, a creek or bay.

**Ord, The:** probably the hammer-shaped hill. G. *ord*, a hammer.

**Ormigill:** O.N. *ormr*, a serpent; *gil*, a ravine. But *Ormr* can be a proper name or a nickname.

**Ousdale:** (1198 *Øysteinsdalr*) Oystein's dale. Here the value of an early version of the name is evident.

**Oust:** O.N. *aust*, east; Near it is Westfield.

**Papigoe:** the priest's geo. O.N. *papi*, priest of the old Celtic Church; *gyá*, a geo.

**Pentland Firth:** O.N. *pettaland fjörthr*, Pictland Firth. 'petta' was the genitive plural of *pettr*, a Pict.

**Philip's Haven:** named after Louisa Philips, daughter of Sir George Philips and wife of the 14th Earl of Caithness. Originally Wester Haven.

**Portnellan:** G. *port an eilein*, port of the island. Originally applied to an island bay in Loch Calder in which there was a landing place used for transporting peats across the loch. Name transferred to the hill overlooking the bay.

**Quiniclave:** O.N. *krernar-kleif*, quern cliff. There was a water-mill here at one time.

**Ramscraigs:** raven's rocks. O.N. *hramn*, a raven.

**Reisgill:** O.N. *hrís*, brushwood; *gil*, a ravine.

**Reiss:** rising ground. Icelandic. *rísa*, to rise.

**Riera Geo:** the cairn geo. O.N. *reyrr*, a heap or cairn.

**Rigifa:** O.N. *hryggjar-fjall*, ridge hill.

**Roster:** horse stead. O.N. *hross*, horse; *bólstathr*, homestead.

**Russl Hole:** rubbish hole. O.N. *rusl*, rubbish.

**Sannick:** O.N. *sand vík*, sand bay.

**Sarclet:** O.N. *saur*, mud, or *sauthr*, sheep; *hlíth*, slope.

**Scarskerry:** O.N. *skarfr*, shag or cormorant; *sker*, a rock.

**Scarmclate:** sheltered slope. O.N. *skerme*, shelter; *hlíth*, a slope.

**Scouthal:** O.N. *skógr*, wood; *dalr*, dale.

**Sellifer:** O.N. *sela-fjara*, seal shore.

**Shinnery:** the old sheiling. G. *sean*, old; *airigh*, a sheiling.

**Shurrery:** O.N. *sjóvar-erg*, sea sheiling. *sjó*, sea; *erg*, sheiling (from G. *airigh*). The 'sea' is the Loch of Shurrery.

**Sibster:** O.N. *suthr-bólstathr*, south homestead.

**Skerry Neavain:** the pearl skerry. G. *sgeir*, rock; *neamhain*, a pearl.

**Skinnet:** (1223 *Scynend*). O.N. *skinandi*, the shining one, referring to the Thurso River which flows by Skinnet.

**Slickly:** O.N. *slakka-hlíth*, slope of the hollow in the high ground. cf. slack.

**Sordale:** O.N. *saurr*, damp ground; *dalr*, dale.

**Stannergill:** possibly *stein-garthr*, the (standing) stone enclosure + *gil*, a ravine.

**Staxigoe:** O.N. *stakkr*, rock stack; *gjá*, geo.

**Stroma:** the island in the stream (from the strength of the current). O.N. *straumr*, the stream; *ey*, island.

**Stroupster:** O.N. *stór*, big; *bólstathr*, homestead. (*stór > stró*).

**Swarthouse:** O.N. *svartr*, black; *áss*, ridge.

**Swilkie, Swelkie:** O.N. *svelgr*, a whirlpool.

**Taldale:** O.N. *hallr*, sloping; *dalr*, dale. The intrusive initial 't' is due to Gaelic influence.

**Tannach:** G. *tamhnach*, a green or fertile field in heath land.

**Thrumster:** the homestead at the outskirts. O.N. *thruma*, outskirts; *bólstathr*, a homestead.

**Thurdistoft:** O.N. *Thurdi's toft* or home-site. Thurdi was a female personal name; *toft* was a version of *topt*, site, farm.

**Thurso:** O.N. *Thór's-a*, *Thor's* river, and *thjórs-a*, bull river, both have their supporters but lately Professor Thorson put forward *Thors-haugr*, Thor's mound, based on some 13th century spellings (Thurseha, Turishau, Thorsau). He points out that a Scandinavian river name containing the name of a god is unusual indeed.

**Tobar Acraig:** the well of Halkirk, a medicinal well. Acraig comes from the local pronunciation of Halkirk (Haakreeg) which has developed under Gaelic influence.

**Toftgunn:** Gunn's site. The story goes that the Great Gunn was banished to this spot by his disgusted followers after he had caused the ship conveying his bride to Caithness to be wrecked. He was more interested in securing the dowry than the bride to be.

**Torr A' Gharaidh:** the hillock of the enclosure. G. *torr*, a hill; *garadh*, an enclosure. There is an old wall which once enclosed a stackyard.

**Torranshondall:** hillock of the tarn dale. G. *torr*, hill; O.N. *tjörn*, tarn or pool; *dalr*, dale.

**Torvaich:** hillock of the byre. G. *torr a' bhathaich*.

**Traigh nan Ron:** the seal' shore. G. *traigh*, shore; *ron*, a seal.

**Troupa, Hole of:** the trows' pool. O.N. *troll*, a trow; *pollr*, a pool.

**Ulbster:** the wolf homestead. O.N. *úlfr*, a wolf; *bólstathr*, a homestead. But *Ulfr* was a common personal name.

**Utterquoy:** the old name of Holbornhead Farm. The outer quoy. O.N. *útarr kví*.

**Warehouse:** O.N. *vargr-áss*, wolf ridge.

**Warth Hill:** the beacon or watch hill. O.N. *vartha*, a beacon, or possibly Icelandic. *varthe*, a watchtower.

**Wathegar:** the enclosure at the ford. O.N. *vath*, a ford; *garthr*, an enclosure.

**Whilk, Moss of:** O.N. *vilkit*, dismal.

**Wick:** O.N. *vík*, a creek or bay.

**Winless:** the pasture slope. O.N. *vin*, good grassland; *hlíth*, a slope.

**Yarrows:** O.N. *japr-áss*, serpent ridge.

CHAPTER 27

# SOME EMINENT CAITHNESSIANS

Many born within the boundaries of the County have by their endeavour, astuteness or inventive genius made their mark in the world. Conversely, Caithness has benefited from the skills of many from south of the Ord. The first part of this chapter summarises in chronological order the lives and achievements of some such eminent men, who, for reasons of birth or association with the County, we can consider to be Caithnessians. The concluding section gives, in alphabetical order, less detailed notes on men born in the County who in some chosen field have made contributions worthy of note.

## SWEYN ASLIEFSSON

In the 12th century, when fighting, raiding and plundering were commonplace among the Viking Jarls of North Scotland there was born in Caithness, Sweyn, son of Aslief and her recently slain husband Olaf. This Sweyn Asliefsson, as he was called, became one of the most notorious and feared men of his time. Many pages of the Orkneyinga Saga record his dark exploits. He robbed whom he pleased, created and deposed Jarls as he chose and was the friend or tool of the Scottish monarchy. The great castle of Lambaborg (later Bucholie) at Freswick was Sweyn's stronghold.

Sweyn, to avenge the death of his father, slaughtered the murderer's descendants and put fire to their homes. From then on, he plundered and killed throughout the British Isles and is reputed to have had constantly at his call a fighting force of 80 men.

He was a good strategist, for he constantly attacked his enemies from an unexpected position, often travelling miles overland to surprise his adversaries, while they vainly awaited his arrival by sea.

In 1171 he captured Dublin but was killed as the result of a strategem against him as he landed to receive ransom money for the town.

The Swansons and Gunns of Caithness can claim descent from the Asliefssons of the 12th century.

## GILBERT OF MORAY, BISHOP OF CAITHNESS

Gilbert of Moray, saint, social worker, and ecclesiastic was one of the most outstanding men in the unreformed Church in Scotland. Born towards the end of the 12th century, he ultimately became Bishop of Caithness and died in 1st April, 1245.

Gilbert was educated at the Cistercian Abbey of Melrose, then served at several other Church establishments until in 1203 he became Archdeacon of Moray, from whence he took his name. In 1222 he became bishop-designate of

229

Caithness, where the Cathedral was the "High Kirk" of Halkirk. Gilbert's claim to be remembered rests on what he did to keep religion alive and to preserve civilisation, after both had been threatened with extinction by the Norse invaders.

It is said that Gilbert translated the Psalms into Gaelic but this statement does not rest on very good authority. What he probably did was to encourage the use of the psalms in the native dialect. One important aspect of Gilbert's episcopate was that he could speak to the people in their own tongue, which was more than his predecessors could do, since it was the policy of the Roman Church to appoint Englishmen or other foreigners to the bishoprics.

Gilbert died peacefully in his palace at Scrabster, a sure sign that he had achieved so much more than his predecessors who had suffered mutilation and death at the hands of their unruly parishioners.

## JAN DE GROT

From Jan de Grot, who may have been granted land in Caithness in 1489, the name John o' Groats is said to derive. It has been suggested that Jan's surname came into being because in his job as a ferryman he charged a "groat" for the journey from Huna to Orkney.

Another tale relates how each year he had a reunion with his sons, and how during one such family gathering the sons quarrelled about who should have precedence and sit at the head of the table. Jan resolved the dispute by building an eight-sided house; each room was octagonal and into the dining room with its eight-sided table led eight doors. On arrival, the sons entered the dining room by individual doors, each one sitting down at the 'head of the table'.

The flagpole near John o' Groats Hotel is believed to mark the site of Jan de Grot's house. Excavations made at this site some years ago revealed a rectangular building, but no evidence of an octagonal room was found. To perpetuate the legend, the hotel has an eight-sided room.

Set into the outside wall of the south transept of Canisbay Church a peculiarly lettered red sandstone slab commemorates various members of the Grot family. Part of the inscription on the stone reads, "Jhone Grot laid me heir April XII Day 1568."

## TIMOTHY PONT

Timothy Pont (born c.1560) was the elder son of Robert Pont the Scottish Church reformer. Timothy graduated from St Andrew's University in 1583-4 and in 1601 was appointed minister of Dunnet. It is not known how long he remained in that charge but he had certainly been replaced by 1614, when the name of William Smith appears as minister of the parish.

Pont, an accomplished mathematician and cartographer, was the first projector of a Scottish Atlas. In connection with this work he made a complete survey of all the counties and islands of the kingdom, "visiting even the most remote and savage districts". He died, probably in 1614, having almost completed his task.

The originals of his maps, which are preserved in the National Library of Scotland, Edinburgh, are characterised by their neatness and accuracy. King James I gave instructions that the maps were to be purchased from Pont's heirs and published. Owing to public disorders of the period this task was never carried out. The maps were, however, revised and published in 1654 in Volume V of Blaeu's Atlas.

In 1850 another of Pont's surveys was published under the title, "Topographical Account of the District of Cunninghame, Ayrshire, compiled about the year 1600 by Mr Timothy Pont." In 1968 a document relating to Pont's grant of authority to search out the mineral resources in Orkney and Shetland was discovered among his maps.

## RICHARD OSWALD

Richard Oswald (1704-1784) was the son of George Oswald, minister at Dunnet.

Oswald became a well-known Scottish merchant in London. Later, he went to Germany and became Commissary-General of the army, to the Duke of Brunswick. In 1759 he purchased the estate of Achencruive, in Ayrshire.

He married Mary Ramsay, through whom he acquired extensive estates in North America and the West Indies. Because of his connection with these lands he had been frequently consulted by the British Government during the War with the American Colonies.

In the published papers of Lord Shelburne there is an account of his employment of Richard Oswald to negotiate peace with the rebelling Colonies after hostilities had ceased. Shelburne called him, 'a practical man and conversant in those negotiations which are most interesting to mankind.' The ensuing negotiations were brilliantly conducted by Oswald who received high praise for the diplomacy which culminated in his signing the treaty of peace with Benjamin Franklin, acknowledging the independence of the United States of America.

## REV. ALEXANDER POPE

Alexander Pope (1706-1782) was the eldest of a large family whose father was a minister at Loth. He received a liberal education and was reputed to be "an accomplished classical scholar, an intelligent antiquary and was intimately conversant with science".

When a young man, he travelled to England to meet his eminent namesake and kinsman the poet Alexander Pope — and was reported as having had a "cordial" meeting after a "stiff and cold" start.

It was as a minister in the Parish of Reay that Pope made a name for himself. He was inducted to Reay on 5th September, 1734 and found his parishioners were "not only ignorant, but coarse in their manners and vicious in their dispositions, and Episcopalians in name but heathens in reality."

Pope was a man of fervent piety and tireless energy — characteristics much needed to tame his wild parishioners.

The Kirk records show that at that time the habits of the people were such that they would on a Sunday: go to sea to fish, fee a servant, drink during a sermon and winnow corn.

To deal with such unruly people the minister adopted methods which would be considered outrageous by any minister today. For instance, he normally carried a stout cudgel with which he protected himself and administered retribution to his rebellious parishioners. As time went on Pope's influence was felt and the tone of the parish was considerably improved.

Pope ultimately suffered from paralysis and had to be carried to his pulpit to deliver his sermons.

Contemporary writers have likened Pope to a pioneer working in a difficult part of a vineyard; a man who turned a barren wilderness into a fruitful field.

## MAJOR-GENERAL A. ST. CLAIR

Born in Thurso about the year 1734, St. Clair emigrated to the American colonies some 20 years later and enlisted in the army. Soon he was promoted to lieutenant and under General Wolfe carried the colours on the Plains of Abraham.

Following the siege of Quebec he worked unhappily for a time in civil life and with relish accepted the invitation to raise a regiment and be its colonel in 1755. The following year, as a Brigadier-General he joined General George Washington and became one of the most trusted advisers of the Commander-in-Chief. For his distinguished service under Washington he was promoted to Major-General.

Returning to civil life, he was elected President of Congress and Governor of the North-West Territories. His wise administration was invaluable in the early days of independence.

He died, a poor man, in 1818.

## SIR JOHN SINCLAIR

John Sinclair, only son of George Sinclair of Ulbster — whose ancestors had held the earldoms of Caithness and Orkney — was born at Thurso Castle on 10th May, 1754. He was educated at the High School of Edinburgh and then at the Universities of Edinburgh, Glasgow and Oxford.

He was elected Member of Parliament for Caithness in 1780 and as an Independent Member in an evenly balanced Parliament he soon gained considerable influence.

In 1782 he obtained a grant of £15,000 towards the relief of a serious famine in the North of Scotland.

In 1786, the Prime Minister, Pitt, rewarded him with a baronetcy for his political services, with the privilege that the patent should include the male posterity of his daughters should he die without an heir. Some time later, open disagreements with Pitt led to Sir John's attempting to form a third political party.

As President of the Highland Society Sir John took a great interest in investigating the relative qualities of sheep and their wool. A very methodical observer, he was one of Britain's earliest statisticians. In fact, he was responsible for introducing the words "statistics" and "statistical" into the English language. A "Statistical Account of Scotland", which he compiled in 1790, was derived from data obtained from all the parish ministers in the country.

Despite his active public life, he gave much time to the improvement of his estates, which he had inherited at the age of sixteen. He abolished the open-field system, introduced a regular crop rotation as well as encouraging the cultivation of turnips, clover and rye-grass. He improved the breeding of livestock and introduced the Cheviot sheep to the County.

The town of Thurso was largely rebuilt by Sir John; its wide streets, spacious squares and well-built houses are a tribute to his foresight. The main square in the town has been re-named "Sir John Square" in his honour. His rectilineal layout of Halkirk village was community planning far in advance of its time.

By the end of the 18th century the French Wars had caused a financial crisis in Britain. Sir John was given the task of steering a Select Committee on Commercial Credit in an attempt to save the economy. As a reward for this service, Pitt, in 1793, made him the first President of the Board of Agriculture — an organisation for which Sir John had striven for some time.

In 1784 at the request of Pitt, Sir John raised and was appointed Colonel of a regiment of 600 men. It was known as the Rothesay and Caithness Fencibles. He subsequently raised a regiment, known as the Caithness Highlanders, which served in Ireland.

Made a Privy Councillor in 1810, he was subsequently offered the Post of Commissioner of Excise — a sinecure which obliged him to resign his seat in Parliament.

Withdrawing into private life, he went to reside in Edinburgh. Here on the 21st December 1835, died perhaps the most eminent son of Caithness.

## JAMES BREMNER

James Bremner, engineer and ship-raiser, was born at Keiss in 1784 and died in Wick in 1856. He received such education as his mother could afford until, as a 15-year-old, he was apprenticed to Robert Steele and Sons of Greenock, whose shipyard gave him the opportunity of both theoretical and practical instruction. There he remained for $6\frac{1}{2}$ years while learning his trade.

After making two voyages to North America he returned to Wick to operate his own shipbuilding business. During the next 50 years he built 56 vessels. He also engaged in designing and building harbours and piers on the Caithness coast. He constructed Keiss harbour and renovated those at Pulteneytown and Sarclet. Outwith the County, Bremner built harbours at Lossiemouth and Pitullie, near Fraserburgh.

In addition to his skilled craftsmanship he showed considerable ingenuity and enterprise in raising and recovering 236 ships wrecked round the treacherous Scottish coastline from Aberdeen to Skye. However, his greatest triumph was raising the huge ship "Great Britain" which had run aground at Dimdrum Bay in Ireland.

In 1833 Bremner was elected a corresponding member of the Institution of Civil Engineers and 11 years later he was awarded the Telford medal for his many important papers on harbour construction and the raising of wrecks.

## ALEXANDER BAIN

Alexander Bain was born in the parish of Watten in the year 1810. He made many important inventions in the field of telegraphy, the chief of which was the automatic chemical telegraph.

After having served an apprenticeship to a clockmaker in Wick, he went to London as a journeyman in 1837. There he attended lectures on the applications of electricity to the working of clocks. He was one of the first to devise a method by which a number of clocks could be worked electrically from a standard time-piece. This claim was disputed, as was the credit he sought for being the inventor of the first printing telegraph. Independently, he discovered the use of the earth circuit, but again his claim was anticipated. However, what cannot be disputed was the fact that he was unquestionably very early in the field. The wide range of his inventions also includes electrically operated fire alarms and their associated equipment.

His most important invention, made in the year 1843, was the chemical telegraph, a full description of which can be found in the Society of Arts Journal 1866, Volume 14, page 138.

This apparatus could be worked at a speed previously impossible, and its invention certainly entitles Bain to the credit of being the pioneer of modern high-speed telegraphy. Perhaps the most valuable part of the invention consisted of the use of strips of perforated paper for the transmission of the message. This contrivance was long after adopted by Bain's rival, Wheatstone, and is in use in all existing high-speed systems of telegraphy.

Bain received £7,000 for his patents, but the money was wasted in litigation regarding his claims and he died a poor man.

In 1873 he received a grant of £150 from the Royal Society and at the time of his death in 1877 he was supported only by a government pension of £80 per year.

A memorial commemorating his work has been erected in his native Watten.

## ROBERT DICK

Robert Dick was born at Tullibody, in Clackmannanshire in January 1811. Although a promising scholar he was not sent to higher education. Instead at the age of 13 (mainly through the influence of his step-mother who made home life miserable) he was apprenticed to a baker.

Despite the hard work and long hours at the bakehouse, he read widely, acquiring a deep knowledge of botany and making an impressive collection of plants while he was still an apprentice.

After serving as a journeyman in Leith, Glasgow and Greenock, he went, in 1830, to Thurso, where his father was Supervisor of Excise. There, Robert Dick set up a baker's business, as, at that time there were only three bakers' shops in the County. While building up his business he still 'made' time to study geology and natural history and soon had a comprehensive collection of rocks, insects and plants. In 1834 he re-discovered the Northern holygrass, a plant which had been thought extinct in Britain.

The appearance of Hugh Miller's book 'Old Red Sandstone' in 1841 led Dick to make further researches for fossils, and ultimately, to correspond with the author. This correspondence caused Miller to make considerable modifications to his book. Miller later wrote, 'He (Dick) has robbed himself to do me service'.

Dick's extreme modesty prevented him from writing for publication, but nevertheless he became a recognised authority on the geology and botany of Caithness and assisted a number of notable scientists in their researches.

Robert Dick's studies show a record of unceasing perseverance under poverty, pain and illness. To gather specimens he walked distances of 80 km to 130 km (50 miles to 80 miles) after completing a hard day's work.

Solitary in his habits, Dick never married. His character is revealed in his letters, which show him to have had a deep love of nature and a desire to find facts at first hand.

Increasing competition in the baking trade and a shipwreck in which the cargo of flour was lost, ultimately ruined him and he spent his last years in great privation. Despite this, it was with difficulty that he was persuaded to sell his fossils; indeed, he gave many away to researchers who, he felt, were entitled to them.

Prematurely aged, Dick died on 24th December, 1866. His fellow townsmen gave him a public funeral to testify their recognition and later had erected in Thurso churchyard a large obelisk to his memory.

In Thurso museum the Dick collection of plants, fossils and shells has been recently restored to public display. The collection is a remarkable testimony to the zeal and prowess of this dedicated, self-taught amateur.

## ALEXANDER HENRY RHIND

Alexander Henry Rhind, a banker's son, was born in Wick on 26th July 1833. He became a well-known antiquary whose writings about ancient Egyptian tombs were regarded as standard works on the subject. In addition, he published many papers on British antiquities several of them relating to the County of Caithness.

Rhind went to school in his native Wick and then continued his studies at Edinburgh University. From an early age he was interested in natural history, Scottish history and antiquities. The visible remains of ancient dwellings and burial mounds fascinated him and in 1851 he supervised the opening and examination of several archaeological sites near Wick.

In 1852 Rhind sent to the Society of Antiquaries in Edinburgh "rubbings" made of a slab of stone from Ulbster. He later presented the Society with bone remains from a broch at Kettleburn, near Wick. For his work and interest in antiquities the Society elected him a Fellow. In order to furnish an index for archaeological inquiry, Rhind proposed that 'all primeval vestiges should be carefully laid down on the ordnance map of Scotland'.

Dogged by ill-health Rhind gave up the idea of a legal profession and instead sought warmer climates. Initially, he moved to the south of England and later to Egypt where the wealth of archaeological remains absorbed his attention and led him to make many worthwhile observations — in particular, of the tombs at Thebes. In 1862 he again visited Egypt but the following year, after a serious illness, he decided to return to Britain. Unfortunately, he died en route, in Italy, on 3rd July, 1863.

Rhind's bequests reflected his interests; he left considerable capital for scholarships to Edinburgh University, as well as large sums of money to the Society of Antiquaries. He left a valuable library of some 1600 volumes and said that the money from Sibster Estate (which belonged to the family) was to be used to found a lectureship in archaeology.

## WILLIAM MILLER

William Miller, one of three brothers, was born in Thurso on 13th January, 1838.

Following a brilliant career at Aberdeen University and New College, Edinburgh, he went overseas to work at Madras. His task was no easy one; the influence of the School to which he had been appointed had sadly waned. Through Miller's energy and devotion the School made astonishing progress and within four years was presenting candidates for University degrees.

In 1874 Miller sent home to the Free Church Foreign Mission Committee a proposal that his School (the Free Church Institution) in Madras should become the Central Christian College for the whole of India. In 1877 Madras Christian College was officially opened. Many years later a writer commented that, "The Madras Christian College is the lifework of one of the greatest missionaries Scotland ever sent to India, William Miller."

Many honours were conferred on him not only for his work in the College but his many writings on educational and missionary subjects. He was awarded the D.D. by Edinburgh University and the LL.D. by both Aberdeen and Madras Universities. In 1901 a huge crowd assembled in Madras to watch the unveiling of a statue in his honour.

William Miller retired to Edinburgh. He died in 1923, aged 85 years, certainly one of the most inspiring men the County has produced.

## SIR WILLIAM SMITH

William Alexander Smith, founder of the international youth organisation, the Boys' Brigade, was born in Thurso, on the 27th October, 1854. Not much is known of his earlier childhood except that he came from a devout and God-fearing home, that he was the eldest of four children and longed to be a soldier.

On the death of his father, William Smith then only 13 years old, was sent to Glasgow to be cared for by his uncle. On completing his education Smith entered his uncle's business and settled down to the drudgery of a commercial life. His leisure time was devoted to study, participation in church affairs and serving with the 1st Lanark Rifle Volunteers — in which battalion he ultimately gained the Queen's Commission and later became its Colonel.

It was a result of his military training and his religious beliefs that the idea of forming a "Boys' Brigade" first came to Smith.

On 4th October 1883 at North Woodside Hall, in Glasgow he founded the Boys' Brigade, with the object of instilling "Discipline and Religion" into the life of every boy. The object of his organisation was "The Advancement of Christ's Kingdom among boys and the promotion of the habits of Reverence, Discipline, Self-Respect and all that tends towards a true Christian Manliness".

After a slow start the Boys' Brigade grew, and spread throughout Britain, until in 1887 Smith was asked to give up his own business and become full-time Brigade Secretary, an office which he accepted with alacrity.

The organisation of the Boys' Brigade gradually spread overseas: to Jersey in 1887, to Ireland in 1888 and ultimately, to nearly every country in the world, regardless of race or colour.

In 1909 the name of William Alexander Smith appeared in the Honours' List to receive a Knighthood in recognition of his work for the Brigade.

Sir William died in May 1914 after collapsing at his desk while working to the end for the organisation which he set up and is now known throughout the world.

A granite memorial bearing the crest of the Boys' Brigade and dates of the birth and death of its founder is let into the wall of his birthplace — Penny-land House, Thurso.

## GENERAL THE LORD HORNE OF STIRKOKE

Henry Sinclair Horne was born in 1861 and died in 1928. He came from a family which for several generations had been one of the best known in Caithness and had a long association with Stirkoke.

Having completed his education at Harrow, he was commissioned into the Army in 1880 and later, as a major, fought in the African Campaign.

In 1914 he left for France as a Brigadier-General, making a name for himself as a bold, experimental and resourceful commander. Throughout the first battle of Ypres when the fate of Britain hung in the balance, Horne was Sir Douglas Haig's chief gunner. Subsequently, he was appointed Major-General for 'Distinguished Service in the Field.'

In November 1915 Lord Kitchener selected Horne to accompany him to the near East as his chief military adviser concerning the evacuation of the Dardanelles.

Horne, in September 1916, was appointed to the command of the First Army in France. During an important advance, with telling effect, he used his Artillery in a dual role: covering the forward movement of his infantry as well as dealing with hostilities on its lengthening flank, it became known as the "creeping barrage".

When war ended, Horne, for his services to the Nation, received the thanks of both houses of Parliament and was raised to the Peerage as Baron Horne of Stirkoke. Parliament granted him £30,000 and conferred on him the G.C.B. In addition, he was made a C.B. (1914) and a K.C.M.G. (1918). Lord Horne was mentioned in nine despatches and received many military decorations from a number of Allied Nations. The honorary degrees of D.C.L. (Oxford) and LL.D. (Cambridge and Edinburgh) were conferred on him.

## JOHN HORNE

John Horne was born in Louisburgh, Wick and served his apprenticeship on a local paper the 'Northern Ensign,' now defunct.

His heart was set on the Baptist ministry, so he went to train at the Spurgeon Pastors' College, in London, where he gained high merit as a student. He ministered most successfully to a number of congregations in Lowland Scotland and wrote extensively on religious matters. As he was often dogged by ill health ('since cradle time I have been little more than a weakling'), he resigned his pastorate in 1909 and until his death in 1934 devoted the remainder of his life to literature mainly centred on his home County.

When Horne began to write, no one else at that time was writing about Caithness, and his poems, one-act plays and essays on the County became a symbol of the Homeland to those from 'Over the Ord.' His publications included 'A Canny Countryside,' 'Round the Old Home,' 'Caithness Originals,' 'Red Apothecary,' 'Ma Rachel and other Originals' and 'The County of Caithness' — the only comprehensive account of the area which has, as yet, been published. Among Caithnessians of his day he was unequalled for the excellence of his literary works and his deep knowledge of the County and its people.

Apart from his ministerial and literary achievements, he carried out a number of local enterprises, being responsible for the memorial stone at the site of Altimarlach, the Calder statue, the Caithness Soldiers' Tower at the North Head and the 'Donald Horne Room' in the Wick Library.

## VISCOUNT THURSO OF ULBSTER

Born in 1890, an only child whose parents died when he was very young, Archibald Sinclair, was brought up by his grandparents and other relatives.

He was educated at Eton and Sandhurst and entered the army in 1910. As a major, he was for some time second in command to Winston Churchill. On the death of his grandfather he succeeded to the baronetcy in 1912.

His long and distinguished career in politics began, when from 1919-21 he was appointed personal military secretary to the Secretary of State for Colonies.

In 1922 he became M.P. for Caithness and Sutherland and served the constituency until the 1945 election.

During these 33 years in the Commons, Sir Archibald held many high offices, such as:

1930-31 Liberal Chief Whip
1931-32 Secretary of State for Scotland
1935-45 Leader of the Parliamentary Liberal Party
1940-45 Secretary of State for Air

As Lord Rector of Glasgow University from 1938-45, Sir Archibald must have been one of the longest serving Rectors.

In the New Year Honours' List of 1952, Sir Archibald Sinclair became Viscount Thurso of Ulbster.

This honour was the highlight of a lengthy, variegated and eminent political career, a feature of which was his close association with Winston Churchill in two World Wars as well as the intervening period.

## BRIGADIER "BIG JOCK" CAMPBELL

'Jock' Campbell was born in Traill Street, Thurso in 1894.

He attended the Royal Military Academy at Woolwich and was commissioned in 1915. He originated the Rover tank columns which played such a prominent part in the Libyan campaign. During the '14-'18 War, "Big Jock" was awarded the M.C.

In the 2nd World War he was awarded the D.S.O. and later a Bar was added to it.

The 'Gazette' of November 21, 1941 announced that 1.9 m (6 ft 4 in) Brigadier 'Big Jock' Campbell had been awarded the highest military honour the nation can bestow — the Victoria Cross (He is the only Caithnessian to have gained the V.C.). Part of the citation read, "his magnificent example and his utter disregard of personal danger were an inspiration to his men and to all who saw him. His brilliant leadership was the direct cause of the very heavy casualties inflicted on the enemy."

It was said of Brigadier Campbell, "he wins V.C. s all the time." The Victoria Cross was pinned on Campbell's breast in Cairo, by General Auchinleck. Tragically, a month later, "Big Jock" was killed in a motoring accident.

## NEIL M. GUNN

Neil M. Gunn is well known throughout the country as a writer of good Scottish fiction, and in Caithness especially, as the man whose book was made into the successful film "The Silver Darlings".

Neil Gunn hails from the Dunbeath area of Caithness. The rivers and glens depicted in many of his stories reflect his adoration of the scenery he lived among for many years.

Yet though his love of the country is predominant, he does not exclude the city from his works, as a significant part of some of his novels is set in the metropolitan areas of Edinburgh and Glasgow.

"Gunn describes the traditional observances, beliefs and superstitions of the people," says J. B. Caird in his pamphlet on the novelist. This, indeed, is the mainspring of his writing: the vivid portrayals of the crofters and fishermen in their loved but often harsh environment.

To compile a list of this author's titles is not the purpose of this summary but a mention must be made of some of his more outstanding successes which have been appearing since 1926. "The Silver Darlings" depicting the herring fishing was perhaps his best-known book; but many others such as "The Drinking Well", "Highland River", "Morning Tide", "The Grey Coast", "Butchers' Broom" and "Green Isle of the Great Deep" have stood the test of time.

**DR JOSEPH ANDERSON** (1832-1916) was at one time editor of the John O'Groat Journal. He became an eminent antiquarian, excavated many cairns and brochs in Caithness and wrote extensively on Stone and Bronze Age times.

**JAMES, 14th EARL OF CAITHNESS** (1824-1881) patented many useful and ingenious inventions including a loom, a gravitating compass and a steam carriage.

**JAMES TRAIL CALDER** (1784-1864) of Castletown, schoolmaster at Canisbay, was author of the "History of Caithness".

**REV. D. DAVIDSON** (1781-1858) of Wick, an eminent theologian, was editor and compiler of several Bible Dictionaries and Commentaries.

**JOHN FINLAYSON** (1783-1860) became a Government calculator and actuary of the National Debt Office, London. He was one of a distinguished Thurso family.

**DR ALEXANDER GUNN** (1844-1914) who was born at Lybster became a famous surgeon and assisted Lord Lister in his researches into the use of antiseptics.

**CAPT. JOHN HENDERSON** (1759-1828) an authority on statistics and agriculture, was born in Thurso. He published, in 1812, a work of considerable merit, "A General View of the Agriculture of Caithness."

**JOHN HENDERSON** (1800-1883) of Thurso, an authority on genealogy, published "Caithness Family History."

**REV. JAMES IVERACH** (1839-1922) of Halkirk became Moderator of the United Free Church. A gifted writer, he published many works on a variety of subjects.

**REV. JOHN MACDONALD** (1779-1849) of Reay, the well-known Gaelic scholar and poet, was called "The Apostle of the North."

**JOHN M. MACKAY** (1856-1931) of Lybster was Professor of History at Liverpool University for 30 years until he retired in 1914, He devoted his life's work to building up the University system of a Senate and a Faculty.

**JOHN NICOLSON** (1843-1934) who was born at Canisbay but lived most of his adult life at Nybster did important work in the recording, cataloguing and collecting of Caithness antiquities. His antiquarian relics form a collection in a museum near his house.

**JOHN RAE** (1845-1915) of Wick was one of the best-known economists of his day. He was the biographer of Adam Smith and published many political works.

**SIR WILLIAM SINCLAIR OF KEISS** (circa 1700-1767) was founder of the Baptist Church in Keiss, the first in Scotland. He published a hymnal of some sixty songs of his own composition.

# CHAPTER 28

# A SELECTION OF CAITHNESS DIALECT WORDS

To use the term "Caithness dialect" implying that such a dialect ever was common to the whole County would be incorrect. The south and west of the County came under the influence of Gaelic, the north and east under the influence of Norse, and it is the north-east corner of Caithness that is the true home of the dialect.

Many variations exist in pronunciation, in word forms and word meanings, and words used in one district may be quite unknown in another: boys, from places as far apart as John o' Groats and Dunbeath, who travel to Wick for their secondary schooling, even today remark on the different elements in each other's vocabulary. This indicates that the rapidly disappearing dialect still has considerable currency at least in rural districts.

And yet, for many generations the dialect words and phrases which enriched the everyday conversation of natives of the County must have remained almost unchanged. It is only in comparatively recent times that the rate of disappearance of dialect words has been rapidly accelerated.

In "An Introductory History of Scotland" published in 1937 the authors, Davidson and Oliver, quote a children's "counting-out" rhyme which consisted of the numbers one to nine and was "a tiny little bit" of the language of the early Britons. From what the authors say we deduce that this rhyme survived in Dumfries-shire until about the middle of the 19th century. A similar counting-out rhyme with the same words hove (hover) and dove (dover) for 'eight' and 'nine' was in everyday use by children in the village of Lybster and perhaps elsewhere in the parish of Latheron in the earlier years of the present century and is known to have survived at least until the decade immediately following the Second World War.

Scott describes in "Waverley" how Davie Gellatley was maintained at "heck and manger" — a phrase still used some thirty years ago in the same parish.

Such examples illustrate how ancient forms could survive as long as the way of life remained with little change from generation to generation.

The words which follow are a selection only of dialect words gathered from various sources many of them by school children from their grandparents.

Finally, a word on pronunciation. There are many variations of pronunciation with consequently corresponding variations of spelling in different parts of the County. The main characteristics are as follows:

Broad 'a' becomes 'aa', e.g. walk, talk, etc.
'i' as in pig, big, jig, etc. becomes 'ee' as in seed.
'oo' becomes 'ee' in certain words: e.g. 'feel' for 'fool', 'feet' for 'foot'.
Diphthongs 'ae', 'ay', 'ea', 'ai', 'oy' become 'ey': e.g. chair, seat, boy, etc.
'j' and soft 'g' become 'ch' at the beginning of a word.

'ch' becomes 'sh' in Canisbay district.
'th' is sometimes elided, e.g. 'the' becomes 'e'; 'this' becomes 'iss'.
Final '-et' becomes '-ad'; and '-nd' becomes '-n'.
Final 'ing' becomes 'an' e.g. singan, walkan, lookan.
Initial 'wh' becomes 'f' e.g. 'who' becomes 'fa'; 'when' becomes 'fan'; 'Whaligoe' becomes 'Faligoe'.

**Aans:** Beard of bere or barley.
**Ablach:** a clumsy, ungainly person.
**Acht:** to own, to be the parent of. "Fa achts ye?"—"Who's your father?"
**Aifrins:** the last milk taken from a cow.
**Aig:** to work at eagerly.
**Aicher:** an ear of barley.
**Aik:** to fling, to hit.
**Aikle:** a molar tooth.
**Ailiss:** a hot blazing—"An ailiss o' a fire".
**Aince-Errand:** a journey for a special purpose. A Keiss man went aince-errand to Wick for a big needle.
**Airch:** an aim. " 'At wis a poor airch ye made".
**Aise:** ashes. An **Aise-Packad** was a wooden box-shovel for lifting the ashes and the **Aisy-Pow** was the 'pool' where the ashes were deposited.
**Aishan:** stock, family (usually disrespectful), "He comes o' a bad aishan".
**Amadan:** a foolish or stupid person.
**Ammel:** a swingletree.
**Andoch:** small, insignificant.
**Aneval:** lying on one's back, in a helpless position. Used of sheep and intoxicated people.
**Anno:** to row against the wind or tide to prevent drifting. **Annosman,** the rower.
**Antle:** to keep on complaining, arguing.
**Antran Ane:** one among many.
**Ask:** a cow's chain or tie in the byre.
**Attry:** ill-natured, bad-tempered.
**Awms:** a kindly, deserved deed. "Id wid be awms till help 'im".
**Awmry:** plate-rack.
**Awpie:** a guillemot.
**Ayest:** to covet, envy. "Them 'at'll ayest 'e silk goon 'll get 'e sleeve o'd".
**Baak:** (1) any beam or rod of wood; (2) a ridge in ploughed land; (3) a stone or bit of wall behind the fire when it stood in the middle of the room (also **Brace),** (4) the bolt-rope to which herring nets were attached.
**Baan:** snow hardened on the soles of boots.
**Baglin:** a puny or misgrown child.
**Backie:** the stake to which an animal is tethered.
**Backin:** the address on a letter.
**Baffle, Baffin:** scroll paper (once used by school children).
**Bard:** a scolding woman.
**Bare-Feeted Broth:** broth made without meat.
**Bare-Tail:** left with less than one's due or with nothing.
**Barken:** to encrust, plaster over with dirt, etc.
**Barlan:** land for growing bere (barley).
**Barm:** to rage, storm noisily (of a person). "a barman' targe"—a raging woman.
**Barriemasherie:** skimmed milk.
**Bauchle:** originally a worn-out shoe, extended to an old worn-out man.
**Beddacks:** hop scotch.
**Beem:** to steep barrels, tubs, etc., to make them tight.
**Beenich:** the salted stomach of a calf for rennet.
**Beerach:** a string tying a cow's tail to her leg at milking to prevent switching. "Yield kye need no beerach".
**Beesty Milk:** the first milk from a cow after calving.
**Begood:** began. " 'E tide hed begood till ebb."
**Begotted:** bewitched, obsessed.
**Beheave:** advantage. "A good wife pits ivrything till beheave".
**Bollwaar:** tangle and seaweed growing in deep water.

**Belly:** to bellow, roar.
**Bellygut:** greedy, avaricious.
**Belshach:** talking rapidly and almost incoherently.
**Benlin:** a stone hung on straw or heather ropes to secure the thatch of a roof.
**Bevil:** to arrange, make to fit. "Setterday nicht can be lek Sunday moarnin' if ye bevil id richt"
**Bielan:** festering, suppurating.
**Bick:** a female dog, bitch.
**Bicker:** to run quickly, with clatter of feet.
**Bing:** run, come, go, etc. (Tinkers' cant) "bing till yer trampers"—jump to your feet.
**Bink:** (1) shelf or plate-rack; (2) stone shelf for water supply; (3) shelf on hillside.
**Birk:** birch spars laid horizontally on couples of roof.
**Birss:** temper, anger. "Ye pit his birss up".
**Birth:** current formed by a very strong tide—in the opposite direction.
**Birze:** to squeeze or press.
**Bitlag:** a stone, round not flat and slaty. "Herts as hard as bitlags".
**Bissy:** cow's bed in a byre.
**Black Gait:** an ill road.
**Blackjack:** a fish, the saithe.
**Blaidies (Healan'):** leaves of certain plants, used to poultice wounds.
**Blainag:** a pimple or small pustule.
**Blawn:** a preparation of sour milk.
**Blearach:** defective in sight.
**Bleems (Tattie):** potato shaws.
**Bleeter:** a sharp, passing shower.
**Blin-Buck:** blind man's buff.
**Blin-Siv:** a blind sieve, one without holes.
**Blin-Swap:** an exchange carried through with the eyes closed.
**Blinner:** to blink, see obscurely.
**Blockie:** a small cod.
**Bloodshed:** bloodshot.
**Blown:** applied to land over-manured by seaweed.
**Blown-Milk:** a preparation of sour milk (see **Blawn**).
**Blost:** to boast.
**Bodach-Back:** the outside peat in a bank.
**Boch:** an untidy person, a mess.
**Boachie:** a child's toy.
**Bobantilter:** a hanging ornament. An icicle.
**Boke:** to retch.
**Boltie Lairag:** a corn bunting.
**Bool:** a round stone.
**Bools:** the hinged handle of a lugged pot.
**Boorach:** a mess, an untidy place or situation.
**Boorag:** a turf or peat from near the surface of moss. cf. **Booragtoon** in Thurso.
**Booran':** lowing, of cattle.
**Borag:** a bradawl.
**Borray:** a bird, the razorbill.
**Bowd:** a billow, wave.
**Bowg:** stomach, belly.
**Brain:** to stun, not necessarily by a blow on the head.
**Braingel:** a confused crowd, sometimes a dance.
**Braggal:** (1) boastful talking; (2) a boastful talker.
**Brander:** girdle with bars only.
**Branks:** pieces of wood, part of the halter of a cow's tether. Facetiously, the mumps.
**Bran'le: Branstickle:** a stickleback.
**Brat:** a rough apron.
**Brawd:** to jerk the hook into a fish.
**Breenge:** a clumsy, violent rush forward.
**Breeshle:** to hurry, rush.
**Breether:** first shoots of grain.
**Brile:** a very strong outburst.
**Brime:** to haul a boat out of the sea.

**Brither-Bairn:** cousin; **Brither-Dochter:** niece; **Brither-Sin:** nephew.
**Broachan:** oat-meal gruel, or thin porridge.
**Broachle:** a belching.
**Brocht:** to eruct.
**Brock:** (1) kitchen refuse for pigs; (2) bits of straw raked up after harvest.
**Brockie:** with face streaked (with dirt) like a brock or badger.
**Brod:** a mother goose.
**Brolach:** a mess, a failure.
**Bron:** glowing cinders or peat.
**Bronach:** sad, listless.
**Broon Plate:** porridge made of sowens of the thick sort.
**Brot:** a rag; **Brotach:** ragged.
**Brotag, Hairy Brotag:** caterpillar of the drunken—or tiger-moth.
**Browg:** bradawl.
**Bruffle:** bungler.
**Brulie:** a noisy quarrel.
**Brunt:** (1) cheated, swindled; (2) keen, eager.
**Brumple:** a fish; the blenny.
**Buckiefaalie:** a primrose.
**Bug (Dinna Let/Say):** don't say a word about . . .
**Bugglin':** straw on the bottom of a boat to help with the transport of animals.
**Bulder:** a blustering lie. **Bulders:** a rough-spoken bully.
**Bulliwan:** stalk of the docken.
**Bummler:** a blockhead, a bungler.
**Burgess Threed:** a very strong kind of thread once much used. It came from Bruges.
**Burn-Sae:** a cask for holding water, carried by two people who passed a pole (a **Sae-Tree**) through two handles on the cask or tub.
**Bursen:** fastidious, difficult to please (with meat).
**Burstin:** the hot meal obtained when, early in the harvest, sheaves were thrashed and the corn dried in an old pot and ground in a quern.
**Bushy-Muck:** a fish, the wrasse.
**Buttery:** a limpet, the interior of which was more yellow than normal—attractive bait.
**Butts:** chums, companions. "They're great butts". Diminutive **Buttie.**
**Bous:** a sulky mouth. "Look at 'e bous on 'im!"

**Ca'a:** a path or road left between fields to give access to hill pasture.
**Cabbag:** a fisherman's small basket (made of heather) to hold bait.
**Caff-Seck:** ticking filled with chaff to serve as a mattress.
**Caibie:** a hen's stomach.
**Caikal:** a voracious worm.
**Cairie:** a type of sheep once common in the north-east corner of Caithness.
**Caisie:** a wicker basket or creel.
**Cairlin:** an old woman. In the phrase "to go hom' wi' 'e cairlin", said of e.g. a fisherman who goes home without catching anything.
**Calach:** cockerel.
**Calmy Ston':** a kind of stone once used by children as a slate-pencil.
**Camsterious:** frisky (of a horse).
**Cann:** knack, know-how.
**Cark:** to complain peevishly.
**Carran:** spurrey (spergula arvensis).
**Carrant:** a journey or expedition.
**Carrie Elt:** a thick, ill-baked oat bannock—extended to a clumsy woman.
**Carrieshang:** a noisy brawl of words.
**Carriewattle:** a general scrimmage.
**Carvey:** caraway seeds.
**Cashal:** a cobbler's knee-strap.
**Castan' 'E Hert:** an old cure for fright or illness. Molten lead was poured through the eye of a pair of scissors into a basin of spring water where it spluttered into small bits. If one bit resembled a heart, it was sewn into the patient's clothing and recovery was assured. If it failed it was repeated every second day.
**Catmar:** a fish, the catfish.

**Chalouse (Jalouse):** guess, surmise.
**Chief:** very friendly, "As chief as dowgs' lougs".
**Chinny Lin:** daddy-long-legs (crane fly).
**Claggan:** a stiff lump of anything. Thick brose would be a "raw claggan".
**Claik:** one who gossips in a sly reprehensible manner.
**Claister:** smear.
**Clamsh:** to splice two pieces of wood together to make a rough temporary mend.
**Clapshot:** potato and turnip mashed together and seasoned.
**Clev:** to sort out and make up a fishing line after use.
**Clew:** ball of wool.
**Clibber:** a wooden pack-saddle.
**Clink:** a heavy fall.
**Clipe:** to scratch with the finger-nails.
**Clit:** a cow's hoof.
**Clivs:** claws, facetiously the hands.
**Clocher:** to cough, clear the throat noisily.
**Clock:** a black beetle.
**Clockan (hen):** broody (hen).
**Clookan:** huddling for warmth.
**Cloor:** to dent, smash in.
**Cloorer:** a mason's hammer.
**Clunkertonie:** a jellyfish.
**Coachie:** soft and spongy (used of turnips).
**Cockiloorie:** any bright plaything.
**Cole:** haycock.
**Coom:** dust from the grain when first passed through the mill in the process of shillin'.
**Coolye:** to talk round plausibly. "He wid coolye 'e egg fae 'e craw".
**Coonye:** an awkward corner.
**Cootrie:** a bird, the puffin.
**Corrag:** the fore-finger.
**Corse:** the starfish.
**Cowmags:** fish, small cuddings.
**Cown:** to weep.
**Crackins:** oatmeal heated to a frizzle in fat.
**Craig:** palate, throat.
**Craishan':** a withered shrunken person.
**Craithan':** swarming.
**Crawspurse:** the ovarium of a skate.
**Crampard:** iron guard on the end of a staff.
**Crang:** body or carcass.
**Creepie:** a three-legged stool.
**Creesh:** grease.
**Crellag:** a blue-bottle fly.
**Croch:** to make a noise in the throat as from a severe cold.
**Crockan:** any black object.
**Crockle:** knuckle.
**Croil:** a broken-down person, animal or thing. The broken-down state.
**Cromags:** the points of all the fingers and the thumb brought together. **Cromags-Fu':** the amount that can be lifted by such a hand.
**Crooban:** part of the harness of a pack-horse.
**Crooner:** a fish, the gurnard.
**Crossag:** the starfish.
**Croze:** to make a pleased noise in the throat, as infants do.
**Cruise Up:** to cheer up, buck up.
**Cudge:** a small room or corner.
**Culk:** a large piece or lump.
**Cundy:** a covered drain, a conduit.
**Curr:** a touch, to move with a touch. Also used in 'knotty' to represent running away with the ball from your opponent's club.
**Curriewumple:** a melee.
**Cut:** mood, usually unpleasant. "She's in a bad cut ivenow".

**Cuttag:** an unruly girl. Also **Cutty.**
**Cuttie:** a small, thick cake of oatbread, usually with a hole in the middle.
**Cuther:** to nestle in.
**Cyard:** a despicable person.
**Cyarr:** to antle (q.v.) with a snarl in the voice.

**Daa:** a lazy idle woman.
**Daad:** (1) a blow; (2) a lump of something. "Gee's a daad o' 'at".
**Daak:** a brief let-up in a storm, a fight etc. To abate.
**Daaken:** to dawn. The early dawn is the **Dawkenin'.**
**Daat, Daatie:** darling. "Ma daatie—my dear, my darling".
**Daffins:** the cords by which nets are tied to the backrope.
**Dainler:** a river eel, not full grown. (Thurso word?).
**Daivered:** fatigued (with walking against the wind), confused.
**Dashag:** a small screw built from the ground.
**Day 'Moung 'E Dockans:** a day spoilt by, say, bad weather or some unexpected interruption. The idea is of uselessness or waste of time.
**Daynettle:** a whitlow.
**Dayset:** the end of the evening twilight; "**Efter-Dayse**" is the period between dayset and bedtime.
**Denshach, Denshag,** finicky; particular about food.
**Deugind:** obstinate, "thrawn".
**Dey:** dairymaid.
**Dird:** a fuss, a showy way of walking. "He's dirdan' awey 'ere".
**Dirdy-Lochrag, Dirdy-Wachle:** a lizard.
**Divaal:** a stop, give up. "He noor divaals".
**Divider:** ladle.
**Dode:** a slow person, mentally and physically.
**Dooal:** an earwig.
**Doo-Dockan:** the burdock.
**Dort:** to sulk, not to be friends temporarily.
**Doss Up:** to dress up showily. **Doss:** an ornament.
**Dossan:** a forelock left after the rest of the head has been closely cut.
**Dowed:** of fish, dried for a day or two but only partially dry.
**Dowg Afore His Maister:** the roll and noise of the sea that foretells a storm.
**Dowgston':** the spotted orchid.
**Dozent:** stupid.
**Dracht:** a boundary, usually a ditch, between two farms or crofts.
**Draffy:** awkward, stiff on the legs.
**Dreefle:** a crowd.
**Dreich:** dreary, dull and uninteresting.
**Droke:** (1) meal mixed with water; (2) to drench; (3) a silly-looking person.
**Drooggle:** to be engaged in wet dirty labour.
**Drunt:** (1) to nod, sleeping in a chair; (2) a slow. dull person.
**Droich:** a dwarf.
**Drooked:** soaked to the skin.
**Ducksies:** stones used in a boy's game.
**Dudder:** a soft, unmanly person.
**Durken:** to get disheartened. "He durkened on 'e chob".
**Dwan:** swoon.
**Dwannie:** weak, sickly.
**Dyochree:** a kind of sowens.

**Eem:** a rising misty vapour, of heat or even of frost.
**Efterwal:** (1) leavings, refuse; (2) land that has been impoverished.
**Eidistreen:** the night before last.
**Elt:** to mix meal and water to form dough, the dough so made; hence **Carrie-Elt,** a thick, ill-baked oatcake. **Muckle-Elt:** a stout clumsy woman.
**Etchal:** a small quantity.
**Ettercep:** a spider.

**Faap:** a bird, the curlew.

**Faagal:** an excessive burden, carried because of greed or to avoid another journey.

**Fae:** from.

**Faik:** the strand of a rope. Also **Faith.**

**Fa-in:** meal of poor quality made from unripe grain.

**Fann:** a large wreath of snow.

**Farand:** fashioned; **Owld-Farand:** old fashioned.

**Far-Drachted:** subtle (of a remark), also long-headed, long sighted.

**Farlie:** something to be wondered at.

**Fascal:** a straw mat hung up as a draught screen.

**Fassag:** a hassock of straw; if broad and thin used on a horse's back below the saddle

**Feek-Fikes:** small household chores.

**Feerach:** a state of bother and confusion. "He's in a richt feerach".

**Feese:** to adjust.

**Feet-Ale:** a drink to seal a sale of cattle, paid for by the seller.

**Feint:** a very positive negative. "Feint a thing did a see".

**Feint Perlicked:** absolutely nothing. "A got feint-perlicked for ma pains".

**Feltie:** a bird, the fieldfare.

**Feochled:** tired, worn out.

**Fettle:** a loop of rope to secure a burden on one's back.

**Fillad:** the thigh.

**Fi-Arter:** a slovenly person.

**Filthy Wamlin:** a small, troublesome person.

**Flacht:** a handful of wool before it is carded.

**Flaff:** a sudden gust of wind.

**Flam:** to blow in strong gusts; the blow itself. "A flam o' win' cam' doon 'e lum".

**Flate:** a straw mat. See **fascal** above.

**Fleep, Fleeps:** a feeble, useless woman.

**Flipe:** (1) to work with a brush as in whitewashing; (2) to ruffle the skin.

**Flist:** to boast, brag.

**Flor:** to strut or move in boastful manner.

**Floss:** rushes with the pith removed, used for making small simmans.

**Fluchter:** a frightened person or animal.

**Flummery:** humbug, flattery. "Non' o' yur flummery here!"

**Fluther:** a soft piece of ground, a bog.

**Forkytail:** an earwig.

**Forenent:** in front of.

**Follow:** person or type. A good follow—a generous person. A bad follow—the opposite.

**Folp:** whelp.

**Foosim:** filthy, fulsome.

**Footre:** to overcome by ridicule.

**Forebait:** limpets, usually chewed and spat into the sea about the fishing lines, to attract fish.

**Forfochen:** weary, all in.

**Forrow:** a single load or lift of anything. See **fraucht.**

**Fraik, Fraikas:** a fuss or ado, in a flattering way.

**Fraucht:** a burden of water, peats, etc.—as much as one can carry on one trip.

**Freet:** when the witches took the freet, it meant that they got the milk from other folk's cows (from a distance) and left the other folk milkless. Fruit?

**Fren:** anyone except one's own family and relations; outsiders.

**Fuffle:** to shuffle in one's walk.

**Fummle:** to tumble, to upset.

**Funseless:** sapless, insipid.

**Fupag:** a worthless woman.

**Fushionless:** sapless (See **funseless**).

**Futterag:** a weasel.

**Futtle:** to make a bad job of any piece of work; the person or tool responsible.

**Fykan':** Working handlessly at anything. Often applied to children.


**Gailan':** smarting hotly, as a sore.

**Gaat:** a gelded pig.

**Gainer:** a gander.

**Galtag:** a small sore, a pustule or boil.

**Gandygows:** nonsensical pranks.

**Gangs:** spring-shears for clipping sheep.

**Gant:** to stammer, a stammer.

**Gapaaz:** a fool.

**Garrybag, Garbal:** the abdomen of an unfledged bird. Extended to apply to a young fellow who is not as grown-up as he thinks.

**Gaun-'Gither:** a form of sowens.

**Gavelock:** an earwig.

**Geedin:** the carting of dung, seaweed, etc., the spread dung, etc.

**Geeg:** to giggle, titter.

**Geetsher:** a grandfather.

**Geik:** hemlock; extended to any hollow plant stem used by children as a squirt.

**Gerr:** clumsy.

**Gilpan:** an unfledged sparrow.

**Gilt:** a stack of hay on a rectangular base.

**Gird:** a hoop.

**Girn:** to complain with facial expressions of displeasure.

**Girn:** bird-trap.

**Girnal:** a sore swelling in the armpit, usually due to blood-poisoning in the hand.

**Girss:** grass.

**Givelag:** earwig.

**Gizzend:** shrunk by heat, no longer watertight. "'E barrel's 'at gizzened id'll no haad in shore bools".

**Glack:** the angle between the thumb and forefinger. " 'E glack o' 'e han'."

**Glaikit:** vacant, foolish.

**Glaip On:** to attack eagerly, to gulp down (usually of food).

**Glamp:** practically the same as glaip.

**Glape:** to glower, to frighten.

**Gleed:** a spark of fire, a streak of light.

**Glide:** cross-eyed. Glide Annag was a well-known nomadic character.

**Glounk:** the sound of air replacing liquid in a bottle.

**Glowsteran':** blusteran'.

**Gloy:** cleaned straw used for weaving straw articles, e.g. caisies.

**Gluff:** to scare, frighten. A fright.

**Gluffus:** a scary, excitable person.

**Gollan:** (1) a daisy; (2) the end of a rainbow which is incomplete. There is usually an end at each side of the horizon. They indicate broken weather.

**Gomeral:** a foolish person.

**Gornal:** a (trouser) button.

**Gosk:** chickweed.

**Gowf:** a bad smell or obnoxious vapour.

**Gowff:** a guffaw. "He let oot a great gowff".

**Gowpen:** the two hands cupped together. **Gowpen-Ful':** as much as these hands will hold.

**Gowrag:** a small cole of hay.

**Gray:** (1) a dram of whisky; (2) a slight breath of wind.

**Graylord:** a large saithe.

**Greith:** soapy water.

**Grice:** a young pig.

**Groff Write:** writing with large characters.

**Gromish:** to crush (usually a part of the body). " 'E cairt-wheel gromished his feet".

**Groo:** ugly.

**Grone:** a pig's snout.

**Groot:** the refuse left from melted livers originally; now extended to other refuse.

**Grop:** the refuse from straw, oatmeal, etc. now extended to other refuse. (A Caithness man described the Dundee mill workers as a lock o' grop).

**Greep:** the surface drain or waterway in a byre.

**Grum:** dregs, small potatoes, etc., extended to general leavings.

**Grumly:** muddy, or liquids.

**Gudge, Gunch:** a squat, thickset person.

**Gug:** the slime of fish.

**Gumph:** a bad flavour.
**Gundy:** toffee.
**Gurr:** matter in the corners of the eyes.
**Gurrag:** a small boil.
**Gushel:** to work untidily and messily; such a worker; extended to a choppy sea.
**Gwich:** sound made when swallowing.
**Gyacher:** churlish, testy.
**Gyte:** foolish.

**Haal:** hold, grip. The expression "to had haal" means to stand up to. Clothes will "had haal" to rough usage, food to the teeth or stomach, etc. "To go by haal" means to proceed by holding on to something, as of a child.
**Haavers:** halves. Boys would call "Haavers" to claim a half of anything found.
**Had Till Id:** stand up to it. "How're ye haddan' till id?"
**Hagger:** a condition of the sea when it is broken by wind and rain.
**Hail:** a small quantity, a drop, of a liquid.
**Hale-Heid Errand:** whole-head, an errand for a specific purpose cf. Aince-errand.
**Hammel:** kindly, homely.
**Hanteran':** a short period of time. "A'll be 'ere in a hanteran'."
**Hantle:** a large number, plenty. "A hantle o' fowk wis 'ere".
**Harns:** brains.
**Hattle:** a sea bottom rough with stones and sea-ware.
**Head:** in the usage "He's a good heid till bairns", i.e. kind and helpful to bairns.
**Heck:** a wooden frame for holding hay, etc. for cattle.
**Hecked:** white-faced, of a cow.
**Heck Hen:** a hen to feed hawks—part of the rent once paid by tenants.
**Heckin:** the distance the lead is raised above sea-bottom in handline fishing.
**Henware:** a kind of seaweed.
**Heuky:** itchy.
**Hiller:** a stout, untidy person.
**Hinnyware:** (honeyware): a kind of seaweed.
**Hippal:** rheumatic pains.
**Hivad:** a mass. " 'At's a hivad o' hair for ye!"
**Hix:** the sound of convulsive weeping.
**Hizzel:** a big gnarled stick.
**Hoarnygollach—** a centipede.
**Hobbled:** perplexed, worried.
**Hoolipan:** rolling gait.
**Horsegollan:** the ox-eye daisy.
**Hullerz:** a big, hulking fellow.
**Hummelt:** hornless, polled.
**Hurl:** a deep, hollow sound.
**Hushle, Heishle:** a confused heap or group.

**Ile:** oil, but used to describe the fishing ground between the shore and a current.
**Ingy: Ingle,** to lamb.
**In-Sook:** a touch of frost.
**Isk:** to be breathless through sobbing.
**Ivenow:** just now, even now.

**Jaabard:** a debilitated animal—specially applied to a lean cod.
**Jabble:** a weak fluid or mixture spoiled by shaking. Applied to the sea, it has the same meaning as **hagger** above.
**Jeeg:** a sudden jerk or pull.
**Jockhasty:** a coarse riddle for rough-dressing grain.
**Jondal:** a young farm-servant.
**Jowp:** the head or skull.
**Jiffire:** the action of flinging away from one an article such as a book.
**Jeckiebeet:** a bird, the stonechat.
**Jeckie Forty-Feet:** the centipede.

**Jeckiemill:** the death-watch beetle. Its ticking in the wall was a presage of death.
**Jenny Spinner:** the mayfly.

**Kaaz:** calves.
**Kaaran:** a worn-out horse.
**Kaim:** to rear, the action of rearing horse.
**Kair:** to clean up and remove broken straw after threshing.
**Kaivel:** to cast lots, usually when sharing a catch of fish. Each person selected a stone or small article, the owner of each being known. Then one person who did not know the owners, placed one on each share, allotting them thus to the owners of the stones. Also **Kaivel Stone.**
**Keek:** to steal a glance at.
**Keet:** the ankle. "Better till be oot o' 'e keets than oot o' 'e kind".
**Keltry:** porridge stick.
**Kemp:** dog's tail grass.
**Kerant:** a ploy, a prank.
**Kettle:** to kitten. A kitten was a **Ketlin'.**
**Kilk:** the roe of white fish.
**Kimpal:** a truss of straw prepared for thatching; extended to an untidy mass, even an untidy woman.
**Kinch:** a twist; the doubling of a rope when fastening it to anything. "A gied masel a nesty kinch".
**Kirsan:** an inedible crab.
**Kithan:** an ill-tricked youngster. Term of reproach.
**Kittle:** tickle.
**Kittyfake:** a bird, the kittywake.
**Klyer:** (1) an unsound spot in an animal's fat; (2) an unwholesome secret, a source of grievance, i.e. something that festers.
**Knappal:** a boy, a lad.
**Knapper:** to jolt, as of a vehicle on a rough road.
**Kned:** of animals, to breathe with effort.
**Knib:** a piece of wood acting as a swivel between two ropes.
**Knidge:** a stockily built person or animal.
**Knivel:** the horn of a young beast.
**Knotty:** a game, a form of shinty.
**Knowsh:** a lump, a hump.
**Kooshie:** a cry to a cow.
**Kowley:** a strong, strapping fellow.
**Krank:** unstable (used of a boat).
**Krumban:** a bent or deformed attitude brought on by an ailment. "A chicken wi' 'e krumban"
**Kudge:** a small corner.
**Kullyan:** a soft, effeminate person.
**Kyowtach:** trim and neat. "A kyowtach wifie".
*(Some words which could begin with k- will be found under c-)*

**Laager:** to besmear.
**Lairag:** lark, laverock.
**Laiteran:** the elders' pew in a church; a lectern in a church.
**Lamper:** (of milk) to coagulate naturally.
**Land Sea:** a sea where heavy waves break on the shore.
**Langal:** a hobble for sheep.
**Langersome:** tedious, dreary.
**Lay:** (1) to weld a piece of iron on an iron implement to replace a worn bit; (2) to thresh; (3) an instrument for sharpening a scythe; (4) a lull in the waves during stormy weather, hence a chance.
**Lay Off:** to talk at great length. "He's fairly layan' hid off him".
**Layr:** a habit (usually bad). "Ye'll gie 'e bairns a bad layr wi' 'at carry on".
**Lee-A-Lally:** children's game.
**Leem:** a wide-mouthed containing vessel.
**Leep:** to heat or steep. Usually of limpets, to separate them from the shells for bait. hence **a Leepan' Day,** a hot muggy day. **Leepadie:** a person fond of the fireside.

**Libbag:** a horn spoon with a short handle.
**Lild:** a dry cow.
**Limmerach:** club moss.
**Linn:** a piece of wood placed below the keel of a boat to help draw it up on shore.
**Linn:** to cease.
**Lippen:** to trust. "Dinna lippen till him!"
**Lipper:** a small movement on the surface of the water.
**Lirrip:** to strike.
**Lit:** indigo blue.
**Lith:** a gate or gap in a fence.
**Liv:** palm of the hand. **Liv-Fu'**—as much as the palm will hold.
**Liverin':** a mixture of meal and water used to thicken soup etc.
**Lock:** a lot. **Lockie:** a small quantity.
**Loogard:** a slap on the ear.
**Long:** in the expression **Takkan' Long**—longing for, equivalent of homesickness.
**Loot:** to go about in a slouching manner.
**Lowper, Lowperdowg:** a porpoise.
**Lowse:** to unyoke horses, thus to stop work.
**Lundie:** a strong, strapping fellow.
**Lunt:** to smoke a pipe, especially a clay pipe or 'cutty'.
**Lurks:** folds in material or fabric that require to be smoothed out.
**Lyapach:** raw, half-baked or badly baked (of bread).
**Lyatt:** a small quantity of liquid or semi-liquid.
**Lyper:** a mass of sores, scabs, etc.

**Maa:** a bird, the seagull.
**Maak:** fish milt.
**Maithe:** a maggot.
**Maivie:** (1) the maw of a fish; (2) the stomach of a small animal; (3) a **yirnin'** (rennet bag)
**Mar:** to annoy.
**May Gobs:** a cold spell of weather early in May.
**Maysie:** a pack saddle.
**Meanie:** a bent awl.
**Meddem:** a tickling in the nose, supposed to foretell a visit from a man.
**Meef:** faint.
**Meel:** a bone button.
**Meese, Meeze:** a fisherman's bearing mark.
**Mein:** weak, feeble. "To make mein" is to sympathise with.
**Mell:** heavy hammer used to drive in fence posts.
**Ment:** to make a threatening gesture; such a gesture.
**Merrigle:** a mischievous boy.
**Mersgim:** a fish, the angler-fish.
**Meugle:** to besmear with mud.
**Millary:** a fish, the bass.
**Milleli:** a plant, 'Queen of the Meadow'.
**Minshach:** mean, shabby.
**Mishacker:** to maul, disfigure.
**Mistimeous:** clumsy, untidy.
**Mitch:** the crutch on which the mast of a fishing-boat rested when it was horizontal.
**Moch:** a moth.
**Mocher:** to cuddle, to soothe. Often applied to the soothing of animals.
**Mogre:** to make a mess of, to spoil; a mess or botch.
**Mogs:** clumsy hands.
**Moniment:** an insignificant person.
**Moogans:** stockings without soles used as a leg covering, with a 'latchard' round a toe.
**Moogard:** a mess.
**Moogart:** a plant, the mugwort.
**Mools:** pulverised earth or peat.
**Moot:** to mention.
**Moozhe:** to grow mouldy.
**Mucher:** to graze a cow, holding on to the tether.

**Muggy:** liver.
**Muiran:** generic name for wild game.
**Muldoan:** the basking shark.
**Mull:** the mouth; to feed a child from the mouth.
**Mullach:** used as a term, almost of endearment, among women. Originally sorrow.
**Mullach:** a knee-shaped bit of wood used at the bow and stern of a boat to fix the keel to the stem and the sternpost.
**Muller:** to break into crumbs; **Mullers, Millers:** small crumbs.
**Mulliwark:** the mole.
**Munt:** to walk with an effected gait.
**Murt:** the root of couch-grass.
**Myavenned:** peevish.
**Myuggle:** to make a mess of, to botch.

**Naitie:** neat, clever—especially with the hands.
**Nap:** hoax, in the phrase 'to take one's nap of someone'.
**Nashag:** the bearberry.
**Neb:** nose.
**Neever Day:** New Year's Day.
**Nether:** an adder.
**Newins:** the quality of newness. The newins of a new garment was exchanged usually for a kiss.
**Niaff:** (1) to yelp or bark; (2) a pert saucy person (indicating contempt).
**Nibbie:** crook with a hooked head.
**Noor:** never. "A noor let on".
**Nupes:** the fruit of the cloudberry.
**Nyattry:** grumbling, complaining continually. cf. 'attry'.
**Nyack:** a tinker.
**Nyams:** of a bad disposition.
**Nyonyach:** just perfect.
**Nyorned:** thrawn.

**Oakie:** a guillemot. At one time the term 'Oakies' was applied to the Castletown folk.
**Oast:** a place dug out on the shore to hold a boat.
**Ochanie. Ochanie Got I:** an exclamation of various moods, but usually of surprise.
**Ochnin':** the last stage of darkness, the morning gloaming.
**Oddle:** the dividing of a tide in a tideway.
**Ondocht:** a mean, puny creature.
**Onfa':** the evening gloaming.
**Onmark:** a mischievous person or animal; an oddity.
**Ootcome:** what is given in excess of what is due or expected.
**Ootrook:** the backward rush of water after a wave has broken on the shore.
**Oot-Shookimers:** outsiders; those outside an estate who used the estate mill; incomers, especially fishermen, who secured work or opportunities at the expense of the locals.
**Owse:** (1) to bail a boat; (2) to spill water in large quantities from a container.
**Oxter:** armpit.
**Oy:** a grandchild.

**Paal:** to puzzle. "A'm fair paaled wi' 'at", but "No' paaled" means not particular, not interested.
**Paalie-Maalie:** sickly.
**Paat:** to walk in a heavy, noisy way.
**Paiferal:** a stupid person.
**Pailag:** a porpoise. "Pechan' lek a pailag".
**Palch:** to mend roughly and temporarily.
**Palmer Scarf:** a bird, the guillemot.
**Panner:** a big shot of herring.
**Partal Waal:** the wall between the dwelling and the byre in a 'long hoose'.
**Partan:** an edible crab.
**Pech:** to breathe heavily.
**Peedie, Peerie, Peerie-Wee:** small.
**Peedle:** to play truant. Till peedle fae 'e school. Confined to Thurso.

**Peegie, Peegan:** a greybeard jar. **Peeg:** was a hot-water bottle.
**Peepag:** a sounding reed made from oat-straw.
**Peeser:** an unfledged pigeon.
**Pelcher:** a fish, the mullet.
**Pellad:** the tadpole.
**Pells:** rags, tatters.
**Peltag:** a year-old coal-fish.
**Perjink:** polite, very correct.
**Persians:** the name applied to the inhabitants of Canisbay.
**Piavie:** a sick turn; **Piavan':** sickly.
**Pike-Thanks:** bare thanks or hardly any thanks.
**Pilk:** to shell peas.
**Pingies:** broken pieces of china children used as playthings.
**Pirk:** (1) to trifle; (2) a small wooden skewer or peg.
**Pirkas:** (1) an affected girl; (2) something insignificant, not worth having or being interested in.
**Pirkles:** a halter with iron spikes on it, used to prevent a calf from sucking a cow.
**Pirl, Pirlag:** a pellet of sheep dung.
**Pitchers:** children's game.
**Pickencyarr:** a bird, the guillemot; a quarrelsome person.
**Pictarnie:** a bird, the tern.
**Pillar:** a kind of crab.
**Pingelty:** a difficulty.
**Pizz:** what is small and worthless. " 'E tatties are fair pizz 'iss year".
**Ploog:** a pimple.
**Plowter:** to walk or work in an ungainly fashion.
**Pluck:** (1) the moult; " 'E hens hev takken 'e pluck"; (2) a broken herring, broken because of having been plucked from the net.
**Plucker:** a fish, the fasher-lasher. "As mad as a plucker".
**Pints:** boot-laces (points).
**Poll:** to cut the hair. " 'He's gettan' his heid polled for 'e show".
**Pooper:** in earlier days a pupil who helped the schoolmaster in small jobs and got his education free.
**Pooshan:** poison. Used as an adjective. "He's a pooshan moniment".
**Poot:** young bird in the nest.
**Powl:** a crutch, support.
**Preef:** to check the amount of grain in a sack; also **Preefsman:** a form of 'proof'.
**Preeg:** plead.
**Preen:** a pin.
**Pron:** oatmeal or similar substance coarsely ground or crushed.
**Prong:** to prick.
**Prontag:** a crumb of dough in baking.
**Prot:** (1) a trick or prank; (2) a counting-out-rhyme.
**Puckle:** a small amount, e.g. of potatoes, straw, etc.
**Puddag:** a frog.
**Purk:** to prick.
**Purn:** reel of thread.
**Purr:** to prick; a prick. "A purred masel on 'e nettles".
**Pursiewan:** bog-myrtle.

**Quearn:** the turbot.
**Queeblins:** small herring.
**Queeze:** to question.
**Quey:** heifer.
**Quine:** a girl, young woman.

**Rachle:** in the phrase 'a rachle o' bon's', a lean emaciated person or animal.
**Rachled:** (of faces) wrinkled and worn.
**Rackle:** to take the kinks out of a simmans rope when rolling it into a clew.
**Raik:** a person working with fuss and effort but little care. "A raik o' a worker".
**Raintree:** a beam to which the crook of the fire was hung.
**Raip:** to make a rough and temporary sewing of a tear.

**Rake:** a load. Generally applied to peats.
**Ramgoose:** a bird, the diver.
**Rander:** to darn, to thicken the heels of stockings.
**Rapach:** too talkative and indiscreet.
**Rawn:** herring roe.
**Ree:** of weather, clear and frosty with wind. "Hid's a ree day".
**Redder:** a fine-toothed comb for the hair
**Reend:** a cloth or wooden border to anything.
**Reeskie:** the uncultivated strip of land between two fields.
**Reested:** dried over the fire; a form of 'roast'.
**Reet:** to turn things over clumsily; a form of 'root'.
**Reeze:** to praise, to flatter.
**Riddlan' Heids:** refuse separated from grain with a riddle.
**Rillins:** old shoes or strips of hide from which they were roughly made; extended to any old tatters. "His coat wis aal in rillins".
**Ringan':** an intensive word. "He's a ringan' divil".
**Risban's:** the cuffs of a shirt. Probably wristbands.
**Risk:** light drizzle.
**Risp:** a few stalks of straw or hay.
**Rit:** to tear, to mutilate.
**Rit-Fur:** the first furrow opened in ploughing; a furrow made to run off water.
**Rive:** to burst from over-eating. "A'm lek till rive efter 'at feed".
**Robbie-Boy:** a tomboy, a hoyden.
**Roche:** a bird, the little auk.
**Ronyal:** a clumsy, ungainly person.
**Roo:** a small heap of peats during the drying process.
**Roog:** to tear, to pull to pieces.
**Roolyin-Pin, Roolyin-Tree:** a stick for stirring potatoes during the washing of them.
**Roopid:** hoarse.
**Rooze:** to cure in brine.
**Rorie:** a cabbage without a heart.
**Rowars:** rolls of wool prepared for spinning.
**Rownkas:** an animal that has or can assume a hump.
**Roy:** milk in the udder of a new-calved cow.
**Rowth:** a strip of iron on a boat where the oars rest on the sides.
**Runk:** a shrivelled person or animal.
**Runkar:** a fish, the lump-fish.
**Ruthag:** a small, reddish crab.
**Ruthe:** seeds of spurrey.
**Runshag:** wild radish.
**Ryrachan:** a cow which has made many visits to the bull.

**Sall:** a rope binder for a calf.
**Sand-Lairag:** the ringed plover.
**Saye:** a tub or large container.
**Scaad:** to heat, scald. "A scaad o' heit", a spell of hot weather.
**Scaap:** crustacea between high and low water marks.
**Scaddan:** herring.
**Scag:** to spoil the look of.
**Scam:** to burn the outside of, to overheat.
**Schochad:** the green plover.
**Schochle:** to walk clumsily, with a rock.
**Schooshle:** to walk awkwardly.
**Scloug:** a blow on the ear.
**Scodge:** to wear out a good suit. **Scodged:** partly worn.
**Scodger:** to sneak about. **Scodger:** a lazy lounger.
**Scon:** to flatten.
**Scoo:** a large, flat basket.
**Scoor:** 'A scoor o' hail' is a heavy, sweeping shower; 'to scoor aboot' is to range about with a suggestion of looking for something to one's advantage.
**Scoorins:** a home-spun cloth, like a twill.

**Scoorag:** a bannock made of unleavened bere-meal.
**Scoort:** an armful—a scoort o' peats.
**Scoot:** (1) to run away with speed; (2) to project water from the mouth or some narrow instrument; (3) the tail rush of water over a rock, cf. the Scoot o' Scartan in Stroma.
**Scootie Allan:** a bird, Richardson's skua.
**Scorrie:** a bird, a young seagull, under a year old.
**Scowth:** scope, room to manoeuvre.
**Scravole:** to crawl.
**Scravvle:** a thin sprinkling of fish in a net.
**Scrayed:** dried up.
**Screever:** a strong wind.
**Screw:** a stack of corn, etc., on a circular base in the stackyard.
**Scroit:** a crowd of worthless, vulgar children.
**Scrowg:** a lean, hard person.
**Scruff:** scurf, a thin membrane.
**Scud:** a blow.
**Scuddle:** to wander away, usually with speed, to avoid a duty. (Mostly of children).
**Scuff:** a glancing blow.
**Scutter:** a slight drought.
**Scuttle:** an egg shell.
**Sea-Cockie:** a bird, the puffin.
**Sea-Dowg, Sea-Dae:** the dogfish.
**Sea-Hen:** the starfish.
**Seean:** a fish, the saithe or fully-grown coalfish.
**Seet:** a cover in the bottom of a boat over the wedge at the keel.
**Segg:** the iris.
**Sellag:** young coalfish.
**Semmle:** to fix together, by sewing etc., probably from 'assemble'.
**Sen:** to bless. "Sen 'e bairn".
**Senshach:** sensible, intelligent (usually of a child).
**Shag:** an old bull.
**Shaltie, Sheltie:** a Shetland pony or a pony of like type.
**Shangie:** a rope on the mast to hold the lower end of the sprit.
**Shannag:** an ant.
**Sharrow, Shant:** bitter in taste. " 'At's gey sharrow sooans"
**Sharl-Pin:** a wooden pin acting as a hinge.
**Sharn:** cow dung.
**Shawn:** scarce (of fish). (Exclusive to Wick fishermen).
**Shiel:** a peat-cutting spade.
**Shilfa:** the chaffinch.
**Shincough:** the whooping cough.
**Shither:** people, folk—usually associated in some way.
**Shochlan:** shuffling.
**Shon:** a bog, soft ground.
**Shoo:** in a boat, to backwater.
**Shoodie:** a swing.
**Shookie:** a call to a horse.
**Shoot:** posture. "He had a richt shoot on him at 'e sy'."
**Shottle:** a division in a wooden kist.
**Sib:** related.
**Sile:** signs of herring at sea.
**Silkie' Selchie:** a seal.
**Simmans:** ropes of twisted straw or heather.
**Simmans-Crank:** an implement for twisting the straw or heather. cf. 'thrawcrook'.
**Sind:** rinse (clothes).
**Sindry:** gone to pieces. " 'Iss tub hes gone aal sindry wi' 'e drocht".
**Sinkler:** a long, lean cod with a big head. cf. sooshler.
**Sistance:** the smallest possible quantity of anything.
**Skail:** (1) to spill; (2) to disperse, to empty. " 'E school's skailan'."
**Skalders, Skulders:** the jellyfish.
**Skeechan:** treacle ale.

**Skeel:** to shelter from the wind.
**Skeer:** to join a broken thing with nails or string.
**Skeet:** to throw flat stones on the water to make them skip.
**Skeet:** diarrhoea.
**Skeeter:** the cuttlefish or ink fish
**Skelach:** country bumpkin.
**Skelf:** splinter of wood driven into the finger.
**Skellad:** a tin vessel with a long handle. cf. Skillet.
**Skelp:** (1) a slap; (2) a piece, a chunk. "Gee's a skelp o' 'at cheese".
**Skeoche:** a fissure in the rocks.
**Skibbielickie:** children's game, tig.
**Skimmer:** little bits. "Id's in skimmer".
**Skin-Revach:** a piece of hide used as a valve on the plunger of a boat's pump.
**Skint:** (1) a small drop; (2) to besplatter someone or something with liquid.
**Skifter:** a light covering—"a skifter o' snow".
**Skiollag:** wild mustard.
**Skite:** the spree. "He wis on 'e skite last nicht".
**Skleetan-Feeted:** splay-footed.
**Sklent:** a breeze helping a boat tacking to windward.
**Skook:** to move with a stooping, cowering motion.
**Skow:** anything small and broken such as barrel staves after the barrel is broken.
**Skutch:** to move quickly and industriously; a quick turn in such movement. "Ye's better pit a skutch on ye passan' 'e hoose".
**Skutchens:** a busybody.
**Skybal:** poor soil. "He's got a richt skybal o' a place".
**Skybaleer:** to abuse, criticise meanly.
**Slag:** a soft mire.
**Slammag:** a handful of anything soft and mushy.
**Slant:** a puff of wind.
**Slap:** a gap in a wall or fence.
**Slaister:** to work clumsily. Also heavy, fatiguing work.
**Slewed:** drunk, intoxicated.
**Slater:** the woodlouse.
**Slent:** a lull between showers.
**Slie:** fungus on a damp wall.
**Slither:** a lazy person.
**Slitter:** a tear in cloth; an untidy worker.
**Sloch:** the core of a horn; the sheath of a straw.
**Slock:** to put out, of a fire; to ease, of a thirst. Also **Slocken.**
**Slooan:** a lazy hulk.
**Slop:** a sore disappointment. "He got a richt slop fan his lass didna turn up".
**Slot:** a wooden bar on a barn door.
**Slounk:** a lazy person.
**Smagan:** a toad.
**Smelt:** an oily patch in the sea.
**Smiach:** sense, gumption.
**Smouch:** to burn slowly.
**Smyagger:** to besmear.
**Soarn:** to go about seeing what one can pick up, with or without actually begging.
**Sochan:** drawing breath with difficulty.
**Sochrach:** placid, complacent.
**Sodgers:** ribgrass.
**Sookid:** slightly damp. Sookid fish has not been completely dried; sookid clothes are not quite dry enough to take off the line.
**Sool:** a swivel.
**Soolye:** a family with an indifferent reputation.
**Sooph:** to burn slowly.
**Soorag:** the sorrel.
**Sooroo Tak' Ye, Sooroo Swall Ye:** maledictions.
**Soord:** the cross-bar between the legs of a chair or table.
**Sooshler:** a long, lean cod.

**Sowans:** a mixture prepared from the finer husks or 'sids of the oat.

**Snaik:** a slug.

**Sneecan:** an ant.

**Sneed:** a horse-hair line or leader in fishing.

**Sneeg:** to jerk.

**Sneerag:** a child's plaything.

**Snirie:** to toss the head.

**Snock-Snorles:** kinks or knots in a thread during the spinning process.

**Snooie:** a sharp pull. " 'E coo gied a snooie an' A lost haud".

**Snuffle:** a bird, the snow bunting.

**Spangs:** long strides.

**Spannel:** sand eel.

**Spart:** to spread or scatter. Survives in 'spartan' dung'.

**Speeler:** a toy boat made of wood with a feather for a sail.

**Speet:** a stick for carrying fish by passing it through their gills.

**Speet An' Spang:** quite new. cf. Spleet-new.

**Speldag:** a fish, split and dried.

**Speurd:** a contemptible person.

**Spilk:** see "skelf".

**Spoot:** dart quickly.

**Spoug:** a hand or limb. "A hit 'im wi' ma left spoug".

**Spoug-Shave:** spoke-shave.

**Spootcher:** a bucket with a long handle.

**Spoung:** a leg or arm.

**Spounk:** (1) a match; (2) spirit or 'go'. "He hes no spounk in 'im".

**Sprool:** a cross-piece of wire in a fishing line.

**Sprowg:** a sparrow.

**Spulger:** bailer for a boat.

**Spundie:** a spent herring.

**Spanner, Spunner:** to gallop.

**Squaar:** a swathe in mowing.

**Squaw:** infertile (of eggs). Also appears as **jaw**.

**Squeever:** a squall of wind.

**Staig:** a colt.

**Stab:** a wooden fence post.

**Stangfish:** the weever.

**Staidle:** the foundation of a stack of grain, etc.

**Stan' O' Gloes:** a suit of new clothes.

**Stap:** a boiled cod head with the bones removed and stuffed with 'liverin'. **Stappid Heid.**

**Starnfa':** jelly tremella.

**Starnies:** stars.

**Starrach:** cold weather.

**Stick:** of an animal, to push with the horns.

**Stilties:** an inclusive term for small wading birds, especially redshanks and greenshanks.

**Steethe:** the foundation of anything, but usually a building.

**Stoit:** nonsense

**Stolm:** a dip of ink, that adhered to the nib. (Used in Wick schools).

**Stoater:** to stagger.

**Stonner:** a stone foundation, on or below the surface of the ground.

**Stoog:** the centre of a boil.

**Stoon:** a sudden attack of pain; a whim. "He's in a bad stoon ivenow".

**Stonechecker:** a bird, stonechat.

**Story:** the grub of the crane-fly.

**Straeffin:** a thin skin, a membrane.

**Stran:** gutter along the side of a paved street.

**Stravaig:** to wander aimlessly.

**Strintle:** the flow of a small stream of water.

**Stroop:** pipe down the side of a house, draining water from the roof.

**Stroosh:** to walk with long, swinging steps: such a manner of walking "She hes a richt stroosh on 'er 'e nicht".

**Strump:** broken bits of straw.

R

**Stryth:** the working animals on a farm, at one time horses and oxen.
**Sudgess:** subject to.
**Sumph:** a soft, silly person.
**Styme:** usually of fire or light, the faintest trace. "Id's 'at dark A canna see a styme".
**Styal:** a growth on the eye. A stye.
**Swaadge:** to grow empty.
**Swaats:** the liquid on sowens.
**Swack:** lithe, active.
**Swartheid:** the black root of a tangle, seaweed.
**Sweel:** to rinse or wash without being particular. "He gies his feice a sweel".
**Swere:** reluctant.
**Swey:** the movable horizontal bar of the fire-brace.
**Swilkie, Swelchie:** a whirlpool. Cf. The Swilkie of Stroma.
**Swink:** to leak (of a tub, etc.)
**Sy:** (1) a scythe, to scythe; (2) a strainer or syer, to strain (commonly of milk).

**Taa:** (1) a thread; (2) a stolon of grass.
**Taajer:** a termagant of a woman.
**Taat:** a matted tuft of wool, hair, etc.
**Tack:** to burn or shine brightly. " 'E stars are tackan' 'e nicht".
**Tak' 'E Get:** to run away. " 'E coo took 'e get on me".
**Tammie-Louper:** a child's toy carved from black tangle.
**Tanyaird:** the poor-house, on the analogy of old horses going to the tanyard to be put down.
**Taptyre:** a state of agitation. "Ye're in a fair taptyre 'e day".
**Tartan Purry:** dish of red cabbage and oatmeal.
**Tarter:** the noise of scrambling about. "Fitna tarter 'e bairns are makkan".
**Tee-Look:** a look-to. "Gie a tee-look till 'e beyce".
**Teetlan', Teetlag:** the meadow pipit.
**Teistie:** the black guillemot.
**Thaar:** need, in phrases such as "Ye thaarna fash, ye needna bother".
**Theedle, Theevil:** porridge stick.
**Thief-Lookan' Sky:** a threatening type of sky, one that will steal the good day.
**Thingment, Thingiment:** something of which the real name has been forgotten.
**Thistlecock Lairag:** a bird, the corn bunting.
**Thorny Sellag:** a fish, the lesser weever.
**Thram:** a malediction. "I'll . . . ye!"
**Tiachersome:** ill-disposed.
**Timmer-Towngue:** timber-tongue, a disease of animals.
**Tirr:** to remove the top of, say, the turf over a peatbank, the earth over a quarry, etc.
**Tirrywirry:** fit of passion.
**Tirvin':** the sod from the top of a peat bank, cf. turf.
**Tobless:** unsteady on the feet (of a child).
**Tochie:** a call to a calf.
**Tod-Tail:** Indian file, used by children in their games.
**Tommienorrie:** a bird, the puffin.
**Totem:** a spinning top made from a bobbin.
**Traap, Traapach:** a slovenly woman, a slut.
**Trachled:** fatigued.
**Traik:** tiring walk.
**Threep:** to assert, brooking no contradiction. "He threeped doon my throat that . . . ".
**Trailey-Wallads:** lagging behind.
**Trefalyegan:** (1) a tangled mass of wool, string, etc.; (2) a long, rambling speech.
**Treffis:** the wooden partition between stalls in a stable.
**Tret:** a strip of cotton dipped in mutton fat, and then dried and stored to act as a poultice.
**Trink:** an opening between rocks, usually under water.
**Trock:** rubbish.
**Trosk:** a stupid, useless person.
**Trot:** to play truant from school (Wick area).
**Trou(v)ag:** term of commiseration. "Poor trou(v)ag".
**Trow:** to play truant from school (elsewhere.)
**Trowgs:** a derisive perjorative word added to a Christian name.

**Truggs:** a lazy worker.
**Tuag:** a small knob on a hilltop, e.g. Corbie Tuags in Stroma.
**Tulgans:** what is being carried, a burden.
**Turse:** (1) to arrange a dress; (2) a stout, ungainly person.
**Tuskar:** a peat-cutting spade.
**Twilt:** quilt.
**Twin:** to part. "A canna stan' till twin fae ye".
**Twine At:** to work perseveringly at.
**Twirk:** to twist; a twist. "There's a lock o' twirk in 'at cheil".
**Twite:** to whittle a piece of wood.
**Tworrow:** an odd corner of ploughed land.
**Tyangersome:** quarrelsome.
**Tyarr:** to quarrel.
**Tyauve:** to mix leaven in baking.


**Ugg:** the pectoral fin of a fish and the area around it.
**Unresty:** unsettled, restive.
**Uphaud:** the cost of upkeep.
**Ush:** the entrails of an animal killed for food.


**Waa-Drap:** a delicate person.
**Waal:** a stroke of the oar.
**Waal-Watter-Wake:** as weak as well-water.
**Waan:** hope, prospect. "A heve no waan o' gettan' anither horse".
**Waariebowg:** (1) the bladder of a seaweed; (2) the grub of the warblefly.
**Waffle:** slender, pliant.
**Wait:** a mill-lade.
**Wamling:** an ill-grown, emaciated person.
**Wap:** (1) a row or quarrel; (2) a smart blow.
**Warsie:** sick from want of food.
**Watter-Thraw:** water brash.
**Wattle:** to twist or ravel; a revel or entanglement. " 'E coarn's fair wattled".
**Waz:** a straw collar for a horse; extended facetiously to a man's collar. **Wazzan:** is the throat, a form of weazand.
**Weal:** a plentiful supply, probably a contraction of wealth. Used by Keiss fishermen who talk of 'a weal o' fish' when they get a good catch.
**Weathermooth:** an open place in the sky, at the horizon, from which clouds radiate.
**Wee-Weet:** birds, the redshank and greenshank.
**Weicht:** weight, deserts—in the phrase "At's yer weichts". "You deserved that".
**Weint:** a moment. "A'll be wi' ye in a weint.
**Wift:** to influence someone to leave what they are at to serve your own purposes. To take an unfair advantage in bargaining.
**Willie-Beebs:** birds: the common sandpiper and the purple sandpiper.
**Willie-Roozer:** a specimen of anything larger than usual, a 'thumper'.
**Willie-Weet-Feet:** a bird, the sandpiper.
**Winlin:** a bundle of straw.
**Winner:** an insignificant creature.
**Winstrae:** a grass, holcus lanatus.
**Wisk:** anything bulky and untidy rolled round the neck.
**Wisp:** the nest of a wild bee if on the surface of the ground.
**Witchag:** the swallow.
**Wittans:** information. "A hev no wittans o' 'at".
**Wowgie:** lively, dashing.
**Wraxed:** over-strained or stretched.
**Wugrum:** dampness on the interior walls of a house from a leak in the roof.
**Wursum:** the festering matter in a sore.
**Wyeck:** feeble, very ill.

**Yaa:** an eel.
**Yallar:** to bark noisily; the noisy barking of a dog in pursuit of something.
**Yarfal:** poor peat, peat combined with clay or sand.
**Yarwins:** a revolving frame to hold the hasps to be wound.
**Yowlie:** a native of Aukengill, perhaps from high-pitched voice.

## NOTES

(1) There is no standard spelling of the Caithness dialect.

(2) Pronunciation may vary from district to district, as may the meaning.

(3) Some words common to many Scottish dialects have been included.

(4) A few words in this list can be recognised as corruptions of Standard English, e.g. Naitie, wazzan, but most such words have been omitted.

(5) Many of the words, perhaps the greater part, are obsolete or at least obsolescent, but they have their value and so are included.

# Bibliography

The following selected list of references provides useful additional material.

### Part 1

| | | | |
|---|---|---|---|
| ALEXANDER | Birds of the Ocean | Putmam | 1928 |
| BAXTER ET ALIA | The Birds of Scotland | Oliver & Boyd | 1953 |
| BROWN ET ALIA | The Hamlyn Guide to the Birds of Britain and Europe | Hamlyn | 1970 |
| CLAPHAM ET ALIA | Flora of the British Isles | Cambridge University Press | 1962 |
| CRAIG (EDITOR) | The Geology of Scotland | Oliver and Boyd | 1965 |
| CRAMPTON | The Vegetation of Caithness | Edinburgh | 1911 |
| CRAMPTON ET ALIA | The Geology of Caithness (Memoir of the Geological Survey) | HMSO | 1914 |
| DORST | The Migration of Birds | Heinemann | 1962 |
| DUKE OF PORTLAND | The Red Deer of Langwell | | 1936 |
| EASTWOOD | Radar Ornithology | Methuen | 1967 |
| HARVIE-BROWN ET ALIA | A Vertebrate Fauna of Sutherland, Caithness and West Cromarty | Douglas | 1887 |
| HOLLOM | The Popular Handbook of British Birds | Witherby | 1960 |
| HOLLOM | The Popular Handbook of Rarer British Birds | Witherby | 1960 |
| MANLEY | Climate and the British Scene (New Naturalist Series) | Collins | 1952 |
| MILES | The Acanthodian Fishes of the Devonian Plattenkalk of the Raffrath Trough in the Rhineland. Akiv For Zoologi, Kuel, Svenska Vetenskaps—Akademien. | Ser. 2, Vol. 18, No. 9 | 1966 |
| O'DELL ET ALIA | The Highlands and Islands of Scotland | Nelson | 1962 |
| PERRING ET ALIA | Atlas of the British Flora | Nelson | 1962 |
| PETERSON ET ALIA | The Field Guide to the Birds of Britain and Europe | Collins | 1954 |
| RAYNER | The Stratigraphy of the British Isles | Cambridge University Press | 1967 |
| SAXON | The Fossil Fishes of Caithness. Caithness Notebook. No. 6 | Caithness Books | 1967 |
| SCOTTISH BIRDS | The Journal of the Scottish Ornithologists' Club | | |
| | Report of the Scottish Peat Committee—Scottish Home Department | HMSO | 1954 |
| SCOTTISH PEAT | Second Report of the Scottish Peat Committee. Department of Agriculture and Fisheries for Scotland | HMSO | 1962 |
| SCOTTISH PEAT SURVEYS VOLUME 4 | Caithness, Shetland and Orkney Department of Agriculture and Fisheries for Scotland | HMSO | 1968 |
| SISSONS | The Evolution of Scotland's Scenery | Oliver & Boyd | 1967 |
| WEATHER | The Monthly Magazine of the Royal Meteorological Society | | |
| WITHERBY ET ALIA | The Handbook of British Birds (5 Volumes) | Witherby | 1940 |

# Bibliography

### Part 2

| | | | |
|---|---|---|---|
| BEATON | Ecclesiastical History of Caithness | Rae | 1909 |
| BRONSTED | The Vikings | Penguin | 1960 |
| CALDER | Civil and Traditional History of Caithness | Murray | 1861 |
| CHILDE ET ALIA | Illustrated Guide to Ancient Monuments; Vol. VI—Scotland | HMSO | 1967 |
| CORDINER | Remarkable Ruins of North Britain | London | 1780 |
| CRAVEN | A History of the Episcopal Church in Caithness. | Peace | 1908 |
| CRUDEN | The Scottish Castle | Nelson | 1960 |
| CURLE | Inventory of Ancient Monuments in the County of Caithness | HMSO | 1911 |
| DONALDSON | Caithness in the 19th Century | Moray Press | 1938 |
| FEACHEM | Prehistoric Scotland | Batsford | 1963 |
| FIRST STATISTICAL ACCOUNT | | | 1794 |
| GRANT | Old Thurso Caithness Notebook No. 4 | Caithness Books | 1966 |
| GRAY | Sutherland and Caithness in Saga Time | Oliver & Boyd | 1922 |
| HAMILTON | Jarlshof | HMSO | 1956 |
| HAMILTON | Clickhimin | HMSO | 1968 |
| HENDERSON, I. | The Picts | Thames and Hudson | 1967 |
| HENDERSON, J. | Caithness Family History | Douglas | 1884 |
| HENSHALL | The Chambered Tombs of Scotland, Vol. 1 | Edinburgh University Press | 1907 |
| HORNE | County of Caithness | Wick | 1963 |
| McGIBBON ET ALIA | The Castellated and Domestic Architecture of Scotland from the 12th to the 18th Century | Douglas | 1889 |
| MACKENZIE | The Medieval Castle in Scotland | Methuen | 1927 |
| MACKIE | The Origin and Development of the Broch and Wheelhouse Building Cultures of the Scottish Iron Age | Proceedings of the Prehistoric Society for 1965, Vol. 31 | |
| MACKINLAY | Ancient Dedications in Scotland | Douglas | 1914 |
| MOWAT | The Story of Lybster | Wick | 1959 |
| NEW STATISTICAL ACCOUNT | | | 1841 |
| PENNANT | A Tour in Scotland | London | 1771 |
| RIVET (EDITOR) | The Iron Age in Northern Britain | Edinburgh University Press | 1966 |
| ROSS INSTITUTE SOUVENIR | Ye Booke of Halkirk | | 1911 |
| SIMPSON, D. | Scottish Castles: An Introduction to the Castles of Scotland | HMSO | 1959 |
| SIMPSON, J. | Everyday Life in the Viking Age | Batsford | 1967 |
| SIMPSON, W. D. | The Ancient Stones of Scotland | Hale | 1965 |
| ST CLAIR | The St Clairs of the Isles | Brett, New Zealand | 1889 |
| THOM | Megalithic Sites in Britain | Oxford University Press | 1967 |
| WAINWRIGHT (EDITOR) | The Northern Isles | Nelson | 1964 |
| WAINWRIGHT | The Problem of the Picts | Nelson | 1955 |

# *Bibliography*

## Part 3

| | | | |
|---|---|---|---|
| BEATON | *Ministers and Men of the Northern Highlands* | Northern Counties Newspapers | 1929 |
| BEDFORD-FRANKLIN | *A History of Scottish Farming* | Nelson | 1952 |
| CALDER | *Loc.sit.* | | |
| DONALDSON | *Loc.sit.* | | |
| DOUNREAY HANDBOOK | | U.K.A.E.A. | 1965 |
| GENERAL REGISTRY OFFICE | *Census Scotland* 1961, *Vol.* 1, *Part* 12 | HMSO | 1961 |
| HENDERSON | *General View of the Agriculture of the County of Caithness* | London | 1812 |
| HORNE | *Loc.sit.* | | |
| MITCHINSON | *Agricultural Sir John* | Bles | 1962 |
| PENNANT | *Loc.sit.* | | |
| REGISTRAR GENERAL, SCOTLAND | *Annual Estimates of Population* | HMSO | 1966 |
| SMILES | *Robert Dick, Baker, of Thurso, Geologist and Botanist* | London | 1878 |
| STAMP (EDITOR) | *The Land of Britain (Part 15, Caithness—Vince)* | London | 1944 |

## Glossary and Abbreviations

*The following is a list of some technical terms used in the book*

AEROBIC:    (opposite ANAEROBIC) requiring free oxygen for respiration.

AKROSE:    A sandy sedimentary rock containing, usually, a high percentage of felspar.

ARTEFACT:    A man-made stone implement.

BRECCIA:    A coarse-grained sedimentary rock consisting mainly of angular fragments of pre-existing rocks.

COLLOID    A substance in a state in which, though it appears to be dissolved, cannot pass through a membrane.

CONGLOMERATE:    A cemented sedimentary rock consisting of rounded fragments of pre-existing rocks.

CURRENT-BEDDING:    Inclined beds of rock which have been deposited in shallow water under strong current action.

DIP:    The inclination of the beds of rock (STRATA) to the horizontal.

ECOLOGY:    The study of organisms in relation to their environment.

ERRATIC:    An ice transported rock which has been stranded far from its original source.

EVAPORITES:    Minerals formed from solution, followed by subsequent evaporation.

GRANULITE:    A granular-textured metamorphic rock.

KITCHEN-MIDDEN:    The dumped material, often shells and bones, marking the site of a settlement of early man.

LACUSTRINE:    Pertaining to a lake.

MACHAIR:    Fairly level stretches of calcareous sand occurring inland of sand dunes.

MONOLITH:    A single detached pillar or block of stone.

NOTOCHORD:    A simple cellular rod, foreshadowing the spinal column.

OPERCULUM:    The gill cover of fishes.

OROGRAPHIC:    Relief.

SCARP:    The steep face of a tilted bed of rock.

SCREE:    An accumulation of angular debris strewn on a hillside or at a mountain foot.

STRIKE:    The horizontal direction which is at right angles to the dip of the rocks.

UNCONFORMITY:    A breach of continuity in the sequence of rocks.

### ABBREVIATIONS

| | |
|---|---|
| G. | Gaelic |
| H.W.M. | High Water Mark |
| L.W.M. | Low Water Mark |
| O.D. | Ordnance Datum |
| O.N. | Old Norse |

### ORDNANCE SURVEY REFERENCES

So that sites may be accurately located, six figure Ordnance Survey references (readily applicable to the 7th Series 1″=1 mile maps) have been frequently used, e.g. Keiss Broch (ND 353611).

# *Index*